W9-AXF-988

Dramma per musica

Dramma per Musica
Italian Opera Seria of the Eighteenth Century

Reinhard Strohm

Yale University Press
New Haven and London

Set in Ehrhardt by Best-set Typesetter Ltd, Hong Kong
Printed in Great Britain by Redwood Books, Wiltshire

Library of Congress Cataloging-in-Publication Data
Strohm, Reinhard.
    Dramma per musica: Italian opera seria of the eighteenth century/
    Reinhard Strohm.
    Includes bibliographical references and index.
    ISBN 0–300–06454–3
    1. Opera—Italy—18th century.   I. Title.
  ML1733.3.S87   1997   97–27576
  782.1'0945'09033—dc21   CIP

A catalogue record for this book is available from the British Library

10 9 8 7 6 5 4 3 2 1

Contents

LIST OF ILLUSTRATIONS vi

PREFACE vii

1 Introduction: the *dramma per musica* in the eighteenth century 1

Court and city opera

2 A context for *Griselda*: the Teatro Capranica in Rome, 1711–1724 33

3 The Neapolitans in Venice 61

4 The crisis of Baroque opera in Germany 81

5 Francesco Corselli's *drammi per musica* for Madrid 97

Tragédie into *dramma per musica*

6 Apostolo Zeno's *Teuzzone* and its French models 121

7 Antonio Vivaldi's setting of *Teuzzone*: dramatic speech
and musical image 134

8 Antonio Salvi's *Amore e maestà* and the *funesto fine* in opera 165

9 *Amore e maestà*: the emancipation of an opera libretto 177

Theory and practice

10 *Tolomeo*: Handel's opera and the rules of tragedy 201

11 *Arianna in Creta*: musical dramaturgy 220

12 Sinfonia and drama in opera seria 237

Themes and dreams

13 Handel's *Ariodante*: Scotland and Arcadia 255

14 Rulers and states in Hasse's *drammi per musica* 270

15 The Earl of Essex, *servitore di due padrone* 294

BIBLIOGRAPHY 306

INDEX 317

Illustrations

1a. Filippo Juvarra, 'Arco trionfale e scalea': stage design (draft) for
    Tito e Berenice, Teatro Capranica, 1713. Biblioteca Nazionale, Turin,
    Ris. 59,4.   44
1b. Filippo Juvarra, 'Arco di Tito': stage design for *Tito e Berenice* (?),
    Teatro Capranica, 1713. Biblioteca Nazionale, Turin, Ris. 59,4.   45
2a. Alessandro Scarlatti, *Arminio* (III, 13), opening of the quartet 'Al
    valore del mio brando'. Yale University, Music Library, Misc. MS 75.   58
2b. Alessandro Scarlatti, *Arminio* (III, 13), quartet 'Al valore del mio
    brando', middle section. Yale University, Music Library, Misc.
    MS 75.   59
3. Interior of the Teatro S. Giovanni Grisostomo, from *Venezia
    festeggiante* (Venice, 1709). Museo Correr, Venice.   68
4. Travelling opera troupes in central Europe, 1724–54.   94
5. Pierre Corneille; engraving by Michel Lasne.   128
6. Jean Racine; pen and wash portrait by his son Jean-Baptiste.
    Bibliothèque Nationale, Paris.   132
7. Apostolo Zeno, *Teuzzone*, music by Antonio Vivaldi (Mantua,
    1719); title-page of the libretto.   135
8. *Le comte d'Essex*, painting by Nicolas Lancret representing Act V,
    scene 6 of the play by Thomas Corneille. Hermitage, St Petersburg.   180
9. A performance of Antonio Salvi's *Arsace*, Turin, 1740: painting by
    Pietro Domenico Olivero. Museo Civico, Turin.   197
10. Franciscus Lang, *Dissertatio de actione scaenica* (Augsburg, 1727):
    figures showing indicative and expressive gestures.   225
11. Antonio Galli Bibiena, stage design for *Adriano in Siria*, Vienna,
    1732?. Gabinetto delle Stampe, Rome, F.N. 407 (10447).   242
12. Faustina Bordoni as Ginevra in *Ariodante*, Venice, 1716; caricature
    by Antonio Maria Zanetti. Fondazione Giorgio Cini, Venice.   264
13. Pietro Metastasio, *Opere* (Venice, 1781); frontispiece and title-page
    of volume I.   285
14. Giovanni Carlo Galli Bibiena, stage design for Metastasio's
    La clemenza di Tito, Lisbon, 1755. Biblioteca S. Cecilia, Rome.   289

Preface

No matter what the critics of our century have decreed on the Italian *dramma per musica*, its own contradictions and oscillations between irrationality and rationality, between spectacularity and spirituality, kept it alive at the time. It was enormously successful and in a permanent state of expansion and transformation. It was being enjoyed by its audiences.

This enjoyment seems to have flowed from two main sources. First, the genre's spectacularity, and its artistic use of the human voice and body, celebrated a power over nature which seemed unheard of in the history of civilization. Secondly, the plot structures and the behaviour and speech of the dramatis personae also suggested that Reason had gained a control over human passions and social relationships which, had it been real, would have ensured a golden age.

The ambition to control nature, including human nature (mind, body and voice), was often expressed in the precept that the visual arts, but also the theatre and music, should 'imitate nature': this precept assumes that whoever is able to paint an object also understands and controls it. It was an artistic as well as a technological challenge.

The early eighteenth century has given us opera as we know it: a unified and artistically designed, dramatic enactment of human stories, expressed by the human voice and underscored by orchestral heartbeats. The sensuousness of its performance encouraged the spectators to identify themselves emotionally with the characters, and the artistic stratagems of libretto and musical form appeared enjoyable to the mind. Opera therefore shared the goals of enlightenment theatre: it participated in the taming of the passions through the ritualistic and beautified reenactment of human conflicts, and it shared the desire to develop society through rational designs. The fact that the happy endings of the plays did not occur in reality has been held against the whole tendency. This is perhaps unfair: even if the social choreographies of the early enlightenment met with an increasingly critical echo, the efforts to dig ever further into the unknown vaults of the mind and of nature, something already set in motion, carried emancipation forward.

The conviction – or some may say, the prejudice – that Italian opera of this period was theatre in the first place and music in the second has guided me in the exploration of the cultural and literary dimensions of this art-form, and has perhaps taught me some new approaches, to the drama as well as to the music.

The essays in this book have been selected from a larger number of my writings on opera produced in the years 1986–96; the plan to put this selection together in one volume and under a common heading arose only retrospectively. A list of the original versions is given below. The essays have been slightly revised, whether in the course of translating and updating, or with the aim to make them fit together in the new context. The translations are my own. The references and bibliography take into account research published before 1996.

Since I am keen to investigate any of the themes that may still be under-represented in our view of this art-form, the subject matter of the essays is not restricted to any particular aspect of the *dramma per musica*, except that they focus on the period of the early eighteenth century. The introductory chapter draws together many of the suggestions made individually in the other chapters. The first group of essays, entitled 'Court and City Opera', concerns the contemporary reception and environment of the *dramma per musica*. It attempts to recover something like a collective feeling of being 'within' this artistic tradition, through the analysis of social and repertorial patterns of which audiences would have been aware. The four-part study '*Tragédie* into *dramma per musica*' seeks new ways of reading the latter as an emerging genre of its own, by comparing it with its models and measuring it against contemporary theories. Obviously, the roles of French spoken drama and of the Italian libretto reform come into focus here. This study is an effort to meet the genre on its own terms, rather than on those of later practicians and critics who erroneously claim to have spoken the last word about the 'essence' of opera. The following three essays, exemplifying the interaction of 'Theory and Practice', are detailed if selective studies of principles observed by the poets, composers and actors which our age needs to learn about: verisimilitude, *decorum*, gesture, rhetoric and the meaningful handling of stereotypes. These principles are as relevant for performance today as are the texts.

The 'Themes and Dreams' announced in the last section are mainly my own: above all, the dream of being able to read the *dramma per musica* for what it communicated rather than what we may need it for. I happily admit that these and similar attempts at 'decoding' works of the past are ultimately elusive.

The pleasure of studying these operas is exceeded only by experiencing good performances of them, and therefore my acknowledgements ought to start with the names of the performers whom I have admired. The list, in order to be fair, would become too long to be included here. But I may mention some friends and col-leagues for whose expert advice or practical help I am personally grateful: Mario Armellini, Heinz Balthes, Lorenzo Bianconi, Melania Bucciarelli, Ian Caddy, Juan-José Carreras, Winton Dean, Francesco Degrada, Antonio Fanna, Francesco Giuntini, Giovanna Gronda, Anthony Hicks, John Hill, René Jacobs, Nicholas John (+), Reinhold Kubik, Ortrun Landmann, Lowell Lindgren, Candace Marles, Hans Joachim Marx, Lucia Mencaroni, Pierluigi Petrobelli, Curtis Price, Michael Talbot and Thomas Walker (+). I am also indebted to the intrepid editors of the original versions of these essays: David Bryant, Thomas Bauman, Tim Carter,

Rainer Kleinertz, Max Lütolf, Annegrit Laubenthal, Hans Joachim Marx, Marita Petzold McClymonds, Christoph Wolff and Alina Zórawska-Witkowska. Research for 'Tragédie into dramma per musica' has been supported by a research fellowship of the National Endowment for the Humanities (1988) and by small grants from Yale University and King's College London. Time spent in the great music and theatre collections in the libraries of London, Munich, Rome, Venice, Bologna, Wolfenbüttel, Münster, Vienna, New Haven, New York, Chicago and Berkeley has always been a rewarding experience, thanks to the efforts of those who still dare to care about books. I have particularly enjoyed working, in 1988 and 1991, with students at the Department of Music and Theatre (directed by Professor Pierluigi Petrobelli) of the University La Sapienza, Rome, and teaching guest seminars and lectures on Baroque opera at the universities of Cremona/Pavia, Wisconsin, Chicago, Zaragoza and Paderborn/Detmold. Malcolm Gerratt, the editor of these revised versions, takes all the credit for their re-appearance in the real world.

To express all these acknowledgements is a great pleasure because it makes me feel that there is a future to these studies, and that our own drama 'per musica' is open-ended. May it have a *lieto fine* for everyone.

First versions of the essays published in this volume

1. 'Dramma per musica B. 18. Jahrhundert (opera seria)', in *Die Musik in Geschichte und Gegenwart*, ed. by Ludwig Finscher, vol. 2 (Sachteil) (Kassel, etc.: Bärenreiter, 1995), cols 1479–93 and 1498–1500. Republished with permission of Bärenreiter Verlag.

2. 'A Context for Griselda: the Teatro Capranica, 1711–1724', in *Alessandro Scarlatti und seine Zeit*, ed. by Max Lütolf (Berne: Haupt, 1995), pp. 79–114. Republished with permission of Verlag Paul Haupt.

3. 'The Neapolitans in Venice', in *Con che soavità: Studies in Italian Opera, Song, and Dance, 1580–1740* (Essays Dedicated to Nigel Fortune), ed. by Iain Fenlon and Tim Carter (Oxford: Clarendon Press, 1995), pp. 249–74. Republished with permission of Oxford University Press.

4. 'Die Epochenkrise der deutschen Opernpflege', in *Johann Sebastian Bachs Spätwerk und dessen Umfeld: Bericht über das wissenschaftliche Symposion (61. Bachfest Duisburg 1986)*, ed. by Christoph Wolff (Kassel, etc.: Bärenreiter, 1988), pp. 155–66. Republished with permission of Bärenreiter Verlag.

5. 'Francesco Corselli's Operas for Madrid', in *Teatro y Música en España (siglo XVIII)*, *Actas del Simposio Internacional Salamanca 1994*, ed. by Rainer Kleinertz (Kassel-Berlin: Edition Reichenberger, 1996), pp. 79–106.

6–9. 'Tragédie into "Dramma per musica"' I, *Informazioni e studi vivaldiani* 9, 1988, 14–24; II, ibid., 10, 1989, 57–101, III, ibid., 11, 1990, 11–25; IV, ibid., 12, 1991, 47–74. Republished with permission of the Istituto Italiano Antonio Vivaldi and Casa Ricordi – BMG Ricordi S.p.A.

10. 'Händel-Oper und Regeldrama', in *Zur Dramaturgie der Barockoper: Bericht über die Symposien 1992 und 1993*, ed. by Hans Joachim Marx (Laaber, 1994) (Veröffentlichungen der Internationalen Händel-Akademie, vol. 5), pp. 33–54. Republished with permission of Laaber Verlag.

11. 'Zur musikalischen Dramaturgie von *Arianna in Creta*', in *Gattungskonventionen der Händel-Oper: Bericht über die Symposien 1990 und 1991*, ed. by Hans Joachim Marx (Laaber, 1992) (Veröffentlichungen der Internationalen Händel-Akademie, vol. 4), pp. 171–88. Republished with permission of Laaber Verlag.

12. 'Sinfonia and Drama in Early Eighteenth-century Opera Seria', in *Opera and the Enlightenment* (Essays Dedicated to Daniel Heartz), ed. by Thomas Bauman et al. (Cambridge: Cambridge University Press, 1995), pp. 91–104. Republished with permission of Cambridge University Press.

13. 'Schottland und Arkadien: Zu Händels *Ariodante*', in *Studien zur Musikgeschichte: Eine Festschrift für Ludwig Finscher*, ed. by Annegrit Laubenthal et al. (Kassel, etc.: Bärenreiter, 1995), pp. 238–47. Republished with permission of Bärenreiter Verlag.

14. 'Rulers and states in Hasse's *drammi per musica*', in *Johann Adolf Hasse und Polen*, ed. by Irena Poniatowska and Alina Zórawska-Witkowska (Warsaw: Instytut Muzykologii Uniwersytetu Waszawskiego, 1995), pp. 15–35. Republished with permission of Warsaw University.

15. 'The Earl of Essex, *servitore di due padrone*', written for forthcoming volume of studies in honour of Pierluigi Petrobelli on his 60th birthday, and published in advance with permission of the Forschungsinstitut für Musiktheater, University of Bayreuth.

1

Introduction: the *dramma per musica* in the eighteenth century

The concept

Dramma per musica ('drama for music')[1] was the most usual name for Italian operas from the seventeenth to the early nineteenth century. It appeared most often on the title-pages of printed librettos, less frequently in musical sources. A number of librettos carry synonymous names such as *dramma da recitarsi in musica*, *dramma da cantarsi* ('drama to be recited', '. . . to be sung') or the term *melodramma*, which alluded to the concept of *melos* in Greek antiquity. When the term was quoted together with an author's name, this was with few exceptions that of the librettist, as for example in *dramma per musica di Paolo Rolli*. Sometimes, the specification *per musica* was omitted, serving the literary pretensions of the librettist and possibly alluding to the habit of reading dramas. The massive survival of librettos in private collections is one of the signs that *drammi per musica* were widely read at home, like other dramatic literature. Librettos were also published in collected editions, usually under the title *Poesie drammatiche* or a similar one.

In other sources such as contemporary writings, archival documents, letters and travel diaries, the name *dramma per musica* is rare. Here we find more often the colloquial term *opera*, particularly when the subject referred to is the production or musical performance as a whole. Until about 1730, the term *commedia* is also found, regardless of serious or comic content. Sources from outside Italy record 'opera', 'drama', 'singspiel' and other translations of the Italian word *opera*. 'Serious opera' or *opera seria* becomes a more standard term in the later eighteenth century, distinguishing the serious variant from the comic, now usually labelled *opera buffa*. In Italy itself, the specifications *seria* and *buffa* were used well before 1800, as shown in the title *L'opera seria* which Raniero de' Calzabigi gave to his opera buffa of 1769 and elsewhere.

It therefore seems that the colloquial name for the operatic genre in the eighteenth century was *opera*, which in the course of time became diversified into *seria* and *buffa*. *Dramma per musica*, however, was used throughout this period (and

---

1. *(Il) dramma* is a masculine noun in Italian; the plural is *(i) drammi*.

already in the seventeenth century) as an official designation for the genre, with special emphasis on the literary aspect.

The *dramma per musica* of the period c. 1690–c. 1790 can be regarded as a relative unity. Despite the significant changes described below, it was characterized by aesthetic attitudes and practical conditions which then formed a continuous tradition all over Europe. Some of its hallmarks distinguishing it from opera in other periods were the competition, or coexistence, with ideas of enlightened absolutism, with forms of the European spoken drama (both tragedy and comedy, courtly and bourgeois), and with the reception of antiquity.

The seventeenth century had not favoured a terminological or factual distinction between serious and comic operas. The dualistic concept of heroic (serious) and comic dramatic genres, which implied a difference of rank, derived from the classicist (Aristotelian) theory of drama, which from c. 1690 gained influence on Italian opera. This theory rigorously distinguishes tragedy and comedy, but not so much according to the plots as to the social status of the characters. Tragedy (called *tragedia* or often simply *dramma*) required mythical or royal characters, extraordinary events, heroic attitudes; comedy presented ordinary, contemporary and sometimes low-minded people. In the early eighteenth century, comic operas usually carried the name of the 'low-class' variant, *commedia per musica*, and were thus clearly separated from the heroic or mythological *dramma*. Not by coincidence, it is in this phase that comic scenes or *intermezzi comici per musica*, which could be full of slapstick humour, often appeared for the sake of contrast in musical *drammi*, but rarely in *commedie*. From about 1740 onwards, librettists of comic operas usually called their products *dramma giocoso per musica*, presumably to lend them a higher literary status. The first known appearance of this term belongs to Giovangualberto Barlocci's libretto *La libertà nociva* (Rome, 1740, music by Rinaldo da Capua).[2] This new designation then seems to have run parallel with *opera buffa* just in the same way as the term *dramma per musica* was shadowed by *opera seria*. Analogous specifications of the serious genre as *dramma serio*, *dramma eroico* or *dramma tragico per musica* were to complete the terminological symmetry towards the end of the century.

Differentiation into sub-genres, whether by content or by form, often depended on individual tastes or local conditions. Not always did diverging names refer to clearly distinguishable things. It is possible, however, to isolate the type of pastoral opera, which continued the seventeenth-century tradition of the *favola pastorale* and was now usually called *dramma* (or *melodramma*) *pastorale per musica*. The latter term appears, for example, with Francesco Silvani's *Ama più chi men si crede* (Venice, 1709, music by Antonio Lotti). Critics of the time rated this subgenre rather near that of comedy, whether because of the rural setting or the non-royal characters, who might also be royals disguised as shepherds. Heroic themes could in any case be introduced here, as had already been done in Renaissance drama; this led to hybrids such as the *pastorale eroica per musica* or *melodramma*

---

2.   Piero Weiss, 'La diffusione del repertorio operistico nell'Italia del settecento: il caso dell'opera buffa', in *Civiltà teatrale e settecento emiliano*, ed. by S. Davoli (Bologna: Mulino, 1986), pp. 241–56.

eroico pastorale – the name of Antonio Maria Lucchini's *Dorilla in Tempe* (Venice, 1726, music by Vivaldi). Pietro Metastasio used pastoral themes or settings in some of his *drammi per musica* without referring to the fact in the designation: for example in *L'Olimpiade*, *Ciro riconosciuto*, *Il Re Pastore*.

Occasionally, pastoral operas were labelled 'satyres': an example is *Il Dafni* by Girolamo Frigimelica-Roberti, designated a *tragedia satirica* (Venice, 1705, music by Carlo Francesco Pollarolo). Satirical works in the modern sense, such as parodies of heroic operas, were frequent in Venice before c. 1740, but no music is extant. Later, this variant merged with opera buffa in general.[3]

Genuine musical tragedies with unhappy endings – sometimes in a pastoral setting – were written mainly around 1700–30 and after c. 1760. The earlier of these phases seems indebted to Italian humanist ideas; conspicuous contributors were Girolamo Frigimelica-Roberti, for example with *Il trionfo della libertà*, a *tragedia per musica* (Venice, 1707, music by Alessandro Scarlatti), and Agostino Piovene, for example with *Nerone* (Venice, 1721, music by G. M. Orlandini). The later phase was triggered by French influences and the reforms advocated by Raniero de' Calzabigi. One of the earliest musical tragedies of this phase was Mattia Verazi's *Sofonisba* (Mannheim, 1762, music by Tommaso Traetta).

Mixtures of tragic-heroic and comic elements were achieved in various ways.[4] Pietro Pariati, in his *tragicommedie per musica*, liked to lead aristocratic characters into ridiculous situations, as in his *Don Chisciotte in Sierra Morena* (Vienna, 1719, music by Francesco Conti). Many other librettists simply juxtaposed noble and ridiculous characters, for example in *Angelica ed Orlando*, a *dramma per musica* by Francesco Antonio Tullio (Naples, 1735, music by Gaetano Latilla). An outcome of these experiments later in the century was the development of *opera semiseria* and of the partly parodistic *dramma eroicomico per musica*, exemplified by Carlo Francesco Badini's *Le Pazzie d'Orlando* (London, 1771, music by Pietro Guglielmi), which was also set as *Orlando Paladino* by Joseph Haydn (Eszterháza, 1782).[5]

Variants of the genre can also be distinguished by their form. Most important were the shorter types of opera, known as *azione teatrale per musica* or *festa teatrale per musica*, which were often monosectional or divided in two parts only. The courtly theatres of Europe regularly produced them on festive occasions. They belonged, properly speaking, to the tradition of the *componimento drammatico per musica*, as the genre is called in most older librettos. It had been available since the seventeenth century as a more restrained or more exclusive kind of entertainment, for example in the private quarters of the Roman popes, where of course no operas could be performed.

---

3. See Silke Leopold, 'Einige Gedanken zum Thema: Komische Oper in Venedig vor Goldoni', in *Bericht über den internationalen musikwissenschaftlichen Kongress Bayreuth 1981*, ed. by C.-H. Mahling and S. Wiesmann (Kassel, etc.: Bärenreiter, 1984), pp. 85–92.
4. It must be kept in mind that the Italian term 'tragicommedia' could be understood as the equivalent of the French 'tragicomédie' or 'comédie héroïque', a heroic drama with a happy ending.
5. Helen Geyer-Kiefl, *Die heroisch-komische Oper, ca. 1720–1820* (Tutzing: Schneider, 1987) (Würzburger musikhistorische Beiträge, 9).

The formal distinction of the shorter types of opera corresponded to a differentiation of content, whether it be the lack of a love story, or of a secondary conflict, or of architectural stagecraft. Many *componimenti drammatici per musica* were in fact celebratory, allegorical, pastoral or comic; in the last case they were sometimes called *scherzo drammatico per musica*. They could have mythological and therefore sometimes tragic *sujets* such as Acis and Galatea, Pyramus and Thisbe, and so on. The relatively simple plots and lack of historical intrigue enabled this conservative sub-genre to become, paradoxically, a vehicle for opera reform in Calzabigi's and Gluck's *Orfeo ed Euridice*, a *festa teatrale per musica* (Vienna, 1762).[6] The reverse example is provided by Metastasio, who treated heroic-historical themes even in some of his *azioni teatrali*, as in *Il sogno di Scipione*, 1735, and *Atenaide*, 1762.

Genre-transfer between the *dramma per musica* and smaller forms occurred as well, involving even non-dramatic genres such as *serenata* and *cantata da camera*. Silvio Stampiglia's *Imeneo* (Naples, 1723, music by Nicola Porpora) originated as a *componimento drammatico per musica* in two parts, but was also cast into three-act opera form (as in Handel's setting, 1740). *Medonte re d'Epiro*, a *dramma per musica* by Giovanni de Gamerra (Florence, 1777, music by Giuseppe Sarti), appeared in Florence, 1782, as a two-part *cantata* with choruses. It is probable that unstaged performances of operas – under names such as *serenata* or *cantata* – were frequent, particularly in ecclesiastical institutions.

The *dramma per musica* in contemporary society

In contrast to its status today, opera in eighteenth-century Italy was almost a regular theatrical entertainment, whereas literary spoken theatre was rather a speciality. In the earlier part of the century, the cultivation of spoken drama was confined to a few centres and circles of patrons, above all the academies of Rome, Modena, Parma, Bologna, Siena and Florence. Spoken comedies in verse and prose, and the improvised performances of the commedia dell'arte, were widely enjoyed, but did not really compete with opera.

Until about the middle of the century, the *dramma per musica* was the dominating operatic form. From 1701 to 1745, the theatres of Venice staged more than 450 different operas, i.e. ten per year: of these, eight or nine in each year were *drammi per musica*, the others comic operas or pastorals.[7] Beginning with the advent of opera buffa in 1743, the total number of operas rose at first to about fourteen per year, without a reduction of *drammi per musica*. From about 1750 onwards, a balance was maintained of performing about eleven operas per year, five or six each in the two main types. Except for variations in the years 1756–60, this balance still functioned until c. 1790. The situation in other major cities was presumably analogous. An observer wrote in 1756 that Italy as a whole was producing fifty new operas each

6. Raymond Monelle, 'Gluck and the Festa Teatrale', *Music & Letters* 54 (1973), pp. 308–25.
7. The following statistics for Venice are mainly derived from Taddeo Wiel, *I teatri musicali veneziani del settecento* (Venice, 1897), repr. ed. by R. Strohm (Leipzig: Peters Reprints, 1979).

carnival season, and if the *burlette* or comic operas were counted as well, over a hundred.[8] In Venice, the *dramma per musica* probably had a fixed clientele and certainly a fixed opera house, the Teatro S. Benedetto, which from 1755 performed serious operas exclusively, continuing the earlier social role of the S. Giovanni Grisostomo and S. Cassiano theatres.[9]

Tickets for admission to theatres specializing in opera seria were expensive.[10] Everyone had to buy them, whether being a subscriber or owner of a box (*palco*), or seeking admission only to the stalls (*platea*), which provided unnumbered benches or no seats at all. The uppermost tier and gallery were often accessible to the common people and servants, who had free entrance if they accompanied persons of rank. This unequal tripartite division of the auditorium approximately reflected the social structures of the audience. The stalls were populated by younger and often fanatical supporters, mostly men, from the privileged classes (and possibly by courtesans), the boxes were used by the court, aristocracy and patrician families, and the upper tier and gallery by the common people. It was normal to see up to ten or twenty performances of the same opera in a season if the piece was successful. To a large extent, visits to the opera were used for social intercourse and the boxes were aristocratic meeting places. Guests and foreign visitors were regularly invited to the opera house.

The most important patrons of the *dramma per musica*, the wealthy aristocracy and the courts, influenced operatic life after the middle of the century predominantly in favour of the serious genre. Thus they stood against a more general trend favouring opera buffa. Enlightened princes did no more than to strive for a certain balance of genres, as for example Archduke Peter Leopold of Tuscany, who in 1776 liberalized a public opera system which had previously obliged the impresarios to provide a minimum number of opera seria productions (more than half the annual performances).[11] There were no significant regional differences in the cultivation of the various operatic genres, except perhaps that some provincial centres turned to opera buffa more decisively, because specialized buffa troupes operated without castratos and were therefore cheaper to hire than the opera seria personnel.

Nevertheless, the *dramma per musica* in eighteenth-century Italy had the cultural significance of a national art-form. Italian opera was capable of suggesting a national unity which in political terms seemed unattainable. It inherited much of the aura of *italianità* which the Italian language and poetry had possessed since the times of Petrarch. The 'national' quality of the operatic genre itself, and of its means of expression (belcanto, recitative, da capo aria, and so on), was intensely discussed

---

8. Henri Bédarida, 'L'opéra italien jugé par un amateur français en 1756', in *Mélanges de musicologie offerts à M. Lionel de la Laurencie* (Paris: Droz, 1933), p. 190.
9. See T. Wiel, *I teatri musicali*, and Nicola Mangini, 'I teatri Veneziani al tempo della collaborazione di Galuppi con Goldoni', in *Galuppiana*, ed. by M. T. Muraro et al. (Florence: Olschki, 1986), pp. 133–42.
10. For more detailed information (largely relevant to the eighteenth century), see Lorenzo Bianconi and Thomas Walker, 'Production, consumption and political function of seventeenth-century Italian opera', *Early Music History* 4 (Cambridge, 1984), pp. 209–96, especially pp. 221–43.
11. Marcello De Angelis, *La felicità in Etruria. Melodramma, impresari, musica, virtuosi: lo spettacolo nella Firenze dei Lorena* (Florence: Ponte alle Grazie, 1990), pp. 113–17.

by contemporaries. For example, critical comparisons of French and Italian art, music or literature often mention opera in nationalist terms (see also below). The classicizing plots of the *dramma per musica* frequently touched upon peninsular history, particularly that of the Roman Republic and Empire. These national interpretations of the past also tended to involve, towards the end of the century, operatic calls for freedom, and criticism of foreign European powers, for example in librettos featuring Cato or Horatius. In contrast to comic opera, the *dramma per musica* was written exclusively in Tuscan, the dominant literary idiom; in its historical aloofness it also ignored other regional differentiations, for example of costume. This helped to assure it a high cultural reputation and wide reception among both local audiences and foreigners. Tourism was a vital source of income for Italy's cities at the time. The carnival celebrations, not only of Venice, had attracted foreigners since well before 1700 and were significantly interrelated with opera. Despite potential conflicts between the opera business and the ecclesiastical authorities, at least the subjects of the *dramma per musica* were mostly taken from pre- or non-Christian civilizations and could therefore be used to promote enlightened tendencies without openly contradicting the Church. As the most splendid and yet non-ecclesiastical art-form in Italy at the time, opera in general fostered the secularization of art and of creative thought.

On the other hand, there had always been a solid alliance between opera and political absolutism. The hierarchic structures and the celebratory, ritualistic character of the *dramma per musica* as well as its apparent freedom and spontaneity of personal artistic expression had come to symbolize aristocratic norms of morality and rulership. In the eighteenth century the *dramma per musica* aimed at social modelling rather than the self-glorification of power as it had done in the preceding century, but in representing rulers who conformed to general human norms, it helped to legitimize their actual power. Even the eighteenth-century reforms of opera, welcome to the courts, did not break this ideological alliance.

Other cultural trends for which the *dramma per musica* served as a vehicle were exoticism, pastoral tastes and a general nostalgia which typified the escapism of an urban society more and more entangled in bureaucratic concerns. Voltaire's or Rousseau's idea of the 'noble savage' was preceded in the *dramma per musica* by librettos acknowledging the dignity of the ancient Chinese or Central American civilizations (Apostolo Zeno's *Teuzzone*, 1706, exemplifies the former, Girolamo Giusti's *Montezuma*, 1733, the latter). The Romantic interest in ancient ruins, in archaic customs and archeology, is already well developed in Pietro Metastasio's earlier librettos – for example in dramas set in Roman times, where famous rituals and sacred monuments were shown. These tastes, anti-rationalist at least in tendency, were by 1780–90 transformed into the Romantic types of 'rescue-' und 'terror-opera'.

In the eighteenth century the reception of Italian music in the rest of Europe concentrated more on opera than had been the case in the seventeenth. The *dramma per musica* was a European art-form as well as a major representative of Italian culture, which it helped to disseminate. By comparison, the European reception of French culture and customs did not depend on the distribution of French music but rather supported it in turn. The fame of the *dramma per musica* abroad overshadowed that of other Italian musical genres (oratorio, cantata, concerto), and its heroic historical *sujets* themselves illustrated the importance of supranational dynasties and their interactions. The system of the European political territories offered Italian opera a wide and deep market, opening up second or even first career chances to many *operisti*: musicians, poets, scene-painters, architects, impresarios. In addition to the Italian court poets of Vienna, Mannheim, Munich, Berlin and other centres, who often had much wider duties than that of writing librettos, some of the most important singers and composers spent decisive years abroad: for example Agostino Steffani (Hanover, Düsseldorf), Attilio Ariosti and Giovanni Bononcini (Berlin, Vienna, London), Carlo Broschi detto Farinelli (London, Madrid), Nicola Porpora (London, Vienna), Antonio Caldara, Antonio Salieri (Vienna), Faustina Bordoni (London, Dresden), Francesco Corselli (Madrid), Niccolò Jommelli (Vienna, Mannheim, Stuttgart), Regina Mingotti (Dresden, Berlin, London), Baldassare Galuppi (London, St Petersburg), Giuseppe Sarti (Vienna, Copenhagen, St Petersburg). Handel, Hasse, Gluck and J. C. Bach went to Italy for professional training and returned to the north almost like native Italian *operisti*. The opera careers of Fux, Karl Heinrich Graun, Joseph Haydn and Mozart, which were mostly spent outside Italy, demonstrate the enormous receptivity of Central Europe to the genre. Since the dynastic network of opera patronage connected other parts of Europe with Italy itself, for example through the Habsburg dominion of Lombardy, Naples and then Tuscany, or the Bourbon administrations in Parma and Naples, major developments of the genre occurred both inside and outside Italy, as with the almost simultaneous reform initiatives of Du Tillot/Frugoni/Traetta in Parma, 1759–60, and Durazzo/Calzabigi/Gluck in Vienna from 1761. These circumstances, however, should not be used to downplay the role of Italy itself in the development of the genre, as has sometimes happened.

Civic and aristocratic patrons of opera, particularly in Central Europe (Bohemia, Leipzig, Hamburg and elsewhere), often hired opera seria specialists who had come from Italy as a travelling troupe: the Denzios, Mingottis, Peruzzis, Nicolinis, Bambinis, Locatellis and yet others. Many of these troupes converted to opera buffa after c. 1750. In London and other northern cities, Italian impresarios were active on their own or on behalf of the courts, and were supported by the native aristocracy sometimes into the nineteenth century. The *dramma per musica* spearheaded Italian opera when it was established, between c. 1710 and c. 1760, in the kingdoms of Britain, Spain, Portugal, Sweden, Russia and Denmark. In France, where Italian opera was traditionally excluded, the French-texted *drammi per musica* by Gluck, Sacchini and Piccinni performed after c. 1770 exemplified the major achievements of the genre.[12] A mutual interaction between *dramma per musica* and *tragédie lyrique*, as well as other French and Italian forms, can also be gathered from the French

---

12. On critical reception in France, see Bianca Maria Antolini, 'L'Opera italiana in Francia: intorno all'"Essay sur l'union de la poésie et de la musique" di François-Jean de Chastellux (1765)', in *Napoli e il teatro musicale*, ed. by B. M. Antolini and W. Witzenmann (Florence: Olschki, 1993), pp. 69–96.

critical debates on opera and music in general. The readers of the time, especially in England and France, favoured memoirs, letters and travel accounts, genres which typically discussed opera as performed in many European centres. Competent and critical remarks about singers, music and theatres are found in authors such as De Brosses, Montesquieu and Burney. The European discussion of opera seria was, in any case, one of the liveliest intellectual debates of the period. In this respect, the *dramma per musica* exceeded even opera buffa in public acclaim.

Management and production

The *dramma per musica* was the most expensive form of opera for whose production the most demanding specialists, such as castratos and theatre architects, had to be hired. It required a considerable investment and was cultivated more in big centres than in small towns, and more as a long-term than short-term undertaking.[13] Unforeseen circumstances, however, often cut the activities short. The theatres had to be built or rebuilt for the specific needs of the genre, particularly the movable scenery which was not yet the rule in other theatres and genres including that of opera buffa. The auditoria were usually large for the standards of the time, larger for example than in French opera, as reported by Charles de Brosses (1739). Furnishings and lighting were opulent. In addition to the opera houses at courts and in cities, occasional venues for opera were, as often in the seventeenth century, summer palaces (Pratolino, near Florence; Salzdahlum, near Braunschweig) and country seats of nobles (*villeggiature*) or of academies (S. Giovanni in Persiceto, near Bologna).

The patrons of the *dramma per musica* were, first of all, the princes of various ranks, who considered opera as their own business and had it managed by court theatre directors, majordomos or other court employees as part of the household, often financing it from the private purse. Secondly, the opera houses were increasingly managed by associations and corporate bodies – noble, civic, academic or even ecclesiastical – in the larger cities such as London, Rome, Milan, Turin, Bologna and Prague. These managements often needed princely guarantees or subventions to be viable.[14] In Venice, leading patrician families controlled certain opera houses and sometimes owned the building itself. In addition, the civic administration (city council, police) had a controlling function or financial interest (Hamburg, Bologna, Reggio Emilia). In a few places (Vienna, Madrid), a civic opera house existed alongside the court opera.

In all these cases the actual productions could be entrusted to professional impresarios who might work as court employees or as leaseholders. The third type

13.   L. Bianconi and T. Walker, 'Production, consumption and political function of seventeenth-century Italian opera'; Franco Piperno, 'Il sistema produttivo, fino al 1780', in *Storia dell'opera italiana*, ed. by L. Bianconi et al., vol. 4, 1987, pp. 1–75
14.   On this matter, see Franco Piperno, 'Impresariato collettivo e strategie teatrali: Sul sistema produttivo dello spettacolo operistico settecentesco', in *Civiltà teatrale*, ed. by S. Davoli, 1986, pp. 345–65.

of management, that of the free impresario working for his own benefit, was rare because of the high risks involved, and was at first concentrated on a few centres (Venice, Hamburg) and travelling troupes. After c. 1700, however, these forms of business were made more efficient, for example by spreading the productions over a whole region (Orsatti in the Veneto region) or by combining seasonal trips with a fixed base (the Prague impresarios).

The seasonal pattern in Italy was the same as for other forms of theatre. Carnival lasted from 26 December (St Stephen's Day) to Ash Wednesday; many centres also had a spring season around Ascension, and possibly an autumn season which in Naples and Venice was sometimes extended into Advent. At court, operas or smaller dramatic performances could be used to celebrate the birthdays and namedays of their sovereigns, in whatever part of the year. This also happened in allied territories (for example in Naples or Milan for Habsburg or Bourbon rulers), or at the Roman embassies of the European powers. In Protestant centres such as Hamburg and London, operas were performed from about October to July, with a short break in Lent.

Italian opera required many specialists, particularly among the singers. In the eighteenth century their careers focused on either the comic or the serious genre; castratos specialized only in the latter.[15] The leading singers enjoyed a high social status and were much better paid than the composers. Some castratos had parallel careers as composers, art-dealers and booksellers, court secretaries or impresarios.[16] National and increasingly international circulation led to the development of a European 'labour market' for opera singers. Its relatively standardized tasks and conditions furthered the standardization of the *dramma per musica* itself, or vice versa. From c. 1725 to c. 1800 this trend corresponded to the universal applicability of Metastasio's librettos. The careers of some singers suggest that they knew the most suitable roles in his *œuvre* by heart and only learned the music afresh for each production. But it is also known that individual singers performed, in successive seasons, different roles of the same drama. Singers were often chosen and paid according to a rough classification into categories such as 'prima, seconda (etc.) donna', 'primo, secondo (etc.) uomo', 'tenore', which in the course of the century became more refined and adapted for use in opera buffa. This so-called 'role

15. Sergio Durante, 'Il cantante', in *Storia dell'opera italiana*, ed. by L. Bianconi and G. Pestelli, vol. 4, 1987, pp. 349–415; idem, 'Alcune considerazioni sui cantanti di teatro del primo settecento e la loro formazione', in *Antonio Vivaldi*, ed. by L. Bianconi and G. Morelli, vol. 2, 1982, pp. 427–81; Robert S. Freeman, 'Farinello and His Repertory', in *Studies in Renaissance and Baroque Music in Honor of Arthur Mendel*, ed. by Robert Marshall (Kassel, etc.: Bärenreiter, 1974), pp. 301–30; John Rosselli, 'The Castrati as a Professional Group and a Social Phenomenon, 1550–1850', *Acta Musicologica* 60 (1988), pp. 143–79. On buffo singers, see Reinhard Strohm, 'Aspetti sociali dell'opera italiana del primo Settecento', *Musica/Realtà* 2 (1981), pp. 117–41; Franco Piperno, 'Buffe e buffi (Considerazioni sulla professionalità degli interpreti di scene buffe ed intermezzi)', *Rivista Italiana di Musicologia* 18 (1982), pp. 240–84. Generally on singers, see also John Rosselli, *Singers of Italian Opera: The History of a Profession* (Cambridge: Cambridge University Press, 1992).

16. See, for example, Lowell Lindgren, 'La carriera di Gaetano Berenstadt, contralto evirato (ca. 1690–1735)', *Rivista Italiana di Musicologia* 19 (1984), pp. 36–112; Elvidio Surian, 'L'operista', in *Storia dell'opera italiana*, ed. by L. Bianconi and G. Pestelli, vol. 4, 1987, pp. 293–345.

hierarchy' is said to have influenced the dramaturgy of the *dramma per musica*. It certainly had an effect on the number of arias given to each singer, sometimes in contradiction to the dramatic weight of his or her role.[17]

Instrumentalists and *maestri di cappella* of opera seria were often simultaneously employed in church or as chamber musicians. Most composers also wrote sacred music; after c. 1750 many contributed to opera buffa as well. Composers who specialized in opera seria after c. 1750 were Johann Adolf Hasse, Davide Perez, J. C. Bach, Niccolò Jommelli and Francesco di Majo: whether they did this voluntarily or conformed to institutional requirements is not entirely clear.

An Italian impresario was able to hire all the performers, including the composers, from anywhere, according to what his financial resources, taste and patronage would allow. The contract of work, called *scrittura*, concerned a single production or more often a whole season, the latter particularly when it came to singers, scenographers and costume designers. At court, existing employees could be 'borrowed' for the opera productions, for example the court poet, architect, the chapel singers and trumpeters, or the prince might impose his favourite chamber artists on the opera management.

Composers, if hired from elsewhere, usually arrived within four to six weeks before the first performance; they composed or arranged one or two opera scores while in residence. The total annual programme of a leading opera house (for example in Venice) might comprise as many as five or six different operas written by three to four *maestri di cappella*. The composers normally had to conduct the premières but not the subsequent performances. Stage rehearsals, directed by the *maestro* at the first harpsichord, lasted for a few weeks at most. There were also many private rehearsals, and negiotiations over substitute arias or costumes, for example. The singers' agents, mothers, patrons and friends might be involved in these, as is vividly satirized in Benedetto Marcello's *Il teatro alla moda* (Venice, 1720). The custom of holding private auditions with potential patrons before the première is documented as well. The stage rehearsals were partly concerned with stage action and movement, the direction of which was the responsibility of the librettist.[18] Recitative performances may sometimes have been improvised; the setting of recitatives is said to have occasionally been devolved to composition students.

When a production ceased to draw audiences, it was simply discontinued. If this happened towards the end of a season when no other production was scheduled, ad hoc performances of serenatas or pasticcio operas might be put on as stop-gaps. The musical settings, stage-sets, costumes, librettos and other parts of discontinued productions were henceforth available for other operas or productions, although the authors or managers sometimes tried to prevent this. The recitatives mostly required new settings for a new cast. Individual arias, however, were frequently

---

17.   In Leonardo Leo's *Catone in Utica* (Venice, 1729), for example, Farinelli had only the secondary role of Arbace but sang by far the most arias.
18.   See Gerardo Guccini, 'Direzione scenica e regía', in *Storia dell'opera italiana*, ed. by L. Bianconi and G. Pestelli, vol. 5, 1988, pp. 123–73.

copied and reused, as they circulated among professional copyists, composers, singers, patrons and members of the audience. Pasticcio operas are those which contain a large number of arias already used in other operas (whether or not by the same composer). Furthermore, in 'original' scores a few borrowed arias from earlier works of the same composer can often be found. Singers travelled around with their favourite arias (*arie di baule*, i.e. 'suitcase arias'), aiming at inserting them into new productions. The majority of the complete opera scores extant today were never used for performances but copied for purposes of documentation. This is even true of the few large collections comprising copies of instrumental parts as well (for example, the former Imperial Library of Vienna or the Biblioteca de Ajuda, Lisbon).

Ballets were added to all operatic genres, depending on taste and resources. Opera seria performances of the later eighteenth century were frequently combined with splendid ballet-pantomimes which could have an independent *sujet*, whether heroic-historical, pastoral or mythological.[19] Ballet producers such as Gasparo Angiolini or Jean-Georges Noverre were actively involved in the opera reforms around 1760–70. Scenographers and theatre architects also had much impact on the history of the *dramma per musica*, to name only the Piedmontese architect Filippo Juvarra, or the families (Galli) Bibiena, Galliari and Quaglio, who first contributed representative courtly architectures for historical *drammi*, and later created evocative images for classicist and pre-Romantic works. Librettists were aware of this contribution and may have planned their dramas also as visual sequences.[20] Famous painters and draftsmen, for example the Roman caricaturist Pierleone Ghezzi, or the Venetian families Canal and Mauro, also painted stage-sets for *drammi per musica*. Too little is known about these, or about the style and significance of costume designers.[21]

Drama and music

The so-called 'conventions of opera seria' have been described many times, often with a critical or satirical intention. This is a tradition which goes back to the period itself (see also below). All the same, even the wittiest satires (such as Benedetto Marcello's *Il teatro alla moda*, 1720) or the most engaged polemics (such as Calzabigi's *Risposta di Don Santigliano*, 1790) did not strive to present these conventions as a self-contained, authoritarian system of strict rules – an image conveyed by

19. See, generally, Kathleen Kuzmick Hansell, 'Il ballo teatrale e l'opera italiana', in *Storia dell'opera italiana*, ed. by L. Bianconi and G. Pestelli, vol. 5, 1988, pp. 175–306.
20. Mercedes Viale Ferrero, 'Luogo teatrale e spazio scenico', in *Storia dell'opera italiana*, ed. by L. Bianconi and G. Pestelli, vol. 5, 1988, pp. 1–122; eadem, 'Le didascalie sceniche nei drammi per musica di Zeno', in *L'Opera italiana a Vienna*, ed. by M. T. Muraro, 1990, pp. 271–85; Elena Sala Di Felice, *Metastasio: Ideologia, drammaturgia, spettacolo* (Milan: Franco Angeli, 1983), pp. 109–47.
21. See William L. Barcham, 'Costume in the Frescoes of Tiepolo and Eighteenth-Century Italian Opera', in *Opera and Vivaldi*, ed. by M. Collins and E. K. Kirk, 1984, pp. 149–69.

some twentieth-century commentaries.[22] It is rather that the cultivation of this ubiquitous genre favoured conformism but also a thousand variants, that it aimed at rationality but lacked a pervasive system. Many a convention, well established later, was at the beginning of this period only an ideal which supporters of the *dramma per musica* hoped to promote. They urged, in particular, the elimination of the 'irregularities' of seventeenth-century practice – such as the mixing of tragic and comic elements – and recommended the return to good taste, to dramatic verisimilitude (for example by omitting spectacle and supernatural appearances) and generally the imitation of nature, which in turn was being measured against the principle of verisimilitude. These ideals had been developed by French critics on the basis of the classical poetics, and had been used in evaluating spoken *tragédies* by Pierre Corneille, Jean Racine and others. The *dramma per musica* also imitated the French in heeding the social norms of the *bienséances* (*decorum*), which were thought to be just as relevant for characters on stage as for people in the auditorium.

The primary matter of the *dramma per musica* was the poem. It consisted of *versi sciolti* (heptasyllables and hendecasyllables in free succession) for the recitatives, and of lyrical verse in many different metres for the arias (also called *ariette* or *canzonette*). A *dramma per musica* usually had three Acts (five Acts indicated a more classicist or French-influenced variant), each with up to twenty 'scenes' which were defined by the entrance of new characters. Usually, two or more different stage-sets were shown in each Act. The five to eight characters of a drama (Metastasio mostly had six) appeared on stage in a well-planned succession aimed at continuity: leaving the stage empty within an Act or unit was avoided (*liaison des scènes*). This principle was related to the ideal of verisimilitude, as interruptions in the sequence of events were deemed to be improbable.

According to the conventional view, recitatives and arias were contrasting but complementary means of expression, of which the former had to present the action, the latter the affections and thus the essential dramatic message. This separation of dramaturgical functions, and as a result the scenic type of the exit aria – which prevailed from c. 1690 onwards – was rooted in the theory of the genre itself. The *dramma per musica* rarely admitted events which could not be expressed on stage through monologue or dialogue. On the other hand, there were traditional doubts concerning the probability of singing on stage, particularly for the purpose of ordinary communication.[23] This meant that arias – sung verse – were not simply employed to function as ordinary dialogue, but had to be either monologues or quasi-monologues carrying special significance, being declarations to the audience, public speeches, invocations of supernatural powers, visions, soliloquies, confessions of love. Furthermore, 'sentence arias', i.e. quotations of traditional popular sayings, mostly directed to the audience, were welcome. The often-cited 'simile arias' (which also existed in bourgeois musical comedy) usually combined the

22. For example in Marita P. McClymonds and D. Heartz, 'Opera seria', in *The New Grove Dictionary of Opera*, ed. by S. Sadie (London: Macmillan, 1992), vol. 3, pp. 698–707.
23. On the problem of singing on stage, see Piero Weiss, 'Baroque Opera and the Two Verisimilitudes', in *Music and Civilization: Essays in Honor of P. H. Lang* (New York, 1984), pp. 117–26, and the essay '*Tolomeo*: Handel's opera and the rules of tragedy', chapter 10 in this volume.

expression of a commonplace truth with a metaphorical depiction of an emotional situation, which had to be addressed to the audience. The imagery of these statements was related to Baroque emblematics. The dramaturgical space which could accommodate all these expressions with their music was typically found on the edges of the drama, as it were: in locations where ordinary dialogue has not yet begun or has just finished. An ideal place for arias was, for example, the moment when one of the dialogue partners has 'hit the nail on the head', making further discussion unnecessary: we may call this an 'aria threshold'.

Entrance arias, especially those interrupted by recitative, and shorter aria forms (such as the *cavatina*) were still regularly used about 1720 but then fell into disfavour, probably because they did not sufficiently allow for immediate applause. Between c. 1680 and c. 1720, the number of *ariette* in a typical *dramma per musica* decreased from about fifty to about thirty. At the same time, their length and expressivity was greatly enhanced.

It would be an exaggeration, however, to claim that the recitatives in the *dramma per musica* presented only actions, the arias only feelings. Metastasio, for one, enumerates several other expressive functions of the aria: 'character, situation, affections, opinion and reasoning'.[24] The French term *sentiment* (Italian: *sentenza*), in any case, denoted both 'feeling, emotion' and 'thought, reasoning'. Librettists liked to alternate between strongly expressive and less expressive arias. Drama theorists generally recommended the variation between extreme and moderate colours, calling it *chiaroscuro*, as in painting.[25] Certain arias communicated ideas or ideals, others suggested the pleasures of nature or sensual enjoyment, yet others presented the ethos or pathos of the characters. To conquer this variety, the eighteenth century developed pragmatic or theoretical aria classifications involving categories such as *aria cantabile*, *aria di bravura*, *aria parlante*, and so on. These aria typologies may have been useful, at least for impresarios and listeners, as a rough guide through the immense variety of poetic expressions, singing styles and dramatic situations the genre could offer. Aria typologies have also been seen as the vehicle for the practice of borrowing and transferring arias from one dramatic context to another, if necessary with parody texts, because it was assumed that in a stereotypical dramatic situation, any aria belonging to the same category could be sung. But arias were frequently transferred into quite dissimilar dramatic situations, and the reasons for the transfer often concerned other textual or musical aspects.[26] The practice of aria transfer and parody was gradually replaced by individualized reworkings in the operas of Gluck and other reformers.[27]

There was a general consensus that imitation of nature in the aria was best achieved through natural declamation and a lively musical support for the recited words. Particular stress was laid on the poetic variety of metaphors and metres, and

24. 'Caratteri, situazioni, affetti, senso, ragione': quoted after Paolo Gallarati, *Musica e maschera: Il libretto italiano del settecento* (Turin: EdT, 1984), p. 60.
25. For example by Pier Jacopo Martello, *Della tragedia antica e moderna* (Rome, 1714), in P. J. Martello, *Scritti critici e satirici*, ed. by Hannibal S. Noce (Bari: Laterza, 1963).
26. R. Strohm, *Italienische Opernarien*, vol. 1, pp. 245–60.
27. Klaus Hortschansky, *Parodie und Entlehnung im Schaffen Chr. Willibald Glucks* (Köln: Volk, 1973).

on musical inventiveness in rhythm and melody. Both Martello and Metastasio emphasized the rhythmic variety of different arias.[28] Contemporary and later critics (such as Chastellux and Planelli) praised 'simple and periodical vocal melody' – articulated, for example, in four-bar groups – which they considered an innovation of the 1720s.

One might think that the imitation of nature was most hampered by the so-called da capo form (ABA), inherited from the previous century. This poetic refrain form was derived from the traditional *canzonetta* and consisted of a single stanza (middle section) and a refrain (*intercalare*, da capo section) sung before and after. The da capo repetition of the text was increasingly criticized around 1740–60, or suggestions were made for making it appear 'natural' or dramatically probable.[29] Nevertheless, it remained in use for longer than the musical da capo form itself, until c. 1780, when modified or climactic musical repetitions had become the norm. In the reform operas of the Gluckian tendency, strophic and other repetition schemes are frequently employed for dramatic effects.

Ensembles were rare in the *dramma per musica*, partly because they had no analogy in spoken drama. Whereas the love duet and the chorus were tolerated as legitimate forms of simultaneous speaking, the dramatic ensemble – regularly found already in Alessandro Scarlatti's operas – was like a multiple, sung dialogue with interaction of the characters and was therefore seldom introduced. The typical seria-ensemble of the later eighteenth century was more like a simultaneous *a parte* indicating a stalemate of conflicting affections, with expressive functions quite comparable to those of an aria.[30]

The core of the matter was the developing ideal of dramatic identification through the means of music: the fiction that the character on stage creates, in the very moment of performance, the words that are musically recited, whether to interact with a partner on stage or to arouse the feelings of the spectators who are made to participate in the same fiction. This dramatic identification was pursued, in the earlier phase, almost entirely through the delivery of words clothed in music, but in the later phase increasingly through the medium of the instrumental sounds of the ritornellos and accompaniments, which the listeners had learnt to accept as representing the innermost tones of the heart. This aesthetic, which since the generation of C. P. E. Bach was also transferred to pure instrumental music, has remained a natural supposition in opera until the twentieth century.

The development of this progressive personalization and 'dramatization' of music in the *dramma per musica* may be exemplified with a standardized situation such as the *ombra*-aria, where the poetry depicts emotions aroused by a vision, usually in terms of an almost physiological sensation (its congruence with the

---

28. Pietro Metastasio, 'Estratto dell'arte poetica d'Aristotile e considerazioni su la medesima' (1773), in Pietro Metastasio, *Tutte le opere*, vol. 2 (Milan, 1965), p. 964.
29. For example by Mattheson, Algarotti and Krause. Jean François Marmontel, on the other hand, defended the text repetition caused by the da capo.
30. See Daniel Heartz, 'Hasse, Galuppi, and Metastasio', in *Venezia e il melodramma del Settecento* [I], ed. by M. T. Muraro (Florence: Olschki, 1978), pp. 309–39; Reinhard Wiesend, 'Zum Ensemble in der Opera seria', in *Colloquium 'Johann Adolf Hasse'*, ed. by F. Lippmann, 1988, pp. 187–222.

Passions de l'âme described by René Descartes is striking). Until and including Metastasio, the poetry of such arias was a succinct, rhetorically formulated image or tableau, as for example in *Siroe re di Persia*:

'Gelido in ogni vena
scorrer mi sento il sangue,
l'ombra del figlio esangue
m'ingombra di terror.'

('Ice-cold in my veins/ I feel my blood running,/ the shadow of my murdered son/ fills me with terror.')

To give vivid embodiment to such an image was a challenge that could already be met by Hasse's instrumental textures (*Siroe re di Persia*, 1733).[31] His technique of figurative tone-painting could penetrate into the far corners of Metastasio's verbal structure, without endangering the fiction that the character was making a spontaneous statement about his or her feelings.

Further musico-dramatic development was sought in two directions. On the one hand, there was the cultivation of accompanied recitative, usually performed as a preparative *scena* for an aria and depicting the spontaneous surge or fluctuation of feelings. The words of such recitatives often assert the unpredictability of the experience itself, as in 'Non sò che mi nasce in petto . . .', or 'Oh dei! che mai sarà?'; the musical setting indulges in interruptions and surprises. On the other hand, composers of the generation of Niccolò Jommelli and later endeavoured to make the discourse of the aria itself appear 'dramatic', or even to present the musical flow as if it were an acting partner (see also below). The task was to present the often well-known verse as if it were freshly created on the stage, here and now. Under these conditions, the individualization of the musical form had to exceed that of the words by far.[32]

The instrumental and, generally, musical component in the performance of the drama became overwhelming. A 'dramatization' of music was taking place which was at the same time a 'musicalization' of the drama, as the music transgressed the poetic borders assigned to it. In the aria 'Non ti minaccio sdegno' from Metastasio's *Catone in Utica* (Rome, 1728), Leonardo Vinci solidifies the energetic declamation of the words into a terse rhythmic-melodic contour which is also heard at once in the accompanying bass, doubling or echoing the effort of the singer. In the setting by J. C. Bach, however (Naples, 1761), voice and orchestra pursue separate initiatives, the orchestra being the more determined and stronger of the two. The soprano, on the other hand, spontaneously extends her phrase at 'non ti prometto

31. See Helga Lühning, 'Cosroes Verzweiflung: Regel und Erfindung in Hasses Seria-Arien', in *Colloquium 'Johann Adolf Hasse'*, ed. by F. Lippmann, 1987, pp. 79–130. Another good example of this musical approach is Vivaldi's setting of 'Non sò d'onde viene' in his *Olimpiade* (Venice, 1734).
32. For an example from Mozart, see Stefan Kunze, 'Die Vertonungen der Arie "Non sò donde viene" von J. Chr. Bach und W. A. Mozart', in *Studien zur italienisch-deutschen Musikgeschichte II*, ed. by H. Hucke (Cologne-Graz: Böhlau, 1965) (Analecta Musicologica, vol. 2), pp. 85–111.

Example 1a. Leonardo Vinci, *Catone in Utica* I, 2 (Rome, 1728): aria of Marzia

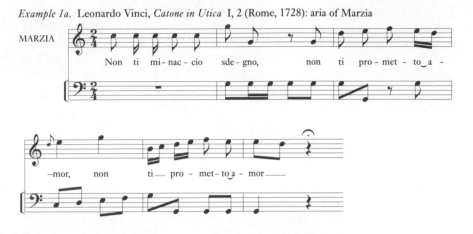

Example 1b. Johann Christian Bach, *Catone in Utica* I, 2 (Naples, 1761)

amor', lyrically deflected by the word 'amor'. The phrase as a whole appears generated, here and now, from the interaction of two unequal partners, whereas Vinci's melody is more easily heard as a song invented by the singer alone (see music example 1). Even so, both artists would still have agreed that the music had to express the feelings of the dramatic character as if experienced at that moment.

A more controversial problem concerns the significance and purpose of the *dramma per musica* as a dramaturgical structure. Around 1690–1700 librettists became more and more influenced by the classicist precepts of tragedy but, not surprisingly, never entirely subscribed to them. The so-called 'three Aristotelian unities' of time, place and action, for example, were felt to be useful to ensure consistency and 'necessity' (i.e. verisimilitude) of the dramatic action, while their rigid application – especially that of the 'unity of place' – was mostly rejected. Other relatively accepted dramaturgical patterns were those of *intrigue* and *dénouement*, and the Aristotelian concepts of *catastrophe* (reversal of fortune) and *catharsis* (purification of the passions), for example through the impact of an unexpected rescue or peaceful solution at the moment of greatest tension.[33] The happy ending (*lieto fine*) remained a principle of the genre until the late eighteenth century (see also above).

The contents of a drama (or tragedy) were usually classified into six categories (*parties intégrantes*), as developed by Pierre Corneille[34] from the model of Aristotle's *Poetics*: they were, in descending order of importance, fable (*sujet*), ethos, pathos, diction, music and scenography. Each of these categories was, in the course of time, turned into a subject which music could express: whereas in the seventeenth century music was regarded as subsidiary and a vehicle of poetry, composers of the eighteenth century made increasing efforts to give musical representation to affections, ethos, *sujet* and setting. This trend was related to the formal emancipation of the aria: the structural weight of the arias increased in the same measure as their capacity to express new aspects of drama increased. The later phases of this development have been characterized above as a 'dramatization' of music, and as a 'musicalization' of drama at the same time. Until about c. 1730, however, the decisive factor was the rhetorical significance of the poetic and musical *concetti* (conceits, images) and the theatrical-allegorical language incorporating them. In the universally competitive atmosphere of the dramatic performance by the singers, what counted was not only the convincing identification of the character with her or his role, and thus with the contents of the words, nor only the beauty of the voice, but just as much the unique, convincing recitation (*pronuntiatio*) according to the precepts of rhetoric, vitally supported by the appropriate action, gesture and mimicry.[35] These precepts were by no means restricted to aria-singing, but were equally valid for recitative, whose performance styles are particularly in need of reconstruction today.[36]

33. Although all these precepts were generally considered valid only in tragedy, librettists of the *dramma giocoso per musica* such as Lorenzo Da Ponte often endeavoured to approximate one or more of the 'unities', or to provide the comic equivalent of a catastrophe.

34. Pierre Corneille, 'Trois discours sur le poème dramatique (1660)', in P. Corneille, *Œuvres complètes*, vol. 3, ed. by Georges Couton (Paris: Gallimard, 1987), pp. 117–90, especially pp. 123–34; these categories of content are contrasted with the categories of form, the *parties d'extension* such as prologue, episode, epilogue.

35. Dene Barnett, *The Art of Gesture: The Practices and Principles of Eighteenth-century Acting* (Heidelberg: Winter, 1987).

36. An important starting point can be the acting directions found in the librettos themselves: see Jacques Joly, 'Le didascalie per la recitazione nei drammi del Metastasio', in *Metastasio*, ed. by Accademia Nazionale dei Lincei, pp. 277–91, also in J. Joly, *Dagli Elisi all'Inferno*, pp. 95–111. On Metastasio's and Hasse's recitatives, in particular, see Raymond Monelle, 'Recitative and Dramaturgy in the Dramma per Musica', *Music & Letters* 59 (1978), pp. 245–67.

Since the time of Monteverdi, the *dramma per musica* had been not only a 'drama of the affections' (Carl Dahlhaus) but also a vehicle for moral edification and intellectual discourse about human nature. Its subjects comprised, in the sense of Aristotle's *Poetics*, both the passions ('pathos') and the virtues or social norms ('ethos'). Its characters were often allegorical representations of them, as in king = power, glory; young hero = valour, honour; princess = honour, fidelity. In the late seventeenth century, however, opera followed European spoken drama in a tendency to loosen these strict analogies between moral precepts and the hierarchy of the dramatis personae. Thus, an ethos such as *gloire* or *virtù* could be personified in several characters at once, although under divergent conditions, as for example in the case of Titus, Berenice and Antiochus in Racine's *Berenice*, or Alexander, Porus and Cleophis in Metastasio's *Alessandro nell'Indie*. In addition, the study of Descartes's *Les passions de l'âme* suggested a more flexible treatment of the interactions between passions and morality.[37] In the *dramma per musica*, the growing tendency towards heroic-historical subjects (as opposed to mythological ones) helped to make characters appear more human, more 'psychologically' motivated, even more sentimental. The spectator was now encouraged to identify with the heroes in their humanity: of the two traditional purposes of tragedy – to arouse fear and compassion – the eighteenth century greatly privileged the latter.

These 'enlightened' tendencies led, on the other hand, to some fragmentation of expression. It could endanger dramatic coherence if single emotional phases or fleeting thoughts were separately displayed, for example one by one in a succession of monologues or arias. This problem has given rise to a modern interpretation of the *dramma per musica* of c. 1690–1740 as a succession of potentially unrelated affective situations (comparable to 'monads'), each represented by an aria.[38] If the drama as a whole were indeed only a kaleidoscope of self-contained affections and situations, unity of 'character' should not be sought in it. In comparison with older interpretations of the *dramma per musica* which looked for the verbal and musical expression of 'psychology' and character development, this theory had the advantage of dismissing overly organicist views of the total structure, and of emphasizing the formal unities, such as the aria, to which the genre was tied. Robert S. Freeman, discussing Apostolo Zeno's librettos and their settings, even coined the formula 'opera without drama' and spoke of opera seria as an 'aria concert', implicitly denying the coherence and goal-directedness of the opera as a whole.[39]

It may be objected, first, that aria texts very often project several conflicting feelings, not just one, or illustrate doubts and expectations which leave the situation open to change. The degree of interaction between affections as well as characters,

---

37. Don J. Neville, 'Moral Philosophy in the Metastasian Dramas', in *Crosscurrents and the Mainstream*, ed. by D. J. Neville, 2 vols (London, Ontario: Faculty of Music, 1982) (= Studies in Music from the University of Western Ontario, 7/1–2), pp. 28–46.
38. See, for example, Donald J. Grout, *A Short History of Opera*, 2nd rev. edn, 2 vols (New York: Columbia University Press, 1965), p. 187; Carl Dahlhaus, 'Zum Affektbegriff der frühdeutschen Oper', in *Die frühdeutsche Oper*, ed. by C. Floros et al., 1981, pp. 107–11.
39. Robert S. Freeman, *Opera without Drama: Currents of Change in Italian Opera, 1675–1725* (Ann Arbor: UMI Research Press, 1981) (Studies in Musicology, vol. 35)

involving also their musical presentation, is easily underestimated. For example, librettists liked to design hierarchies between a main plot (*azione principale*) which was taken to be historical, and sub-plots added by poetic invention ('si finge . . .'), which suggests a formal model not of isolated monads, but of centre and periphery. Musically, the most important analogy to such designs was the pattern of keys (or 'tonalities'). Analyses of operas demonstrating hierarchical and cumulative key-schemes are often successful, for example when arias are shown to be contrasting in their immediate succession and yet related to a central key once they are all heard. Their distribution among the singers (and thus their melodic styles, ranges, degrees of virtuosity, and so on), their orchestration and rhythmic features were further musical parameters which could strengthen the coherence and convergence of the whole structure.

In any case, it would not be wise to deny the coherence of a theatrical genre which abounds in complicated intrigues waiting to be resolved, favours scenic cohesion in the appearance of characters (*liaison des scènes*), avoids unmotivated breaks or reversals in the action, and in every Act builds up towards a climax in the last aria of a leading singer. In fact, the principle of goal-directedness was perhaps never stronger in European opera. Some *drammi per musica* appear to be constructed with the sole aim of bringing about the demonstrative reenactment of a famous historical event or *dictum*.[40] In others, the only novelty of treatment of a well-known fable was a changed ending. The strongest dramatic change was expected towards the very end, when dangers and temptations are successfully overcome by the hero. The final reversal of fortune (the *catastrophe*) was also usually the moment when the *dramma per musica* followed its typical preference for the *lieto fine* and so revealed its true identity.

Establishment of the genre

The beginning of the *dramma per musica*, in its more recent form described here, may be placed around 1690. The leading members of the Accademia dell'Arcadia, founded in Rome in 1690, and authors such as Apostolo Zeno, Domenico David, Silvio Stampiglia, Carlo Sigismondo Capeci and Antonio Salvi among the librettists, Carlo Francesco Pollarolo, Alessandro Scarlatti, Francesco Gasparini, Giovanni Bononcini and Antonio Lotti among the composers, strove from then onwards to depart from Baroque taste, as referred to above. They were influenced, at least indirectly, by French debates about spoken drama and about the conflicts between 'anciens et modernes'. French tragedies by Pierre and Thomas Corneille, Philippe Quinault, Jean Racine, Nicholas Pradon and others became the models for some of the most famous librettos in the years around 1700 – including Zeno's *Faramondo* and *Lucio Vero*, David's *La forza della virtù*, Girolamo Gigli's *La fede ne'*

---

40. For an example, see Reinhard Strohm, 'Metastasio's *Alessandro nell'Indie* and its earliest settings', in R. Strohm, *Essays on Handel*, 1985, pp. 232–48.

tradimenti, Salvi's *Arminio* and *Astianatte*.[41] But these years were a period of experimentation. While the foremost patron of the Roman Arcadia, Cardinal Pietro Ottoboni, harvested little more than courteous praise for his own reform librettos, several only superficially 'reformed' poets such as Francesco Silvani were generally popular (for example with his *La fede tradita e vendicata*, Venice, 1704). Everyone liked pastoral dramas, and there were also strong undercurrents of unheroic, spectacular and fantastic dramaturgy, especially in Naples, Venice and the smaller theatres of the Veneto and Romagna. Librettists adhering to these tastes included Grazio Braccioli (Vicenza, Venice), Antonio Maria Lucchini and Giovanni Palazzi (Venice), and Giuseppe Maria Buini (Bologna), who also led a travelling company. Some of these collaborated with Vivaldi, whereas his closest competitors in Venice (Tommaso Albinoni, Giuseppe Maria Orlandini and Giovanni Porta) had more to do with the dissemination of the reformed style. Individual composers or librettists of the period cannot usually be identified with one stylistic orientation only, since theatrical taste notoriously depended on audiences, patrons and singers as well.

Among the most single-minded reformers were the Venetian nobles Girolamo Frigimelica-Roberti and Agostino Piovene, who both offered *tragedie per musica* with unhappy endings, and the classicist Benedetto Pasqualigo, who sought to revive the perceived *decorum* of Greek dama (*Antigona* and *Ifigenia in Tauride*, Venice, 1718 and 1719, music by Orlandini). Apostolo Zeno dominated Venetian opera from c. 1695 to c. 1730: his merits concerning the literary improvement of the *dramma per musica*, which were singled out by Pier Jacopo Martello in 1715, were in certain ways a shared achievement with his friend and collaborator Pietro Pariati and others.[42] Pariati and then Antonio Salvi were also the most important early authors (from 1706) of *intermezzi comici per musica*, a genre which originated in Zeno's own circle through extraction of the comic roles and scenes from the thus purified *dramma*.

An already lively exchange of operas and personnel between Venice and Vienna was strengthened in 1718 when the Habsburg court appointed Zeno as court poet and historian (at first serving alongside Pariati).[43] Pietro Metastasio (Trapassi) succeeded Zeno in 1730 and held the position until his death in 1782. The *drammi per musica* written by Zeno and Metastasio for the Imperial court enjoyed an almost limitless distribution in Europe, which was by no means the case with their first

41. On librettos of this period generally, see Carlo Caruso, 'Italian Opera Libretti, 1679–1721: Universality and Flexibility of a Literary Genre', in *Alessandro Scarlatti und seine Zeit*, ed. by M. Lütolf, 1993, pp. 21–37.

42. On Zeno, the reform and Martello, see R. S. Freeman, *Opera without Drama*; Piero Weiss, 'Pier Jacopo Martello on Opera (1715): An Annotated Translation', *Musical Quarterly* 66 (1980), pp. 378–403; C. Caruso, 'Italian opera libretti'; on Pariati, see Giovanna Gronda, 'Per una ricognizione dei libretti di Pietro Pariati', in *Civiltà teatrale e settecento emiliano*, ed. by S. Davoli, 1986, pp. 115–36; and eadem (ed.), *La carriera di un librettista: Pietro Pariati da Reggio di Lombardia* (Bologna: Il Mulino, 1990).

43. Elena Sala Di Felice, 'Zeno: da Venezia a Vienna: Dal teatro impresariale al teatro di corte', in *L'Opera italiana a Vienna*, ed. by M. T. Muraro, 1990, pp. 65–114.

musical settings created in Vienna (by Francesco Conti, Antonio Caldara, Johann Joseph Fux and others).[44]

The achievements of Pietro Metastasio for the *dramma per musica* are unparalleled. In many areas, the success of his dramatic works wiped out not only the competition but the mere possibility of competition. Matters were different only at the beginning and towards the end of his career. The poet benefited very much from the models provided by the previous generation, above all by the Florentine Antonio Salvi, whose *Amore e maestà* (Florence, 1715, music by Giuseppe Maria Orlandini), with its tragic ending, directly influenced Metastasio's first original libretto, *Didone abbandonata* (Naples, 1724, music by Domenico Sarri).[45] Another model was probably Carlo Sigismondo Capeci, for example with his *Telemaco* (Rome, 1718, music by Alessandro Scarlatti). Metastasio was also well aware of the Neapolitan *commedia per musica* with its mannerist and partly folkloristic style which he could experience in his early years in Rome and Naples (1718–30).

It is possible to draw a distinction between Metastasio's eight *drammi per musica* written in Italy in the years 1724–30 and the nineteen others almost exclusively written in and for Vienna. Although the aesthetic and ideological categories of his *œuvre* did not change much, there are drastic differences between individual works as well as groups. His early librettos elaborate on deceit and suffering (*Siface, Didone abbandonata, Siroe re di Persia*), on rebellion against weak or tyrannical rulers (*Catone in Utica, Ezio*), or dynastic crises (*Semiramide riconosciuta, Alessandro nell'Indie, Artaserse*). His most characteristic statements, although not necessarily simple ones, about society and individual life, nature and reason, are contained in some *drammi* of the Viennese period, particularly of the early years under Emperor Charles VI (1730–40): *Demetrio, Adriano in Siria, L'Olimpiade, Demofoonte, La Clemenza di Tito, Attilio Regolo*. Many further differentiations between individual dramas can be made in view of their special circumstances, for example public and carnival occasions versus private performances in the Imperial family circle. *Il re pastore* and *L'Eroe cinese*, intended for the latter, were nevertheless written to demonstrate both the pastoral and the heroic orientations.[46]

What has later come to be regarded as a 'Metastasian type' or even 'Neapolitan type' of opera seria was first created by the poet in collaboration with his singers and composers in Naples and Rome, Marianna Benti-Bulgarelli, Niccolò Grimaldi und Domenico Gizzi being the most significant among the former, and Domenico Sarri, Nicola Porpora, Leonardo Vinci und Leonardo Leo among the latter. From 1725 his librettos were enthusiastically received in Venice, where – thanks to the support of the ex-Neapolitan librettist Domenico Lalli and local impresarios – the interna-

---

44. Klaus Hortschansky, 'Die Rezeption der Wiener Dramen Metastasios in Italien', in *Venezia e il melodramma del Settecento* [I], ed. by M. T. Muraro, 1978, pp. 407–24; and Reinhard Wiesend, 'Metastasios Revisionen eigener Dramen und die Situation der Opernmusik in den 1750er Jahren', *Archiv für Musikwissenschaft* 40 (1983), pp. 255–75.

45. See chapter 8 in this volume, p. 174.

46. On the courtly *festa teatrale* and its significance for Metastasio, see Jacques Joly, *Les fêtes théâtrales de Métastase à la cour de Vienne (1731–67)* (Clermont Ferrand: Presses de l'Université II, 1978).

tional success of these operas was prepared.[47] The Metastasio settings by Leo, Porpora and especially Vinci soon circulated everywhere in Europe, from Vienna and Hamburg to London, where Handel developed his own approach to the genre but also offered his audiences the works of Italian composers in pasticcio form. His rivals at the Opera of the Nobility (1734–7), and later managers, made much use of the scores of Porpora, Hasse, Pescetti, Pergolesi and Lampugnani.

Vinci's music was still being performed in various parts of Europe around 1760, although the composer had died in 1730. This was due to an idealization of the match of words and music heard in these settings – a persistent value judgement which also benefited the posthumous reputation of Giambattista Pergolesi and which corresponded to the nostalgic view that the genre was now past its prime.[48]

The distribution of Vinci's operatic type after 1730 was already the work of a second generation of artists, prominent among whom were vocal stars such as Carlo Broschi detto Farinelli, Gaetano Majorano detto Caffarelli and Faustina Bordoni Hasse. In this phase, composers trained in Naples – Johann Adolf Hasse, Pergolesi, Gaetano Latilla and Rinaldo di Capua – still made much impact, but Metastasio's *drammi* were now also cultivated by the best northern composers, including Antonio Vivaldi, Geminiano Giacomelli and Baldassare Galuppi. Hasse, who had come to Italy in 1724, began to set Metastasio's *drammi* only in 1730 (with *Artaserse*, for Venice), thereafter becoming their most prominent composer. His direct collaboration with the poet, however, was restricted to a few occasions (*Ipermestra*, 1744, and other works for Vienna after 1760). Most of Hasse's stage works originated for the Dresden court, where he was the first *maestro di capella*; in contrast to Vienna's Caldara, Berlin's Karl Heinrich Graun or Stuttgart's Jommelli, Hasse was able to travel much and so to enhance the radius of his operas significantly, especially in Italy itself (for example in Venice, Naples, Bologna and Milan).

The poets of the *dramma per musica* besides Metastasio are studied too little today. In Berlin, Dresden and Vienna, Giovanni Claudio Pasquini and Giovanni Ambrogio Migliavacca worked at first very much in the master's shadow: they corresponded with him and even had their texts corrected by him. More independent but stylistically comparable librettists were Carlo Innocenzo Frugoni in Parma, Leopoldo de Villati in Munich, Giovan Pietro Tagliazucchi in Berlin, Mattia Verazi in Mannheim and Carlo Francesco Badini in London. Migliavacca, Frugoni and, above all, Verazi then became involved in the reform tendencies around 1760 (see also below).

During the years 1740–63, amidst political crises and wars, especially in central Europe, a new generation of composers became established, creating much of what was later exploited or indeed challenged by the reforms. A typical figure was the Venetian Baldassare Galuppi, whose *opere serie* written after c. 1748 (*Demetrio* and *Artaserse*, Vienna, 1748 and 1749) aroused as much rejection as enthusiasm, since

47.   See chapter 3 in this volume, 'The Neapolitans in Venice'.
48.   Reinhard Strohm, *Die italienische Oper im 18. Jahrhundert* (Wilhelmshaven: Heinrichshofen, 1979), pp. 172–6.

the 'musicalization' in his arias – abstract musical rather than dramatic-expressive invention, mechanical word-setting, mixture of seria and buffa idioms – seemed to defy Metastasio's dramatic intentions.[49] By contrast, the Neapolitan Niccolò Jommelli greatly developed the dramatic expressivity of voice and orchestra in his earliest *drammi per musica* (*Ezio*, Bologna, 1741; *Merope* (Zeno), Venice, 1742). He liked to transform the aria texts by fragmentation, 'analysis'[50] and word repetitions into scenic rhapsodies which seemed to represent each character's fluctuating emotions. Jommelli complained about the compactness of Metastasio's four-liners, as he then had to disfigure them to create space for expression. Metastasio, in turn, criticized Jommelli's musical excesses, nevertheless acknowledging his dramatic genius.[51]

Composers working in similar directions were Domenico Terradellas, Davide Perez (from 1752 in Portugal) and Francesco Corselli (from 1734 in Madrid). Christoph Willibald Gluck was the most determined anti-conformist of this chronological group. Having been moderately successful in Italy and London (1743–6), he worked for the travelling troupes of Mingotti and Locatelli in Dresden and Prague. Early proof of his artistic personality was his *Semiramide riconosciuta* for Vienna, 1748, whose apparently crude simplicity was indignantly rejected by Metastasio as *arcivandalica insopportabile* ('arch-primitive, intolerable').[52] This marks the beginning of the last crises and reforms of eighteenth-century opera seria.

Criticism, reform and survival

The eighteenth century is distinguished in the history of opera by a lively and continuous debate, which spread beyond specialist circles, about the *raisons d'être*, practice and aesthetics of opera. The criticisms expressed did affect the development of the genre, although they did not entirely change its course. Reformist and conservative tendencies were parallel streams in the great river-bed of operatic life; opera criticism was a tradition as was opera itself.

As said above, the eighteenth-century *dramma per musica* was a genre born from a reformist tendency, striving for the ideals of noble simplicity,[53] imitation of nature and human dignity. The critics of the new reformist tendencies subscribed, in many respects, to the same ideals. Three main types of criticisms and reforms can be distinguished.

49. Generally on Galuppi and Metastasio, see Reinhard Wiesend, *Studien zur opera seria von Baldassare Galuppi: Werksituation und Überlieferung – Form und Satztechnik – Inhaltsdarstellung*, 2 vols (Tutzing: Schneider, 1984).
50. *Zergliederung*, a term used in Christian Gottfried Krause, *Von der musikalischen Poesie* (Berlin, 1752). On this interesting critic, see Gloria Flaherty, *Opera in the Development of German Critical Thought* (Princeton: Princeton University Press, 1978), pp. 167–75.
51. Paolo Gallarati, *Musica e maschera: Il libretto italiano del settecento* (Turin: EdT, 1984), p. 59.
52. Letter of 29 June 1748 to G. C. Pasquini, in P. Metastasio, *Tutte le opere*, vol. 3, p. 353.
53. *Noble simplicité*, a formula already found in François Raguenet, *Parallèle des Italiens et des François en ce qui regarde la musique et les opéra* (Paris: Moreau, 1702).

a) The classicizing criticism of literary academies such as the Accademia dell'Arcadia in Rome, which was inspired by the French *Querelle des anciens et des modernes*, regarded opera as an unreasonable, degenerate form of genuine tragedy. Its right to exist was challenged by such influential minds as Lodovico Antonio Muratori,[54] Gian Vincenzo Gravina (the teacher of Metastasio),[55] Joseph Addison,[56] Saverio Maffei (in the preface to his *Teatro Italiano*, 1723)[57] and Johann Christoph Gottsched.[58] Their decisive argument was the alleged improbability of singing on stage, particularly when it was part of a dialogue. The argument implied, of course, that the entire theory of sung recitation in ancient tragedy – the foundation myth of opera – had to be denied.[59] Giovanni Maria Crescimbeni, a leader of the Accademia dell'Arcadia, wished to accord the musical drama – almost as a price for its toleration – only a niche among the pastoral and mythological types of literature, restricting opera to a minor role beside spoken drama.[60] This would have corresponded to the model of the French theatrical genres, clearly separated into the heroic-historical *tragédie* (which was spoken) and the spectacular, mythological or pastoral *tragédie lyrique* (which was sung). The taste for the *merveilleux* in French opera remained sheltered from rationalist criticism until about the mid-eighteenth century.

Another serious challenge to Italian opera and operatic practice put forward by the same generation concerned its morality: the genre itself and some of its social circumstances, for example the involvement of castratos, or alleged prostitution, were denounced by theologians and moralists in Catholic as well as Protestant regions of Europe.[61]

Against these objections, the proponents and practicians of the genre (they included Pier Jacopo Martello, Aaron Hill, Johann Mattheson and leading librettists) had to show plausibly that the heroic-historical *dramma per musica*, when stripped of supernatural or spectacular elements, did not contradict reason or verisimilitude, and was more than a disfigured branch of tragedy which needed to be pruned. They also had to demonstrate the moral correctness or at least indifference of the genre, and to emphasize its claim to literary status, distancing it from the improvised and potentially immoral *commedia dell'arte*. The genre they proposed was subject to the principles of verisimilitude and *decorum*.

---

54. Lodovico Antonio Muratori, *Della perfetta poesia Italiana spiegata, e dimostrata con varie osservazioni* (Modena: Soliani, 1706).
55. Gian Vincenzo Gravina, 'Della ragion poetica', in G. V. Gravina, *Scritti critici e teorici*, ed. by Amadeo Quondam (Bari: Laterza, 1973).
56. On Addison, Dennis and other English critics, see Lowell Lindgren, 'Critiques of Opera in London, 1705–1719', in *Il melodramma italiano*, ed. by A. Colzani, N. Dubowy et al., pp. 145–65.
57. Laura Sannia Nowé, 'Una voce sul melodramma nelle discussioni del primo settecento (S. Maffei)', in *Metastasio e il melodramma*, ed. by E. Sala Di Felice and L. Sannia Nowé, 1985, pp. 247–70.
58. See Gloria Flaherty, *Opera in the Development of German Critical Thought* (Princeton: Princeton University Press, 1978), and chapter 4 in this volume, 'The Crisis of baroque opera in Germany'.
59. See also P. Weiss, 'Opera and the Two Verisimilitudes', and C. Caruso, 'Italian opera libretti', pp. 25–8.
60. See R. S. Freeman, *Opera without Drama*, pp. 11–22.
61. See, for example, L. Lindgren, 'Critiques of Opera', pp. 146–7.

b) A second type of criticism, virulent throughout the eighteenth century, sub-scribed to exactly these principles but regretted that opera seria, after all, did not live up to them. This criticism was expressed with various degrees of severity and has, in some respects, aided the survival of the genre. It addressed negative side-effects of the opera business including the cult of castratos and primadonnas, or dramaturgical defects such as improbabilities of plot, mixture of styles, or excessive musical effects in comparison with dramatic ones. Early examples are found in the writings of Raguenet and Martello, otherwise intended as apologies of the genre.[62] Benedetto Marcello's famous *Il Teatro alla moda* (Venice, 1720) castigates absurdi-ties of the musical production;[63] the elaborate singing treatise by Pier Francesco Tosi (*Opinioni de' cantori antichi e moderni*, 1723), whose title alludes to the same rivalry between old and new as does Martello's, complains about the arrogance of singers and urges the return to proper declamation and good action. Carlo Goldoni's *Mémoires* (Paris, 1787) expose, in an episode presented as autobiogra-phical, unreasonable precepts of libretto-writing.[64] Operatic satires frequently mocked the immoral or irrational behaviour of professionals, from Girolamo Gigli's intermezzi *La Dirindina* (Rome, 1715, music by Domenico Scarlatti; withdrawn before the first performance) or Pietro Metastasio's intermezzi *L'impresario delle isole Canarie* (Naples, 1724, music by Domenico Sarri), via Antonio Palomba's well-travelled musical comedy *L'Orazio* (Naples, 1737, music by Pietro Auletta) to Calzabigi's opera buffa *La critica teatrale* (*L'opera seria*) (Vienna, 1769, music by F. L. Gassmann) and Giovanni Battista Casti's *Prima la musica e poi le parole* (Vienna, 1786, music by Salieri). The last-named title refers to the claim of these critics that the words should have priority over the notes, whether simply to ensure intelligibility of the drama, or to achieve expressive congruence of music and word. Such criticism was endorsed, of course, by Metastasio as well.

Other themes were the improbability of the da capo repetition (see above), the incoherence of the many intrigues, the excessive amount of *arie di bravura*, unre-lated ballets and similar attractions, the endless ritornellos and text repetitions in arias, the undramatic noise of the sinfonia. We read about these matters in Giuseppe Riva, Evandro Edesimo, Christian Gottfried Krause, Francesco Algarotti, Giovanni Maria Ortes, Raniero de' Calzabigi (in his preface to the Collected Works of Metastasio, Paris, 1755, an *éloge* of the poet), François-Jean de Chastellux, Antonio Planelli, Antonio Eximeno, as well as the bibliographer Francesco Saverio Quadrio and the conservative historiographer Stefano Arteaga, in whose *Le rivoluzioni del teatro musicale italiano*, an apology for Metastasio's *drammi per musica* (1783–8), most of the cited objections have found a home. It is significant how much

---

62. F. Raguenet, *Parallèle des Italiens et des François*; Pier Jacopo Martello, *Della tragedia antica e moderna* (Rome, 1715).

63. Benedetto Marcello, *Il teatro alla moda* (Venice: Pinelli, 1720), ed. by Andrea d'Angeli (Milan, 1927); Eleanor Selfridge-Field, 'Marcello, Sant'Angelo and *Il Teatro alla Moda*', in *Antonio Vivaldi*, ed. by L. Bianconi and G. Morelli, 1982, vol. 2, pp. 533–46. Johann Mattheson's *Die neueste Untersuchung der Singspiele* (Hamburg, 1744) contains a consenting paraphrase.

64. See Carlo Goldoni, *Tutte le opere*, ed. by Giuseppe Ortolani (Verona, 1959), vol. 1, p. 129; Remo Giazotto, *Poesia melodrammatica e pensiero critico nel settecento* (Milan: Bocca, 1952), chapter 3.

this critical tradition ended up in defending its target. Some of the observers after c. 1740 attempted a distinction between the original achievements in the genre (by Metastasio, or Vinci, Hasse and Pergolesi) and an alleged decline afterwards, advocating for example a revision of the musical complexities introduced by Galuppi or Jommelli.[65]

The encyclopaedists and protagonists of the Parisian *Querelle des bouffons*, and other French authors such as Voltaire (in the preface to his tragedy *Sémiramis*, 1748), Jean François Marmontel or André-Ernest-Modeste Grétry, included opera seria in their largely positive evaluations of Italian music.[66] German enlightened and pre-Romantic intellectuals such as Johann Adam Hiller, Christian Friedrich Daniel Schubart, Wilhelm Heinse and Johann Friedrich Reichardt (in his early writings) combined criticism of the practical conditions and side-effects with sometimes enthusiastic acknowledgment of the important aspects of the *dramma per musica*.

c) Whereas the first type of criticism was overtaken by the development of the genre itself, and the second turned out to be its watchful supporter, a third critical tradition advocated real change. Defects and negative side-effects were noted by these critics not in order to eliminate them, but to promote a contrasting idea of musical drama. This third tradition branched off from the second around 1750–5, with Francesco Algarotti at the court of Frederick II in Berlin (*Saggio sopra l'opera in musica*, Livorno, 1755) and with the court theatre director Giacomo Durazzo and Gluck in Vienna. These men offered practical realizations almost from the outset. The Berlin circle comprising the king, his court poet Tagliazucchi, the Kapellmeister K. H. Graun, and Algarotti, created *Semiramide* (1754, after Voltaire)[67] and *Montezuma* (1755) as formal and ideological alternatives to Metastasio. Durazzo's and Gluck's *L'innocenza giustificata* (Vienna, 1756) demonstrated anti-Metastasian dramaturgy while employing his lyrical verse.[68] Further points of crystallization were the courts of Mannheim with Mattia Verazi (*Ifigenia in Aulide*, Rome and Mannheim, 1751, music by Jommelli; *Sofonisba*, Mannheim, 1762, music by Traetta) and of Parma, under minister Guillaume-Léon Du Tillot, with Frugoni, who adapted Rameau's *tragédies lyriques Hippolyte et Aricie* and *Castor et Pollux* as *Ippolito e Aricia* and *I Tindaridi*, respectively (set to music by Tommaso Traetta, 1759–60). Mattia Verazi's name may be singled out, as he experimented with dramatic innovations not only in Mannheim and Stuttgart under favourable governments, but also later in Milan from 1770 in his own right,

---

65. On this group of critics, see R. Giazotto, *Poesia melodrammatica*, and B. M. Antolini, 'L'opera italiana'.

66. Jean François Marmontel, *Essai sur les révolutions de la musique Française* (Paris, 1777); André-Ernest-Modeste Grétry, *Mémoires ou essais sur la Musique*, 3 vols (Paris, 1797).

67. See Cesare Questa, *Semiramide redenta* (Urbino: Quattro Venti, 1989), pp. 123–35.

68. In this context, the impact of performance styles and tastes must also be considered. See, for a significant case, Daniel Heartz, 'From Garrick to Gluck: The Reform of Theatre and Opera in the Mid-eighteenth Century', *Proceedings of the Royal Musical Association* 94 (1967–8), pp. 111–27.

introducing radical novelties of structure such as great ensembles in the middle of Acts, ensemble-finales, large choral scenes, and others.[69]

The leading spirit was unquestionably Ranieri de' Calzabigi, who in the 1760s collaborated with Durazzo, Traetta, Gluck and the librettist Marco Coltellini, his former student. Gluck's famous, programmatic preface to the printed edition of his *Alceste (tragedia messa in musica*, Vienna, 1769) was at least inspired by Calzabigi. The poet and his circle cultivated a new, somehow rebellious veneration of antiquity, trying to deepen standard classical myths (Iphigenia, Orestes, Alceste, Paris and Helena) with elements of exoticism and barbarism, inspired by the rediscovered rituals of pre-European cultures such as Scythia, Crete or ancient America. They sought, perhaps subconsciously at first, a certain archaic stillness of dramaturgical form, typified in stark and simple choral movements, and paid the highest tribute to the ideal of *noble simplicité* (for example by eliminating intrigues and secondary plots). Their rhetorical exaggeration of the thesis of the priority of words over music went hand in hand with a clever, theatrical ambition which made sure the effects of spectacular crowd scenes or French ballets were not missing either. The difference was that their choir singers and dancers wore classical Greek robes, displaying a humanistic severity and dignity which the aristocratic patrons had to tolerate in this context.

Algarotti's theory of *recitativo accompagnato*, as a freer and more natural form of expression which was apt to diminish the hiatus between lyricism and dialogue, was seemingly contradicted by Calzabigi's idea of the aria as a contrast to recitative and exclusively dedicated to emotions (whereas Metastasio's sentence and simile arias were totally rejected). What they had in common, however, was the idea of an enhanced scenic identification and 'dramatization' of the performer's art which, despite the slogan of the priority of the words, was being absorbed in the general trend of those decades towards the 'musicalization' of drama. It was the musical setting, not the text, that conquered more and more of the dramatic continuity. It is therefore not surprising that Calzabigi's later, even more radical librettos *Paride ed Elena* (Vienna, 1770, music by Gluck) and *Elfrida (tragedia per musica*, Naples, 1792, music by Paisiello) had no impact on the reform because they were unsuccessful as operas.[70]

It must be obvious that the relationship between conservatism and reform was not one of historical succession but of competition and cumulation. Many European centres were only marginally interested in the Italian works of Gluck, except that conventionalized versions of *Orfeo ed Euridice* were heard, for example, in Naples and London in the 1770s. Until about 1780 the majority of opera houses still favoured Metastasian opera seria in the manner of Hasse or perhaps Galuppi. Innovation was by no means lacking in these works, for example in the melodic style

69. Marita McClymonds, 'Mattia Verazi and the Opera at Mannheim, Stuttgart, and Ludwigsburg', in *Crosscurrents and the Mainstream in Italian Serious Opera, 1730–1790*, ed. by Don J. Neville, pp. 99–136.
70. See also Michael F. Robinson, 'The Ancient and the Modern: A Comparison of Metastasio and Calzabigi', in *Crosscurrents and the Mainstream*, pp. 137–47.

of Niccolò Piccinni, Gian Francesco di Majo, Giuseppe Sarti, Pietro Anfossi and, above all, Johann Christian Bach. They almost completely transferred the principle of emotional identification with the singing character to the musical sphere, developing a 'singing Allegro' style for heroic arias (replacing, for example, the older Maestoso-types) and new forms of the serious Cantabile idiom, for example in a slow 3/4-metre. Arias as well as orchestrated *accompagnato* recitatives were enhanced with rich, characterizing woodwind sounds.[71] As for the contribution of established composers still devoted to Metastasian ideals, that of Hasse must not be underestimated, as his late works show considerable flexibility and even an inclination towards reform. Examples are his *Piramo e Tisbe*, an *intermezzo tragico per musica* (a mythological *azione teatrale*) by Coltellini (Vienna, 1768),[72] and to some extent his setting of Metastasio's *Ruggiero, ovvero l'eroica gratitudine* (Milan, 1771), the last stage-work of both authors. The Venetian Antonio Sacchini may be mentioned in a similar context, as his fairly traditional music impressed opera seria audiences around 1770 in reform dramas such as Verazi's *Calliroe* (Milan, 1770). The only *opere serie* by Joseph Haydn were *Armida* (Nunziato Porta?, 1784) and *L'anima del filosofo* (*Orfeo ed Euridice*) (Badini, London, 1791, not performed), which belonged to the reform tendency and have been counted among his best dramatic works.[73]

The historical impact of these composers, who were either conservative or on the outer periphery of reform tendencies, was particularly great in central Europe, where most of them worked for at least some time, and in the remaining countries: for example in Russia, where Galuppi, Traetta and Sarti worked, or in England, where J. C. Bach settled. They also provided the models for the youngest generation to be mentioned here, that of Wolfgang Amadeus Mozart, Antonio Salieri, Giovanni Paisiello and Domenico Cimarosa. The last-named three composers are distinguished from the previous group in that their operatic style and characteristic effects were entirely at home in opera buffa and their best efforts for the *dramma per musica* (an example is Cimarosa's *Olimpiade*, Vicenza, 1784) were stylistically enriched by this very orientation. It was quite otherwise with Mozart, who drew maximum inspiration from the contrast of genres. Following the vicissitudes of his career, he was able to contribute to the reform tendency as much as to traditionalism (which is also true, to some extent, of Traetta or Sarti), although in his early stage-works for Milan, 1770–2 (*Mitridate, Ascanio in Alba* and *Lucio Silla*), his 'musicalization' of the texts still rather conflicted with the reformist zeal of his librettists Vittorio Amedeo Cigna-Santi, Giuseppe Parini and Giovanni De Gamerra. Later, however, he was able to react with the same sincerity and enthusiasm to a lightly adapted version of Metastasio's *Il re pastore* (Salzburg, 1775) as to the eclectic, overloaded reform drama *Idomeneo* by Giambattista Varesco (Munich,

71. An aspect emphasized by Eric Weimer, *Opera seria and the Evolution of Classical Style, 1755–1772* (Ann Arbor: UMI Research Press, 1984) (Studies in Musicology, 78)
72. Francesco Degrada, 'Aspetti gluckiani nell'ultimo Hasse', in F. Degrada, *Il palazzo incantato*, pp. 133–53.
73. Marita P. McClymonds, 'Haydn and the Opera Seria Tradition: *Armida*', in *Napoli e il teatro musicale*, ed. by B. M. Antolini and W. Witzenmann, pp. 191–206.

1781), thus revealing in these two works the whole stylistic range of the *dramma per musica* of his era.[74] This breadth of dramatic and musical ideas was compressed into a single work in *La Clemenza di Tito* (Prague, 1791), whose text adaptation by Catterino Mazzolà resembles a pitched battle against Metastasio's original. The long posthumous survival of Mozart's setting on the European stages has been explained with its essentially German rather than Metastasian or Italian character – an interpretation that is of course difficult to substantiate.[75]

In any case, at the end of the century what might be called the European landscape of the *dramma per musica* embraced much more than the traditionalist and the reformist camps. A tendency which might rather be called pre-Romantic was developed by poets such as Giovanni De Gamerra, Antonio Simone Sografi, Francesco de Rogatis, Giuseppe Foppa and Ferdinando Moretti, and by composers who had become aware of this new landscape. In the words of Marita McClymonds, dramas such as Foppa's *Alonso e Cora* (1786) and Moretti's *Il Conte di Saldagno* (1787) 'took a giant step beyond the innovations of the past and opened the door to Romantic opera of the nineteenth century'.[76] Epochal themes such as cruelty and terror, religion, and nationalism were presented in theatrical visions (for example, the underground scene in De Gamerra's often-performed *Medonte re d'Epiro*) which were outside the realm of Metastasio's taste, or even outside the rationalist category of 'taste' itself. Other examples of this pre-Romantic trend are, from about 1780, the settings of Shakespeare adaptations, such as Giuseppe Foppa's *Amleto*, Padua, 1792, music by Gaetano Andreozzi.

The *dramma per musica* survived by transforming itself beyond recognition: the 'tightrope-walk between anti-naturalist artificiality and idealist simplicity'[77] had been successful. The elasticity of the genre was its lifeline; had it conformed to a rigid formula such as the separation of drama and music (as claimed by Freeman), it would have ended with Mozart, of course. But it rather seems that the *dramma per musica* reached the nineteenth century alive because it had always been a reform genre striving for an ever-increasing identification of music and drama. Admittedly, its fate was also linked to the social framework of a retrospective court culture, and for that reason opera seria in the narrow sense of the word was, after about 1789, gradually pushed back by bourgeois realities. But opera seria in the wider sense did survive, perhaps even into the age of Hollywood cinema.

74. See Paolo Gallarati, *La forza delle parole: Mozart drammaturgo* (Turin: Einaudi, 1993).
75. Anna Amalie Abert, 'Mozarts italianità in *Idomeneo* und *Titus*', in *Colloquium 'Mozart und Italien'*, ed. by F. Lippmann, 1978, pp. 205–16.
76. Marita P. McClymonds and D. Heartz, 'Opera seria', in *The New Grove Dictionary of Opera*, ed. by S. Sadie (London: Macmillan, 1992), vol. 3, pp. 698–707, p. 706.
77. '... die Gratwanderung zwischen antinaturalistischer Artifizialität und idealer Naivität': Stefan Kunze, 'Die Opera seria und ihr Zeitalter', in *Colloquium 'Johann Adolf Hasse'*, ed. by F. Lippmann, 1987, p. 15.

Court and city opera

2
A context for *Griselda*: the Teatro Capranica in Rome, 1711–1724

The following pages are an attempt to express my gratitude to the organizers of our conference, to the performers of Alessandro Scarlatti's *Griselda*, and, in a sense, to the work itself.[1] I can perhaps do a small service to all of them by bringing together some information about the theatre where *Griselda* was born. There is a chance that we may learn to understand the work better if we know more about its institutional and artistic background. This trivial wisdom seems very justified in our case: the opera was written for people who had seen all the other operas (or most of them) given in that opera house in the preceding years. Most of these people – or at least, most of those who counted – were members of the Roman aristocracy, of wealthy, ecclesiastical or erudite circles. Nevertheless, let us try to put ourselves in their shoes to get to know the Teatro Capranica.[2]

It was in exactly that spot where the modern visitor would suspect it was: in the undistinguished but graceful palace extending along the northern side of the Piazza Capranica, on the first floor. For many years in the twentieth century, the often-rebuilt auditorium had been used as a cinema; in 1988 I found there a self-service cafeteria. Cardinal Domenico Capranica had bought the ground in the fifteenth century. In the seventeenth, the family shared the building and grounds with other owners and tenants, among them the church of S. Maria d'Aquiro. By 1679, *drammi per musica* were performed in the private theatre on the first floor. In 1694 the cousins Pompeo and Federico (Alveri) Capranica became the full owners, and they reopened the theatre in the following January as a public opera house. It had to close in 1698, by order of Pope Innocent XII. In the years 1711–24 there were regular performances of *drammi per musica* in the theatre, precisely two each carnival

1. This essay originated as a paper delivered at the Séminaire International 'Alessandro Scarlatti', 10–14 November 1988, at the Opéra-Studio de Genève. The seminar, organized by Max Lütolf, focused on a performance of Scarlatti's *Griselda* by the Opéra-Studio de Genève (musical director: Jean-Marie Curti).
2. The following two paragraphs are based on Arnaldo Rava, *I teatri di Roma* (Rome: Palombi, 1°53), pp. 47–55, and Costantino Messina et al., *Sogni e favole io fingo: Teatro pubblico e melodramr..a a Roma all'epoca di Metastasio* (Exhibition catalogue, Rome, Palazzo Venezia, 1983–4) (Rome: Ministero per i beni culturali e ambientali, 1983), pp. 108–10 (no. 100). For the repertory, see also Giuseppe Pavan, 'Il teatro Capranica (1711–1800)', *Rivista Musicale Italiana* 29 (1922), pp. 425–44.

season, according to widespread convention in such public opera houses. Also following universal custom, most of the boxes were sold or let to wealthy patrons and institutions (such as the foreign embassies), usually with the *ius redimendi*, which the owners could exert only rarely because of their financially precarious state. Thus, the owners of the boxes had an important part of the control over the business and were its supporters. Individual entrance tickets (*bolettini*) were also sold for access to the stalls. To reach the auditorium, the spectators had to go through a downstairs shop which was then let to a carpenter.

The productions were managed according to the impresario system, i.e. there was an attempt to recoup the expenses for each season through income from boxes and tickets, although there must have been subventions from patrons other than through the ownership of boxes. It is not known who the impresarios were for most seasons, but absence of information on that point suggests that the younger of the cousins, Federico Capranica, managed some of the seasons himself. In 1712 Federico bought out his cousin's boxes and other capital. In 1713 Filippo Juvarra enlarged and modernized the auditorium by command of Cardinal Ottoboni, then a patron of the theatre; a design of the new form by Juvarra is known.[3] The business history of the theatre did not change much until 1724, when Federico had accumulated such debts that he had to sell the theatre to another cousin, Camillo Capranica, for 3,000 scudi, except for the 43 boxes already sold to others. After the *Anno Santo*, 1725, when theatres were closed in Rome, the performances resumed under very different circumstances (see also below).

1711–24 was, then, a relatively self-contained period in the history of this theatre. Its opera productions were as shown in table 1.

To start our inquiry, a few generalizations may be in order. I shall organize them in four points.

1. From the point of view of cultural history, we could identify this period as that of 'Arcadian opera before Metastasio'. Members of the Accademia dell'Arcadia were indeed connected with the Teatro Capranica more than perhaps with any other public venture in Rome: as patrons and financial supporters (Cardinal Ottoboni, Prince Ruspoli, ex-Queen Maria Casimira of Poland), as contributing authors (Alessandro Scarlatti, Carlo Sigismondo Capeci, Gaetano Lemer), as stage directors (Paolo Antonio Rolli, at least in 1715) and surely as influential spectators who would comment on the performances publicly and in private *accademie*. This short period was indeed the only episode in Roman opera history when Arcadians influenced a public opera house. Why did they care, and what did they want?

2. The most important issue may be that of a transformation, during these years, of the status of opera in Rome. Patronage of the arts, including music and theatre, was firmly ingrained in the habits of Roman high society, but its exercise had largely been private and volatile. The cardinals, princes, ambassadors and nobles did not

---

3. Reproduced in A. Rava, *I teatri di Roma*, p. 54; Mercedes Viale Ferrero, *Filippo Juvarra scenografo e architetto teatrale* (Turin: Pozzo, 1970), fig. 12.

Table 1. Operas at the Teatro Capranica, 1711–24

(If the libretto or music was imported from elsewhere, the author names are followed by the place and date of the original production)

1711   1ᵃ   *L'Engelberta o sia la forza dell'innocenza*
                Apostolo Zeno, Venice, 1709 / A. Orefice and F. Mancini, Naples, 1709?
                Revision of Naples, Teatro S. Bartolomeo, 1709?
        2ᵃ   *Dorisbe ovvero l'amor volubile e tiranno*
                Giovan Domenico Pioli, Naples, 1709 / Alessandro Scarlatti, 1709
                Revision of Naples, Teatro S. Bartolomeo, 1709
1712   1ᵃ   *La fede tradita e vendicata*
                Francesco Silvani, Venice, 1704 / Francesco Gasparini, 1704?
        2ᵃ   *Ataulfo re dei Goti ovvero la forza della virtù*
                Domenico David, Venice, 1693 / Giuseppe Maria Orlandini
1713   1ᵃ   *L'amor tirannico*
                Domenico Lalli, Venice, 1710 / Orlandini?
        2ᵃ   *Publio Cornelio Scipione*
                Agostino Piovene, Venice, 1712 / (Carlo Francesco Pollarolo, 1712?)
1714   1ᵃ   *Lucio Papirio*
                Antonio Salvi / Francesco Gasparini
        2ᵃ   *Tito e Berenice*
                Carlo Sigismondo Capeci / Antonio Caldara
1715   1ᵃ   *Astarto*
                Zeno and Pietro Pariati, Venice, 1708 / Giovanni Bononcini
        2ᵃ   *Ambleto*
                Zeno and Pariati, Venice, 1705 / Domenico Scarlatti
1716   1ᵃ   *Il Ciro*
                Matteo Noris, Venice, 1703 (*L'odio e l'amore*) / F. Gasparini
        2ᵃ   *Il Vincislao*
                Zeno, Venice 1703 / Mancini, Naples, 1715, and F. Gasparini
                Revision of Naples, Teatro S. Bartolomeo, 1715
1717   1ᵃ   *Il Pirro*
                Zeno, Venice, 1704 / F. Gasparini
        2ᵃ   *Il Trace in catena*
                Salvi, Pratolino 1706 (*Il Gran Tamerlano*) / F. Gasparini and 2 pupils
1718   1ᵃ   *Berenice regina d'Egitto overo le gare di amore, e di politica*
                Salvi, Pratolino, 1710 / D. Scarlatti and Nicola Porpora
        2ᵃ   *Telemaco*
                Capeci / A. Scarlatti
1719   1ᵃ   *Astinome*
                Domenico Antonio Petrosellini / Carlo Francesco Pollarolo
        2ᵃ   *Marco Attilio Regolo*
                Noris, Venice, 1693, altered by Capeci? / A. Scarlatti
1720   1ᵃ   *Tito Sempronio Gracco*
                Silvio Stampiglia, Naples, 1702 / A. Scarlatti, 1702
                Revision of Naples, 1702
        2ᵃ   *Turno Aricino*
                Stampiglia, Pratolino, 1704 / A. Scarlatti, 1704
                Revision of Pratolino, 1704
1721   1ᵃ   *Crispo*
                Gaetano Lemer / Giovanni Bononcini
        2ᵃ   *Griselda*
                Zeno, Venice, 1701 (revised) / A. Scarlatti
1722   1ᵃ   *Nino*
                Ippolito Zanelli, Reggio Emilia, 1720 / Orlandini

Table 1. *Continued*

	2ª	*Arminio*
		Salvi, Pratolino, 1703 / A. Scarlatti, 1714
		Revision of Florence, 1716
1723	1ª	*Oreste*
		Giangualberto Barlocci / Benedetto Micheli
	2ª	*Ercole sul Termodonte*
		Girolamo Bussani, Venice, 1678 / Antonio Vivaldi
1724	1ª	*La virtù trionfante dell'amore e dell'odio overo il Tigrane*
		(Silvani, Venice or Mantua?) / B. Micheli, Vivaldi and N. Romaldo
	2ª	*Giustino*
		Nicolò Beregan, Venice, 1683 / Vivaldi

owe anything to the 'public' at large; they could make up their minds each year whether they wanted to have opera or oratorio or perhaps only chamber works in their private palaces. Public opera houses, on the other hand, needed to produce regularly to keep their audience, and to prevent litigation over the return for the money paid for the boxes. Both systems of patronage had been tried, and very intensely, during the 1690s. From the 1697–8 season until 1709, opera was forbidden in Rome, and the final showdown between the two systems was still overdue when theatres opened again about 1710. Not that the patrons themselves thought of it necessarily in that way; but rivalry and competition were at the basis of the opera-game. Everybody wanted to show off and display taste, intelligence, connections, power and wealth. It is therefore natural that the public opera house – the Capranica – attracted from the beginning not only condescending remarks but also very active support. Whereas the private palace theatres were the homeground of each of the competing patrons (to which they regularly invited each other as peaceful guests), the public theatre became their amphitheatre. Everybody was there and could be seen.

Some useful secondary functions of the public opera houses included that of the 'fall-back' opportunity: when artists and staff were no longer needed, they could be hived off to the public theatre. It may also sometimes have been cheaper to sponsor a good public production than to mount a mediocre private one. In 1711 the Queen of Poland had a private performance arranged all for herself and a few friends in the Teatro Capranica (see below). But as these opportunities were being seized, the ground imperceptibly shifted: the more the patrons reckoned that they could always rely on public opera being available for their needs and ambitions, the more they had already become its customers. Within less than five years (1711–15), the glamorous tradition of palace opera in Rome had died out. It took much longer for impresario opera to establish itself; it never grew entirely independent from sponsorship, and in this sense the business of opera has perhaps never entirely left the semi-private limbo.

3. In one particular respect, public opera could not catch up with its private counterpart. Its business was considered on the edge of morality, and it lived under the spell of excuses. Women were not allowed to appear on the public stage in the

papal territories, owing to the old chauvinistic fear of uncontrollable prostitution. This benefited, in turn, the careers of castratos: in proportion to the growth of public opera, their field of activity opened up. Their quality, specialization, range of employment and salaries also developed.

Over and above the concerns for social peace and political stability – which also legitimized censorship and inquisition – the morality issue was extremely important for Italian opera at the time, particularly in Rome.[4] Conservative commentators rejected opera outright for moral reasons; liberals struggled to demonstrate that the genre could be used to educate and better people. Almost half the opera titles of our repertory list show the concern for moral values, and many others from the same period could be quoted. The mingling of aesthetic and social norms is, of course, a characteristic of the humanist tradition, and especially of the Aristotelian views of the theatre, which were dear to the Arcadians and the libretto reformers of the earliest eighteenth century. Combined with a still predominantly allegorical imagery (which was also fuelled, presumably, by education in ecclesiastical institutions), we see the public opera house populated with personified values. The characters on stage are for ever torn between yielding to their instincts and obeying moral restrictions. Love invariably becomes *tiranno amore*, death for honourable causes a recommended goal. But honour and friendship blossom, presumption is punished, and innocent beauty is allowed to seduce.

4. What did *not* really occur in this period was the advent of a freelance type of artistic business. The impresario might have wished to go out in the wide marketplace of Italy's cities to find the best scenographer, dancing master, the best singers, poets, composers, instrumentalists that he could afford. But he had to listen to a hundred friends and patrons of these scenographers, dancing masters, singers, and so on, who all tried to make a deal involving the placement of their protégés. He had to compromise between his resources and the wishes of a clientele that cultivated its own tastes and commitments. As a result, the Teatro Capranica, with all its patronal support, presents a repertoire reflecting not the best, nor the average, of Italian opera, but the best of Italian opera according to certain identifiable tastes.

Taking these four points together, we might call this stretch of institutional history the one in which 'Arcadian opera went public'. Its aesthetic and social norms, its dreams and superstitions went public, too. From an organizational point of view, this was not a complete transition to the impresario system, but a transition to a state in which the most brilliant opera productions could take place in a public theatre. From the aesthetic-humanistic point of view, this transition was an inestimable gain for Italian civilization.

Scarlatti's *Griselda* is something like a miracle when viewed from a seventeenth-century standpoint. The exquisiteness and magnificence of its poetry and music, the whole aura of refinement, spontaneity, style and subtlety which it exudes, must have made some of its patrons (or even authors) wish the common people were not there.

4. See Bruno Cagli, 'Produzione musicale e governo pontificio', in *Le Muse galanti*, ed. by B. Cagli, 1985, pp. 11–21.

We do not precisely know if they were; but it is of the highest significance for later opera history that such a work had been performed in public. Whoever compares it with Apostolo Zeno's original libretto version will notice how much less rigorous, how much richer, warmer and more appealing the opera is. The opera's 'message' could be spelled out in a title such as *Il trionfo dell'amore, e dell'innocenza* (which was actually once given to the libretto). In 1721 that triumph was made artistically enjoyable, for all the people.

Let us now follow the vicissitudes of the Teatro Capranica through its single seasons.

1710

The reopening of the theatre was originally planned for the carnival season of 1710. At that time the War of the Spanish Succession was still raging (not in the papal territories), and the supporters of the Bourbon and Habsburg causes, foremost among them the ambassadors of these nations, conducted a mini-war of succession within Rome: each of them claimed the right to inherit the theatre boxes once occupied by the Spanish ambassador.[5] The preparations for the actual season were fairly advanced by the end of January 1710. The planned opera was *Dorisbe* by the Roman poet Giovan Domenico Pioli, with music by Alessandro Scarlatti. Most of the boxes had been paid for. But on 7 February the Government prohibited the performances because of the continuing row. By that time, the libretto had been printed; Pioli dedicated it to the 'nobiltà Romana'.[6] The libretto names as the principal singer (in the role of Dorisbe) Giovanni Rapaccioli, who in the carnival of 1711 appeared at the Teatro S. Bartolomeo in Naples, and as scenographer Nicola Michetti, 'virtuoso del cardinale Ottoboni'. Pietro Ottoboni, then, had already offered his support to the new public opera house, as he was to do several times afterwards.

The Capranica enterprise was from the very beginning an object of rivalry between a number of princes who in 1709–11 began to have operas played also in their own private theatres: Cardinal Pietro Ottoboni at the Cancelleria, Queen Maria Casimira of Poland in her Palazzo Zuccari, and the newly-promoted protégé of Pope Clement XI, Prince Francesco Maria Ruspoli, in his Palazzo Bonelli.[7] It may satisfy a sense of balance that the task of contesting for boxes at the Capranica in 1710 was left to the ambassadors of Spain and Austria. In reality, however, they

5. Specific information is found in Francesco Valesio, *Diario di Roma*, ed. by Gaetano Scano and Giuseppe Graglia, 6 vols (Milan: Longanesi, 1977–81), vol. 4, pp. 364, 369, 374–81.
6. This libretto, which cannot be of the 1711 season, is the only one transcribed in Claudio Sartori, *I libretti italiani a stampa dalle origini al 1800*, 6 vols (Cuneo: Bertola and Locatelli, 1993). I have not been able to identify a reprint for the 1711 season; perhaps none was made. Of the first opera given in 1711, *L'Engelberta*, no 1710 printing exists.
7. A list of all Roman opera productions for 1710–32 is in Reinhard Strohm, *Italienische Opernarien des frühen Settecento (1720–1730)*, 2 vols (Cologne: Volk, 1976) (Analecta Musicologica, 16), vol. 2, pp. 293–321. For Alessandro Scarlatti's contributions, see also Lowell Lindgren, 'Il dramma musicale a Roma durante la carriera di Alessandro Scarlatti (1660–1725)', in *Le Muse galanti*, ed. by B. Cagli, 1985, pp. 52–4.

represented the interests of the Roman patrons as well. The party of the Bourbons was Ottoboni's: the cardinal had been made protector of the affairs (i.e. ambassador) of France in July 1709, and his influence on the Capranica competed directly with that of the Habsburg establishment, including the former Imperial ambassador Vincenzo Grimani, now viceroy of Naples, like Ottoboni himself a Venetian cardinal and an experienced supporter and author of opera. Grimani was, from 1708 until his premature death on 26 September 1710, the main protector of Alessandro Scarlatti, whom he had recalled to the position of Maestro della cappella reale of Naples.

1711

The first season which actually took place shows Alessandro Scarlatti as the exponent of Neapolitan influence at the Capranica. Both operas given were imported from Naples. The first, *L'Engelberta o sia la forza dell'innocenza*, was an arrangement of *Engelberta*, performed at the S. Bartolomeo on 4 November 1709 (the feast of San Carlo, i.e. the name-day of Charles III of Habsburg) with music by Giacomo Orefice and Francesco Mancini. Whereas the Neapolitan score survives,[8] that of the Roman production is lost, so that it cannot be determined what changes were made to the music. It is intriguing to speculate whether Alessandro Scarlatti had anything to do with this score. The opera was first mentioned by Valesio on 7 January, dress-rehearsed on 13 and premièred on 14 January.[9] The second Capranica opera, *Dorisbe*, was Scarlatti's *L'amor volubile e tiranno*, given at Naples on 25 May 1709; in this case, too, only the Neapolitan score exists.

In the carnival season of 1711 all the three palace theatres presented operas, in addition to the Capranica, and this was understood by many as direct competition.[10] National jealousy or aristocratic prejudice, or both, may have coloured a report published among those made by the director of the French Academy in Rome, Poërson:

17 janvier 1711.

Nous avons actuellement trois Théatres ouverts. Ils ont tous trois un égal concours, quoy que l'on dise dans le public qu'il faut voir celui du Cardinal

---

8. *A-Wn*, MS 18057, including the intermezzi *Pimpinone* by Pariati/Albinoni. This score was probably presented to Charles III or sent directly to Vienna. On the intermezzi, see Michael Talbot, 'Tomaso Albinoni's *Pimpinone* and the Comic Intermezzo', in *Con che soavità*, ed. by I. Fenlon and T. Carter, 1995, pp. 229–48.

9. F. Valesio, *Diario di Roma*, vol. 4, pp. 420–3. The diarist notes that theatre bills on the day of the première promised free admission, if the tokens (*bolettini*) were acquired in a shop underneath the auditorium. This was not true (possibly the work of a practical joker), since the *bolettini* really cost 4 and 5 *giulini*. The carpenter's shop underneath had to be passed by everybody to enter the auditorium.

10. Details on the operas given by Ruspoli and Ottoboni are assembled in Franco Piperno, 'Crateo, Olinto, Archimede e l'Arcadia: Rime per alcuni spettacoli operistici romani (1710–1711)', in *Händel e gli Scarlatti a Roma*, ed. by N. Pirrotta and A. Ziino, 1987, pp. 349–65.

Ottoboni, entendre celui du Prince Ruspoli, et s'abstenir de celuy de Capranica qui en effet réussit mal; mais c'est le Théâtre du public. . . . Le Prince royal de Pologne dispose pour lundy de faire paroistre l'Opéra de la Reyne sa mère. . . .[11]

Ruspoli had opened the season on 4 January with *L'Anagilda ovvero La Fede nei tradimenti* (Gigli/Caldara), Ottoboni on 11 January with *Teodosio il giovane.*[12] The cardinal's architect and scene-painter Filippo Juvarra is the obvious reason why the French correspondent recommends seeing the production at the Cancelleria.[13] Less obvious, but easy to explain, is the way he compliments Ruspoli: his opera deserved to be heard because he employed women sopranos, the famous Anna Maria de Piedz and Catterina Petrolli, and excellent intermezzo singers, the young Annibale Pio Fabbri (still a soprano, later a famous tenor) and the bass buffo Giovanni Battista Cavana. Ruspoli enriched his seasonal programme on 16 January with a production of the spoken *commedia in prosa* (i.e. drama) *Attilio Regolo*, which Girolamo Gigli had adapted from the French playwright Jean-Nicholas Pradon. Even this work – dedicated to Roman virtue and honour – was interlaced with musical fun: the intermezzi *L'Astrobolo.*[14]

Maria Casimira's theatre opened on 19 January with *Tolomeo et Alessandro, ovvero la corona disprezzata*, by the Queen's household artists Carlo Sigismondo Capeci and Domenico Scarlatti. The stage sets by Filippo Juvarra rivalled his own (more splendid) decorations for Ottoboni. The same three artists produced Maria Casimira's second opera of this carnival, *L'Orlando ovvero la gelosa pazzia.*[15] The Queen of Poland employed female singers as well: Anna Maria Giusti and Paola Alari. Altogether too much of a competition for *Engelberta*!

The second half of the season went much better for the Teatro Capranica. Its production of *Dorisbe* was first given privately on 3 February at the special request of the Queen of Poland for her granddaughter Maria Casimira, to whom the librettist Pioli had dedicated the dramma. Valesio reports that Her Majesty was present in the stalls, with four cardinals, without admission of further public ('senza bolettini').[16] This recalls pictures of private opera performances at the Parisian court of Anne of Austria and Cardinal Mazarin seventy years earlier.

11. Quoted after Roberto Pagano, Lino Bianchi and Giancarlo Rostirolla, *Alessandro Scarlatti* (Turin: ERI, 1972), p. 207.
12. Libretto perhaps by Vincenzo Grimani, but altered; a version of the drama was given in Naples, 1709, with music by Alessandro Scarlatti. The music of 1711 was composed by Ottoboni's cellist Filippo Amadei, a friend of Domenico Scarlatti who later went to London.
13. See M. Viale Ferrero, *Filippo Juvarra*; Maria Letizia Volpicelli, 'Il teatro del cardinale Ottoboni al Palazzo della Cancelleria', in *Il teatro a Roma nel settecento*, 2 vols (Rome: Istituto della Enciclopedia Italiana, 1989), pp. 681–782.
14. Details in Ursula Kirkendale, *Antonio Caldara: Sein Leben und seine venezianisch-römischen Oratorien* (Graz: Böhlau, 1966) (Wiener musikwissenschaftliche Beiträge, vol. 6), pp. 56–60.
15. Details in Malcolm Boyd, *Domenico Scarlatti – Master of Music* (London: Weidenfeld, 1986), pp. 47–9; M. Viale Ferrero, *Filippo Juvarra*, ch. 9; Reinhard Strohm, 'Scarlattiana at Yale', in *Händel e gli Scarlatti a Roma*, ed. by N. Pirrotta and A. Ziino, 1987, pp. 115–18. A celebratory broadsheet for *Tolomeo* says that the plot of this opera symbolized the renunciation of the Polish throne by Maria Casimira's son, Alexander Sobieski.
16. F. Valesio, *Diario di Roma*, vol. 4, p. 428.

The production of *Dorisbe* shared in a type of common programme of the Roman patrons: everybody had decided to offer pastoral operas.[17] Maria Casimira's *Orlando* – a relatively rare subject for opera in Italy at that time was countered by Ruspoli with the famous pastoral *La costanza in amor vince l'inganno*, with new music by Antonio Caldara. Ottoboni's contribution was intended to be his own pastoral drama *Ciro*, for which the preparations took too long. *Ciro* then opened the 1712 season with music by Alessandro Scarlatti.[18]

The fashion of the pastoral, particularly suitable to the aspirations of the Arcadia, was given systematic treatment elsewhere, for example in London, 1712–13, where both new operas were pastorals: Scarlatti's *La fede riconosciuta* (of Naples, 1710) as *Dorinda*, and Handel's *Il pastor fido*. It is peculiar to the Roman season of 1711 that the pastorals occupied the second carnival position usually reserved for more lavishly staged operas; their staging was indeed magnificent.

As stated above, the Teatro Capranica enterprise had been expected to open in January 1710, with the pastoral opera *Dorisbe* by Alessandro Scarlatti. Therefore the other pastoral operas mounted in the 1711 season must have followed Capranica's lead, not vice versa. This 'concerted action' might have been an idea developed between Cardinal Ottoboni and Scarlatti.

1712

In the carnival of 1712 Ottoboni produced two operas: he offered *Ciro* (see above), followed by the adventurous drama *Eraclio* by Pietro Antonio Bernardoni (presumably after Pierre Corneille), a version of which had been given at the S. Bartolomeo of Naples at the beginning of the same season (26 December 1711). Ruspoli did not produce any more operas, and Maria Casimira only one, *Tetide in Sciro*, by Capeci and Domenico Scarlatti, with stage-sets by Juvarra and with two new singers from Venice.[19] The production had been planned since May 1711. The classicizing *sujet* of Achilles in Skyros contrasted with an extremely complicated plotline, full of disguises and intrigues.

The Capranica operas were more inclined towards the Venetian/Florentine libretto reform. *La fede tradita* was one of the most successful Silvani librettos, sentimental, heroic and spectacular, with one of those Gothic tyrant-dagger-dungeon plots which the Venetians loved.[20] *Ataulfo* was based on a famous Venetian reform libretto by Domenico David, with an Iberian setting, but Gothic taste had

---

17. F. Valesio, *Diario di Roma*, vol. 4, pp. 376 and 427; M. Boyd, *Domenico Scarlatti*, p. 48.
18. F. Piperno, 'Crateo, Olinto, Archimede', pp. 360–5. On Ottoboni's authorship of the libretto, see also L. Lindgren, 'Il dramma musicale', p. 53, n. 63. On Juvarra's pastoral stage designs for *Ciro*, see Mercedes Viale Ferrero, 'Scenotecnica e macchine al tempo di Alessandro Scarlatti', in *Alessandro Scarlatti und seine Zeit*, ed. by M. Lütolf, 1995, pp. 55–77.
19. See M. Boyd, *Domenico Scarlatti*, pp. 49ff.; M. Viale Ferrero, *Filippo Juvarra*, ch. IX. Domenico Scarlatti's score of this opera is, exceptionally, extant today.
20. Although a derivation of the libretto from Genoa, 1709 (music by Giuseppe Maria Orlandini), is possible, the Venetian version was more probably the model. The drama was often given as *Ernelinda*, for example in London, 1713.

invaded the Capranica so much that the setting was now changed into a Gothic one. Also, independent intermezzi were added: in the first opera, *Madama Dulcinea ed il cuoco* by the Marchese Trotti, possibly written expressly for the production, and in the second, *La Birba* (Despina-Gildone). *Ataulfo*, furthermore, had *balli*. Some excellent singers were hired, among them Cavana and the later famous Domenico Giacinto Fontana 'detto Farfallino' ('Butterfly') for the intermezzi, and for the serious parts Antonio Bernacchi, Giovanni Antonio Archi detto Cortoncino, Domenico Tollini (a virtuoso of the new emperor, Charles VI) and Gaetano Borghi.

Giuseppe Maria Orlandini, then resident in Florence, is named as composer in the libretto of *Ataulfo*, and I suspect that he was responsible for the anonymous *La fede tradita* as well, whether by composing it himself or by arranging it as a pasticcio. In a production of this drama in Bologna in the following August, 'most of the music' was by Orlandini, according to the libretto. Gaetano Borghi sang the role of Rodoaldo in both the Roman and Bolognese productions. The stage-sets at the Capranica were by Pompeo Aldobrandini of Bologna, and the *ingegnere* was the architect Domenico Paradisi, who had worked for Ottoboni in 1695.[21] As with all productions before 1718, we do not know who the impresario was. Although it is possible that Federico Alveri Capranica was himself responsible in some ways, the styles of the productions in 1711 and 1712, at least, are so contrasting that they seem directed by different people.[22]

1713

In 1713, only the Queen of Poland was still producing palace operas of which librettos are extant: the twin set of *Ifigenia in Aulide* and *Ifigenia in Tauri* by the usual authors.[23] Two operas on texts by Antonio Ottoboni (father of Pietro) were privately given in this carnival, perhaps in Ruspoli's theatre, but no librettos were printed: *Giulio Cesare nell' Egitto* and *Proserpina rapita*.[24] Lalli's *L'amor tirannico*, at the Capranica, has possibly higher aspirations to a heroic tragedy in the manner of French drama. Piovene's *Publio Cornelio Scipione* was possibly more comparable to the 'Roman taste' of *Giulio Cesare*, but it was the most recent libretto by a radical Venetian 'reformer'. Its subject, also tried by Zeno and Salvi, had obvious symbolic implications at the end of the Habsburg war in Spain, since it constructed an analogy between 'Roman' and 'Imperial' virtue and wisdom.

21. See M. L. Volpicelli, 'Il teatro del cardinale Ottoboni' (n. 13 above), passim.
22. The libretto of *La fede tradita* has no dedication. *Ataulfo* is dedicated, by the bookseller Pietro Leone, 'alle Dame'.
23. See M. Boyd, *Domenico Scarlatti*, pp. 56ff.
24. See Mercedes Viale Ferrero, 'Antonio e Pietro Ottoboni e alcuni melodrammi da loro ideati o promossi a Roma', in *Venezia e il melodramma nel Settecento*, ed. by M. T. Muraro (Florence: Olschki, 1978), pp. 271–94; Michael Talbot and Colin Timms, 'Music and the Poetry of Antonio Ottoboni (1646–1720)', in *Händel e gli Scarlatti a Roma*, ed. by N. Pirrotta and A. Ziino, 1987, pp. 367–437, especially pp. 377–9.

The Capranica team was similar to that of 1712, with Aldobrandini as scene painter, and the singers Tollini and Archi, as well as Cavana for the intermezzi. Neither libretto names the composer. The first opera was only a pasticcio, probably arranged by Orlandini.[25] *Publio Cornelio Scipione* may have been played with the Venetian music of Carlo Francesco Pollarolo. This great old master had maintained close connections with Pietro Ottoboni; he was the composer of both the new Ottoboni operas, as well as of one of the acts of *Eraclio* given at the Cancelleria in 1712. Pollarolo must have been in residence in Rome for at least part of the carnival. The Teatro Capranica, therefore, seems to have benefited from Ottoboni's patronage for Pollarolo in this season and received from him either the original score or an arrangement of his opera. An arrangement of the music was surely necessary, since the libretto itself is altered from three to five acts, to achieve a more 'classical' form.

1714

Pietro Ottoboni's renewed interest in the Capranica began about February 1713 at the latest. The cardinal went so far as to commission his architect Juvarra to rebuild the Capranica stage. Planning must have begun in May 1713 and work was carried out in October–November. Juvarra also produced the stage-sets for the two Capranica operas of 1714; several of his sketches are extant.[26] The only contestant in the private theatres was, in this season, Maria Casimira's pastoral drama *Amor d'un ombra e gelosia d'un aura* (by Capeci and Domenico Scarlatti), to which a French correspondent awarded the prize, remarking however that none of the productions was lavishly staged and that there were few performances altogether; they were over by 13 February.[27]

The Teatro Capranica seems to have inherited, in this season, the support and some of the artistic status which had previously been distributed among the private theatres. The two Capranica operas were designed to complement each other in a common plan, and their authors were carefully chosen. Antonio Caldara, free from the duty of opera-composing for Ruspoli, provided the first work, *Tito e Berenice*, to a new libretto by Capeci. The recently arrived Francesco Gasparini, connected with the Principe Borghese,[28] set *Lucio Papirio*, a newly-written libretto by the Medici court poet, Antonio Salvi. Juvarra was the scenographer for both works. The guiding hand behind this assembly of artistic forces was Ottoboni's.

One of the French correspondents' reports claims that the new Capranica opera in January would have but little success, 'n'estoit l'égard que l'on a pour le Cardinal

25.   Orlandini's name was first suggested by G. Pavan, 'Il teatro Capranica (1711–1800)' (n. 2 above). See also R. Strohm, *Italienische Opernarien*, vol. 2, pp. 190–1.
26.   Mercedes Viale Ferrero, 'Scene di Filippo Juvarra per il *Lucio Papirio* di Francesco Gasparini (Roma, Teatro Capranica, 1713–1714)', in *Francesco Gasparini*, ed. by F. Della Seta and F. Piperno, 1981, pp. 245–57, with plates.
27.   M. Boyd, *Domenico Scarlatti*, pp. 60ff.
28.   See Fabrizio Della Seta, 'Francesco Gasparini Virtuoso del Principe Borghese?', in *Francesco Gasparini*, ed. by F. Della Seta and F. Piperno, 1981, pp. 218–19.

1a. Filippo Juvarra, 'Arco trionfale e scalea': stage design (draft) for *Tito e Berenice* (I, 1?), Teatro Capranica, 1713, but not used ('Capranica non in opera').

Otthoboni', and adds that the patron had personally interfered with Capeci's libretto.[29] Even more interesting is a press announcement of 8 August 1713, first noticed by Fabrizio Della Seta: 'Cardinal Ottoboni has taken over the protection of the Teatro Capranica, by having new boxes added and [the auditorium] re-decorated, and by having ordered the two Arcadian Academies to write two operas, and to the one who does better he'll present a gift to their community. The music of the one [opera] will be by Caldara, the other by Gasparino.'[30]

29. M. Viale Ferrero, 'Scene di Filippo Juvarra', pp. 245–6.
30. 'Il Cardinale Ottoboni ha preso la protettione del Teatro Capranica, con far accrescere altri palchi, e farvi di nuovo le apparenze, avendo ordinato alle due Accademie degli Arcadi di componere due Opere, e per quella farà migliore corrisponderà con un regalo alle Università, la Musica d'una sarà del Caldara, e l'altra del Gasparino.' Rome, Bibl. Angelica, MS Arcadia 19, fol. 274v; quoted here after F. Della Seta, 'Francesco Gasparini Virtuoso del Principe Borghese?', p. 223, n. 23.

1b. Filippo Juvarra, 'Arco di Tito': stage design for *Tito e Berenice* (?), Teatro Capranica, 1713, not used.

So this was a prize-winning contest! It was like a social game, cleverly planned and widely enjoyed by those in the know. An important implication, which has not yet been investigated, concerns the Accademia de' Quirini, the separatist branch of the Arcadia. Since Capeci's *Tito e Berenice* must be identified as the contribution of the Arcadia proper, Salvi's *Lucio Papirio* was sponsored by the Accademia de' Quirini. A leading figure of the 'Quirini', Gian Vincenzo Gravina, was a known opponent of melodramma and yet the teacher of Pietro Metastasio (then still called Pietro Trapassi). One of Antonio Salvi's dramas which impressed the young poet was *Amore e maestà* of 1715, which had a totally tragic ending and may have been acceptable to his teacher Gravina.[31] Other members of the 'Quirini' were Paolo Antonio Rolli and Gaetano Lemer, whom we shall meet in due course.

31. Further on this libretto, see chapters 8, 9 and 15 in this volume.

The poets Capeci and Salvi probably knew of each others' tasks, as there is a 'concerted' relationship between the two librettos. Both represent heroic self-sacrifice, the respect for the laws of Rome, and a victory over oneself, *Tito* in Imperial Rome, *Lucio Papirio* in Republican Rome. In the former case this virtuous act conflicts with erotic love, in the latter with paternal love. The distribution of the characters among the singers shows the same hierarchy of roles in both operas, although the two leading castratos, Matteo Berscelli and Domenico Tempesti, seem to switch first and second place. Berscelli is Domiziano (secondo uomo) and Quinto Fabio (primo uomo), respectively; Tempesti is Tito (primo uomo) and Lucio (secondo uomo). Capeci derived his drama from the 'Titus and Berenice' dramas of both Pierre Corneille and Jean Racine, compounding their intrigues and affections; Salvi seems to have worked independently.

The Roman productions of these years had increasing repercussions elsewhere, for example in London. *Amor d'un ombra e gelosia d'un aura* was repeated there in 1720 under the title *Narciso*.[32] Handel used both Capeci librettos of 1711 (*Tolomeo* and *Orlando*) in 1728 and 1733, respectively; he may also have borrowed from *Tito e Berenice* for an unfinished opera project of c. 1731–2.[33] This work, entitled *Titus l'Empereur* in Handel's sketches, begins with a triumphal scene in which Titus is feasted as the new emperor. Such an opening scene occurs neither in Corneille nor in Racine, nor indeed in Capeci's libretto. Among Juvarra's stage designs of 1713–14, however, there are some which were apparently intended for *Tito e Berenice* but subsequently not used. One is entitled 'Veduta del arco di Tito' ('View of the Arch of Titus'), another 'Arco trionfale e scalea' ('Triumphal arch and flight of steps'), with the addition 'Capranica non in opera'.[34] Either design would fit Handel's first scene excellently, although he does not rely on Capeci's libretto as his model but on Racine. He may nevertheless have been aware of the Roman production and Juvarra's stage designs.[35]

1715

In the years 1715–17 the Capranica was the only Roman theatre which presented *drammi per musica*. It had the advantage of drawing together the artistic forces and the patronal support which would otherwise have been spread over the competition; on the other hand, competition and mutual reinforcement in matters of opera was lacking. For example, Carlo Sigismondo Capeci began in these years to devote most of his energies to prose comedy; he might not have done so had his patroness not

32.   Details in M. Boyd, *Domenico Scarlatti*, pp. 61–2.
33.   See Reinhard Strohm, *Essays on Handel and Italian Opera* (Cambridge: Cambridge University Press, 1985), pp. 58–9, 62–3, 65–6.
34.   M. Viale Ferrero, 'Scene di Filippo Juvarra', p. 248 and fig. 3; M. Viale Ferrero, *Filippo Juvarra*, fig. 157. See illustrations 1a and 1b.
35.   This would not be surprising, since there is evidence that Handel's *Giulio Cesare in Egitto*, likewise, is somehow connected with the Juvarra designs for Antonio Ottoboni's Roman libretto of 1713: see M. Viale Ferrero, 'Antonio e Pietro Ottoboni'.

left Rome in 1714, and had opera productions at the Palazzo Zuccari not ceased altogether.

Both the Capranica operas of 1715 were based on Venetian librettos by Zeno and Pariati, belonging to the mainstream of libretto reform. Paolo Antonio Rolli, Arcadia's rhyme virtuoso, arranged the libretto of *Astarto* and also directed the rehearsals (see below). Giovanni Bononcini had moved to Rome and was immediately available to compose a new opera score (like Francesco Gasparini a year before). The Bononcini brothers, Giovanni and Antonio Maria, were then in the service of Count Wenzel Gallas, Imperial ambassador in Rome since 1714, who had already established regular performances of serenatas and other music in his palace.[36] Ruspoli was the employer of Caldara and, at least for occasional poems, of Rolli; Borghese was a patron of Gasparini. The main musical patrons in 1715 can therefore be identified as Gallas, Ruspoli and Borghese. Count Girolamo Gigli of Siena, formerly the educator of Ruspoli's son Bartolomeo, contributed to *Ambleto* with the comic intermezzi *La Dirindina*, causing a famous scandal. The events have often been discussed; it is documented that essentially the singers were unwilling to perform this lascivious satire against operatic vanity and loose morals, so that the intermezzi, already set to music by Domenico Scarlatti, had to be withdrawn on command of the papal administrator, and replaced by *intermedii pastorali* (*Elpina e Silvano*).[37] It is understandable that the castrato singer of the female part (Dirindina), Domenico Giacinto Fontana, feared ridicule by performing the role of a pregnant primadonna.[38]

This is the first Capranica season for which a reasonable amount of music survives.[39] Of Domenico Scarlatti's music, we have *La Dirindina*,[40] and one aria from *Ambleto*. The latter lonely item survives in a Bolognese collection of arias all drawn from the four Capranica operas of 1715 and 1716.[41] It was perhaps copied by a Bolognese visitor to Rome in those years, who may have had ties with the composer Luca Antonio Predieri. Furthermore, there is a complete score of Bononcini's *Astarto* in the Santini collection (*D-MÜs*, MS 4137). Although both libretto and score are anonymous, Bononcini's authorship is secure because of the recurrence of many arias in his other works, including the London revival of *Astarto* itself, 1720. This revival happened through Paolo Rolli and presumably at the

36. On the Bononcinis and Gallas, see Lowell Lindgren, *A Bibliographic Scrutiny of Dramatic Works Set by Giovanni and His Brother Antonio Maria Bononcini*, PhD, Harvard University, 1972 (Ann Arbor: UMI, 74–25,641), pp. 146ff.

37. M. Boyd, *Domenico Scarlatti*, pp. 70ff.; Francesco Degrada, 'Una sconosciuta esperienza teatrale di Domenico Scarlatti: *La Dirindina*', in F. Degrada, *Il palazzo incantato*, pp. 67–97.

38. He was now a pupil and protégé of Francesco Gasparini; see F. Della Seta, 'Francesco Gasparini Virtuoso del Principe Borghese?', pp. 237–8.

39. The musical sources for productions of the Teatro Capranica in this period (except for the new source of *Arminio*, see below) are listed in R. Strohm, *Italienische Opernarien*, vol. 2, pp. 152–303.

40. Discovered and edited by Francesco Degrada (Milan: Ricordi, 1985).

41. *I-Bc*, MS DD 47, fol. 7–69. M. Boyd, *Domenico Scarlatti*, pp. 68–70, presumes that six arias of *Ambleto* were not by Domenico but were taken from Gasparini's original setting of the text, since they are printed with asterisks in the libretto. I doubt this, because of the unqualified attribution of the music to Scarlatti in the libretto.

request of Richard Boyle, Lord Burlington, to whom the London libretto is dedicated. Burlington, well known as a patron also of Vanbrugh, Pepusch and Handel, had visited Rome in 1715 and seen the carnival performances of *Astarto*. Lindgren concludes that 'his enthusiasm for the work extended to attending rehearsals and to bringing Paolo Antonio Rolli, the stage director of the work, with him to England'.[42]

Astarto may be considered one of Giovanni Bononcini's best scores, after the inimitable *Il Trionfo di Camilla* (Naples, 1696). The Venetian libretto – modelled by Zeno after a play by Philippe Quinault – treats the same historical subject as *Abdolomino*, a libretto by Silvio Stampiglia set by Giovanni Bononcini for Vienna (1709). This points to Habsburg influence through Count Gallas. A singer of Gallas's household appeared in the productions, the soprano Domenico Genevesi. The tenor Giovanni Paita, who studied with Francesco Gasparini, was highly praised for his part in *Astarto* in a letter by Gallas's secretary Primoli.[43]

Pietro Pariati, the co-author of both *Astarto* and *Ambleto*, had just been appointed Imperial poet in 1714, and Zeno himself was to follow in 1718. Zeno's successor-to-be in Vienna, Pietro Metastasio, possibly saw the Roman performance of *Astarto*, on whose plot he much later modelled his *Il re pastore*. He probably knew *La Dirindina* as well, whose *sujet* resembles that of his own only intermezzi, *L'impresario delle Canarie* of 1724.

1716–1717

The common feature of these two seasons is the composer of all four operas, Francesco Gasparini. Neither composer of 1715, Domenico Scarlatti and Caldara, wrote for these two seasons. Gasparini had not been involved in the 1715 season, spending the carnival with operas in Florence, and the spring season in Reggio Emilia. His correspondence with the Borghese family reveals that he was still uncertain whether to return to Venice or settle in Rome in the spring of 1715; the decision for Rome must have been made in the latter half of that year. Apparently the friendship with the Borghese family was a deciding factor.[44] When, however, Antonio Caldara left the service of Prince Ruspoli in May 1716 for a position in Vienna, Gasparini became his successor.[45] He seems to have immediately attracted students in singing, harpsichord and composition. He was able to use the Teatro

42. It is through Rolli's dedication to Burlington of 1720 that we learn of his part in the Capranica production; see L. Lindgren, *A Bibliographic Scrutiny*, pp. 157–8.
43. L. Lindgren, *A Bibliographic Scrutiny*, p. 154.
44. F. Della Seta, 'Francesco Gasparini Virtuoso del Principe Borghese?', pp. 238–9 (letters of 12 and 23 March 1715).
45. U. Kirkendale, *Antonio Caldara*, p. 82; Franco Piperno, 'Francesco Gasparini "virtuoso dell'eccellentissimo Sig. Principe Ruspoli": contributo alla biografia gaspariniana (1716–1718)', in *Francesco Gasparini*, ed. by F. Della Seta and F. Piperno, pp. 191–214. The composer is styled 'virtuoso del . . . Principe Ruspoli' in both libretti of 1717. See also Emilia Zanetti, 'La presenza di Francesco Gasparini in Roma: Gli ultimi anni 1716–1727', in *Francesco Gasparini*, ed. by F. Della Seta and F. Piperno, pp. 261ff.

Capranica as a trial-ground for singers he trained, and even for his composition students.

The most promising of these singers, apart from Fontana who reappeared in 1717, was Giovanni Ossi, who is identified as 'pupil (*allievo*) of Mr Gasparini' in both librettos of 1716. He also sang in Ruspoli's palace. Ossi was a mezzosoprano, excellent in the role of a hero or villain; he dominated this particular field for about fifteen years afterwards in most opera houses of Italy. In the 1717 season, Ossi sang the second female part – an experiment which he was not to repeat often. Among the other performers of 1716, the mezzosoprano Matteo Berscelli and the tenor Giovanni Paita were old associates of Gasparini, at least since Venice, 1709.

The music of *Il Trace in catena* was by Gasparini 'and two of his pupils (*allievi*)'. One of these must have been the young Giovanni Porta, since the texts of two arias of the opera recur in his opera *Teodorico* of 1720, and Porta is identified as Gasparini's student in the libretto of his own *Argippo* of Venice, 1717.

Outside influence on the choice of personnel was surely exerted. The Imperial ambassador Gallas lent his virtuoso Domenico Genevesi. Giovanni Francesco Costanzi was borrowed from the viceroyal chapel of Naples. Prince Ruspoli, on the other hand, seems to have kept a low profile. None of the four libretti bears a dedication – Federico Capranica himself may have acted as impresario. The 1716 operas had intermezzi, the 1717 operas balli, directed by Nicolò l'Evesque (as before). The scenographer of 1716, Francesco Galli Bibiena (replaced by Nicola Michetti in 1717), was an important addition to the Roman circuit in this period. He worked on the construction of the Teatro Alibert from 1717 and was to reappear at the Capranica in the crucial season of 1721.

The whole season of 1716 was affected by the war against the Turks. The pope hesitated to permit the opening of the theatres, so that the first opera, *Il Ciro*, had not yet started on 1 February.[46] The second opera, *Il Vincislao*, was perhaps staged in a hurry. Gasparini simply arranged a Neapolitan production of the previous year, adding some arias of his own to those of Francesco Mancini, the Neapolitan *vicemaestro* under Scarlatti. Existing aria copies drawn from *Il Ciro* seem to attest to its success, whereas of the other three operas of 1716 and 1717 almost no music survives.[47]

The librettos are a different matter. All four hail from the Venetian/Florentine reform circles around 1700–15; I suspect that it was Gasparini's taste which led to this choice. The subject of *Il Ciro*, however, had also been treated in *Il Tigrane* by Domenico Lalli, set to music by Alessandro Scarlatti for Naples in 1715. In effect, the Capranica season of 1716 offered, in terms of opera plots, a replica of the previous S. Bartolomeo carnival. Zeno's *Vincislao* (on murderous intrigues in the Royal House of Poland, interestingly) was an adaptation of Jean Rotrou's tragedy;

46. On that day, Gallas's secretary Primoli writes that the operas will be rather mediocre, and complains: 'Che dite dell'austerità di questa corte che prende ogni picciol pretesto per dare il bando a qualsivoglia allegria?' ('What do you say about the austerity of this court which uses every possible pretext to banish any entertainment?'). See L. Lindgren, *A Bibliographic Scrutiny*, p. 154.
47. R. Strohm, *Italienische Opernarien*, vol. 2, pp. 165–6.

his *Il Pirro* is also indebted to French precedent. *Il Trace in catena* was based on Pradon's tragedy *Tamerlan*. The Roman version of 1717 contains many alterations to Salvi's original of 1706, mostly benefiting the role of Giovanni Ossi. Perhaps Salvi arranged the libretto himself at Gasparini's request when both men met in Florence in 1715.

1718

Domenico Scarlatti's contribution to *Berenice regina d'Egitto* may be the last operatic music he ever composed. The libretto says 'La musica è delli Sgg. Domenico Scarlatti, e Nicolò Porpora'; Domenico's few surviving arias occur in the first Act. The task was probably divided equally, splitting the second Act in the middle, as was sometimes done elsewhere. None of Porpora's music for the opera survives, so that a direct comparison between the two Neapolitan composers – almost contemporaries – cannot be made.[48]

The opening of the Teatro Alibert in 1718 changed the climate of Roman musical theatre by providing significant competition to the Capranica. As if this were not enough, the old Teatro della Pace, rebuilt in 1717,[49] also now started to produce operas.

The opera house of the Conte Antonio d'Alibert was a public theatre as well. Henceforth, there was no more scope in Rome for regular private opera productions. The princes now had to come out of their palaces in order to patronize opera. The artists were redistributed over this wider 'market' that had opened up for their skills. The Teatro della Pace offered only pasticcios in its first season. The Alibert, however, 'poached' both Francesco Mancini, who composed *Alessandro Severo* for the inauguration, and Gasparini, who set *Sesostri*. The Neapolitan *vicemaestro* was rather an outsider, but why did Gasparini leave the Capranica?

Perhaps the answer lies in Naples. On 21 September 1717 Alessandro Scarlatti was given leave from his employment at Naples to spend the whole carnival season of 1718 in Rome, with full continuation of his salary.[50] It seems that Alessandro got himself hired by the Capranica for the whole season, to rival the Alibert enterprise. *Berenice*, the opera jointly composed by his son Domenico – whose participation he may well have suggested – was pitched against Mancini, his deputy at Naples. His own new opera was intended for comparison with that of his friend and rival Gasparini.

Gasparini's employer, Prince Ruspoli, supported the Alibert from at least its second season, 1719. The second Alibert opera of 1719, Gasparini's *Astianatte*, is dedicated to Isabella Cesi Ruspoli, the Prince's wife. It makes sense that Gasparini worked in the opera house then favoured by his patrons. As for 1718, however, it appears that Gasparini moved out of the Capranica (how voluntarily, we do not know) to make room for his illustrious colleague and his son; it seems this was all

48.   For some remarks on both composers, see M. Boyd, *Domenico Scarlatti*, pp. 78ff. The musical source is cited in R. Strohm, *Italienische Opernarien*, vol. 2, p. 226.
49.   By the theatre architect Domenico Vellani of Bologna: see A. Rava, *I teatri di Roma*, vol. 2, p. 114.
50.   Roberto Pagano et al., *Alessandro Scarlatti*, pp. 222–3.

Scarlatti's own design and not a scheme invented by the impresarios. That Gasparini was awarded membership of the Arcadia (of which Scarlatti already was a member) in this same year could have been part of the deal.

1718 is the first season when there is a trace of professional impresarios at the Capranica. The impresarios Bernardo Robatti, Lorenzo Capua and Giuseppe Masini dedicated the libretto of *Berenice* to the wife of the Habsburg ambassador, Wenzel Gallas; Porpora could at this point be considered a Habsburg protégé. The dedication of *Telemaco* is anonymous. I suspect that the impresarios had little influence on the choice of librettos and composers – rather perhaps on that of the singers. Among these, the later famous castratos Carlo Scalzi and Domenico Gizzi stand out. In the 1718 librettos the theatre is identified for the first time as 'sala del sig. Federico Capranica', no longer 'de' signori Capranica'. Pompeo's co-ownership had ceased already in 1712.[51]

Berenice is another Salvi libretto written for the court opera of Ferdinando de' Medici at Pratolino; this is compatible with the idea that Alessandro – who had written operas for Pratolino – influenced the choice of the opera. The piece is lighthearted and legendary, requiring mostly pastoral sets.[52] Salvi may again have been asked to rewrite some of it, as the textual changes against 1710 are significant. *Telemaco* (i.e. Telemachus and Calypso, a subject which could qualify as 'pastoral-magic') is peculiar in that its libretto and scenic style is entirely in the French manner, with a mythological prologue and much emphasis on the *merveilleux*, as the subject requires. Capeci – competing with Salvi just as in 1714 – probably derived his libretto from a pasticcio of the same title by Campra; there had been a similar work in Vienna, composed by Carlo Agostino Badia. Scarlatti displayed the utmost instrumental magnificence, already apparent in the prologue with a triple orchestra including a *coro* of horns, oboes and bassoons. This orchestral style was not unknown in Rome – although somewhat old-fashioned by 1718. The French characteristics of the work were balanced by Italian and Viennese ones, especially in the arias. Scarlatti's autograph, which survives in the Vienna library, was perhaps dedicated to the Habsburg court; there is also a copy in Brussels, with an added French title-page probably of Belgian provenance.[53] We might regard the work as Scarlatti's contribution to 'Les goûts réunis'. It is tempting to think that, as the European wars were reaching an end, an allusion to reconciliation of cultures was intended.

1719

The impresario Bernardo Robatti, now on his own, dedicated *Astinome* to Teresa Borromei Albani; the poet was 'un Accademico Quirino', i.e. Domenico Ottavio Petrosellini da Corneto.[54]

---

51. A. Rava, *I teatri di Roma*, p. 54.
52. The (pseudo-)historical character Berenice is the same as in the Titus opera of 1714, but the events are drastically different.
53. See R. Strohm, *Italienische Opernarien*, vol. 2, p. 224.
54. According to a manuscript note in the libretto copy of the Brussels Conservatoire.

A powerful patron must also have been needed to elicit the music from the famous Carlo Francesco Pollarolo, aged sixty-six: this is one of his very last opera scores. Alessandro Scarlatti could have been instrumental in persuading his old colleague.

He himself wrote the second opera. Its music survives in many good sources, including the autograph score in the British Library, which is labelled 'opera 112' and dated 'Gennaro 1719'.[55]

The composers of this season were the oldest masters of opera still around: the Capranica was 'de-modernizing'. The same may have been true for the librettos. *Astinome* is a classicist-Arcadian exercise in good stage manners during the Trojan War. The author says in the preface that 'a personage of great authority' (presumably the dedicatee, Teresa Albani) had persuaded him to write it, although he had been living in lonely retirement for many years. *Marco Attilio Regolo* was a relatively independent version of a story also treated by Pradon (whose tragedy Ruspoli had presented in 1711) and found in an old libretto by Matteo Noris.[56] The librettist or arranger was perhaps Capeci, whose signed works of these years are mostly prose comedies. Robatti dedicated the libretto to Teresa's husband Carlo Albani, who is identified as a nephew of the pope.

A competition with the Alibert and Pace theatres was almost certainly intended, this time in Roman-Arcadian terms. At the Alibert, Gasparini persisted in his 'Venetian/Florentine' preference by composing, in 1718 and 1719, three historical dramas by Zeno and Salvi. The Pace offered the pastoral *Erminia* and Stampiglia's exotic *Etearco*, both set by Giovanni Bononcini and patronized by the Austrian ambassador. The Capranica productions of 1718–19 were easily the most classicizing and yet old-fashioned works. In all four of them, however, intermezzi or buffo scenes were inserted; all but *Marco Attilio Regolo* contained *macchine*. These attractions, and the choice of the singing cast (among which we note the return of Annibale Pio Fabri, now as tenor), may well have been negotiated by the impresario.

1720

Alessandro Scarlatti monopolized the 1720 season, to be sure. Not only the choice of composer, but even that of subject matter and librettist now lacked the touch of variety or contrast which the Capranica had usually offered. Both operas were

55.   An aria collection now in Cambridge was used by Handel in the 1730s as a source for musical ideas: see John H. Roberts, 'Handel's and Jennens's Italian opera manuscripts', in *Music and Theatre: Studies in Honour of Winton Dean for his 70th Birthday*, ed. by Nigel Fortune (Cambridge: Cambridge University Press, 1987), pp. 159–202, especially pp. 162–3.

56.   Metastasio – the next librettist to use the subject – probably remembered the 1719 version. On its attribution, see L. Lindgren, 'Il dramma musicale', p. 53, n. 66, where there is also a document saying that Scarlatti returned to Naples on 18 February 1719, immediately after the production of the work.

revisions of earlier works by Scarlatti himself. The librettos were Roman-republican dramas written by Silvio Stampiglia, a founder member of the Arcadia, who had never subscribed to Zeno's and Salvi's type of reform libretto.[57] He was still living in Rome and had revised the librettos for the composer. The two operas of 1720 have in common a characteristic subject matter: the triumphs of Latin *virtù*. The plot of *Turno Aricino*, in particular, recalls the heroism of *Lucio Papirio*. As in 1719, the first libretto was dedicated to Teresa Albani, the second to her husband Carlo: the conclusion seems inescapable that the Albani clan was to be celebrated in the guise of Roman heroes (see also below on 1721). *Turno Aricino* celebrates a place in Latium, Aricia under the Albano mountain, which may have had heraldic significance for the family.

The impresario Robatti, who signed both librettos, was concerned not so much with drama and music as with the artistic personnel and similar attractions: for example, with Gasparini's ex-pupil and rising soprano star, Giacinto Fontana, with the Venetian scene-painters Bernardo Canal ('Canaletto') and his son Antonio, and with the ballets and *abbattimenti* (staged battles).

Of particular interest to the musician must be the splendid ensembles (duets and quartets) in Scarlatti's scores. Their number generally increases in his late operas, already in *Telemaco*; it is therefore certain that Stampiglia fulfilled the composer's wish when he added several ensembles to his original librettos. The original version of *Tito Sempronio Gracco* (1702) had contained one quartet and four duets; the 1720 version adds another quartet ('Alma mia – cor del mio seno') and transforms one duet into yet another quartet ('Non potervi vagheggiare'). Otherwise the libretto was changed very little. The original of *Turno Aricino* (1704) contained four duets; in 1720, two duets, two quartets and one sextet were sung, mostly on new texts.[58] The quartets – as far as they express contrasted affections – show Scarlatti's particular mastery of contrapuntal and dramatic tension within a textually regular, closed number. They are not *concertato* ensembles as in later opera; but they stand comparison with Handel's great opera seria ensembles.

Scarlatti himself counted *Marco Attilio Regolo* as his 112th opera, but *Griselda* of 1721 as his 114th; he considered only one of the two productions of 1720 as an independent work. The surviving music for both productions, a total of 51 numbers, was thus only partly new in 1720.[59] The texts and the musical style of these numbers suggest that *Turno Aricino* was newly composed and is therefore the 113th opera; *Tito* was only a revision.

57. His career and works are reconstructed in L. Lindgren, *A Bibliographic Scrutiny*. See also 'The Neapolitans in Venice', in this volume, pp. 61–80.
58. Extant copies include the quartets 'Anima bella' and 'Che fiero pensiero'. See also Edward J. Dent, *Alessandro Scarlatti: His Life and Works* (London, 1905), rev. edn by Frank Walker (London, 1960), pp. 167–8.
59. R. Strohm, *Italienische Opernarien*, vol. 2, p. 225; L. Lindgren, 'Il dramma musicale', p. 53 (quoting Carl R. Morey).

1721

Griselda is not only one of Scarlatti's greatest operas, it is also the culminating effort of a unique theatrical tradition. These two judgements may be interdependent in some way: I believe that it is difficult to appreciate the aesthetic significance of the opera without knowing its institutional context, just as it would be hazardous to judge the Capranica productions of this period without studying the score of *Griselda*.

The first thing to be taken into account in an evaluation of *Griselda* is perhaps the one thing that none of the numerous commentators has considered so far:[60] the other opera of the season, *Crispo*. That the two pieces are related, that the season was a planned competition, that the patrons and artists collaborated, would have been obvious to the contemporary audience.

Scarlatti wrote his opera 'per il Principe Ruspoli', as he noted on the frontispiece of the autograph; the libretto was dedicated to Prince Francesco Maria Ruspoli by Federico Capranica. Federico's extremely adulatory language almost suggests that the Prince himself had written the libretto. At least it shows who was behind the planning of this season.[61] *Crispo* is dedicated to Ruspoli's wife, Isabella Cesi Ruspoli, by 'the author'. He was Gaetano Lemer, of the Quirinian Academy, a friend of Rolli. We know this from a remark by Rolli himself, which has been discovered by Lowell Lindgren. Together with it, Lindgren found a key to the Roman opera-game, provided in far-away England in a prose comedy by Richard Steele (1724).[62]

A passage in Steele's play, translated by Rolli, alludes to the universal discussions about the two operas performed at London's Haymarket theatre in the season of 1722, making great furore: *Crispo* and *Griselda*. These corresponded to the two Capranica productions of 1721. I quote from Steele's dialogue in Rolli's translation:

(*Lelio, Signora Indana*)
Lelio. Voi che non siete mai parziale alle Mode, stimo che siate il Giudice più conveniente della gran Disputa fra le Dame, qual'Opera sia la più gradevole: o il Crispo o la Griselda.

60.   I do not exclude myself from this criticism: R. Strohm, *Die italienische Oper*, pp. 73–94. Other comments on the opera are in Hermann Junker, 'Zwei Griselda-Opern', in *Festschrift Adolf Sandberger* (Munich, 1918), pp. 51–64; Donald J. Grout, 'La *Griselda* di Zeno e il libretto dell'opera di Scarlatti', *Nuova Rivista Musicale Italiana* 2 (1968), pp. 207–25; idem, 'The original version of Alessandro Scarlatti's '*Griselda*', in *Essays on Opera and English Music in Honour of Sir Jack Westrup* (Oxford: Blackwell, 1975), pp. 103–14; idem, *Alessandro Scarlatti: An Introduction to His Operas* (Berkeley: University of California Press, 1979). The opera has been edited by Donald J. Grout, in *The Operas of Alessandro Scarlatti*, vol. 3 (Cambridge, Mass.: Harvard University Press, 1975) (Harvard Publications in Music, 8).
61.   On the basis of the dedication, I had earlier suggested that Ruspoli himself also arranged Zeno's libretto text. The full wording of the dedication, quoted by L. Lindgren, 'Il dramma musicale', p. 53, n. 70, is perhaps better understood as an extreme hyperbole emphasizing the patron's involvement in the preparations. As such, it has to be taken seriously enough. As for the question who wrote the actual verse, see below.
62.   *The conscious lovers/Gli amanti interni: Commedia inglese del Cavaliere Riccardo Steele* (London, 1724), pp. 57 and 161–2. See L. Lindgren, 'Il dramma musicale', p. 43, n. 42.

Sigra. Indana. Scusatemi, (. . .)ho parzialità (. . .) per quella pastorale Capanna di Griselda; l'abbandonata sua condizione, la Povertà, la Rassegnazione, quell'innocente suo sonno, e quel soporifero 'Dolce sogno' cantato sopra lei che dorme, fecero tale effetto in me, che, per abbreviarla, non sono stata mai così bene ingannata ad alcun'altra opera.

Lelio. Oh, dunque io posso adesso dar qualche conto di questa Disputa. Pare che in Griselda si vegga la Disgrazia d'una innocente ed ingiuriata Donna, ed in Crispo quella d'un Uomo nella medesima condizione; e per ciò gli Uomini sono per il Crispo, e per naturale Condescenza, ambo i sessi per la Griselda.[63]

Rolli annotates this passage, explaining that *Crispo* was the title of a drama by Signor Gaetano Lemer, a highly-reputed member of the Accademia de' Quirini, and that *Griselda* was a drama written by him – Rolli – for the Royal Academy of Music in London, for which he had also revised *Crispo*.[64] In the London version of *Crispo*, Bononcini's music for Rome was retained and only revised, whereas Rolli's new *Griselda* libretto necessitated entirely new music by Bononcini.

Apart from the superb final twist of Steele's dialogue – by 'natural inclination' only the woman finds universal support – Lelio's interpretation of the two plays as a balanced, complementary pair symbolizing the genders is surely correct also for Rome, 1721. Let us consider, too, that the libretto of *Crispo* is dedicated to Isabella Cesi Ruspoli, *Griselda* to her husband; that Bononcini and a 'Quirinian' wrote the first opera, two Arcadians the second; that *Crispo* is set in Imperial Rome, *Griselda* a pastoral; that the former subject comes from history via a French tragedy (Racine's *Phèdre*), the latter from medieval legend via Italian prose (Boccaccio). The very idea of these contrasts and parallelisms must have been exciting. The 1721 Capranica season is intended to be in itself a work of art.

The scenographer Francesco Galli Bibiena, the *maestro de' balli* Antonio Sarò, and the extremely distinguished singers were, of course, common to both productions. Nevertheless, a subtle balance was achieved by redefining the hierarchy within the cast. The tenor Pacini is the elderly Emperor Costantino in the first opera, but the rather youthful villain Ottone in the second. The mezzosoprano star Antonio Bernacchi is the suffering *primo uomo* and youthful lover Crispo, and the avuncular husband Gualtiero. Giacinto Fontana and Giovanni Carestini (at the beginning of his career) exchange function and rank in the leading female roles: Fontana plays the faithful wife Griselda and the young lover Olimpia, Carestini the guilty Empress Fausta and the innocent girl Costanza. In both operas the famous soprano Bartolomeo Bartoli[65] had dramatically inferior roles, though these were padded out with surplus arias; his Roberto in *Griselda* had nine arias, as many as

63. *The conscious lovers*, p. 57.
64. *The conscious lovers*, pp. 161–2.
65. This Bavarian court virtuoso may play a role in the reception history of *Griselda*. Of the many later settings of Zeno's libretto, only one adopts the Roman text revision of 1721: the Munich production of 1723 (with music by Pietro Torri). I suspect that Bartoli, who sang in that production, took the Roman libretto to Munich.

Griselda. This balancing act also influenced the relationship between drama and poetry.

The libretto arranger of *Griselda* initially provided texts for more than fifty closed numbers; operatic conventions of the time would have suggested a maximum of about thirty-five. Both the score and the printed libretto show drastic revisions of text and music, although it is unlikely that an early version can have been performed separately.[66] I imagine that the libretto arranger of *Griselda* was personally close to Ruspoli, and that he, too, was a Roman Arcadian. Capeci would qualify as the author of the new poetry written for the drama, which replaces almost all the lyrical verse of Zeno's (not mentioned in the libretto). The main dramatic and poetic ideas have shifted from a moralistic, sentimental-heroic fable to a display of verbal and scenic beauty threatened by verbal and scenic cruelty. The more direct appeal to the audience's sentimental sympathy (as volunteered by Steele's Signora Indana, although she reacted to Rolli's new version of the plot) is combined with a sensuousness of words and music that Zeno could not have dreamt of. Roberto's main arias alone, 'Come presto nel porto crudele', 'Amanti che piangete', 'Pace, pupille vaghe' and 'Come va l'ape', evoke in metaphoric images a pastoral world made insidious by cruel forces, so that even the loving bee becomes a raving monster. The symbolic triangle Hunting – Eros – Violence is brought to uncanny effect in the hunting scene of the second Act: Zeno's idea of associating violence and pastoral now receives the poetry it deserves. The pastoral tableau of 'Mi rivedi, o selva ombrosa' had repercussions (textual as well as musical) in Rolli's 'Solitario bosco ombroso' as set by Hasse.[67] Not only this song but the whole pastoral nostalgia that is verbalized here (the self-pity of a soul persecuted by the hostile world) may have found its way from Rome, 1721, to the London of Paolo Rolli and his associates. Here emerges a fear of dehumanization by the rigours of a world of business, power, finance and industry, as was then beginning to develop in metropolitan centres such as Rome and London. Scarlatti's music may reflect this, especially the aria which symmetrically matches 'Mi rivedi': Griselda's sleep-and-death wish, 'Finirà, barbara sorte'. This E-flat major song blossoms serenely on a ground of musical darkness (symbolized by c minor). Beauty cannot survive unless immortalized, and thus 'eternal beauty' exists in 'eternal sleep'.

This transformation of Zeno's tale was perhaps possible only in a city, and in artistic circles, where immortality and death formed a familiar conceptual pair, just like two operas in a season. Everyone knew that Crispo was Hippolytus under a different name, and that Hippolytus had to die – like Galatea's Acis – as a victim of murderous jealousy. Although in Lemer's drama Crispo is reprieved at the last minute, the Roman audiences understood that happy endings often really mean tragic endings. Only conventions distinguished between the two.

66.   An opinion expressed in D. J. Grout, 'The original version of Alessandro Scarlatti's *Griselda*'.
67.   See R. Strohm, *Die italienische Oper*, pp. 91–2; idem, 'Hasse, Scarlatti, Rolli', *Studien zur italienisch-deutschen Musikgeschichte* 10 (Cologne, 1975) (Analecta Musicologica, 15), pp. 220–57.

1722–1724: an epilogue

The last years of Federico Capranica's 'reign' at his family theatre are not discussed here in detail, to avoid an anticlimax. It is possible that Capranica, and his patrons and artists, were dealing with the same problem. A performance of the allegorical opera *La virtù negli amori*, written by Lemer and Scarlatti for the enthronement of Pope Innocent XIII (Michelangelo Conti), may have taken place in the Teatro Capranica on 18 November 1721,[68] but another source names the Palazzo Cesarini, the Portuguese embassy.[69] In carnival 1722, both libretti were dedicated by Federico Capranica to Cardinal Nuno de Cunha, the Portuguese representative. He was otherwise known in Rome as the patron of several spoken tragedies then performed in the colleges; Scarlatti's *Arminio* might have appealed to this taste, as its libretto was based by Salvi on a tragedy by Jean-Gualbert de Campistron. Zanelli's *Nino*, a Semiramis plot, cannot be interpreted in such a way (but does it allude to the Cardinal's name?). The use of Orlandini's music, modern for 1720 when it was first heard, highlights the generation gap with Scarlatti.

Is *Arminio*, rather than *Griselda*, the master's last opera (i.e. his 115th)? It seems that Scarlatti composed much new music for the revision, because none of the surviving five numbers[70] can be found in an earlier work by him. They include the great quartet 'Al valore del mio brando' (see illustrations 2a and 2b on pages 58 and 59) and suggest that his compositional energy was quite unbroken.

After *Arminio*, however, Scarlatti retired from the public stage. Gasparini's retirement followed in 1723, and there was now no opera composer left in Rome of Scarlatti's great generation. The Capranica embarked on an experimental journey. *Oreste* is a classicist drama by two young authors, the librettist Giangualberto Barlocci, who was still completely unknown (but later became famous in the field of opera buffa), and Benedetto Micheli, a composer of respected but minor status in the business of occasional serenatas and cantatas, mainly written for the Habsburg ambassadors. The opera is dedicated to Isabella Cesi Ruspoli. Not she, but the Borghese family is involved in something resembling a coup d'état at least in aesthetic terms: the engagement of Antonio Vivaldi.[71] On the whole, we should not consider Vivaldi's three operatic productions of 1723–4 as the beginning of a new era, although he definitely tried to outdo the achievements of the old one. His *Giustino* is a masterwork of sometimes haunting beauty and richness of invention.

68. See E. Zanetti, 'La presenza di Gasparini' (n. 45 above), p. 275, n. 29. L. Lindgren, 'Il dramma musicale', p. 53, n. 72, accepts this.
69. Montserrat Moli Frigola, 'Fuochi, teatri e macchine Spagnole a Roma nel settecento', in *Il teatro a Roma nel settecento* (n. 13 above), vol. 1, p. 255, n. 144.
70. First announced in R. Strohm, 'Scarlattiana at Yale', pp. 140–1.
71. On this story and its unsolved riddles, see Antonio Vivaldi, *Giustino*, ed. by Reinhard Strohm, 2 vols (Milan: Ricordi, 1991), introduction, pp. 6–10; Fabrizio Della Seta, 'Documenti inediti su Vivaldi a Roma', in *Antonio Vivaldi*, ed. by L. Bianconi and G. Morelli, 1982, vol. 2, pp. 521–32; Michael Talbot, 'Vivaldi and Rome: Observations and hypotheses', *Journal of the Royal Musical Association* 113 (1988), pp. 28–46.

2a. Alessandro Scarlatti, *Arminio* (III, 13), opening of the quartet 'Al valore del mio brandò', Teatro Capranica, carnival 1722.

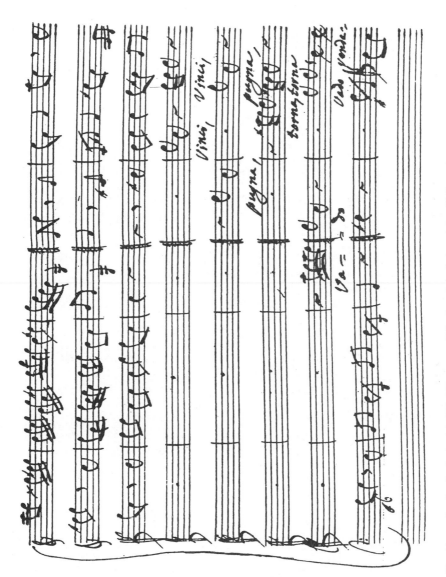

2b. Alessandro Scarlatti, *Arminio* (III, 13), quartet 'Al valore del mio brando', middle section.

But the age of the so-called 'Neapolitan school' around Porpora, Leo, Vinci, Hasse and then Pergolesi, was dawning at the Teatro Alibert, with Porpora's regular appearances from 1722, and Vinci's from 1724.

After the *Anno Santo*, 1725, both the Capranica and the Alibert were rebuilt and reopened under new owners and impresarios: at the former, Camillo Capranica and Giuseppe Pulvini Faliconti were in charge; the latter, the 'Teatro delle Dame', was owned by the Maltese Order and managed by Giambattista Cavana. The Teatro Capranica still had a splendid series of productions for the next decade, but it became secondary in at least one significant way: Metastasio appeared at the Teatro delle Dame.

3
The Neapolitans in Venice

The supremacy of Neapolitan composers in eighteenth-century Italian opera is an established myth in the history of music. Already discussed by contemporary critics (see below), the concept of 'Neapolitan opera' later influenced music historiography for two centuries. Compounding the issue, Francesco Florimo in 1880 propagated the more specific concept of a 'scuola musicale di Napoli' which linked the notion of Neapolitan supremacy to the conservatoire training received by Neapolitan (and immigrant) composers.[1] The idea of a 'Neapolitan school' in the stylistic sense became the working basis for historical interpretation and source studies in the era of Hermann Kretzschmar, Hugo Riemann, Hermann Abert and Rudolf Gerber, whose work was paralleled in Britain by Edward J. Dent and Frank Walker. Most of these writers actually questioned the label 'Neapolitan'. In 1961 the history and problems of the concept were surveyed, under the slightly more cautious formula of a 'Neapolitan Tradition in Opera', by Edward O. D. Downes and Helmut Hucke in a widely-noted IMS round-table.[2] But despite many shifts of opinion concerning the question of geography, international musicology in the early 1960s still favoured an approach which identified chronology, geography and the classification of musical style, an approach which remains apparent in the second edition of Donald J. Grout's successful history of opera[3] and in individual studies of Helmut Hucke, Daniel Heartz, Edward O. D. Downes and others. In 1967 Heartz, while acknowl-

1. Francesco Florimo, *La scuola musicale di Napoli e i suoi conservatorii*, 4 vols (Naples, 1880–3; R Bologna: Forni, 1969). Classifications based on stylistic 'schools' were then used in art criticism and history; the term was adopted by Raphael Georg Kiesewetter in his influential *Die Verdienste der Niederländer um die Tonkunst* of 1829. It is also likely that Florimo inherited the specific concept of a 'Neapolitan school' from German scholarship: for example, Francesco Degrada, 'L'opera napoletana fra Seicento e Settecento', in *Storia dell'Opera*, ed. by Guglielmo Barblan and Alberto Basso (Turin: UTET, 1977), vol. I/1 (*L'Opera in Italia*), pp. 237–332, cites Emil Naumann, *Italienische Tondichter von Palestrina bis auf die Gegenwart* (Berlin, 1876), chapter 'Alessandro Scarlatti und die Schule von Neapel'.
2. Helmut Hucke and Edward O. D. Downes, 'Die neapolitanische Tradition in der Oper/The Neapolitan Tradition in Opera', in *IMS 8th Congress Report New York 1961*, 2 vols (Kassel, etc.: Bärenreiter, 1961), vol. 1, pp. 253–84, and vol. 2, pp. 132–4.
3. Donald J. Grout, *A Short History of Opera* (New York-London, 1947), 2nd, rev. edn, 2 vols (New York, 1965).

edging the problems of a stylistic-geographical periodization of opera, concluded in favour of a Neapolitan-led renewal around 1720–40.[4] Partly concurring with this view, I myself proposed in 1976 that regional traditions such as that of Naples were relevant only until c. 1730–40, and that after that time a more general Italian operatic language had developed, which by force of tradition remained known as 'Neapolitan'.[5] Since the late 1970s, however, the whole question has seldom been mentioned. This is not because more detailed style studies or newly uncovered documents have made it redundant, but because the whole principle of style periodization in music has gone out of fashion.

Meanwhile, scholars such as Francesco Degrada and Michael Robinson had turned their attention to the socio-cultural and economic conditions in Naples itself which made style developments possible in the first place,[6] a successful approach encouraged by the work of Neapolitan cultural historians such as Benedetto Croce and Ulisse Prota-Giurleo. In the 1980s, studies of theatre and social history became more relevant for opera history in general. There was increasing interest in the libretto, as a historical document and occasionally even as a literary work. The types of material studied with the greatest zeal now included librettos, singers, scenography, costume, dramaturgy, theatre management and patronage. Much of this research was not focused geographically. The exploration of individual reper- toires and composers intensified only with respect to some subgenres such as the comic intermezzo, or with only the best-known authors such as Handel, Alessandro Scarlatti, Vivaldi or Pergolesi. The standard *dramma per musica*, and the average 'Neapolitan' composer such as Vinci, Leo, Sarri or Porpora, did not benefit from this expansion of interest. Studies of Johann Adolf Hasse, prompted by his bicen- tenary in 1983, had little to say on his most successful operas, and in any case remained silent on the concepts of style periodization and indeed on the Neapolitan tradition with which he ought to be associated.[7] Pietro Metastasio also received attention in bicentenary conferences of 1982, but his Neapolitan background was again neglected.[8]

Apart from these fluctuations of scholarly fashion, we can still reasonably ask

4. Daniel Heartz, 'Opera and the Periodization of Eighteenth-Century Music', in *International Musi- cological Society: Report of the Tenth Congress, Ljubljana 1967*, ed. by Dragotin Cvetko (Kassel, etc.: Bärenreiter, 1970), pp. 160–8; idem, 'Approaching a History of 18th-Century Music', *Current Musicology* 9 (1969), pp. 92–5.
5. Reinhard Strohm, *Italienische Opernarien des frühen Settecento (1720–1730)*, 2 vols (Cologne: Volk, 1976) (Analecta Musicologica, 16).
6. See, for example, F. Degrada, 'L'opera napoletana'; Michael F. Robinson, *Naples and Neapolitan Opera* (Oxford: Clarendon Press, 1972).
7. A thoughtful assessment of past efforts, however, is Friedrich Lippmann, 'Hasses Arienstil und seine Interpretation durch Rudolf Gerber', in *Colloquium 'Johann Adolf Hasse'*, ed. by F. Lippmann, 1987, pp. 17–65; see also Hellmuth Christian Wolff, 'Johann Adolf Hasse und Venedig', in *Venezia e il melodramma nel Settecento* [I], ed. by M. T. Muraro, 1978, pp. 295–308. Hasse's reworkings of arias by Alessandro Scarlatti are discussed with a view to the problem of a Neapolitan tradition in Reinhard Strohm, 'Hasse, Scarlatti, Rolli', *Studien zur italienisch-deutschen Musikgeschichte* 10 (Cologne, 1975) (Analecta Musicologica, 15), pp. 220–57.
8. Many publications of the years 1982–4 are critically reviewed in Giovanna Gronda, 'Metastasiana', *Rivista Italiana di Musicologia* 19 (1984), pp. 314–32.

what happened to Italian opera – especially opera seria – in the eighteenth century, and whether a qualified case for 'Neapolitan leadership' can be made after all. I believe it can. First, it has always been acknowledged that around 1730 composers, librettists and singers trained in Naples suddenly started to dominate the opera seria repertory in Venice and elsewhere. Secondly, many eighteenth-century observers of Italian opera perceived changes of style and the emergence of a new outlook among composers as well as librettists. They approached the matter in terms of geography: for Diderot, Rousseau, Algarotti, Burney, Grétry, Schubart and Vogler it was the good taste of the 'Neapolitans' which had helped eighteenth-century opera emerge from Baroque dust.[9] It is probably no accident that the term 'Baroque' itself was coined in Paris in 1746 to characterize, pejoratively, an old-fashioned style of music, presumably represented by composers such as Albinoni and Vivaldi.[10] Already in 1739, the Chevalier de Brosses on a visit to Naples had noted the excellence of Leonardo Leo's *La Frascatana*.[11] As is known, Leo's music rivalled Pergolesi's in the Parisian performances leading to the *querelle des bouffons*; Hasse, Latilla, Rinaldo and Auletta were heard there too. As if to increase the Parisians' awareness of Italian composers and genres, Francesco Algarotti in 1754, reflecting the taste of the Prussian court, cited Leonardo Vinci's *Didone abbandonata* as a model setting of a *tragedia per musica*.[12] Thus a relatively small group of composers, all trained in Naples, was singled out for modernity and 'naturalness': a legend was taking shape that equated 'Neapolitan opera' with good taste.[13] We should note that this legend originated in the metropolises of northern and western Europe, not in Italy (nor, incidentally, in Vienna or Dresden). But why did the critics of Paris, Berlin, London and other centres hail a small cluster of Naples-trained opera composers, when there were dozens of other Italians to choose from?

This 'European' acclaim of the 1750s and 1760s was the delayed effect of earlier, equally specific successes – those obtained by some of the same Neapolitans on the Venetian operatic stage in the preceding thirty years. The process began with Metastasian *drammi per musica* in Neapolitan settings performed in Venice in the 1720s and early 1730s, and continued with the Neapolitan intermezzi and *opere buffe* of the 1730s and 1740s. Historical connections between this 'inner-Italian' expansion and later European fame are easily drawn. European cities received most of their Italian musical repertory from Venice, by way of performances attended during the Grand Tour, of manuscript copies acquired, and of the activities of

---

9. For surveys, see D. Heartz, 'Opera and the Periodization', and F. Degrada, 'L'opera napoletana', pp. 237–40. The full story still needs to be told.
10. See Claude V. Palisca, 'Baroque', in *The New Grove Dictionary of Music and Musicians*, ed. by S. Sadie (London: Macmillan, 1980), vol. 2, pp. 172–3.
11. 'Je porterai cet opéra en France . . .'. See Charles de Brosses, *Lettres familières sur l'Italie (1739–40)*, ed. by Yvonne Bézard, 2 vols (Paris, 1931), vol. 1, p. 431.
12. He especially praised the music of the last Act for its accompanied recitatives: '. . . lo stesso Virgilio si sarebbe compiaciuto . . . tanto è animata e terribile.' See Francesco Algarotti, *Saggio sopra l'opera in musica*, 2nd edn (1763), ed. by Giovanni Da Pozzo (Bari: Laterza, 1963), p. 162.
13. Neapolitan church music and vocal chamber works, for example by Scarlatti, Pergolesi and Durante, were awarded the same critical acclaim. Eighteenth-century forgeries, a good measure of popularity, included oratorios and sacred music by Vinci, Hasse and Pergolesi.

travelling opera troupes which were mostly Venetian or north Italian in origin (the Mingotti and Bambini companies, to name just two). The structure of the Italian operatic circuit itself made it almost impossible to succeed abroad without previously having attracted the interest of the Venetian impresarios. The full story of the distribution of Neapolitan *commedia per musica* across the peninsula and then abroad has only recently been told by Piero Weiss.[14] The fact is that serious opera around 1720–50, dominated by Metastasio's *drammi per musica*, travelled on exactly the same south-north routes as opera buffa, and was partly carried by the same travelling companies. The operatic music of Leo, Vinci, Porpora and Hasse found its way to the European centres after it had first been heard in Venice, and after Porpora and Hasse had found employment in that city. Although foreign consumers were of course able to obtain scores or librettos from Naples, Rome or Parma 'at source' (witness Handel or de Brosses), to have dominated a carnival in Venice was presumably the most powerful recommendation an opera could receive. Finally, the engagement of Italian opera composers at foreign courts also tended to follow Venetian successes. Not even Niccolò Jommelli, trained in Naples in the 1730s and brought to Vienna from Rome in 1749, is an exception, since it was in Bologna and Venice in the early 1740s that he became famous in his special field, that of opera seria. It almost seems that whatever the artistic contribution of Neapolitan composers, eighteenth-century opera history was rather made by Venetian impresarios.

What needs to be explained, however, is how Neapolitan composers came to conquer the Venetian *palcoscenico* in the first place. Here I shall attempt to shed some light on the first years of this story, mainly from the angle of operatic practice and business. Although not primarily concerned with questions of style, this factual account might reveal some of the mundane foundations of a grand historiographical theory, while in a sense confirming it.

The chronological outlines of this story are straightforward.[15] Between the time of the 'Febi armonici' (the 1650s) and 1707, no composer or librettist employed or trained in the Spanish-governed Regno di Napoli had more than one opera performed on the Venetian stage.[16] This is not surprising, since there were few resident composers or librettists employed in the south before the early eighteenth century. Even Alessandro Scarlatti, a native of Palermo and the famous Maestro della cappella reale, had to wait (or chose to wait) until 1707 for Venetian performances of two of his operas. The opera repertory of the Teatro S. Bartolomeo and the Royal Palace in Naples was a mixture of local and imported material, with Venetian imports dominating. Such imported works were invariably adapted to local requirements. Frequent exchanges of operatic repertory, and to some extent of singers, also connected Naples with Rome, until public opera was forbidden in the papal states

14. Piero Weiss, 'La diffusione del repertorio operistico nell'Italia del settecento: il caso dell'opera buffa', in *Civiltà teatrale e settecento emiliano*, ed. by S. Davoli, 1986, pp. 241–56.
15. The main source for the following opera performance statistics is Taddeo Wiel, *I teatri musicali veneziani del settecento* (Venice, 1897), R ed. by R. Strohm (Leipzig: Peters Reprints, 1979).
16. See the chronological table in Lorenzo Bianconi, 'Funktionen des Operntheaters in Neapel bis 1700 und die Rolle Alessandro Scarlattis', in *Colloquium Alessandro Scarlatti Würzburg 1975*, ed. by W. Osthoff and J. Ruile-Dronke (Tutzing: Schneider, 1979), pp. 91–116.

(in 1698). But in this respect, too, the operas performed in Naples, and their composers, were more often of Roman origin than vice versa. *Gli amanti generosi* (1705) by Francesco Mancini, then *vicemaestro* of the royal chapel, surprisingly reached London's Haymarket theatre in 1710 and Genoa in 1711, but it never appeared in Venice.

Between 1707 (when the Austrians conquered Naples) and 1720, matters changed inasmuch as the activities of native or locally trained opera composers were now increasing rapidly. Domenico Sarri, Francesco Mancini, Antonio Orefice, Giuseppe Vignola, Nicola Fago, Nicola Porpora, Leonardo Leo and Carmine Giordano began to emulate Alessandro Scarlatti. Neapolitan singers also appeared more regularly in Venice and elsewhere in the north, for example the famous Nicolò Grimaldi (Nicolini), who was made a Knight of the Order of St Mark. A wave of emigration was fuelled by the War of the Spanish Succession (1700–14); in this context, some singers (Matteo Sassani) and composers (Giuseppe Porsile) got as far as Venice and Vienna. But not a single *dramma per musica* of Neapolitan origin was heard in Venice between 1707 and 1720. Sarri managed to have his intermezzi *Barilotto e Slapina* performed at the Teatro S. Angelo in 1712 (although nowhere else), but this is an isolated event, as yet unexplained. On the other hand, of the seventy-six *drammi per musica* publicly performed in Naples between 1707 and 1720, about sixteen were imported from Venice, and about six from other centres including London (Handel's *Rinaldo*). The remainder were local settings, about thirty of texts imported from Venice and about ten from other centres. Most of the imported works were adapted by local artists, however, an activity which seems to have provided a livelihood for several minor librettists and composers, and which perhaps created some of the know-how needed for the reversal of fortunes that followed in the 1720s.

The last Venetian opera performed in Naples for a long time to come was *Tito Manlio* by C. F. Pollarolo, adapted (for perhaps the twentieth time) in 1720 by the local musician Ignazio Prota. From 1721 until 1736, when again the government changed, no Venetian opera was performed in Naples,[17] although of the seventy local settings still about thirty used Venetian librettos. In Venice, on the other hand, of the seventy-eight *drammi per musica* assigned to the years 1721–36 in Wiel's catalogue, as many as thirty were by composers educated in Naples: Porpora (7), Hasse (7), Leo (5), Vinci (4), Sellitti (2), Araya (2), Fiorillo, Sarri and Broschi (1 each). It is more difficult to define Neapolitan origin for librettos. In any case, eighteen librettos were based on *drammi* by Metastasio, twelve of them on those written during his residence in Naples (1720–9), and two had been written for Naples by the Roman poet Silvio Stampiglia, who had long-established contacts with the city (where he died on 26 January 1725).

At least as regards operatic composition, the relationship between Naples and Venice was thus completely reversed in the third decade of the century. It seems to

17. Leonardo Leo provides an only partial exception: he revised his own *Argeno*, Venice, 1728, for a performance in Naples in 1731.

be this process which decided about the future of operatic styles – although the genres of the comic intermezzi and of opera buffa were not yet involved – and which later gave rise to the international fame of Italian and 'Metastasian' opera throughout Europe.

A postscript to the above statistics will lead directly into our story. In addition to Metastasio and Stampiglia, another 'southerner' – a native Neapolitan, even – contributed a total of twenty-two newly written or arranged librettos to the Venetian stage in the years 1710–36. This was Domenico Lalli, born in Naples in 1679 (his real name was Sebastiano Biancardi). He was a cashier at the Banco di SS. Annunziata when, apparently in 1706, the discovery of an enormous gap in the bank's balance forced him to flee the city, leaving wife and family behind. The story of his flight, subsequent wanderings – mostly undertaken in the company of the aristocratic composer Emanuele d'Astorga – and final arrival in Venice in 1710 under the new name has been told by Roberto Pagano on the basis of Lalli's own autobiography (printed in Venice in 1732).[18] Lalli was able to consolidate his position in Venice thanks to his acquaintance with influential Venetian families and to his friendship with the famous librettist Apostolo Zeno, a contact which led to the production of his first *dramma per musica*, produced at the Teatro S. Cassiano in autumn 1710, entitled *L'amor tirannico*.

Other aspects of Lalli's Venetian career include his libretto *Elisa* (S. Angelo, autumn 1711), according to Bonlini the first 'true musical comedy' seen in Venice; his collaborations and apparent litigations with Antonio Vivaldi; his connection with the Teatro S. Angelo, where he played some kind of official role throughout the years 1719–26, and later on, his influential position as house-poet of the Grimani theatres (S. Giovanni Grisostomo and S. Samuele). In this capacity, he was to bring Vivaldi together with the budding librettist Carlo Goldoni to prepare the opera *Griselda* (S. Samuele, 1735).[19]

As a resourceful poet, manager and career-maker, Domenico Lalli hardly surprises us by being involved with the arrival of Neapolitan opera in Venice in the carnival of 1723. This happened at the Teatro S. Angelo. The first opera of the season, *Timocrate*, had a libretto by Lalli, derived from *Amor vince l'odio, overo Timocrate* by Antonio Salvi, first given at Florence in 1715 (which in turn was based on Thomas Corneille). The composer of the new version was, surprisingly, Leonardo Leo, to whom the libretto gives the exaggerated title of 'primo organista della Real Cappella di Napoli'.[20] Of Leo's setting of *Timocrate*, only two arias and a duet have survived.[21] Around that time, Lalli had made himself popular at the Bavarian court: he wrote opera librettos for the wedding of the electoral prince, Karl

18.   Roberto Pagano, *Scarlatti Alessandro e Domenico: due vite in una* (Milano: Mondadori, 1985), pp. 253–7.
19.   Goldoni's own account is translated in Michael Talbot, *Vivaldi*, 2nd edn (London: Dent, 1993), pp. 61–2.
20.   He had held the position of 'supernumerary organist' of the Cappella Reale since 1713 and was made first organist in 1725.
21.   One aria, 'Mi va serpendo in seno', is printed and discussed in R. Strohm, *Italienische Opernarien*, vol. 1, pp. 42–4 (text), and vol. 2, no. 104 (music). Vol. 2 also mentions sources for most of the following operas.

Albert, in Munich in 1722. One of these works was *I veri amici*, Lalli's revision of a libretto by Francesco Silvani loosely based on Pierre Corneille's *Héraclius*.[22] The music was by Tommaso Albinoni, who composed other works for the wedding celebrations, and with whom Lalli often collaborated in those years. The Munich opera was repeated in slightly revised form at the Teatro S. Angelo in the carnival of 1723. Of the arias which were then newly inserted into the score, two musical settings survive with ascriptions to Leonardo Leo.[23] Thus, Leo seems to have been the resident composer of the S. Angelo in this season.

It is worth noting the dedicatees of the two Lalli/Leo librettos of the S. Angelo season in 1723, although they may not have had anything to do with Leo. *Timocrate* was offered to an apparent patron of Lalli's, Prince Johann Philipp Franz von Schönborn, Bishop of Würzburg; and *I veri amici* was dedicated by N. N. (either Lalli or the impresario) on 23 January 1723 to Fra Camillo, Duke of Pola, General Receiver of the Order of the Knights of Malta in Venice.[24]

More importantly, there may have been a previous connection between Lalli and Leonardo Leo (born S. Vito, near Bari, 1694). Leo was educated in 1709–12 at the Conservatorio de' Turchini, Naples, under Nicola Fago and Andrea Basso, and had produced some oratorios before composing his first opera, *Pisistrato*, in May 1714 for the Teatro S. Bartolomeo. This opera uses one of the least-known librettos by Lalli, also printed in Venice for a performance at the Teatro 'Al Dolo' (in Venice?) in June 1711. (In 1736, Lalli had the *dramma* revived in an adaptation by Goldoni.) It is possible that Lalli was acquainted with Leo and had sent him his libretto.

By way of caution, it must be noted that Venetian opera houses were often frequented by 'foreign' composers in those years, and particularly the Teatro S. Angelo. Leonardo Leo may have gone almost unnoticed in the influx of non-Venetian artists, who included the composers Orlandini, Chelleri and Porta, the Bolognese opera troupe Belisani/Buini, and many North Italian and Tuscan singers. Some of them had in fact been satirized in Benedetto Marcello's *Teatro alla moda* of 1720.[25] In any case, it does not seem that Leo's contribution left the special mark on Venetian opera that his involvement might have led one to expect.

The next appearance of a Neapolitan composer in Venice happened under

22. On the libretto, see Anna Laura Bellina, 'Dal mito della corte al nodo dello stato: il "topos" del tiranno', in *Antonio Vivaldi*, ed. by L. Bianconi and G. Morelli, 1982, vol. 2, pp. 297–313, esp. 305–9. Silvani's libretto had been written for the Teatro S. Cassiano in 1713 and repeated elsewhere, including at Naples (carnival 1716, with music by Antonio Maria Bononcini). Bibliographers give Lalli's name in addition to that of Silvani already for the 1713 production, but I rather suspect that Lalli's revision originated in 1722.

23. *BRD-MÜs*, MS 2362, fols 9 and 23. No doubt these settings originated for the S. Angelo production, since the musical copies also name the singers performing the arias on that occasion (Nicolino Grimaldi and Antonia Cavazzi).

24. This prelate was befriended by Johann Baptist Colloredo-Wallsee, the Imperial ambassador to Venice. Both patrons commissioned music for political and other occasions (from various composers including Albinoni), but not, so far as is known, other operas. See Eleanor Selfridge-Field, *Pallade Veneta: Writings on Music in Venetian Society, 1650–1750* (Venice: Fondazione Levi, 1985), p. 332, with further literature.

25. On non-Venetian singers and composers in Venice in those years, see Sergio Durante, 'Alcune considerazioni sui cantanti di teatro del primo settecento e la loro formazione', in *Antonio Vivaldi*, ed. by L. Bianconi and G. Morelli, 1982, vol. 2, pp. 427–81, and Eleanor Selfridge-Field, 'Marcello, Sant'Angelo and *Il Teatro alla Moda*', ibid., vol. 2, pp. 533–46.

3. Interior of the Teatro San Giovanni Grisostomo, from *Venezia festeggiante* (Venice, 1709).

very different circumstances, probably in connection with the Venetian librettist Benedetto Pasqualigo. This *nobile veneto* – a member of the Accademia degli Animosi (as 'Merindo Fesanio') – had since 1718 been providing the Venetian stage with his special brand of classicizing dramas, sometimes even with tragic endings, on Greek mythological subjects. His *Antigona* of 1718 (S. Cassiano) gained extraordinary success with the music of the Florentine Giuseppe Maria Orlandini; the opera had to be revived four times in the following seasons in Venice alone. A *tragedia da cantarsi* by the same authors, *Ifigenia in Tauride* (1719, S. Giovanni Grisostomo), tried to follow up on the success. But neither this nor Pasqualigo's other librettos of classicist inspiration – such as *Il pastor fido* (1721, S. Angelo; after Guarini), *Cimene* (1721, S. Angelo; based on Pierre Corneille's *Le Cid*) – nor even *Giulio Flavio Crispo* (1722, S. Giovanni Grisostomo) or *Mitridate re di Ponto, vincitor di se stesso* (1723, S. Giovanni Grisostomo), both based on Jean Racine (*Phèdre* and *Mithridate*, respectively) and both set to music by the Parmesan composer Giovanni Maria Capelli, seems to have engaged the Venetian audiences. This perhaps explains Pasqualigo's attempt, in the carnival of 1725, to better his lot with 'Neapolitan' imports. There is evidence that the Grimani family, owners of the S. Giovanni Grisostomo, supported Pasqualigo's plans, or that he acted as their literary adviser for this season. The first three librettos used at this theatre in the autumn/carnival season in 1724–5 were all ostensibly noble, literary works, answering to the classicist notions of *gravità e decoro* considered by some contemporaries to be a trend of the times. The autumn opera, *Il trionfo della virtù* by Pietro d'Averara, was based on the Roman Republican subject of Lucius Sulla and P. Cornelius Scipio.[26] The first carnival opera was a revival of Pasqualigo's tragedy *Ifigenia in Tauride*, dedicated by him to a young son of Giovanni Carlo Grimani, Vincenzo, and rewritten for a new setting by Leonardo Vinci. The second carnival libretto was a new effort by Pasqualigo, a heroic drama *Berenice* based on Pierre Corneille's *tragicomédie* (rather than Racine's *tragédie*) on this Roman Imperial subject. It involved a new *scrittura* for the formerly so successful Orlandini. A third carnival opera followed: the Neapolitan maestro, Vinci, was asked to set – perhaps at short notice – *Partenope* by the famous Arcadian Silvio Stampiglia. This libretto, now entitled *Rosmira fedele*, was dedicated by the impresario (not Pasqualigo) to Don Nicolò del Tocco, Duke of Sicignano – apparently a Neapolitan nobleman.[27]

If it is correct that *Ifigenia in Tauride*, just like *Berenice*, mainly served Pasqualigo's poetic and aesthetic ambitions, why was *Rosmira fedele* put on? The extra chance for Vinci of setting a second complete opera proved perhaps decisive for his reputation in Venice. *Rosmira fedele* was definitely not a 'grave and noble' work. The opera was produced 'in the last days of carnival', as mentioned in a letter of 24 February 1725 by Apostolo Zeno to his brother Pier Caterino. Three carnival operas were not the norm at the S. Giovanni Grisostomo, but examples occurred from time to time, especially if the second opera did not 'draw'. On this occasion, however, an additional if not the only motivation must have been the death of the famous Stampiglia, a founding member of the Arcadian Academy, in Naples on 26 January 1725. Apostolo Zeno's letter of 24 February comments in fact on Stampiglia's death, also assessing his merits as a librettist.[28] It seems that audiences were talking about the poet, whose name was better known in Venice than his works.

Partenope had been written by Stampiglia in 1699 for and about Naples, being a love-and-adventure story loosely woven around the legendary foundation of the city by the eponymous heroine. Many revivals in other cities followed, including one in Venice in 1708 with music by Antonio Caldara.[29] But it is remarkable that in the whole time between 1700 and 1725 – when *Partenope* was presented again – no other libretto by this very popular author had been heard in Venice. Stampiglia was not a natural preference of the Venetian theatres, and certainly for the 1720s lacked

26. The composer of this opera, Giovanni Francesco Brusa, earned praise for his next opera, *L'amore eroico* (S. Samuele, spring 1725), in Johann Mattheson's journal *Critica musica* (Hamburg, 1725), vol. 2, pp. 286–7.

27. A certain Leonardo Tocco, Prince of Montemiletto, had been the dedicatee, at his wedding to Camilla Cantelmi in Naples in 1723, of Silvio Stampiglia's last libretto *Imeneo* (music by Nicola Porpora). Marianna Benti sang the primadonna role.

28. Apostolo Zeno, *Lettere*, vol. 2 (Venice, 1752), p. 181. According to Zeno (who succeeded him as Imperial court poet), he had been more *ingegnoso* than *dotto*, and his libretti had more *spirito* than *studio*. In other words, he was a lightweight poet and not a classicist. I am grateful to Dott. Mario Armellini for helping me to identify Zeno's letter.

29. For the various libretti and musical settings, see Robert S. Freeman, 'The travels of Partenope', in *Studies in Music History: Essays for Oliver Strunk*, ed. by Harry S. Powers (Princeton: University Press, 1968), pp. 356–85.

some of the fashionable *gravità e decoro*.[30] This and the demonstrative homage to Naples implied in the 1725 production – plot, poet, musician and dedicatee all being from that city – fit together if the opera was meant to honour the poet, more out of respect and curiosity than from aesthetic inclination. One wonders whether in this case the dedicatee, Don Nicolò del Tocco, had any influence on the choice of opera.

Thus, Vinci was chosen among the many Neapolitan composers to 'represent' his city on the most noble Venetian stage.[31] His reputation, barely established in Naples and Rome by one opera each in 1724, was now quickly spreading across Europe. An example is the pasticcio–opera *Elpidia*, given at London's Haymarket theatre on 11 May 1725. The score of this work is a musical anthology of the three S. Giovanni Grisostomo operas of this carnival, drawing at least fourteen arias from Vinci's *Ifigenia in Tauride* and *Rosmira fedele*, plus perhaps the overture from the former work. Only three arias were taken from Orlandini's *Berenice*.[32] The transfer from Venice to London seems to have been arranged by the opera manager Owen Swiney.[33]

Vinci did have a recent connection with Stampiglia: for the autumn season of 1724 in Naples, he had set his *Eraclea*, revised for the occasion by the author himself. He had also arranged (together with Leo) a pasticcio on Stampiglia's *Turno Aricino*, which had been revised by the poet's son, Luigi Maria Stampiglia. But more opera houses seem to have cultivated Stampiglia's librettos in the years 1724–7, involving also other Neapolitan composers. Vinci was indeed not the most obvious choice for the Venetian initiative. A much more senior member of the royal chapel, Domenico Sarri, had set *Partenope* in 1722 in a new version likewise provided by Stampiglia himself, and with great success; it was repeated in Rome in the

30.   Wiel lists only six Venetian operas on libretti by Stampiglia in the whole of the eighteenth century. Three of these were versions of *Partenope* (1708, 1725 and 1753), two of *Imeneo* (1726, 1750) and one of *Camilla regina de' Volsci* (1749). The seventh, a *Cirene* given in 1742, is probably not authentic.

31.   Charles Burney characterized the Venetian season of 1725 thus: '. . . in 1725 the Venetian theatre first heard the natural, clear, and dramatic strains of Leonardo Vinci, in his two operas of *Ifigenia in Aulide* [sic] and *La Rosmira Fidele* [sic]'. Charles Burney, *A General History of Music from the Earliest Ages to the Present Period (1789)*, ed., with notes, by Frank Mercer (London, 1935), vol. 2, p. 108. Much valuable information on Vinci's operas is offered in Kurt Sven Markstrom, 'The Operas of Leonardo Vinci, Napoletano', PhD diss. (Graduate Department of Music, University of Toronto, 1993).

32.   On this pasticcio, see Reinhard Strohm, 'Handel's pasticci', in R. Strohm, *Essays on Handel and Italian Opera* (Cambridge: Cambridge University Press, 1985), pp. 164 -211, especially 167–9 and 200–1. The material sent to London may have been connected with preparations for the opera *I rivali generosi* (Apostolo Zeno's original title, of 1697, for *Elpidia*) given with music by Giuseppe Vignati at the S. Samuele in May 1726 but perhaps planned already in 1725. The traditional view that Handel was responsible for the London pasticcio has recently been challenged by John H. Roberts (unpubl. conference paper).

33.   See Elizabeth Gibson, *The Royal Academy of Music, 1719–1728: The Institution and its Directors* (New York and London: Garland, Inc., 1989), pp. 362ff. and 372ff., quoting letters by Swiney of 15 March 1726 and 23 January 1727. It is worth noting that Swiney detested the libretto of *Partenope*; see ibid., p. 369 (letter of 13 August 1726): '. . . it is the very worst book (excepting one) that I have ever read in my life: Signor Stampiglia . . . endeavours to be humourous and witty, in it: If he succeeded in his attempt, on any stage in Italy, 'twas, meerly, from a depravity of Taste in the audience – but I am very sure that 'twill be received with contempt in England.'

carnival of 1724. Sarri was the only Neapolitan opera composer of those years who could rival the reputation of Alessandro Scarlatti while being considered a representative of the modern style. He was the first composer to set Metastasio's *Didone abbandonata*, in Naples in 1724.

If the decision to put on *Partenope* was caused by Stampiglia's death, then the *scrittura* for the music would have been extended at very short notice. Perhaps Sarri was invited to offer his *Partenope* at the end of carnival but could not come, leaving Vinci, who was already on the spot, to take advantage of the opportunity. The preferment of Vinci over Sarri may seem rather unfair when one notes that Vinci used his senior rival's music to carry out the commission – as shown by Vinci's own autograph score of 1725.[34] Most of the recitatives are borrowed or derived from Sarri's score of 1722. Vinci copied as much as possible from the original (key, rhythms, bass-lines, etc.) and adjusted only as much as necessary, for example the tessitura for those singers who in the Venetian performance had a different register. This is scarcely a common phenomenon in early eighteenth-century recitative composition (or perhaps better, we have yet to uncover a similar case). Also the few, short sinfonias and acclamatory choruses are virtually identical with Sarri's. An explanation, although not an excuse, would be pressure of time. Vinci had more time, by contemporary standards, for the preparation of his *Ifigenia*, since the *Avvisi di Napoli* inform us with reference to 29 November 1724 that the composer was already in Venice.[35]

Nevertheless, Leonardo Vinci's compositional achievement is not in doubt. Musically, neither the recitatives nor the choruses counted in a *dramma per musica*, only the arias – and Vinci's arias in this opera are consistently superior to Sarri's.[36] His mastery of declamatory verse-setting as well as of graceful melody, his superbly characterized, dramatically compelling music was at that point the best Naples had to offer. Perhaps music history would have developed somewhat differently if Sarri had been chosen in 1725, but even a Venetian success would not ultimately have made up for the fact that Hasse and Pergolesi, to name but two, were to follow the style of Vinci and not that of Sarri.

In the same Venetian carnival season of 1725, the Teatro S. Cassiano repeated Pietro Metastasio's *Didone abbandonata*, the *tragedia per musica* which Sarri had composed for Naples a year before – but with new music by Albinoni. Metastasio was apparently present, having revised his text for the occasion; the libretto contains a dedicatory sonnet by the poet addressed 'to the Ladies of Venice'. Sarri's own setting of *Didone abbandonata* was given in Venice as late as 1730 and remained his only work ever heard there.

---

34. This is the only surviving autograph of an opera seria by Vinci: *GB-Lbl*, Add. MS 14232. It is inscribed *Partenope* (Sarri's original title) and signed by Vinci. On the libretto, music and autograph score, see K. S. Markstrom, 'The Operas of Leonardo Vinci', pp. 86–95.
35. Ulisse Prota-Giurleo, 'Leonardo Vinci', *Il Convegno musicale* 2 (1965), pp. 3–11.
36. See, for example, their respective settings of 'Al mio tesoro' and 'Ardi per me fedele' as compared in R. Strohm, *Italienische Opernarien*, vol. 1, pp. 45–50 (text), and vol. 2, nos 105–7 (music). The score of *Ifigenia in Tauride* is lost, although single arias survive, including those used for the London *Elpidia*.

Didone abbandonata was a drama with an unhappy ending (*funesto fine*) like several other Venetian librettos, for example by Pasqualigo and Salvi.[37] The S. Cassiano theatre, the only one competing with the social prestige of the Grimani theatres, had taken up their 'noble' literary and classicist orientation, now also shared by the young Metastasio. But the difference between the S. Cassiano and the S. Giovanni Grisostomo was, in this season, that the latter, in addition, imported Neapolitan music. This combination was going to succeed. By the end of 1725, the upper-class theatres of Venice were prepared to accept other imported, tragic and classical dramas, written as well as composed by southerners.

In the season of 1725–6, the Grimani theatres adopted Metastasio and his Neapolitan circle. This circle included the poet's friend and Muse, the famous soprano Marianna Benti Bulgarelli *detta* la Romanina, and the famous castrato Nicolò Grimaldi. Grimaldi had already performed in both Leo operas given at the S. Angelo in 1723, and had therefore initiated the performances of Neapolitan operas in Venice. Benti was a member of the royal chapel of Naples and the main singer in the earliest Metastasio settings: the serenatas *Angelica* (Porpora, 1720), *Endimione* (Sarri, 1721), *Gli orti Esperidi* (Porpora, 1721) and *La Galatea* (Comito, 1722), and the *drammi per musica Siface* (Feo, 1723) and *Didone abbandonata* (Sarri, 1724). Benti's stable association with Nicolò Grimaldi had begun in (1717)–1718, when they appeared together twice in settings of Antonio Salvi's famous *tragedia per musica*, *Amore e maestà* (both times renamed *Arsace*). They sang the main roles of Statira and Arsace, respectively, in carnival 1718 at the S. Giovanni Grisostomo (in Michelangelo Gasparini's setting), and in December of the same year at the S. Bartolomeo of Naples, in the setting by Domenico Sarri.[38] Benti and Grimaldi collaborated again in Naples in 1723, and from 1724 onwards all their shared operas involved Metastasio and a small group of Neapolitan composers:

Siface, Metastasio/Feo, S. Bartolomeo, May 1723 (Viriate; Siface)

Silla dittatore, Cassani/Vinci, S. Bartolomeo, 1 October 1723

Amare per regnare, Passarini/Porpora, S. Bartolomeo, December 1723

Didone abbandonata, Metastasio/Sarri, S. Bartolomeo, carnival 1724 (Didone; Enea)

Didone abbandonata, Metastasio/Albinoni, S. Cassiano, carnival 1725 (Didone; Enea)

Didone abbandonata, Metastasio/Porpora, Reggio E., fiera 1725 (Didone; Enea)

Siface, Metastasio/Porpora, S. Giovanni Grisostomo, carnival 1726 (Viriate; Siface)

Siroe re di Persia, Metastasio/Vinci, S. Giovanni Grisostomo, carnival 1726 (Emira; Siroe)

Siroe re di Persia, Metastasio/Sarri, S. Bartolomeo, carnival 1727 (Emira; Siroe).

37. See chapters 8 and 9 in this volume.
38. On the two productions, see pp. 171–2 in this volume.

This last production apparently saw Benti's final public appearance. Grimaldi went on singing at a rapid pace until his death early in 1732.[39] With other partners – in Venice, often the soprano Lucia Facchinelli – he appeared as Enea also in Sarri's *Didone abbandonata* in Venice, 1730, and as Siroe also in Porta's setting in Milan, 1727, and with Vinci's music in its Venetian revival, 1731. He furthermore created the Metastasian roles of Catone (*Catone in Utica*), Ezio (*Ezio*), Scitalce (*Semiramide riconosciuta*) and Artabano (*Artaserse*) for their Venetian premières. His other favourite roles included Arsace – which he repeated in Milan in 1725 (music by Brusa) and Faenza in 1726 (Orlandini) – and Theseus in Pariati's *Arianna e Teseo* (1721, Naples, Leo; 1728, Venice, Porpora; 1728, Florence, Porpora).[40]

One other singer belonged with Benti and Grimaldi to a team for Metastasian opera: Domenico Gizzi of Naples, member of the royal chapel. He sang the *secondo uomo*, Araspe, in four different productions of *Didone*: in Naples (1724), Venice (1725), Reggio (1725) and Rome (1726; Vinci). He also sang at Naples in Metastasio's *Angelica* (1720) and *La Galatea* (1722) with Benti, and at Venice in three later Metastasian operas with Grimaldi.

The S. Giovanni Grisostomo season of 1725–6 offered only two *drammi per musica*, both in the carnival and both by Metastasio (the only ones extant at the time besides *Didone*): *Siface* and *Siroe re di Persia*. There was not even an autumn production to contrast with them. *Siface*, the poet's early effort based on an old libretto by Domenico David, was given with music by Nicola Porpora (it had first been set by Francesco Feo for Naples in 1723). There are two different scores by Porpora, both from 1725–6: one was performed in Milan, the other at the same time in Venice. In the Milan score, the composer used many of his older arias to suit the singers, almost as in a self-pasticcio. In Venice, the original text by Metastasio was largely restored.[41] Almost certainly this was due to the poet himself, who had been asked to contribute to the production in person. That he was present is shown by a letter he wrote to his brother from Venice (16 February 1726): 'My *Siroe* is being raised to the stars much more than *Didone* was last year.'[42] This also implies that Metastasio had seen the *Didone* production in 1725. What Metastasio reports here clinches the main argument of this essay: the reputations of Stampiglia and Metastasio, of Naples in general, of Benti and Grimaldi were insufficient for a full Venetian success without the music of a superior Neapolitan composer.[43]

39.   See Eugenio Faustini-Fasini, 'Gli astri maggiori del "bel canto" Napoletano', *Note d'Archivio* 12 (1935), pp. 297–316.

40.   Thus, Grimaldi repeated his dramatic roles, whether with the same or different music. This pattern is also found with other singers.

41.   See Elena Zomparelli, 'Il Siface di P. Metastasio', unpubl. dissertation, Laurea in Lettere (University of Rome, 'La Sapienza', 1988).

42.   'Il mio Siroe è alle stelle molto più che non fece la Didone l'anno scorso.' Pietro Metastasio, *Tutte le opere*, ed. by Bruno Brunelli, vol. 3, 2nd edn (Milan: Mondadori, 1954), no. 25.

43.   Johann Joachim Quantz also reported in his autobiography that *Siroe* was more successful than *Siface*; he evaluates the singers and mentions that the two composers were present: see K. S. Markstrom, 'The Operas of Leonardo Vinci', p. 158 nn. 73 and 79. Further remarks by Burney on the Venetian season of 1726 confirm the idea of a rivalry between Vinci and Porpora: see C. Burney, *A General History of Music*, vol. 2, p. 108, and K. S. Markstrom, 'The Operas of Leonardo Vinci', pp. 137–47.

Siroe re di Persia is a problematic libretto and by no means one of Metastasio's best: the gloomy, psychologically depressing atmosphere contrasts with the somewhat lighthearted handling of disguise, agnition and happy ending. The influence, again, of Salvi's *Amore e maestà* (Siroe, like Arsace, spends most of his time in prison) and certain Racinian motives (for example, the jealousy between two terribly unequal brothers, as in *Mithridate*) may have been obvious to contemporaries. But Vinci's music demonstrated a unity of conception between declamation, painting of affections and dramatic pace which, I believe, was achieved through direct collaboration with the poet and presumably the lead singers.[44] This collaboration may well have started in Naples in the autumn of 1725, with work on *Didone abbandonata*, given in Rome in January, and *Siroe*, given in Venice in February. What caused this poet-composer partnership which was to flourish until Vinci's death in 1730? Since the main venue of the partnership's successes, the Teatro delle Dame in Rome, was the property of the Order of the Knights of Malta, we may wonder about the Order's receiver-general Fra Camillo Pola, a patron of Lalli and perhaps Leo in 1723. I suggest, rather, that both Metastasio and Vinci had independently attracted the interest of the patrons and impresarios in Rome and Venice, and that the two rival *scritture* from the two cities were coincidental.[45] Not that they remained isolated. Barely recruited to the 'Neapolitan fashion', the Venetians already had to compete with Rome, in addition to Naples itself and to secondary centres of the Italian circuit such as Reggio or Florence, for these coveted productions. In successive seasons from 1726 to 1732, Venice and Rome produced rival performances of the following librettos, composers or plots (revivals are omitted):[46]

Didone abbandonata, Venice, carnival 1725, Albinoni; Rome, carnival 1726, Vinci
Siroe, Venice, carnival 1726, Vinci; Rome, carnival 1727, Porpora
Catone in Utica, Rome, carnival 1728, Vinci; Venice, carnival 1729, Leo
Ezio, Venice, autumn 1728, Porpora; Rome, carnival 1729, Auletta
Semiramide riconosciuta, Rome, carnival 1729, Vinci; Venice, carnival 1729, Porpora
Artaserse, Rome, February 1730, Vinci; Venice, February 1730, Hasse
Alessandro nell'Indie, Rome, carnival 1730, Vinci; Venice, carnival 1732, Pescetti
Mitridate, Venice, carnival 1730, Zeno/Giay; Rome, carnival 1730, Vanstryp/
    Porpora
Annibale, Rome, carnival 1731, Vanstryp/Giacomelli; Venice, autumn 1731,
    Vanstryp/Porpora[47]

44.   See also Reinhard Strohm, 'Leonardo Vinci's *Didone abbandonata* (Rome 1726)', in R. Strohm, *Essays on Handel*, 1985, pp. 213–24.
45.   Charles Burney, *Memoirs of the Life and Writings of the Abate Metastasio* (London, 1796), p. 36, reported that the Venetian Ambassador to Rome brought about the commission to Metastasio for Venice after hearing Sarri's *Didone abbandonata*; see K. S. Markstrom, 'The Operas of Leonardo Vinci', p. 136, noting that Burney mistook the place of performance of Sarri's opera (Rome instead of Naples).
46.   Most of these performances took place at the Teatro delle Dame, Rome, and the Teatro S. Giovanni Grisostomo, Venice; exceptions are *Didone* (Venice, S. Cassiano), *Mitridate* and *Annibale* (Rome, Teatro Capranica), *Annibale* and *Alessandro* (Venice, S. Angelo).
47.   The non-Metastasian operas of 1730 and 1731 could pass as stylistic continuations of Metastasio's Italian series (the poet had by then left for Vienna). *Annibale* and *Mitridate* by the Roman Arcadian Filippo Vanstryp are directly modelled after Racine and Corneille.

The *drammi* by Metastasio in this series constituted his complete Italian output. Venice and Rome had both 'adopted' him. The first edition of his collected works was begun in 1732 by Bettinelli in Venice.

Nicola Porpora plays a somewhat special role in Venice because since 1726 he had been *maestro del coro* of the Ospedale degl' Incurabili there. This position was surely owed to his fame as a singing teacher rather than that of an opera composer. But the *scrittura* for *Siface*, his Venetian operatic début, may have been due to his Neapolitan connections with Metastasio: he had set the early serenatas *Angelica* and *Gli orti Esperidi* (see above) and may originally have been asked, before Feo, to set the libretto of *Siface* in 1723 for Naples.[48] Furthermore, Porpora shared Leo's privilege of being a friend of Domenico Lalli. Porpora and Lalli may already have collaborated in Naples; they certainly did so after 1720, for example in the opera *Damiro e Pitia* written for Munich in 1724. Porpora's most successful dramatic work of those years was the serenata (*componimento drammatico*) *Imeneo* of 1723, to a text by Stampiglia. When Cardinal Pietro Ottoboni, reconciled with his native city, arrived for an extended visit to Venice in the summer of 1726, the Consiglio dei Dieci decreed that an opera was to be performed in his honour on 20 September at the Grimani theatre of S. Samuele: Porpora's *Imeneo*, now revised in three Acts (rather than two *parti*) and retitled *Imeneo in Atene*. I suggest that Domenico Lalli was the reviser of the libretto. The performance presumably happened at the request of the cardinal himself; one singer of his personal household, Domenico Rizzi, appeared in the main role of Tirinto.[49] Did the cardinal also choose either librettist or composer? As for the latter, he had scored a moderate success with *Siface* at the Teatro S. Giovanni Grisostomo in the preceding carnival; his position at the Incurabili would have recommended him to the civic authority to represent the Republic musically. It is not known whether Porpora had any previous connections with Ottoboni, but Lalli apparently did.[50] The poet also dedicated his own next libretto, *Argeno*, to Ottoboni in 1728.

When the Teatro S. Giovanni Grisostomo opened its 1726–7 season, other 'friends' of Lalli were given a chance. One of them was the north Italian Giovanni Porta, who since 1717 had already set five librettos from Lalli's pen, and who composed the opera of the autumn season, *Il trionfo di Flavio Olibrio*. I suspect that the libretto was an adaptation by Lalli of Zeno's *Flavio Anicio Olibrio*.[51] Porta also composed the second carnival opera in 1727, *Aldiso* (libretto by Claudio Nicola Stampa), but Porpora received the honourable task of writing the first, *Meride e Selinunte* after Apostolo Zeno. It appears that all these librettos were adapted by Lalli. Of Porpora's opera, some of the most important sources are in London, including the autograph (*GB-Lbl*, Add. MS 16111) and a copy presumably brought

48. Metastasio remembered him as late as 1772 in connection with this first performance: see R. Strohm, *Italienische Opernarien*, vol. 2, pp. 160–1.
49. For the Ottoboni visit, see E. Selfridge-Field, *Pallade Veneta*, p. 45, and Michael Talbot, 'Vivaldi's Manchester Sonatas', *Proceedings of the Royal Musical Association* 104 (1977–8), p. 27.
50. R. Pagano, *Scarlatti Alessandro e Domenico*, p. 260.
51. It is just possible that the earlier of two settings by Porpora of this basic libretto, given at the Teatro S. Bartolomeo in 1711, also had some traces of Lalli in it.

from Venice by an associate of the Royal Academy (*GB-Lam*, MS 80). Owen Swiney, writing to the Duke of Richmond, praised the production of *Flavio Olibrio* and commented critically on the cast of the season.[52]

There is evidence, nevertheless, that the season as a whole did not go very well for the Grimani theatres,[53] and that therefore the 'Neapolitan element' was increased again in 1727–8. Only two operas were given, both commissioned from Neapolitan composers. Porpora's *Arianna e Teseo*, in autumn, was based on Pietro Pariati's *Teseo in Creta* (Vienna, 1715), also using an anonymous revision made for the Teatro S. Bartolomeo in Naples in 1721 (the music on that occasion was a pasticcio arranged by Leo). The Venetian score of *Arianna e Teseo* is a remarkably good effort for Porpora; it was repeated in Florence the following summer but not in London in 1733–4 when Handel, for the King's Theatre, used Pariati's libretto but Porpora, for the Opera of the Nobility, had to set Rolli's *Arianna in Nasso* instead.

The second opera of this season, *Argeno*, represented a renewal of Leonardo Leo's collaboration with Lalli as librettist. This opera seems to have been very successful, playing for the whole carnival season. Owen Swiney reports on the success obtained in this and the preceding opera by Nicolò Grimaldi, who had returned to the Teatro S. Giovanni Grisostomo.[54] Leo himself seems to have been pleased with the libretto, which offers a wide range of violent emotions in an exotic (East Asian) setting: he reused it for a largely new setting (*Argene*) for Naples in 1731.[55]

In the Venetian season of 1728–9, all the protagonists of our story are assembled: Lalli and Metastasio, Porpora and Leo, plus in addition Nicolò Grimaldi. But a superior ingredient can now be added. Many contemporary witnesses identify the first appearance in Venice of Carlo Broschi *detto* Farinelli as the main event of the season. The Teatro S. Giovanni Grisostomo had of course outflanked other competitors in hiring this Neapolitan singer and ex-pupil of Porpora. He had a rather late début in Venice – perhaps having been kept away by the jealousy of other singers and their protectors. In any case, his resounding success overshadowed, according to contemporary reports, even the appearances of Faustina Bordoni and Senesino at the Teatro S. Cassiano.

52. E. Gibson, *The Royal Academy*, pp. 371–2 (letter of 29 November 1726).
53. Antonio Conti, in a letter of 23 February 1727 to Madame de Caylus, praised Vivaldi's operas at the Teatro S. Angelo, but said of the competition: 'Le nouveau opéra de San Grisostomo a mieux réussi de l'autre par la magnificence des décorations mais la composition est si détestable et la musique si triste que j'y ay dormi pendant un acte.' ('The new opera of S. Grisostomo had a better success than the old one for its magnificent stage-sets, but the poetry is so contemptible and the music so boring that I slept for a whole Act.') See Remo Giazotto, *Antonio Vivaldi* (Turin: ERI, 1973), p. 214. This suggests that the first S. Giovanni Grisostomo opera, *Meride e Selinunte*, was unsuccessful, and that in the second, *Aldiso* (by Giovanni Porta), the libretto and music still did not please Conti. For this correspondence, see Karl Heller, *Vivaldi: Cronologia della vita e dell'opera* (Florence: Olschki, 1991), p. 45, and Michael Talbot, 'Vivaldi and the Empire', *Informazioni e Studi Vivaldiani* 8 (1987), pp. 39–40.
54. E. Gibson, *The Royal Academy*, p. 377 (letter of 13 February 1728).
55. Also in 1731, Leo composed a totally new setting of Lalli's *I veri amici* for Rome under the title *Evergete*.

Several customers from England were in Venice this season, including Handel, who in fact tried to hire Farinelli for London. One of the directors of the Royal Academy of Music, Sir John Buckworth, seems to have attended the three main operas at the Teatro S. Giovanni Grisostomo – Porpora's *Ezio*, Leo's *Catone in Utica* and Porpora's *Semiramide riconosciuta:* he owned full-score copies of all of them.[56] The libretto of *Semiramide riconosciuta* was dedicated to him by Domenico Lalli. The dedications of *Ezio*, played in autumn, and of *Catone in Utica*, the first carnival opera, were also signed by Lalli.[57]

The significance of these dedications is that all three librettos were new creations of Metastasio, written for the Teatro delle Dame in Rome and set to music by Vinci and Pietro Auletta. Lalli had apparently managed to get hold of the librettos immediately after or (in the case of *Ezio*) even before the Romans could mount their own premières. (See the list of 'rival' productions above.) While it is certain that Metastasio had authenticated and directed the Roman versions of these operas, we can only speculate how the Venetians got hold of his newest dramas: with Lalli's help, and possibly with a large golden handshake.

Leonardo Leo was allowed to use a revision of *Catone in Utica* which the poet himself later acknowledged and printed.[58] This drama had, like *Didone abbandonata*, a tragic ending (Cato's suicide), the staging of which had been criticized in Rome in 1728. Metastasio then wrote a new version in which the suicide happens off-stage. Leo's setting of the revised *Catone* was later used by Handel (where the ending is further conventionalized). Its effect in Venice, however, was perhaps spoiled by the casting. Nicolò Grimaldi excelled in the title role, and Domenico Gizzi sang Cesare. Both were overshadowed by Farinelli's showmanship in the secondary role of Arbace, for which additional arias were inserted which had little to do with the drama. The libretto editions identify these with asterisks, probably out of respect for Metastasio. Some of these arias – not all of them by Leo – were circulated widely. In *Ezio* and *Semiramide*, the forces of the same three men were much better balanced, although fewer of Porpora's arias attained any popularity. Interestingly, Handel chose as the basis for his pasticcio *Semiramide riconosciuta* (1733), the homonymous opera by Vinci, not by Porpora, although he must have had easy access to the latter. To use eighteenth-century metaphors, if Vinci was a true painter of the affections, then Porpora was a skilful decorator. As for Leo, his achievement is for some reason underrated today. But then, he does not seem to have quite seized his chance.

From about 1730 for decades to come, Venetian *scritture* for new opera seria productions tend to strike a fair deal between southern and northern composers: Riccardo Broschi (1730), Sellitti (1733), Araya (1734), Fiorillo (1736), Pergolesi

56. Now *GB-Lam*, MSS 79, 75 and 81 respectively. Buckworth must have lent the score of *Catone* to Handel, who used it to prepare his pasticcio of the same title in 1732: see R. Strohm, 'Handel's pasticci', pp. 179–82.

57. *Ezio* was dedicated to Count Harrach, the Austrian ambassador who later became Viceroy of Naples; and *Catone* to the Neapolitan Don Domenico Marzio Pacecco Carafa, prince of Mataloni.

58. See P. Metastasio, *Tutte le opere*, vol. 1, pp. 1399ff., and R. Strohm, *Italienische Opernarien*, vol. 2, p. 185.

(1738) and so forth alternate with the northerners Cordans (1728), Pescetti and Galuppi (1728), Giacomelli (1729), Ciampi (1729), Giay (1730), Corselli (1732), Schiassi (1735) and so forth. Established local composers such as Albinoni and Vivaldi still dominate the minor opera houses. Of course, such evenhandedness would have been unthinkable around 1720, when the southern element simply was not there.

One composer did not fit even this new pattern: Johann Adolf Hasse. In this last case of a spectacular Neapolitan success, ulterior motives and personal influences may have helped a great musical talent along. Hasse's training with Alessandro Scarlatti (1724) and operatic career in Naples (1725–9) had been rather brief when he attracted the Venetian *scrittura* for Metastasio's newest libretto, *Artaserse*, late in 1729. Just as in the season of 1728–9, the impresario managed to get hold of the freshly written drama, and to have it performed at almost the same time as Vinci's 'official' première in Rome (4 February 1730): I estimate that Hasse's setting for Venice was premièred as soon as two weeks later. The stream of revivals flowing from both Vinci's and Hasse's *Artaserse* settings is in itself the single most substantial tradition in eighteenth-century opera seria.

Hasse's setting was already the fourth opera at the Teatro S. Giovanni Grisostomo this season. The others were Francesco Ciampi's *Onorio*, a humble work actually revived in London in 1736 (Opera of the Nobility); Riccardo Broschi's *Idaspe*, whose major interest lay in the arias for the composer's brother Carlo, i.e. Farinelli; and *Mitridate*, by the Turin composer Giovanni Antonio Giay. All three librettos were written (*Onorio*) or adapted by Lalli; his transformation of Zeno's *Mitridate* into a classicist five-act drama was especially ambitious. For Hasse, Lalli delegated much of the rewriting of arias to an assistant he had been using since 1728, Giovanni Boldini, who succeeded in giving Hasse the basis for such epochal successes as 'Pallido il sole' or 'Lascia cadermi in volto'.[59] To avoid offending Metastasio, a second edition of the libretto was distributed simultaneously, with his unaltered text, to which the revised libretto explicitly refers. One wonders whether this was Metastasio's condition for giving his new drama away: he may have felt that the asterisks in Leo's *Catone* libretto did not suffice to protect his authorial claims.

Further observations, including the striking similarity between some of Hasse's and Vinci's settings of the same aria texts (for example 'Amalo, e se al tuo sguardo'),[60] give the impression that there was some connection between Metastasio, Hasse and Vinci over the planning of both operas. This was technically possible – all three were still resident in Naples in late 1729 – and artistically not unlikely as Metastasio later expressed his high esteem for both composers' music. Hasse had the asset – in the poet's eyes – of composing for Grimaldi and Farinelli; Vinci could rely on Carestini and on Metastasio's darling soprano, Giacinto

59. On these pieces, see Daniel Heartz, 'Hasse, Galuppi, and Metastasio', in *Venezia e il melodramma del Settecento* [I], ed. by M. T. Muraro (Florence: Olschki, 1978), pp. 309–39.
60. See R. Strohm, *Italienische Opernarien*, vol. 1, pp. 141–3 and 149 (text), and vol. 2, nos 73 and 74 (music examples).

Fontana. This hypothesis may further imply that Metastasio himself had given Hasse some help in obtaining the Venetian *scrittura*, since he was obviously asked first for his permission to use the libretto.

Later this spring Hasse married Faustina Bordoni, with whom he collaborated for the first time in his opera *Dalisa*, given in May at the Teatro S. Samuele. The libretto of this superfluous little opera had been revised and dedicated (to Edward Coke) by Domenico Lalli. Faustina had been a mainstay of the Teatro S. Giovanni Grisostomo from 1718 until 1725, when she created all three title roles of the Pasqualigo-Orlandini-Vinci season. On her return from London in 1728, however, she accepted a contract with the Teatro S. Cassiano, together with Senesino. This may have lost her the S. Giovanni Grisostomo engagement in the carnival of 1730, which she spent in Turin (singing Porpora). My suspicion about who brought her back in the fold of the Grimani theatres, and thus possibly acquainted her with Hasse, focuses on Domenico Lalli.

A letter written by Antonio Vivaldi on 29 December 1736 suggests that some type of control over S. Samuele and S. Giovanni Grisostomo productions around 1732–6 was in the hands of Michele Grimani.[61] Thus, the Grimanis themselves probably favoured Hasse, who in 1732 produced Metastasio's *Demetrio* at the S. Giovanni Grisostomo, a particularly successful work, and Zeno's *Euristeo* at the Teatro S. Samuele. Of his many operas heard later in Venice, the most remarkable was a revision of his setting of Metastasio's *Alessandro nell'Indie* in 1736. Leo withdrew to Naples. Porpora found things to do in Turin and Rome, visiting the Teatro S. Angelo (in Vivaldi's absence) in autumn 1731 with an *Annibale* written in Rome (see above); and from 1733 he was in the service of the Opera of the Nobility in London. In 1732 his post as Maestro delle figlie del coro at the Incurabili had gone to Hasse, who managed to reconcile a foreign position (Dresden) with Venetian residency.

Setting librettos by Metastasio was something like a sports competition in which the winner would make music history – provided he was a Neapolitan. Vinci outclassed Sarri, Porpora and even Leo in all the Metastasian operas[62] before 1730, when he had to accept a draw with Hasse, despite the latter's use of a Venetianized *Artaserse*. For the next twenty years or so, Hasse dictated the style of Metastasian opera from wherever he happened to work. The extent to which Hasse was as true a Neapolitan opera composer as all these others is still undetermined. But it is a fact that Venice promoted him, and Neapolitan opera, into the great operatic world of the Settecento.

The underlying question of this study – 'who or what makes opera history?' – has not found a clear answer. The European critics who in the eighteenth century first

---

61. Vivaldi says that the manuscript scores of two operas requested from him were deposited at 'Ca' Grimani' with S. E. Michiel Grimani, and that it was not easy to have them copied: see Francesco Degrada and M. T. Muraro (eds), *Antonio Vivaldi da Venezia all'Europa* (Milan: Electa, 1978), pp. 95–6. The two operas were, in my reconstruction of the events, Hasse's *Demetrio* of 1732 and his *Alessandro nell'Indie* of 1736.

62. Except for *Ezio*, which was not touched by Vinci and remained a risky drama for any composer's reputation, even Handel's.

conceived of the 'Neapolitan myth' were not only guided by taste, but also swayed by box-office successes. These successes, in turn, can be traced with surprising precision to the 1720s, to a tangle of mere accident, individual volition, personal relations, rivalries and careerism, especially that of an exiled Neapolitan who promoted his compatriots. No major pattern of artistic policy or patronage emerges. Strategies were aimed at immediate success and lasted for one to three seasons. Little emerges from the study of the dedicatees of librettos. The impresarios remain in the background, whereas the librettists and composers seem the driving force. These artists, and to a lesser extent the singers, apparently had to face fresh challenges in each new season, playing on audience expectations which we can only identify in the areas of poetic taste and singing ability. But some of them had a luckier hand than others. The verdicts (or canons) later reached by history tend to coincide with the impressions gained by modern musicologists who studied the scores. It is possible that this coincidence is not just a fallacy: the 1720s may have been the moment when criteria of musical and literary content and quality started to 'show through' in the business of Italian opera. Patronage, opportunity and status were still decisive, but those who wrote better librettos and scores at that historic moment became more successful than those who even then remained humble agents of an aristocratic pastime.

4
The crisis of Baroque opera in Germany

I

In his collected edition of plays, *Die deutsche Schaubühne nach den Regeln und Exempeln der Alten* ('The German stage, according to the rules and models of the ancients', 6 volumes, Leipzig, 1741–5), Johann Christoph Gottsched also published, from volume 2 onwards, chronological lists of plays printed in various places in Germany since the end of the Middle Ages.[1] This bibliography of dramatic works, which Gottsched later reedited,[2] was based on his private library. It virtually amounts to a survey of the cultivation of opera in Germany, as the majority of titles are Baroque opera libretti. Gottsched must have realized this, but he may have flattered himself to discover, in the entries of the years leading up to 1741, a welcome tendency which he characterized as follows (referring to the year 1733): 'It will be noticed that operas are now clearly on the wane. Whether this was to be attributed to the new appreciation of spoken tragedies, intelligent people may judge for themselves.' ('Man wird wahrnehmen, daß die Opern nun merklich verschwinden. Ob dieses dem neuen Geschmacke an den Trauerspielen zuzuschreiben gewesen, mögen Verständige selbst urtheilen.')[3]

When referring to the years 1738 and 1740, he gleefully commented that German operas were now 'decreasing and slimming down' ('abnehmen und dünne werden'), and he greeted the opera *Atalanta* (Gdansk, 1741) with the exclamation: 'With this one, German operas are finished altogether.' ('Hiermit hören die deutschen Opern gar auf.')[4] Already, in his *Versuch einer Critischen Dichtkunst vor die Deutschen* ('Essay on a critical poetics for the Germans', Leipzig, 1730), he had been able to remark:

1. 'Verzeichniss aller Theatralischen Gedichte, so in deutscher Sprache herausgekommen', in J. C. Gottsched, *Die deutsche Schaubühne nach den Regeln und Exempeln der Alten*, 6 vols (Leipzig, 1741–5), vol. 2 (1741), pp. 43ff.; addenda in vols 3 (1741), 4 (1743), 5 (1744) and 6 (1745).
2. In his *Nöthiger Vorrath zur Geschichte der deutschen dramatischen Dichtkunst* ('Necessary resource for a history of German dramatic poetry') (Leipzig, 1757–62).
3. Quoted after Arnold Schering, *Johann Sebastian Bach und das Musikleben Leipzigs im 18. Jahrhundert* (=*Musikgeschichte Leipzigs*, vol. 3) (Leipzig, 1941; R Berlin-Leipzig: Merseburger, 1974), pp. 274–5.
4. Ibid., p. 275.

The Leipzig opera house expired many years ago, and the one in Hamburg is on its last legs. The one in Braunschweig has also shut down just recently, and it remains to be seen whether it will ever flourish again. In Halle and Weißenfels, too, there used to be operatic stages, not to mention those at other smaller princely courts, but they have all gradually come to an end. This indicates to me the advancing good taste of our fellow countrymen, on which I congratulate them. (Das Leipziger Operntheater ist seit vielen Jahren eingegangen, und das Hamburgische liegt in den letzten Zügen. Das Braunschweigische hat gleichfalls nur neulich aufgehöret, und es stehet dahin, ob es jemals wieder in Flor kömmt. Auch in Halle und Weißenfels hat es vormals Opernbühnen gegeben, die aber alle allmählich ein Ende genommen haben. Dieses zeigt mir den zunehmenden Geschmack unserer Landleute, wozu ich ihnen Glück wünsche.)[5]

The following is not primarily a discussion of Gottsched's arguments in the contemporary German debate about opera, nor of those of his opponents and supporters who included Lorenz Christoph Mizler, Johann Friedrich Armand von Uffenbach, Johann Mattheson and Johann Adolph Scheibe,[6] but of the historical process to which they apparently referred: a crisis in the German cultivation of opera. Did it really happen? How did it manifest itself? What lay behind it?

Arnold Schering, who collected the quoted excerpts in volume 3 of his *Musikgeschichte Leipzigs*, shared Gottsched's factual evaluation, but recommended further research:

For there had long been a crisis in German operatic life. . . . Around 1740 German opera, as if consumed by a creeping illness, had disappeared almost everywhere. . . . An explanation of this reversal of German operatic practice, as identified by Gottsched on the basis of reliable statistics, is at present fraught with difficulties. The reasons which he himself proposes—an increasing preference for tragedy, rising ticket prices, decline of musical connoisseurship – are insufficient and incorrect. The reasons are buried more deeply and have to be related, if I am not totally mistaken, to sociological and capitalist shifts in the German middle class.

Schering then describes certain aspects of these 'shifts', which will be discussed below, and concludes:

. . . thus it was only natural when Germany opened itself to the nation that was unsurpassed in this regard: the Italians. . . . Gottsched had too little inborn

5. *Critische Dichtkunst*, chapter 12. Quoted after A. Schering, *Musikgeschichte Leipzigs*, vol. 3, p. 275.
6. On them, see Joachim Birke, 'Gottsched's opera criticism and its literary sources', *ActaMus* 32 (1960), pp. 194–200; Gloria Flaherty, *Opera in the Development of German Critical Thought* (Princeton: Princeton University Press, 1978); Ernest Harriss, 'Johann Mattheson, Johann Adolf Scheibe, and Modern German Musicology', in *Bach, Händel, Schütz: Alte Musik als ästhetische Gegenwart*, ed. by Dietrich Berke and Dorothee Hanemann, 2 vols (Kassel, etc.: Bärenreiter, 1987), vol. 2, pp. 287–93.

enthusiasm for music to understand that connoisseurs as well as amateurs were prepared to accept a few dramatic absurdities for the sake of a beautiful voice and artistic presentation.[7]

Despite his seemingly cautious and flexible argumentation, Schering mis-accentuates two of Gottsched's points. First, he presents the whole process as if it had been a crisis only of *German* opera followed by Italian hegemony, a problem of national culture caused, above all, by shifts in the 'German middle class'. The tendency to formulate this segment of opera history in narrow, national terms is also found in Schiedermair, Moser and others who considered this to be a crisis only of German or indeed 'early German' opera, especially that of Hamburg.[8] Second, while ostensibly defending the 'beautiful voice(s)' and 'dramatic absurdities' of the Italians against Gottsched, Schering implies in the last sentence that because of these features Gottsched had attacked *Italian* opera, not German – almost making him an ally.

In reality, Gottsched did not criticize any Italian hegemony, of which he was still unaware in 1741, nor did he welcome the disappearance of German middle-class opera only. Rather, he thought in 1741 that all opera enterprises – those of Leipzig and Hamburg as well as those at the courts of Braunschweig, Halle, Weißenfels and smaller centres – were coming to an end. Although, in the context of a publication dedicated to German drama, he speaks of 'German operas', he was of course equally delighted by the demise of the Italian court operas at Braunschweig, for example. Gottsched was an opponent of the genre of opera as such, regardless of language or social context. He was hardly very interested in the national element so highly rated by Schering, except perhaps that he criticized his fellow countrymen more severely than the Italians when they indulged in irrationality. In his radical opposition to opera, Gottsched was an internationalist; he invoked the testimonies of Saint-Évremond and Muratori, who wanted to get rid of opera altogether, and he did battle with reformers such as Mattheson or his own student Johann Adolph Scheibe, who wished to rescue opera by reforming its taste.[9] Gottsched's factual verdict of 1741 ('. . . German operas are finished altogether', see above) can partly

7. 'Denn längst war eine Krise im deutschen Opernleben angebrochen. . . . Um 1740 war die deutsche Oper, wie von einer schleichenden Krankheit verzehrt, fast überall verschwunden. . . . Eine Erklärung des von Gottsched auf Grund zuverlässiger Statistik festgestellten Umschwungs im deutschen Opernwesen bietet bis zur Stunde Schwierigkeiten. Was er selbst dazu vorbringt: Erwachen stärkerer Neigung für das Trauerspiel, wachsende Höhe der Eintrittsgelder, Abnahme der musikalischen Kennerschaft, reicht nicht aus und stimmt auch nicht. Die Gründe liegen tiefer und sind, wenn nicht alles trügt, mit soziologischen und kapitalistischen Verschiebungen in der deutschen Bürgerschaft in Zusammenhang zu bringen. . . . so war es nur natürlich, wenn Deutschland sich derjenigen Nation öffnete, die in diesem Punkte unübertroffen dastand: den Italienern. . . . Gottsched besaß zu wenig angeborenen Musikenthusiasmus, um zu begreifen, daß Kenner wie Liebhaber um einer schönen Stimme und Vortragskunst willen gern ein paar dramatische Sinnlosigkeiten mit in Kauf nahmen.' Ibid., pp. 275–6.
8. Ludwig Schiedermair, *Die deutsche Oper* (Leipzig, 1930), especially pp. 93–4; Hans-Joachim Moser, *Geschichte der deutschen Musik vom Beginn des dreißigjährigen Krieges bis zum Tode Joseph Haydns* (=*Geschichte der deutschen Musik*, vol. 2), 5th edn (Stuttgart and Berlin, 1930), pp. 126ff.
9. See chapter 1 in this volume, p. 24.

be corrected with the help of modern bibliographies.[10] At that time, court operas still existed in Gotha and Rudolstadt, not to mention the Saxon court which Gottsched passes over in silence, perhaps out of diplomacy. It is more significant, however, that he was as yet unaware of the successful opera troupe of Pietro Mingotti, which began to appear at Hamburg in 1743 and at Leipzig itself in 1744.[11] Nor did he presumably know of the new foundations of exclusive court operas at Bayreuth (1737), Stuttgart (1737) and Berlin (1741), which offered almost the same repertoire as that cultivated by Mingotti – opera seria in the style of Metastasio and Hasse, with the addition of comic *intermezzi* – although the works were performed by much better vocal forces and in magnificent courtly productions. For Schering and his colleagues, the restoration of German court opera on an Italian basis, and the triumphal tours of Italian opera troupes, were symptoms of a crisis: they curtailed the German national opera tradition. For some of Gottsched's contemporaries, they signified, on the contrary, the solution to the crisis: Italian intervention was reforming the genre of opera and thus saved it from extinction.

Among these contemporaries was Johann Mattheson who, at Easter 1744, published his *Die neueste Untersuchung der Singspiele* ('The most up-to-date investigation of the operas').[12] This essay sharply attacks Muratori and Gottsched but, on the other hand, concludes with an annotated translation of Benedetto Marcello's *Il teatro alla moda*, the famous satire of 1720 on the abuses of opera. Because of this combination, and because Gottsched is the main target of the publication, Mattheson's introductory words (p. 1) are worthy of note:

At the end of last year, 1743, an expert troupe of Italian operists arrived here in Hamburg – just as if they had fallen from the sky. These *virtuosi* did not stay long, but they received, as well as merited, great applause by every connoisseur, high and low, of such useful entertainments. (Am Ende des abgewichenen 1743sten Jahres kam eine geschickte Bande welscher Operisten hier in Hamburg an; nicht anders, als wären sie vom Himmel herunter gefallen. Besagte Virtuosen verweilten zwar nicht lange; erhielten aber, und verdienten auch, großen Beyfall vom höchsten bis zum niedrigsten Kenner solcher nützlichen Belustigungen.)

It was in fact the troupe of Pietro Mingotti which Mattheson welcomed (not without a grain of irony) like a gift from heaven. What did he want to prove? Surely the ability of opera to reform itself and thus to survive – albeit in Italian costume. In Mattheson's opinion, the Mingotti productions were largely free of the defects of conventional opera. We may note that their Hamburg repertoire comprised *drammi per musica* by Metastasio as well as Pergolesi's *La serva padrona*.

10.   See Renate Brockpähler, *Handbuch zur Geschichte der Barockoper in Deutschland* (Emsdetten, 1964), pp. 118–19 and passim.

11.   Erich H. Müller von Asow, *Die Mingottischen Opernunternehmungen 1732 bis 1756* (Dresden: Hille, 1915).

12.   Johann Mattheson, *Die neueste Untersuchung der Singspiele, nebst beygefügter musikalischen Geschmacksprobe* (Hamburg, 1744; R Leipzig, 1975).

How did Gottsched react to Mattheson, on the one hand, and to these Mingotti productions when they were repeated at Leipzig in 1744, on the other? In his next publication concerning the opera question (1746), he declared his great respect for 'poets and composers of today', supposed that modern operas are better than older ones (to which his witnesses, Muratori and Saint-Évremond, had referred), and concluded that it was perhaps still possible to 'abolish what is mistaken in the operas, and to develop this species of theatrical poems to greater perfection'.[13] This sudden and almost complete retreat, judged by Joachim Birke to be 'momentary and inexplicable',[14] is only inexplicable if we surmise, with Schering, that Gottsched had attacked merely the Italian operas or had sought a reform on national lines. Admittedly, in 1751 he drifted towards a more negative judgement again. This time, however, he targeted Rameau's *tragédies lyriques* for his criticism, while expressing full praise for two Italian court operas by the Saxon Princess Maria Antonia Walpurgis: *Il trionfo della fedeltà* and *Talestri*, operas which had just appeared in Breitkopf's printing shop.[15] The reason lay not only in diplomacy but in the obvious fact that the new opera seria in Metastasio's vein and the literary *intermezzi comici* were results of the libretto reforms stimulated by the Accademia dell'Arcadia; they had been modelled after the classical French spoken theatre which Gottsched admired. They formed, for him, a contrast to the confused theatricality of the *tragédie lyrique* as well as of the old German Baroque operas. If the new type of opera seria commanded the tolerance even of a Gottsched, then it surely had to be acceptable anywhere in Germany – as indeed it was.

What, then, was the meaning of the crisis? For many contemporaries, it simply consisted in the old Baroque type of opera itself, precisely in its more splendid manifestations; the solution, however, was the reformed opera seria and the *intermezzi* of the Italians. For those music historians of our century who gave priority to the national aspect, the crisis essentially consisted in the decline of German national opera and the transfer of the hegemony to the Italians; the solution, for them, was going to be the establishment of German *Singspiel* and German serious opera over the following decades.[16] It seems that such views would not have been shared by Gottsched's contemporaries. Critics like him considered the closure of the German opera houses as a step in the right direction; even Mattheson cannot have shed many tears over the closure of the Hamburg opera. But some scholars thought they had to diagnose a decline of German opera in particular, a 'creeping illness' (Schering) or an 'artistic decadence' (Schiedermair), which then paved the way for the Italians.

13. See J. Birke, 'Gottsched's opera criticism', p. 195.
14. Ibid., p. 195.
15. Ibid., p. 195.
16. See the works by Schiedermaier and Moser, cited above, and the more recent (and more balanced) studies of Hellmuth Christian Wolff, *Die Barockoper in Hamburg (1678–1738)*, 2 vols (Wolfenbüttel, 1957), and Hans Joachim Marx, 'Geschichte der Hamburger Barockoper: Ein Forschungsbericht', *Hamburger Jahrbuch für Musikwissenschaft* 3 (1978), pp. 7–34; idem, 'Politische und wirtschaftliche Voraussetzungen der Hamburger Barock-Oper', in *Die frühdeutsche Oper*, ed. by C. Floros et al., pp. 81–8. Of these studies, only the one by Wolff follows opera in Hamburg past the year 1738 into the period of the Mingottis: see, in particular, his vol. 1, pp. 341ff.

This 'decadence', and the low artistic achievement of the poets (Moser) or the musicians (Schiedermair, Marx), the devilish opera criticism (Schiedermair, Wolff, Marx), ultimately the 'low state of public taste' (Moser) and the anti-artistic attitude of the public (Wolff) – these all jointly gambled away the national tradition to the Italians. Contemporary critics of opera saw this differently. What Gottsched wished to eliminate was Baroque opera in general, precisely in its more opulent manifestations and in whatever language; what Mattheson satirized were the abuses also of the Italian opera convention, and the public's stubborn adherence to the old, unreformed operatic style. These two critics did not need to reinterpret the economic decline of opera in Germany as artistic decadence, because they did not have to seek an excuse for the imminent Italian hegemony.

II

The fate of the German court operas of the eighteenth century should have demonstrated, in any case, that with such a wasteful form of art, economic and artistic decline do *not* normally coincide. As with other cultural activities of the absolutist regimes, the most ambitious projects were the ones that emptied the princely pockets and damaged the state finances. Between c. 1700 and c. 1740, many court operas had to close at least temporarily, because they had been too wasteful already for two or three generations, and the deficit was building up. The end of the court operas was the inevitable consequence of their bloom, which they had reached around 1700: a bloom that may be characterized by the names of composers such as Johann Sigismund Kusser, Reinhard Keiser, Agostino Steffani, Giovanni Bononcini, Francesco Pistocchi, Luigi Mancia, Attilio Ariosti and Johann Hugo Wilderer. Their productions pursued a 'universal' and eclectic aesthetic, according to which the very best singing, instrumental playing, scenography, ballet and so on that was to be found in Europe was considered just right to demonstrate the glory of the respective princely patrons. Not only did every small German court aspire to imitate Versailles or Vienna: some (Hanover, for example) tried to imitate both of them simultaneously. The reason for the economic crisis of opera was implicit in the eclectic and bombastic conception of the genre that Germany had adopted. All that needs to be explained is why the closures of the opera houses occurred in the period of c. 1700–c. 1740 and not earlier or later, and why they spread over a span of about forty years.[17]

This spread was probably not due to a creeping illness of artistic decadence which advanced with different speed in the various places, and definitely not caused by the increasing voices of adverse critics, but it quite simply arose from the dynastic

17.   Erich Reimer, *Die Hofmusik in Deutschland, 1500–1800* (Wilhelmshaven: Noetzel, 1991), pp. 125–7 and p. 201 n. 2, while rejecting earlier hypotheses of a 'decline', also doubts my suggestion that the opera closures in the different centres can be interpreted as manifestations of a single crisis. Nevertheless, he concedes that the crisis of court opera as discussed by me must not be equated with the fate of court music ('Hofmusik') in general, which is the subject of his own excellent monograph. Even when speaking of the larger concept of 'Hofmusik', he diagnoses a crisis: 'Zu rekonstruieren ist deshalb kein Verfallsprozeß, sondern eine Krise und ein daraus hervorgehender Wandel der Institution Hofmusik' (p. 127).

system itself. Nobody could prevent an individual ruler from indulging in operatic entertainment well beyond an economically tolerable degree. The decision to pull the plug was usually left to a successor who, when coming into power, found the finances ruined. Dismissing all the court musicians was quite normal at the time, even at the Habsburg court; at many smaller courts in Germany, however, this meant the end of the opera performances for good, since the deficit had been accumulating for a while and a short interruption of the productions would not have allowed for a regeneration. The years of closure are distributed over a longer time-span because dynastic successions happened at different times in the various states. Furthermore, their economic power was unequal, and wars affected the regions to different degrees. Even so, the War of the Spanish Succession, 1700–13, in the south, and the Nordic War, 1700–18, in the north, provided a common background for the problems of many territories. In most residences, essentially the same happened: blooming operatic life under an earlier prince, followed by abolition under a successor who often belonged to the generation of J. S. Bach. In the following courts the end of opera coincided with a dynastic succession (in some of them, it happened *de facto* earlier but was confirmed by the new ruler):

Ansbach 1703 (no reopening of the opera house)
Bayreuth 1726 (reopening 1737)
Berlin 1713 (reopening 1741)
Coburg-Meiningen 1724 (no reopening in the eighteenth century)
Düsseldorf-Heidelberg 1716 (reopening at Mannheim, 1742)
Durlach-Karlsruhe 1733 (no reopening in the eighteenth century)
Hanover 1698 (no reopening in the eighteenth century)
Kassel 1730 (reopening 1764)
Salzburg 1727 (from 1737 again isolated productions)
Stuttgart 1726 (reopening 1737)
Weißenfels 1736 (no reopening).

In some residences the periods without opera were bridged by smaller musico-dramatic performances, as for example at Mannheim from 1720. In Stuttgart and Karlsruhe the frequency of performances was reduced before the final closures, though this is not the same as artistic decline. Many courts not mentioned in the list had some isolated productions before c. 1725 but not afterwards. In Darmstadt in 1719 the ruling prince was wise enough to stop the performances during his lifetime. Dynastic rather than economic reasons – but in any case not artistic ones – curtailed the operas at Innsbruck in 1717: the Imperial governor, Count Palatinate Carl Philipp, transferred his residence to Mannheim, and the Tyrol was taken under direct administration by Vienna, as had happened in earlier instances.

The opera closures cited so far form a relatively homogenous picture, nor is this really contradicted by the development in some larger residences, where the crisis was only minimized, delayed or anticipated.

At the Habsburg court the death of Emperor Joseph I in 1711, during the War of the Spanish Succession, caused an interruption of the operas for two years. Joseph's brother Charles VI continued from 1713 to his death in 1740 to maintain a splendid Italian operatic establishment, employing Pietro Pariati, Antonio Caldara, Francesco Conti, Apostolo Zeno, Pietro Metastasio and many other Italians. Only his daughter Maria Theresa, involved in wars with Prussia from the moment of her succession, had to initiate a drastic financial reform, in the context of which the opera business was partly farmed out to the impresarios of the Burgtheater and Kärntnertortheater. The court withdrew to festive productions in the private sphere, and sponsored only occasional gala performances in the Burgtheater or Hofburg. This momentous shift can be interpreted as an incipient decentralization of the court opera system, in which the Baroque claim to universality was given up in favour of a modern pluralism of more clearly separated genre responsibilities.[18]

In Munich the Spanish War caused a hiatus as well, albeit a much deeper one, as Elector Max Emanuel was in Belgian and French exile from 1704 to 1715, during which time no operas were performed in the Munich palace. From 1715 until the prince's death in 1726 everything continued in the customary magnificent style. Max Emanuel's successor Karl Albert, too, ignored financial warnings and imitated the Habsburgs with his court operas until 1740, when he had to stop owing to the wars. He died in 1745. In 1753 Elector Max III Joseph was able to open the Residenztheater, rebuilt by Cuvilliés, and to return to a now retrogressive court opera system which was abolished only in the 1780s under his successor Karl Theodor. Thus the opera crisis itself, its solution through a restoration of the old system, and the appearance of more progressive trends, happened in conservative Bavaria a little later than in other German territories, although everything followed the same pattern.

Braunschweig-Wolfenbüttel, on the other hand, had preceded other courts already in 1690 by establishing the Braunschweig city theatre as a public opera house, which performed during the trade fairs; its box office income helped the dukes to recover some of their own court opera expenses. For this reason, the crisis could be minimized by reducing the number of performances in 1735–49. In the final year the principal of an Italian travelling troupe, Filippo Nicolini, was appointed as 'directeur des spectacles'. He turned this courtly-bourgeois collaboration into a second bloom of Braunschweig opera.

At the electoral Saxon and royal Polish court, the interruption of the operas happened not later but earlier than elsewhere. As in Munich, wars prevented regular performances in 1700–17. The elector and (then) King of Poland, August 'the Strong' (r. 1694–1733), in any case disliked Italian opera, whose isolated splendid moments in this period were entirely due to the patronage of the electoral prince, Friedrich August II. These moments included the famous opera-filled festivities of 1717–19 for the wedding of the electoral prince, and the engagement of the Hasse couple in 1730/1. Thus after August the Strong's abstinence from opera, and perhaps because of his successful economic policies, Dresden became after his

18.   For the situation in Vienna, see also Reinhard Strohm, 'Wien und die mitteleuropäische Opernpflege der Aufklärungszeit', in *Europa im Zeitalter Mozarts*, ed. by Moritz Csáky and Walter Pass (Vienna, etc.: Böhlau, 1995), pp. 391–6.

death in 1733 the seat of a new, stable court opera with Johann Adolf Hasse as Kapellmeister. The stylistic orientation of this new foundation belongs entirely to the new epoch, as symbolized by the name of Hasse himself, by his Metastasio settings and his *intermezzi*. The crisis was overcome while others were still heading into it. Dresden became a model for the subsequently reestablished court operas in Bayreuth, Stuttgart and Berlin, in a stylistic as well as organizational sense. The second Silesian War, 1745–7, caused a short disruption, followed by another innovative measure, when Pietro Mingotti and Gluck together produced the wedding opera for Maria Antonia Walpurgis, and Regina Mingotti left the travelling company to join the court establishment (1747). After this, the series of Italian impresarios in Dresden, who presented mostly *opere buffe*, was hardly interrupted for the remainder of the century, although opera seria was progressively diminished by the wars and changing tastes.

It may be concluded that practically no German court opera was able to escape the financial crisis arising from the gestation of Baroque opera; the court operas either had to shut down altogether or to give up their claims to universality, often after a period of operatic abstinence. After 1740, even the most exclusive and, by comparison, anachronistic court establishments such as Berlin, Bayreuth, Stuttgart and Munich no longer cultivated the musical 'world theatre' of the Baroque, but a few did regularize dramatic genres, whereas the promotion of other forms (of opera buffa, for example) had to be left to other patrons or to be relinquished altogether.

III

Since middle-class tastes had little or no influence on the fate of the court operas (perhaps indirectly in Vienna, Dresden, Braunschweig) and since charges of artistic decline should not be levelled against the court operas without new, more thorough research, the reasons proposed by the music historians cited above for the German opera crisis are, for most of the region, unconvincing. We may for the moment stick to the simple diagnosis of a financial deficit which inevitably resulted from the courtly concept of opera itself. How, then, should we interpret the fate of the civic and bourgeois opera enterprises in Hamburg and Leipzig, to which the whole question has too often been restricted? For them, the support of a ticket-buying public was vital indeed.

I am proposing here that the opera enterprises at Leipzig and Hamburg cultivated the same 'universal conception' of Baroque opera as did the courts, and that therefore they succumbed to the same, economic difficulties as did the court operas.

Opera at Leipzig had been a foundation sponsored by the Saxon court. Under August the Strong its audiences must have included a good many of the opera-loving Dresden courtiers. Its leading artists – Nikolaus Adam Strungk, Daniel Döbricht and his family, as well as Grünewald, Heinichen and Telemann – were all court employees; its repertoire closely followed those of the Bayreuth, Braunschweig and Weißenfels court operas; its student performers were encouraged to regard their participation in opera as a traineeship for courtly careers. The founding patron, Elector Johann Georg IV of Saxony, is even said to have destined the Leipzig opera to be a 'nursery' for his court chapel. The opera house suddenly had to close in 1720, in line with courtly enterprises of similar dimensions and surely for the same economic reasons.[19]

Hamburg carried on until 1738. The financial structure of this opera business was precarious to start with, because the singers' salaries were too low for a living and had to be bettered, as Mattheson reports, through private services for the nobility and guest appearances at the Braunschweig opera house.[20] The impresarios went bankrupt at least twice, in 1707 and 1718. The main rescuers were patricians, nobles and representatives of foreign governments, including the English ambassador Johann von Wich. The numerous celebratory serenata performances for dynastic and political festivities honouring foreign states or princely visits, the selling or letting of the boxes to nobility from out of town and neighbouring princes, the anti-democratic and absolutist bias of historical opera plots, and last but not least the whole repertoire itself, which was derived from the European court operas in Braunschweig, Vienna, London and elsewhere – all these elements combine to characterize Hamburg's opera as a precise imitation of a German court opera, attempted under the less favourable conditions of the impresario system.

There is frequent mention of the comical, histrionic, popularizing and primitive traits of the Hamburg operas, which are usually interpreted as concessions to popular taste.[21] They may have been that as well, but exactly the same traits are amply represented in Viennese court opera under Emperor Leopold I, which was in any case one of Hamburg's models. These traits appealed to the princes and the nobility just as much, or more. The educated middle class, by contrast, might have been keener to cultivate serious loftiness in opera: a suggestion that would be borne out by what is generally known about the European theatre of this period. Such a reformist influence seems to have increased in the later phase of the Hamburg opera, when it was championed by Mattheson and his associates, and manifested itself in his reworkings of operatic tragedies after Handel and Orlandini,[22] in the relatively early acceptance of Metastasio (1727), and in Telemann's 'regulated' comedies which made an end to the slapstick humour of Hamburg's earlier fair-ground- and slaughtertime-revues.

In the light of these facts, the interpretation of Hans Joachim Marx, which despite Wolff's refutation unnecessarily revives Schiedermair's thesis of an 'artistic decline' or even a 'mistaken artistic conception' as the main cause of Hamburg's

19. For opera at Leipzig, see M. Brockpähler, *Handbuch*, pp. 251–9, and Norbert Dubowy, 'Italienische Opern im mitteldeutschen Theater am Ende des 17. Jahrhunderts: Dresden und Leipzig', in *Barockes Musiktheater im mitteldeutschen Raum im 17. und 18. Jahrhundert* (Tagungsbericht, 8. Arolser Barock-Festspiele 1993), ed. by F. Brusniak, vol. 2 (Cologne: Schewe, 1994), pp. 23–48.

20. The fullest documentation of the singers of the Hamburg opera is in Hans Joachim Marx and Dorothea Schröder, *Die Hamburger Gänsemarkt-Oper: Katalog der Textbücher (1678–1748)* (Laaber: Laaber-Verlag, 1995), pp. 439–57; see also Klaus Zelm, 'Die Sänger der Hamburger Gänsemarkt-Oper', in *Hamburger Jahrbuch für Musikwissenschaft* 3 (1978), pp. 35–73.

21. See, for example, Wolff, *Die Barockoper in Hamburg*, vol. 1, pp. 60–196.

22. As described, for example, in Reinhard Strohm, 'Die *tragedia per musica* als Repertoirestück: Zwei Hamburger Opern von G. M. Orlandini', in *Die frühdeutsche Oper*, ed. by C. Floros et al., 1981, pp. 37–54, and Winton Dean, 'Mattheson's arrangement of Handel's *Radamisto* for the Hamburg opera', in *New Mattheson Studies*, ed. by George J. Buelow and H. J. Marx (Cambridge: Cambridge University Press, 1983), pp. 169–78.

opera crisis, cannot be upheld.[23] The late phase of the Hamburg opera does not – *pace* Marx – display a tendency towards the 'showy and decorative' ('das Revuehaft-Dekorative') at the expense of musico-dramatic ideals ('das Dramatisch Musikalische'): on the contrary, showiness and mere decoration were old Hamburg habits and common inclinations of Baroque opera in general. Hardly a better example for them could be found than the Viennese *Il pomo d'oro* by Antonio Cesti of 1668. The musico-dramatic ideal, however, was a reformist tendency of the Italian, particularly Metastasian, opera seria and supported by progressive Hamburg citizens such as Mattheson who opposed the conservatism of most other opera-lovers. This tendency is found, for example, in the concentration on the means of language and on the musical expression of the affections, for it characterizes not only Mattheson's opera reworkings after Handel and Orlandini (1721–3) but even Francesco Conti's *Issipile* (text by Metastasio), performed at Hamburg in 1737. Some operas by Telemann, too, belong to this reformist tendency. That these experiments may not always have pleased the Hamburg public (nor perhaps Reinhard Keiser) seems to be reflected in a critical remark by Mattheson about the Hamburg public of 1728.[24] Besides the ambitious, reformed musical dramas which also included Handel's *Cleofida* of 1732, some concessions to the old histrionic taste remained inevitable. The interests of the Hamburg public, a mixture of middle class and nobility, were so diverse that nobody could satisfy them all.[25] In any case, to serve so many different tastes became ultimately impossible in financial terms. The opera enterprise was brought down by its very ambition to offer, in the old 'universal' manner, everything to everybody under one roof. This was not 'a mistaken artistic conception' (Marx) but the traditional one of Baroque court opera. Hamburg's problem was that its opera could not escape this founding concept, although it was no longer adequate to the circumstances; stylistic and generic diversity had grown too far. Mattheson still attempted, in his *Der Musikalische Kapellmeister* (1739), a classification of the operatic genres into tragedy, comedy and satire, and would have loved to see all these variants regularly performed at the Gänsemarkt, if possible in their most purified incarnations. The enterprise simply was not up to such a task, either technically or in terms of personnel. A glance at the late Hamburg repertoire should suffice to arouse sympathy for the singers, dancers, instrumentalists and scenographers on Hamburg's meagre payroll who within those limits had to manage Handel and Campra, Telemann and Porpora, *intermezzi* and tragedies, German farce, ballet-divertissement, Metastasio and folksong.

In *this* respect, Arnold Schering's analysis hits the target:

> The maintenance of independent civic opera houses, the employment and remuneration of native singers and actors, the commissioning of native composers and much more that was needed to maintain a more than mediocre operatic enter-

23. H. J. Marx, 'Politische und wirtschaftliche Voraussetzungen', pp. 87–8.
24. Mattheson says in *Der Musicalische Patriot* (Hamburg, 1728), p. 199, that operas were not suitable for burghers and merchants, only for princes: see H. J. Marx, 'Politische und wirtschaftliche Voraussetzungen', p. 87 and n. 19.
25. Another reflection of this was the failure of the performances of Karoline Neuber in 1735–40: see Wolff, *Die Barockoper in Hamburg*, vol. 1, p. 343.

prise, had gradually become such an expensive matter that – after the withdrawal
of the originally very active student performers – only court operas could survive.
In addition, German singers were not up to the task. They could not manage
the grand style of dramatic belcanto now in fashion. Germany had neither
conservatoires nor private music schools for singers. There was no firm methodi-
cal tradition. Since the throats trained in this country were sufficient only for
smaller *Singspiele* and *intermezzi*, not for opera seria, it was only natural when
Germany opened itself to the nation that was unsurpassed in this regard: the
Italians.[26]

The ambition of the Germans to emulate the Italians (and the French) in their
own native art-forms led to extraordinary artistic achievements and a rich cultural
life. But in contrast to the field of instrumental music, a 'mixed taste' in opera
('vermischter Geschmack', as Quantz called it) was unaffordable in the long term,
and that was true for the civic opera houses as well as for those at the smaller courts.

IV

The transfer of operatic hegemony to the Italians was, therefore, not so much a
crisis as its solution: a shortening of the path of importation, as it were, by which the
cultivation of certain dramatic genres was again entrusted in full to those who had
created them. But these Italian singers, composers and impresarios would not have
been capable of realizing, in Germany, a 'mixed taste', let alone a 'universal conception' of the musical theatre. Each of the diverging tastes had to be satisfied by the
most suitable specialists: here the Italian *operisti*, there the German comedy troupes,
and so on. The travelling troupes could be hired on an ad hoc basis, even in
competition with each other, since this corresponded to their own system of production. The opera crisis was not an artistic decline but a decentralization of the
forms of operatic patronage and production. The process rather precisely mirrored
that of the transition from a system of mercantilism to one of free trade.

Finally, we have to consider what constituted the advantage of specialization in
opera and how it became established. The system of production of the travelling
troupes – not only in opera – was based on a more efficient exploitation of the
market than was posssible for a single-location enterprise. Even in a big city such as
Hamburg, successful plays could not be repeated ad infinitum: whereas the court
opera did not even attempt to derive profit from them, the travelling troupe could
carry them elsewhere. The main business risk of a standing opera house consisted
in falling ticket sales while the salaries remained payable; the travelling impresarios,
just like the impresarios of Venice and other cities of Italy, made the artists carry
some of the risk by regrouping their whole personnel after each tour or season.
Furthermore, the opera troupes were less exposed to damage through wars – they
could beat a retreat; and when state mourning curtailed their performances, they
could try them out in the next state. Most importantly, they could specialize in

26. See n. 7 above.

genres and modes of performance appropriate to their means. This possibility was open not only to the travelling troupes who produced cheaply and frugally, but also to the most expensive court specialists. The latter could offer brilliant performances of their Hasse or Porpora scores; they were less at ease with Telemann's or Rameau's. In recognition of this, after c. 1740 the most famous court operas chose a path of voluntary restriction of their repertoires, a path which in a few cases – such as Berlin and Stuttgart – later led to one-sidedness and schematicism.

As mentioned above, the formal and aesthetic characteristics of opera seria and comic *intermezzi* had been shaped by the Arcadian opera reform, albeit only in the sense that liberal Arcadians such as Zeno and Pariati, who were interested in the musical theatre, had cautiously injected it with certain innovations they had observed in French spoken drama. The result, a concentration on captivating dialogues in the simplest musical form (recitative) but intersected by ample, emotionally expressive arias, perfectly suited the needs of the impresario system. The continuing rotation of singers on short-term contracts and the need to exploit successful productions further were matched by a relative interchangeability of arias (as in a pasticcio), a certain schematicism of the plots, and a stereotyped usage of orchestra and staging, all of which corresponded to the classicist Arcadian ideals. Zeno's librettos were successful because they could be clad, time and again, in new musical clothes suited to the occasion. His poor aria verse (as far as it was not actually supplied by his lyrically more gifted collaborator Pariati) could be substituted without any complications, since he himself had placed it outside the dramatic structure.[27] Similar observations can be made in the libretti of his Italian contemporaries of northern Italy. The reform, the pasticcio practice and the impresario system belong together.

Not surprisingly, then, the first travelling impresarios from across the Alps were northern Italians and their operas were based on reform librettos. The Venetian impresario Antonio Peruzzi is said to have concluded an opera contract with the city fathers of Leipzig as early as 1722. His first documented production was based on Grazio Braccioli's Venetian libretto *Orlando furioso* of 1713 (music by Giovanni Alberto Ristori, revived in 1714 by Antonio Vivaldi), which was now adapted for a resetting by the Venetian Antonio Bioni. The opera was performed in the summer of 1724 for Imperial Count Franz Anton von Sporck in his country estate of Kuksbad and was chosen to inaugurate Sporck's city opera house in Prague in the autumn of that year.[28] From this moment onwards an army of travelling opera troupes took to the road (see p. 94).

Another Venetian impresario, Antonio Denzio, inherited the impresa of Sporck's opera house, where until 1734 he performed over fifty operas – several of them by

---

27. For a modification of this traditional view of Zeno, see chapters 1 and 7 in this volume, pp. 18–19 and 134–5.
28. Details on the first decade of the Prague opera are found in Daniel E. Freeman, *The Opera Theater of Franz Anton von Sporck in Prague* (New York: Pendragon Press, 1992) (Studies in Czech Music, 2); idem, 'Orlando furioso in the Bohemian Lands: was Vivaldi's Music really used?', *Informazioni e Studi Vivaldiani* 14 (1993), pp. 51–73; idem, 'The foundation of Italian Operatic Traditions in Prague', in *Il melodramma italiano*, ed. by A. Colzani et al., 1995, pp. 117–25.

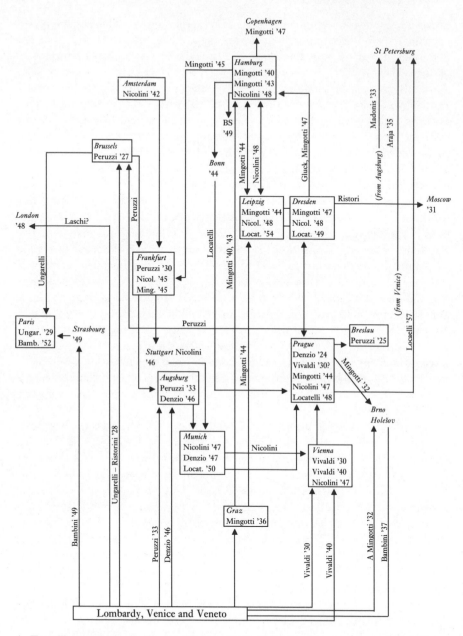

4. Travelling opera troupes in central Europe, 1724–54. Major cities are shown within boxes, with names of opera impresarios (or composers) and the year of their first public appearance.

Vivaldi – and *intermezzi* for the citizens of Prague. Peruzzi began, in 1725, a civic opera in Breslau (Wrocław), but in 1727–9 he visited Brussels and Paris, then Frankfurt, Augsburg and Munich. Members of his cast – many of whom had been contracted afresh each year from northern Italy – went to perform in St Petersburg as early as 1733. As for Denzio, he performed in the 1740s in Augsburg and Munich and later apparently in Mannheim and Lübeck.

Peruzzi's and Denzio's followers were, again starting from the Bohemian-Moravian territories, the Venetians Angelo and Pietro Mingotti, who in the years 1740 and 1743/4 alone criss-crossed Germany several times. Then there appeared Santo Lapis, Eustachio Bambini, Filippo Nicolini with his children's troupe of the 'Piccoli Olandesi' setting out from Amsterdam, and finally the most ambitious of them, Giovanni Battista Locatelli. He had begun his career as a court poet at Bonn in 1741, and in 1745 briefly entered the employ of Pietro Mingotti, but perhaps only with the intention of poaching his two best primadonnas, Giovanna della Stella and Rosa Costa. From 1748 to 1756 Locatelli presented magnificent Metastasio-productions at Prague, commissioning two of the settings from his *maestro di capella*, Christoph Willibald Gluck. He also took the significant decision to adopt Venetian opera buffa, successfully performing such works simultaneously in Dresden and Prague in 1751–5. Although he went bankrupt in 1757 and had to flee to Russia, he founded an impresario tradition in Prague which led without interruption to Bustelli and Guardasoni, and thus to the Prague productions of *Don Giovanni* and *La clemenza di Tito*.

It is known that in 1752 Eustachio Bambini unchained the Parisian *querelle des bouffons* with his *intermezzi* and *opere buffe*; it is less well known that most of these pieces had already been shown by travelling troupes in the German and Czech lands and that Bambini's opera on the subject of Don Giovanni, *La pravità castigata*, had been given in Brno in 1734; the opera's prototype had first been given under Denzio in Prague, 1730.[29]

There is no need to describe in detail how many of the great movements of later eighteenth-century opera had been fostered by the travelling troupes. The important point is that the troupes were more susceptible to innovation than the court opera system was. The history of their repertoires, for example, suggests a determined progression from the north-Italian impresario operas to the *drammi* of Metastasio and his composers, and at the same time from comic *intermezzi* to full comic operas, first of a Neapolitan/Roman variety and then of the Venetian sort; simultaneously from pasticcio practices to individualized settings, as illustrated by Gluck's career as a composer. Nevertheless, his self-borrowings in his later operas recall the techniques which he had learnt while on the road with the troupe. Perhaps that was the background also for his more fundamental musical and dramatic ideas.

---

29.   Tomislav Volek, 'L'opera veneziana a Praga', in *L'opera italiana a Vienna prima di Metastasio*, ed. by M. T. Muraro (Florence: Olschki, 1990), pp. 193–206, especially p. 203. The libretti are listed in P. Kneidl, 'Libreta italské opery v Praze v 18. století, 1', in *Strahovská knihovna* (Prague, 1966) (Památník národního písemnictví, I), pp. 97–131.

The travelling troupe, like no other type of theatre company, depends on professional, convincing stage action. Anybody who wished to interest the German middle class from Graz to Lübeck in an Italian opera had to offer a good deal more than 'a beautiful voice' and 'dramatic absurdities'. This is where Schering is after all unfair to the German bourgeoisie. In the privileged court opera houses, whose expensive stagecraft outshone other dramatic efforts, opera seria was perhaps sometimes enjoyed for what is unfortunately reputed to be its essence: a spectacle for the eye and a concert of select voices. In the makeshift theatres of the civic fairs, however, boring action would not have been accepted for long. I am convinced that the Mingotti troupe, for example, presented Metastasio's *Artaserse* as what it was meant to be: a thriller. Of course, it was a thriller on a high literary level, with a brilliantly constructed, rational plot, in which heroes as well as villains used only the most refined forms of communication. This could be such an exciting theatrical experience that it could make you forget the stage decorations (or the lack of them). And the literary-musical shadow-fencing of *La serva padrona* did not require any decorations, in a sense not even 'beautiful voices'. The words alone carried it all. This may well be judged to be an impoverishment by comparison with the old Baroque opera – but also a humanization. Baroque opera had become enslaved to an apparatus the weight of which finally crushed it. If this was a crisis, then the crisis was solved at the moment when the musical theatre started to consist mainly of people again.

5
Francesco Corselli's *drammi per musica* for Madrid

Francesco Corselli (c. 1702–78) was one of those Italian composers of the eighteenth century whose names have all but disappeared from the history of music as it is written today. He achieved this by joining the royal court of Spain, an institution sufficiently alien to most music historians to grant him, as far as their horizon is concerned, instant invisibility. He compounded the effect by writing mostly vocal music – serious operas and sacred works, which were not printed and for which there was no demand in later centuries. Unlike the keyboard music by Antonio Soler or Domenico Scarlatti, his works have not stood the test of time and prejudice.

These questions set aside, Francesco Corselli was an important figure in European music of his time, not least for having gained an influential position in Spain in a period which was crucial for the future of Spanish opera.[1] The following is an attempt to relate the emigrant son to the mainstream history of Italian opera, by surveying his two *dramma per musica* settings that survive complete: his *Farnace* and his *Achille in Sciro*. These are indeed the works which one might study when asking how relevant the Italian tradition was for music and musical theatre in eighteenth-century Spain.[2]

Francesco Corselli (Courcelle) was born in Piacenza (c. 1702) as a descendant of French immigrants. He may have studied with the widely known opera and church composer Geminiano Giacomelli, also from Piacenza, whom he succeeded in 1727 as *maestro di cappella* at the Steccata church of Parma. His operatic debuts in Venice, *Venere placata* (Teatro S. Samuele, spring 1731) and *Nino* (S. Angelo, carnival 1732), are likely to have been encouraged by Giacomelli, whose stature in Venetian

---

1. Information about opera in Spain and Corselli's career can be gathered from José Subirá, *El teatro del Real Palacio (1849–1851)* (Madrid, 1950), pp. 17–52 (on Corselli, see especially pp. 24–30); Nicolás A. Solar-Quintes, 'El compositor Francisco Courcelle, Nueva documentación para su biografía', *Anuario Musical* 6 (1951), pp. 179–204; Robert Stevenson, 'Corselli [Courcelle], Francesco [Francisco]', in *The New Grove Dictionary of Opera*, vol. 1, pp. 961–2.
2. I owe my thanks to Dr Rainer Kleinertz for having drawn my attention to these works. Manuscript scores of both are extant in the Biblioteca Municipal, Madrid; see Subirá, *El teatro* (see previous note), and José Subirá, *História de la Música Española e Hispanoamericana* (Barcelona-Madrid: Salvat, 1953), p. 477.

operatic life was rapidly increasing in those years. Resident Venetian opera com-
posers might have influenced Corselli as well. Antonio Vivaldi was mostly absent
from the city in 1730–2, but the young Baldassare Galuppi had started his
career there in 1728. Nicola Porpora worked in Venice in 1726–33, his *Annibale*
(S. Angelo, autumn 1731) being written for the same stage and cast as Corselli's
Nino. An arbiter of taste in Venetian opera of those years undoubtedly was Johann
Adolf Hasse, particularly on account of his *Artaserse* (1730), *Demetrio* (1732) and
Alessandro nell'Indie (1736). Corselli's own efforts to get himself known seem to
have had some effect, as two of his arias were performed as far away as London, in
pasticcio operas produced by Handel in late 1733.[3] Corselli apparently arrived in
Spain in 1734 in the service of Don Carlo Borbone, Duke of Parma, later King of
Naples and from 1759 King Carlos III of Spain.[4] Throughout his remaining years,
Corselli served the dynasty as household musician, *maestro di capella* and rector of
the choir school.

The early productions of Italian opera in Madrid[5] were staged in the Coliseo
de los Caños del Peral and the Royal Coliseo del Buen Retiro. In both houses, Italian
opera seria was attempted at least for some time in the 1730s and 1740s, and
partly performed by the same singers. The Italian opera performances at the
Buen Retiro were instigated by the Queen, Elisabetta Farnese, and her adviser
Marchese Annibale Scotti; Carlo Broschi detto Farinelli, the new vocal star and
personal adviser of King Philip V, seems to have had less influence on these early
productions.[6]

Italian operas at the Buen Retiro began during a temporary closure of the Teatro
de los Caños del Peral in the spring of 1738. Corselli as the new chapelmaster of the
court was entrusted with the first opera, a setting of Pietro Metastasio's *Alessandro
nell'Indie* (9 May 1738), which celebrated the wedding (at Naples) of Don Carlo

3.   See Reinhard Strohm, *Essays on Handel and Italian Opera* (Cambridge: Cambridge University Press,
     1985), pp. 206 and 208. The arias were 'Troppo fiere e dispietate', from his *Venere placata* (1731),
     and 'Scherza il nocchier talora', on a text in Metastasio's *Demetrio*. The latter setting originated
     perhaps as an insertion by Corselli in some other composer's opera, just possibly Leo's *Demetrio*
     given in Naples in the spring of 1732 (following a suggestion made by Prof. Lorenzo Bianconi). The
     autograph but fragmentary score of the production (*F-Pc*, MS 2255) does not contain Corselli's aria.
     Of other operatic music by Corselli composed before 1739, very little seems to be extant.
4.   According to R. Stevenson, 'Corselli', it was in 1734 that Corselli was asked to suggest composers
     whose sacred works should be acquired for the royal music library. His list of recommended
     composers (see N. Solar-Quintes, 'El compositor', pp. 189–90) includes famous Italians from
     Alessandro Scarlatti to Galuppi, Leo and Pergolesi, demonstrating his familiarity with the repertory
     but not necessarily his stylistic preferences.
5.   On opera in Spain, see J. Subirá, *El teatro*; José López-Calo and José Subirá, 'L'opera in Spagna',
     in *Storia dell'Opera*, ed. by Alberto Basso, vol. 2/I (Turin: UTET, 1972), pp. 489–536; Manuel
     Carlos de Brito, 'La penisola iberica', in *Storia dell'opera italiana*, ed. by L. Bianconi and G. Pestelli,
     vol. 2 (forthcoming); Juan-José Carreras, 'Opera di corte: Madrid (1700–1759)', in *L'opera italiana
     nei paesi di lingua iberica: Lo stato della ricerca*, ed. by A. L. Bellina and A. Cetrangolo (Padua,
     forthcoming); Juan-José Carreras, 'La compañia de los Trufaldines y la introducción de la ópera
     italiana en España: nuevas fuentes, nuevas perspectivas', in *Il teatro dei due mondi*, ed. by A. L.
     Bellina and A. Cetrangolo (Padua, forthcoming).
6.   See the studies by Juan-José Carreras, quoted above (n. 5); I am grateful to Prof. Carreras for advice
     on these matters.

Borbone with Maria Amalia of Saxony. This work was followed, again on the
occasion of royal weddings, in 1739 by *Farnace*, and in 1744 by *Achille in Sciro*, the
operas to be discussed below.

The music of Corselli's *Alessandro nell'Indie* is lost, but the extant libretto yields
relevant information.[7] The text is said to have been revised by Metastasio himself at
the request of his friend Farinelli. This opera was entrusted to an Italian cast of
modest status. Only truly famous was Annibale Pio Fabri, in the role of Alessandro,
a Bolognese tenor who had been heard on all major Italian stages as well as in Vienna
and London. He remained a fixture of the company in Madrid for at least seven
opera productions. The *prima donna* (Cleofide), the Florentine soprano Rosa
Mancini, had served the court of Parma and had sung secondary roles in Venice
(S. Samuele, 1729) and Naples. The *primo uomo* role of Poro was performed by
the Florentine castrato Lorenzo Saletti, who had appeared in Venetian operas by
Giacomelli, Vivaldi (*Griselda*, S. Samuele, 1735) and Hasse. In an anonymous
Alessandro nell'Indie given at Pisa, 1735, Saletti had already sung Poro, whereas
in Hasse's Venetian *Alessandro nell'Indie* of 1736 he was confined to the
secondary role of Gandarte. In Madrid, Gandarte's role was taken by the Bolognese
contralto Elisabetta Uttini, who in 1736 had sustained the role of Poro in the
provincial opera house of Prato (near Florence). Her other previous appearances
included one at the Teatro S. Samuele in 1728, and one in a minor role (Arasse)
in Hasse's *Siroe re di Persia* at Bologna, 1733. The singer of Alessandro in the
Prato production just mentioned, Maria Marta Monticelli of Bologna, also
appeared in Corselli's cast but was downgraded to the tertiary role of Timagene. To
conclude this little roundabout of *Alessandro* roles – which may be a measure of
the artistic status of the Buen Retiro production – it seems reassuring that a
certain Giacinta Forcellini from Venice, who sang Corselli's *seconda donna* Erissena,
had previously performed that role in Leonardo Vinci's setting as given in Parma,
1736.[8]

The production of Corselli's *Alessandro nell'Indie* was very successful and might
have been seen by contemporaries as a reaction to Hasse's *Demetrio*, produced on 16
February 1738 at the Caños del Peral, and perhaps to Hasse's *Alessandro nell'Indie*,
written for Venice in carnival 1736 and repeated, with alterations, in Naples on 4
November 1736 for Don Carlo Borbone (both times with Vittoria Tesi in the *prima
donna* role of Cleofide). Corselli's setting itself was repeated at the Buen Retiro in
the following December, after the restoration of the opera house. Metastasio and
Hasse now became the most prominent names in the courtly opera repertory. Their
Siroe re di Persia was performed at the Buen Retiro on 24 March 1739, and *La
clemenza di Tito* (where Hasse's authorship is speculative) at the Caños del Peral on
14 May 1739. After that date, the opera company of the Caños del Peral was finally
transferred to the Buen Retiro.

7. A copy is in the University Library, London, Elliot Phelips Collection.
8. On early productions of *Alessandro nell'Indie* and their cast, see Reinhard Strohm, 'Metastasio's
    Alessandro nell'Indie and its earliest settings', in R. Strohm, *Essays on Handel*, pp. 232–48.

Farnace

The season 1739–40 opened with another royal wedding opera, this time for the Infante Don Felipe with the French Royal Princess Luigia Isabella, on the feast of S. Carlo Borromeo, 4 November 1739: Corselli's *Farnace, re di Ponto* (see tables 2 and 3, pp. 103 and 107).

The company hired in 1739 was far superior to that of 1738, not least for the addition of Gaetano Majorano detto Caffarelli, arriving from London. This superb Neapolitan castrato had then reached the height of his career. The other newly engaged singers were the mature contralto Vittoria Tesi, a celebrity and long-standing servant of the courts of Parma and Tuscany, and the Bolognese soprano Anna Maria Peruzzi 'detta la Perucchiera'. These three prominent artists replaced not the better singers of the 1738 season, but the weaker ones (Forcellini and Monticelli), so that there was now a company of seven voices, all with an excellent reputation. The drama newly set by Corselli in 1739, Antonio Maria Lucchini's *Farnace*, was already familiar to some of the performers: Vittoria Tesi had sung Tamiri (*prima donna*) in Leonardo Vinci's setting at Naples, 1729, and Berenice (*seconda donna*)[9] in Giovanni Porta's setting at Bologna, 1731; Rosa Mancini had been Selinda in a Florentine repeat of the same opera, 1733; Elisabetta Uttini had participated in a production of *Farnace* which the travelling company of Pietro and Angelo Mingotti presented in Graz and elsewhere from 1737 onwards. More interestingly, Peruzzi had appeared as the *prima donna* in both Venetian operas by Corselli himself: as Adria in his *Venere placata* and as Zomira in his *Nino*. She had repeatedly sung together with Caffarelli, Tesi and Annibale Pio Fabri. Thus the leading musicans of 1739 knew each other and had been on stage together. Some of them had also performed with Farinelli and may have learnt from him. The more significant previous encounters of members of the 1739 cast were as follows:[10]

Nerina	Pollarolo	Venice	1728	Caffarelli, Uttini
Didone abbandonata	anon.	Milan	1729	Tesi, Caffarelli
Candace	Lampugnani	Milan	1733	Caffarelli, Tesi, Peruzzi
Siroe re di Persia	Hasse	Bologna	1733	Caffarelli, Tesi, Peruzzi, Uttini
Alessandro	Schiassi	Bologna	1734	Fabri, Peruzzi
Clemenza di Tito	Leo	Venice	1735	Fabri, Peruzzi
Demofoonte	Schiassi	Venice	1735	Fabri, Peruzzi
Alessandro	Hasse	Venice	1736	Tesi, Saletti

9. She also appeared as Berenice in Leonardo Leo's opera *Farnace* in Naples, 1736; this was a different libretto with a similar plot.
10. Information on several of these libretti is derived from Claudio Sartori, *I libretti italiani a stampa dalle origini al 1800*, 6 vols (Cuneo: Bertola and Locatelli, 1993).

Achille in Sciro	Sarri	Naples	1737	Tesi, Peruzzi[11]
L'Olimpiade	Leo	Naples	1737	Tesi, Peruzzi
Artaserse	Vinci et al.	Naples	1738	Tesi, Peruzzi
Demetrio	Leo et al.	Naples	1738	Tesi, Peruzzi[12]

The effects on Italian opera of such a circulation of librettos and singers, first nationally and then also internationally, are incompletely known. Much needs to be learned about the practicalities of opera production, from the creation of drama and music to the rehearsing and conducting routine.[13] The 'roundabout' of the *Alessandro* roles, illustrated above, is typical for productions of Metastasio's *drammi per musica* which circulated in many settings. It is possible that the best singers knew entire *drammi* more or less by heart, not just a single role. Male and female roles were equally accessible to the better sopranos and contraltos. That the effects of the circulation would have meant normalization and a relative aesthetic uniformity seems an inescapable conclusion.

Farnace, re di Ponto was a very successful libretto, first given in 1724 at the Teatro Alibert in Rome with music by Leonardo Vinci. For the Madrid production, this original libretto version of Rome, 1724, was chosen as a basis, for reasons as yet unknown. Many other libretto versions would have been available by 1739.[14] Whether Corselli knew Vinci's setting, or indeed any of the others, is not clear. The Venetian librettist Antonio Maria Lucchini (fl. 1714–32) wrote mostly for Venetian composers such as Antonio Lotti and Antonio Vivaldi.[15] Several of his other librettos were pastoral or mythological in character. His *Farnace*, however, is the epitome of the heroic, classicist and historical *dramma per musica* which dominated Italian opera in the first half of the century, and was cultivated by such librettists as Francesco Silvani, Apostolo Zeno, Pietro Pariati, Antonio Salvi, Agostino Piovene, Domenico Lalli and Pietro Metastasio. The last-named, in his early works from *Didone abbandonata* (Naples, 1724) to *Artaserse* and *Alessandro*

---

11. November 1737–June 1738 was the first season of the newly built Teatro S. Carlo of Naples under Don Carlo Borbone as King of Naples. See Helmut Hucke, 'L'*Achille in Sciro* di Domenico Sarri e l'inaugurazione del Teatro di San Carlo', in *Il teatro di San Carlo, 1737–1987: L'opera, il ballo*, ed. by B. Cagli and A. Ziino (Naples: Electa, 1987), pp. 21–32. On the Neapolitan *Achille in Sciro*, see also below.

12. This was the wedding opera for Don Carlo Borbone and Maria Amalia of Saxony, performed at the Teatro S. Carlo on 30 June 1738. It had the same celebratory purpose (although using different singers, of course) as Corselli's *Alessandro nell'Indie* of 9 May 1738, discussed above.

13. Useful material on the social conditions of singers is presented in John Rosselli, *Singers of Italian Opera: The History of a Profession* (Cambridge: Cambridge University Press, 1992).

14. Settings until 1739:
Leonardo Vinci: Rome, T. Alibert (1724), Florence, T. Pergola (1726), and Naples, T. S. Bartolomeo (1729); Antonio Vivaldi: Venice, T. S. Angelo (1727), Prague (1730), Pavia (1731), Mantua (1732), Treviso (1737), Ferrara (1739, cancelled); Giuseppe Maria Orlandini: Milan (1728, as *Berenice*); Antonio Cortona: Brussels (1729); Giovanni Porta: Bologna, T. Malvezzi (1731), Florence, T. Pergola (1733); anon.: Lisbon (1735); anon.: Graz (1737), Vienna, Th. am Kärntnertor (1737); Giuseppe Antonio Paganelli: Braunschweig (1738, 1739); Rinaldo di Capua: Venice, T. S. Giovanni Grisostomo (1739).

15. On his presence in Rome, 1724, and connections with Vivaldi, see Antonio Vivaldi, *Giustino*, ed. by R. Strohm (Milan: Ricordi, 1991) (Istituto Italiano Antonio Vivaldi), text volume, pp. 15–16.

nell'Indie (Rome, 1730), developed antagonistic plots and critical views concerning tyranny and dynastic conflict in a manner quite reminiscent of Lucchini's *Farnace*.

In its setting and main plot, *Farnace* also vaguely resembles Domenico Lalli's *L'Amor tirannico* (Venice, 1711; set to music by Handel in 1721 as *Radamisto*). Farnace, King of Pontus (son and heir of Mithridates, the famous opponent of the Romans), and his wife Tamiri despair of protecting their defeated kingdom from Roman invasion and their infant son from capture. Berenice, Tamiri's mother, hates Farnace and has made peace with Pompeo, the Roman leader; Selinda, Farnace's sister, dallies with the warriors Gilade and Aquilio. The unhappy royal couple, betrayed and persecuted on all sides, decide to die with their son. Tamiri, however, changes her mind and hides the child in an ancient family tomb. Believing each other dead at first, Farnace and Tamiri go through a series of tribulations, mostly caused by the unscrupulous and domineering Berenice. They are finally rescued after Pompeo has persuaded Berenice to forget her hatred; the child is found alive and well.

That this drama served in 1739 as a wedding opera may seem surprising, but in *Alessandro nell'Indie* and *L'amor tirannico* too the trials of a loving couple had involved death and suicide. The triumph of fidelity and heroism of a royal couple over political adversity was found to be a suitable theme for a wedding opera in the case of Antonio Salvi's *Adelaide* (Munich, 1722); his *Arminio*, with a similar plot, was performed in London in 1737 to honour a newly-wed royal couple. The poignant additional motive of the child in peril can be found in traditional heroic or even pastoral operas such as Zeno's *Griselda*. Nevertheless, Lucchini attempts to exploit the contrast of sentimental and cruel effects partly beyond convention, for example in a solo scene of Tamiri with her son ('who does not speak') when she decides she cannot kill him (I, 11). Although he is horrified, she makes him enter the funeral monument and then attempts to kill herself. This whole action is performed as an accompagnato recitative ('O figlio, o troppo tardi nato all'afflitta Patria'), in front of the special stage-set of 'Alleys of plane-trees, alternating with statues, in the midst of which there is a great Pyramid, the funeral monument of the Kings of Pontus'. This image, which is repeated in the second Act, evokes the dynastic glory as well as the sombre recollection of ancient kings and queens, combined here with the presentation of a living mother in despair, encouraging her child to enter the tomb of his ancestors in order to survive and continue the ancestral line.

In the last scenes, Farnace is bound to a big tree next to Berenice's pavilion and is to be executed by arrows, when his supporters suddenly attack and defeat Berenice, threatening her life instead. Pompeo and Tamiri intercede and achieve peace. The *licenza* makes the palace of Hymen descend from the sky; Mars, god of war, joins the royal couple together.

The pyramid, the big tree and the palace of Hymen are only the most characteristic among an extraordinary number of sumptuous stage-sets in this opera (see table 2, p. 103). The arias of all the main characters include heroic and military set-pieces, for example the very first of them, Pompeo's 'Regni ed imperi' (I, 2), or the Trio 'Su, campioni' sung by the Roman leaders when conquering the city (I, 8).

Table 2. The libretto of Corselli's *Farnace*, 1739

(Italian and Castilian on opposite pages:)

FARNACE / DRAMMA PER MUSICA, / TRADOTTO DALL'IDIOMA ITALIANO / al Castigliano d'ordine di S. M. da Don Girolamo Val, / suo Secretario, e del Governo di Castiglia, da rappre-/sentarsi nel Regio Teatro del Bon-Ritiro, in occasione / di solennizare Madrid / LE GLORIOSE NOZZE / DI FILIPPO BORBONE, / INFANTE DI SPAGNA, / CON / LUIGIA, / PRIMA PRINCIPESSA DI FRANCIA. / SI DEDICA / ALLE LORO ALTEZZE REALI. / ESSENDO CORREGITORE IL MARCHESE DI MONTE-ALTO, / ... / LA COMPOSIZIONE DELLA MUSICA È DI D. FRANCESCO CORSELLI / Maestro della Cappella Reale; e l'Invenzione delle Scene di D. Giacomo Bonavia / Custode del Regio Sito di Aranjuez. / In Madrid, nella Stamperia di ANTONIO SANZ. Anno 1739. / /

(Dedicated to 'Altezze Reali' by 'Marchese di Monte-Alto' and 5 others; no date) / /

ARGOMENTO. / Farnace fù uno dè Figliuoli di Mitridate Rè di Ponto ... / ... e ne procurò con ogni suo sforzo la totale ruina. / /

MUTAZIONI / DI SCENE. / NELL'ATTO PRIMO. /

Riviera dell'Eusino con folta Selva d'arbori, che ingombrano tutta la Scena.

Escono Guastatori, che troncando in breve la Selva, la riducono ad un'aperta campagna; nel confine della quale si vede il Mare, ed in esso l'Armata di Berenice.

Approdano le Navi, e gettati i Ponti, espongono sul Lido Cavalleria, e Fanteria.

Dopo l'Esercito, sbarca da ricco Naviglio Berenice con numeroso accompagnamento Reale.

Atrio nel Palazzo Reale di Eraclea.

Pianura in cui si vede la Città d'Eraclea accanto ad una Collina. Bosco da una parte, dove è nascosto Farnace co' suoi Soldati.

Viali di Platani, framezzati di Statove [*sic*], nel mezzo de' quali è una gran Piramide, destinata per Sepolcro de i Rè di Ponto.

Loggie. / /

NELL'ATTO SECONDO. /

Gran Galleria.

Altra veduta della Piramide, destinata per Sepolcro de i Rè di Ponto.

Gabinetti Reali.

NELL'ATTO TERZO. /

Piazza di Eraclea con Archi, e altre pompe trionfali.

Giardini Reali.

Stanza nobile con Baldacchino.

Padiglione Reale di Berenice, dirimpetto al quale è un grand'Arbore isolato. Scende una gran Nube, che s'apre nel Domo [*sic*] delle stanze d'Imeneo ... accompagnato da Marte. / /

ATTORI.[16]

Farnace, re di Ponto	Gaetano Majorano, detto Caffarelli
Tamiri, sposa di Farnace	Anna Peruzzi, detta la Perucchiera
Berenice, regina di Cappadocia	Vittoria Tesi Tramontini
Pompeo, proconsule Romano	Annibale Pio Fabri
Selinda, sorella di Farnace	Rosa Mancini
Gilade, capitano di Berenice	Lorenzo Saletti
Aquilio, prefetto Romano	Elisabetta Uttini
Un bambino che non parla, figlio di Farnace e Tamiri. / /	

(169 pp. Biblioteca Nacional de Madrid, T / 7927)

16.   No singer is given a title in the original libretto.

Berenice introduces herself with a very strong *vendetta* aria in aggressively dotted rhythms, 'Da quel ferro ch'ha svenato' (I, 3). Farnace's (Caffarelli's) most heroic and virtuosic aria, by contrast, is the orchestral and vocal tableau 'S' arma il cielo di tuoni e lampi' (II, 18), which describes a dreadful storm followed by the hope of spring and rejuvenation. The personal conflicts are acted out in the magnificent quartet 'Io crudel? Giusto rigore', in which Berenice insists on her persecution of Farnace and Tamiri even against the intercession of Pompeo (III, 9). This item had been the dramatic and musical climax of Vinci's and Vivaldi's settings, with contrasted and anguished declamation and lively instrumental underpinnings; Corselli lets the voices alone declaim the dialogues, accompanied only by an inexorably walking bass, in a monocoloured f minor idiom reminiscent of church music.

More frequent and more typical for the music as a whole are the galant and tender arias, particularly those sung by the secondary characters. Gilade's declaration of love to Selinda, 'Occhi, voi siete quelle' (I, 9), or Pompeo's graceful nature-minuet 'Senza rugiade, languido cade' (III, 7), as well as most of Selinda's and Aquilio's arias, are typical. Even Berenice, a mixed character, has sentimental arias ('Che giova al mio dolor', III, 1, and 'Non trova mai riposo', III, 13); but the surprise of the opera is the consistently heroic and pathetic style sustained by Tamiri. The conflicts between her duties and affections for her husband, mother and son are concentrated in the great accompagnato 'Dite, che v'ho fatt'io?' and aria 'Dividete, o giusti Dei' (II, 10), the central scene of the opera. Vinci had given Tamiri an almost *preghiera*-like melody of serene simplicity; Vivaldi had maintained the constrained rhythm but introduced sobbing 'lombardic rhythms', a fashionable performance device which Corselli also adopts. Not that Tamiri's heroism is only pathetic and sentimental. In her self-presentation aria 'Combattono quest'alma' (I, 6, solo scene), she is portrayed as a brave warrior between the demands of 'glory, pity, love and cruelty'. (See music examples 2a, b, c.)

Only in Vinci's setting is the 'combattimento' of affections allegorically expressed by a triadic fanfare in the vocal line, after which the competing nouns 'gloria', 'pietà'

Example 2a. Vinci, *Farnace* I, 6 (Rome, 1724): aria of Tamiri

Example 2b. Antonio Vivaldi, *Farnace* I, 2 (Pavia, 1731)

and so on inflect the slightly stiff melodic contours to form a yet graceful line. Vivaldi characteristically paints the battle in an excited perpetuum mobile of the strings: against this background the despairing solo voice articulates abrupt utterings – a typical declamatory show-piece for Anna Girò. Corselli interprets the aria as a lyrical piece, letting the violin sing *colla parte* with the voice and then interrupt her in an almost tender dialogue, giving expression and profile to the words 'amor', 'fedeltà', 'sposo' and 'figlio' but not to 'gloria'. Later on, it is the singer who expresses the agitation of her soul in the coloratura. Vivaldi's solution, the declamatory utterings, is not entirely lost, but the tenderness of individual expression is enhanced. Corselli's choice seems dramatically and stylistically relevant, although the personality, ability or even the explicit wish of the singer may have influenced him.

As shown in table 3 (p. 107), the distribution of arias, ensembles (one trio, one quartet) and accompagnati among the singers followed the usual hierarchical con-

Example 2c. Francesco Corselli, *Farnace* I, 6 (Madrid, 1739)

siderations. Singers and audiences noted the number of arias and ensemble participations, the amount of accompagnati, the question whether arias were part of solo scenes or not, and whether they ended a stage-set or Act. In Corselli's original version of the opera, Caffarelli is favoured before Tesi and Peruzzi; the women have almost equivalent roles, as was sometimes the case (for example in the famous Handel operas of 1726–8 written for Faustina and Cuzzoni), but Peruzzi has most of the accompagnati. This speaks for her acting ambition and, probably, for a good recitative performance.

The opera underwent extensive cuts and changes, however. The surviving non-autograph score, which documents them, suggests that most of the changes were made after the first performance. Only scene I, 18, with a heroic *solo* scene of Berenice

Table 3. The arias of Farnace

1. Arias in libretto sequence

X = present in Vinci's libretto of 1724. * = scenes affected by cuts (see below).
_____ : change of stage set. _____ : change of Act.

I, 2	Pom	Regni ed imperi vuoi debellar?	X
I, 3	Ber	Da quel ferro ch'ha svenato	X
I, 5	Far	Parli di madre amante	X
I, 6	Tam *sola*	Combattono quest' alma	X
I, 7	Pom-Gil-Aq	Su, campioni, su guerrieri	X
I, 9	Gil	Occhi, voi siete quelle	X
I, 10	Sel *sola*	Un caro e dolce sguardo	X
I, 11	Tam *sola*	(*accompagnato*)	
I, 14	Pom	Mi piace, e m'innamora*	X
I, 15	Far	Già per vaga e vezzosa beltà	X
I, 16	Aqu	Bei labri, io penserò	X
I, 17	Gil	Sia l'alma del mio bene	
II, 3	Sel	Lascia di sospirar	X
II, 4	Aqu	Talor due pupillette	X
II, 5	Ber	Colei, che t'invaghì	X
II, 6	Gil *solo*	Anche a Giove io farò guerra*	X
II, 7	Far *solo*	(*accompagnato*)*	
II, 8	Far	(*accompagnato*)	
		Perdona, o figlio amato	X
II, 10	Tam *sola*	(*accompagnato*)	
		Dividete, o giusti Dei	X
II, 11	Gil	Da che volgesti a me	X
II, 12	Far	Spogli pur l'ingiusta Roma*	X
II, 13	Pom	Bella, consolati*	X
II, 14	Ber	Tigre irata, che due prede	X
II, 16	Aqu	Con voi vezzosi rai	X
II, 17	Tam	Forse, o caro, in questi accenti	X
II, 18	Far *solo*	S'arma il cielo di tuoni e lampi	X
III, 1	Ber	Che giova al mio dolor	X
III, 3	Tam *sola*	Numi: se in cielo ancor	X
III, 4	Gil	Chi riprende il mio delitto*	X
III, 5	Sel	Ti vantasti mio guerriero*	X
III, 7	Pom	Senza rugiade (*entrance aria*)	X
III, 9	Ber-Pom-Tam-Far	Io crudel? Giusto rigore	X
III, 10	Aqu *solo*	Rendimi la mia pace*	X
III, 12	Ber	Non trova mai riposo	X
III, 13	Far	Cara destra, io bacio in te	X
III, 14	Tam *sola*	Sbigottisce il pastorello	X
Licenza. Coro		Bella coppia, il fato stenda	

Table 3. Continued
2. Aria distribution among characters

(A = aria, Q = quartet, T = trio)

Caffarelli:	6 A + Q, one *solo, accompagnati*. One A and one *acc.* cut.
Tesi:	6 A + Q, one *solo*, one *acc. Solo* scene with *acc.* and A cut.
Peruzzi:	5 A + Q, five *soli* (!), *accompagnati*. No cuts
Saletti:	4 A + T, one *solo*. One A (*solo*) added, two A cut, including *solo*.
Fabri:	4 A + T + Q. Two A and one scene cut
Uttini:	4 A + T, one *solo. Solo* scene with A cut
Mancini:	3 A, one *solo*. One A cut.

3. Changes in score

I, 13–14:	most of rec. I, 13 and whole scene I, 14 cut from score
I, 16–17:	Act I ended originally with dialogue Ber-Gil and Lucchini's aria for Berenice, 'Chi temea Giove regnante?' Gilade's 'Sia l'alma' is new poetry.
II, 2	whole scene Aqu-Gil cut from score
II, 6	aria (but not rec.) cut from score
II, 7	*accompagnato* cut from score
II, 10	erroneously numbered 'II, 11' in score (etc. to the end of Act II)
II, 12	aria (but not rec.) cut from score
II, 13	aria copy unfinished, probably to be cut
II, 18	erroneously numbered 'XIII' in score
Act III	incompletely copied: arias without violins
III, 4	aria and part of rec. cut from score
III, 5	aria (but not rec.) cut from score
III, 10	whole scene, rec. and aria, cut from score
Licenza.	Score has alternative text = original *Coro* ('Vieni o bella e cara pace').

ending Act I (aria 'Chi temea Giove regnante'), was cut before the libretto was printed; the Act now ends with a substitute aria for Gilade ('Sia l'alma del mio bene', words not by Lucchini), but the music was not bound into the score and is lost. After the printing of the libretto, changes including a radical cutback of the minor roles took place, visible in the score and mostly pencilled into the libretto copy of the Biblioteca Nacional. As table 3 shows, these changes left only the role of Peruzzi unaffected, making her the primary singer of the opera; it is significant that Peruzzi was also the singer who had worked with Corselli in the previous Venetian years.

Achille in Sciro

Pietro Metastasio's *Achille in Sciro*, written for the wedding of Maria Theresa of Austria to Francis Stephen, Duke of Lorraine, and performed in Vienna on 13 February 1736 with music by Antonio Caldara, was a perfect predecessor for the royal wedding opera performed in Madrid on 8 December 1744, when the Infanta Doña Maria Teresa married the Dauphin. This revival emphasized the idea of a peaceful competition between the Bourbon and Habsburg empires.

Table 4. The libretto of Corselli's *Achille in Sciro*, 1744

(P. 1–2: Dedication, in Castilian, to King Felipe V by 'El Marquès de Monte-Alto', dated 'Madrid, 13. de Noviembre de 1744'.) / /

ACHILLE IN SCIRO. / OPERA DRAMMATICA / DI PIETRO METASTASIO / DA RAPPRESENTARSI / NEL REGIO TEATRO / DEL BONRITIRO / PER FESTEGGIARE / J GLORIOSI SPONSALI / DELLA REALE / INFANTA DI SPAGNA / MARIA TERESA / CON IL / DELFINO DI FRANCIA. / Nella Stamperia di ANTONIO SANZ. / Anno 1744. / / ARGOMENTO.[17] / E' per antica fama assai noto . . . / . . . ciò che meglio alla condotta della nostra favola è convenuto. Il luogo dell'azione è la Reggia di Licomede nell'Isola di Sciro. / /

PERSONAGGI. /[18]

Licomede Re di Sciro: Antonio Montagnana, Musico della Cappella Reale.
Deidamia figlia di Licomede, Amante di Achille: Anna Peruzzi, Virtuosa di Camara della Regina . . .
Achille in abito femminile sotto nome di Pirra, Amante di Deidamia: Maria Heras.
Ulisse, Ambasciador dè Greci: Elisabetta Uttini, al servizio di S. M.
Teagene Principe di Calcide, destinato Sposo di Deidamia: Emanuella Trombetta.
Arcade confidente d'Ulisse: Costanza Mancinelli, al servizio di S. M.
Nearco Custode d'Achille: Francesco Giovannini, Musico della Cappella Reale.

La Musica è del Signor Francesco Corselli, Maestro di Musica dè Reali Infanti, e della Cappella Reale: E l'invenzione delle Scene del Signor Giacomo Bonavía Pittore, ed Architetto di S. M. e della Chiesa Metropolitana di Toledo Primata delle Spagne. / /

MUTAZIONI DELLE SCENE. / NELL'ATTO PRIMO. /
Tempio magnifico di Bacco circondato da Portici, che formano una vastissima Piazza, Bosco dal lato destro, e dal sinistro la Marina di Sciro, nella quali [*sic*] vedonsi due Navi, che s'avvicinano navigando.
Appartamenti Reali.
Stanza deliziosa della Reggia.
NELL'ATTO SECONDO.
Logge terrene adornate di Statue rappresentanti varie imprese d'Ercole. Gran Sala illuminata corrispondente a diversi Appartamenti parimente illuminati, Tavola mel mezzo, credenze all'intorno, Logge nell'alto ripiene di Musici, e Spettatori.
NELL'ATTO TERZO.
Portici della Reggia corrispondente al Mare, Navi poco lontane dalla Riva.
Reggia.
Coro di Baccanti. Coro di Cantori.

(68 pp. Biblioteca Nacional de Madrid, T / 13859)

·As mentioned above, *Achille in Sciro* had been performed in Naples in 1737, with music by Sarri, for the inauguration of the Teatro S. Carlo,[19] and repeated in Rome (1738, Arena), Venice (1739, Chiarini) and Turin (1740, Leo) before reaching Corselli. Unusual respect is paid to Metastasio's original text on the title-page of the

17. Identical with Metastasio's *argomento* as printed in *Tutte le opere*, vol. 1, 2nd edn, pp. 754–5.
18. 'Il signor' and 'La signora' omitted.
19. The performance took place on the day of S. Carlo, 4 November. According to H. Hucke, 'L'*Achille in Sciro* di Domenico Sarri', the singers were Anna Maria Peruzzi (Deidamia), Vittoria Tesi (Achille), Angelo Amorevoli (Ulisse), Giovanni Manzuoli (Licomede), Mariano Nicolini (Teagene), Agata Elmi (Nearco) and Cristofano Rossi (Arcade). The score is in *I-Nc*. Peruzzi's appearance in the same role (Deidamia) in both settings, as well as musical similarities of Corselli's setting with aria incipits given by Hucke, suggest a link between the productions of Madrid and Naples.

libretto (see table 4) – perhaps an effect of Farinelli's influence – and the libretto version used in Madrid could hardly have been more faithful to the original. Apart from occasional recitative modifications, the scenes and entrance arias are exactly concordant with the original until III, 2, where a simile aria is inappropriately added for Arcade ('Pensa a fuggire/quell'augelletto'), conceivably a piece borrowed from a different context. After that, only Nearco's solo scene III, 6 is cut, and Teagene has an added aria in III, 7 instead ('Con tromba d'or la Fama'), with an obviously celebratory function. The original final chorus and *licenza* is understandably replaced by another, in praise of the Bourbonic fleur-de-lys.

The dramatic subject of *Achille in Sciro*, derived from Homer and often treated by Baroque dramatists, is the discovery of Achilles among the young girls of the court of Skyros, where he had been hidden in female disguise by his mother Thetis, for fear of an oracle predicting his death before Troy. A Greek delegation, led by Ulysses, arrived from Troy following another oracle predicting that without Achilles the campaign could not be won, and suggesting his hiding-place. The delegation was able to arouse Achilles's masculine enthusiasm over a show of splendid weapons, thus inducing him to reveal his identity. Achilles had secretly been betrothed to the king's young daughter Deidamia and was allowed to marry her, but immediately afterwards he had to join the Greek fleet to conquer Troy.

The suitability of the subject for a dynastic wedding was surely seen in the clichés of male-female behaviour and, to some extent, the conflicts of interest between the sexes, as Deidamia's fear of losing Achilles to a military career and early death in war is known to have been justified. The ethical conflict between love and glory threatens a loving couple; but the young husband's wish to go to war is unstoppable. The matter of the female disguise had served seventeenth-century librettists with welcome opportunities of *double entendre*, and even the Arcadian poet Carlo Sigismondo Capeci wrote on this subject a *Tetide in Sciro* (Rome 1713, music by D. Scarlatti), in which three characters wear the clothes of the opposite sex, one in a compounded double disguise (man = woman = man). Metastasio's drama[20] sheds some of these elements now considered in bad taste, but he still makes Prince Teagene fall in love with the disguised hero. He emphasizes classical motives relating to Achilles's youth and upbringing; the adolescent couple is much tested for mutual honesty, solidarity and trustworthiness. The tasks and dangers of adolescence are repeatedly articulated by Achilles's tutor Nearco. This character replaces the young hero's mythical teacher, the centaur Chiron, who instructed him in music.

The central and critical scene is a musical celebration, during which Achilles exhibits his skills in playing the *cetra* and singing love-songs in response to a chorus. A fake attack of enemies on the royal hall – arranged by Ulysses – changes these

20.   The idea was based, according to the poet's notes, on fable XCVI of Hyginus; see Pietro
        Metastasio, *Tutte le opere*, ed. by Bruno Brunelli, 2nd edn (Milan: Mondadori, 1953–65), vol. 1,
        p. 1501. An Italian dramatic predecessor besides Capeci's drama may have been Ippolito
        Bentivoglio's *Achille in Sciro* (Ferrara, 1663). See also H. Hucke, 'L'*Achille in Sciro* di Domenico
        Sarri', pp. 25–7.

Example 3a. Corselli, *Achille in Sciro* II, 9 (Madrid, 1744): aria of Achille

musical sounds into a 'grande strepito d'armi e di stromenti militari' (II, 7), leading to Achilles's 'discovery'. Thus the poet evokes the traditional antithesis of 'sounds of love' versus 'sounds of war', as Monteverdi had formulated it in his 'Madrigali guerrieri ed amorosi' (1638). In the opera, the initial chorus of this scene, 'Lungi lungi fuggite fuggite/Cure ingrate, molesti pensieri', is set by Corselli with straight trumpets (*trombe lunghe*) and in a heroic idiom. Achilles's love-song, 'Se un core annodi', is a simple minuet accompanied by *lira, o mandolino* and *mandolino, o viola d'amore*. The military music of *trombe, e timbali* which accompanies Achilles's change of mind is not entirely unlike the first chorus, thus making the whole scene appear almost cyclic. A crisis of conscience for Achilles immediately follows, as his newly-found vocation conflicts with his growing remorse for abandoning Deidamia. For the moment, he casts his doubts aside by entrusting Nearco with a soothing message to his bride, 'Dille che si consoli'. The serene minuet character of this

Example 3b. Johann Adolf Hasse, *Artaserse* II, 2 (Venice, 1730): aria of Arbace

aria in Corselli's setting links up with 'Se un core annodi' and emphasizes the courtly conventionality of the whole event, making it seem a prearranged departure to a well-planned war. At the same time, there is a strong musical allusion to other arias beginning with 'Digli' or 'Dille' – for example Cleofide's deeply-felt message 'Digli ch'io son fedele' in Metastasio's *Alessandro nell'Indie*, as set by Leonardo Vinci in 1730.[21] Minuet arias by Hasse can also be cited as models for this melody, for example 'Lascia cadermi in volto' in his *Artaserse* (1730). (See music examples 3a and 3b.)

The flavour of *Achille in Sciro* strongly differs from that of *Farnace*, which had been a violent, gripping drama, set in the historic struggles between Rome and the East, and which barely avoided a tragic ending. Here, the nucleus of the action was an aesthetically slightly ambiguous but pleasing scene of gender revelation, adorned with the trappings of the softer side of a mythical culture. Just as the story had descended from ancient poetry, so the luxurious stage-sets could perhaps be related back to newly-recovered Roman frescoes or Greek vase paintings. Music and femininity really dominate Metastasio's dashing Achilles; the other characters are emblems of human generosity, spontaneity or cleverness. Stage-sets such as 'appartamenti reali', 'portici', 'tempio magnifico', 'riva di mare', 'sala illuminata', and the choruses of 'baccanti' and 'cantori', deliberately turned the performance

21.   See R. Strohm, *Essays on Handel*, pp. 242–5.

into a feast for the eye and ear, even before the vocal virtuosos are considered. The
blending of a real wedding feast and its theatrical enactment was near perfect, from
the opening banqueting choruses to the heraldic *licenza*.

The singers on this occasion, unlike those of the 1739–40 season, had little to do
with Italian opera houses of the time. All but two of them are identified in the
libretto as members of the Royal Chapel or Household; among them we find our old
acquaintances Anna Peruzzi and Elisabetta Uttini, neither of whom seems to have
been back in Italy since 1739. There is no *primo uomo*; the only castrato in the cast,
Francesco Giovannini (soprano), is given the secondary role of Nearco. Apparently
unknown in Italian circuits were the sopranos Emanuella Trombetta (Teagene) and
Costanza Mancinelli (Arcade). The most intriguing figure is the soprano Maria
Heras, who in the soprano role of Achilles was presumably a sight to watch, even if
Achilles, in turn, is disguised as a woman for much of the play. Anna Peruzzi, as
'his' youthful bride Deidamia, was now perhaps in her forties. The Royal Chapel
singer Antonio Montagnana had experienced a brilliant career as one of the rare
lyrical basses of the age, much favoured by Porpora, Handel and Hasse. He was now
past his prime. The role of a slightly slow-witted but extremely benign father and
king in this most enlightened and peaceful reign ever invented by Metastasio must
have suited him perfectly. The contralto Uttini was probably ideal in the role of
Ulisse, a discreet, grey-bearded officer who in reality pulls all the strings.[22]

Corselli's setting, much more assured and inventive than that of *Farnace*, meets
the challenge of the apparently well-chosen cast. He somehow finds music for each
of these singers that makes him or her seem ideally suited to the role. Thus the
poet's dramatic characters are presented as musical entities as well. For example,
the youthful enthusiasm and touch of acerbity in the behaviour of Deidamia and
'Pirra' (=Achille) is conveyed in several brilliant *spiritoso* arias given to the two
sopranos. The musical idioms are typical of the 'galant style' with its dashing
melodies, sighing cadences and simple accompaniments; but Corselli adds strong,
contrapuntally active basses and often 'interlinear' violin figurations between the
colla parte passages, as seen for example in Deidamia's aria 'Del sen gl'ardori' in I,
14. (See music example 4.)

Deidamia bursts forth in anger over the love protestations of Teagene; although
she is indeed not in love with him (nor he with her), the musical character of her
aria, charged with vitality, seems to betray her very real 'ardour' and 'freedom' of
mind. Achille attempts in the same scene to answer Teagene's urgent questions
('Risponderti vorrei'), but his 'lip freezes' because of love, just as love had previously made him eloquent. In Corselli's setting, the youthful enthusiasm of the
Allegro tempo and the vibrating orchestral background is actually maintained while
the singer gets entangled in harmonic wanderings without resolution. (See music
example 5.)

22. Peruzzi, Uttini, Heras and Giovannini were still employed for *La clemenza di Tito*, produced in
    1747 at the Buen Retiro with music by Corselli, Corradini and Mele.

Example 4. Corselli, *Achille in Sciro* I, 14: aria of Deidamia

Vln I

DEIDAMIA

Del sen gl'ar - do - ri nes - sun mi van - ti,

nes - sun — mi — van - ti, non sof - fro a - mo - ri,

non vo - glio a - man - ti, trop - po — m'è — ca - ra, m'è

ca - ra la li - ber - tà

Example 5. Corselli, *Achille in Sciro* I, 14: aria of Achille

Example 6. Corselli, *Achille in Sciro* II, 6: aria of Nearco

Corselli's tendency towards chromaticism, phrase interruptions and surprise harmonies often achieves happy theatrical effects. Another effective musical portrayal of surprise and confusion is Teagene's 'Chi mai vide altrove ancora' (I, 15), a reaction to the preceding aria which is at the same time an *aria brillante* for the soprano Trombetta. This singer's superbly gestural 'Disse il ver? Parlò per gioco' (II, 12), which concludes the second Act, alternates drumming basses with an intricate *perpetuum mobile* in the second violins. The figurations of this piece are modelled on characteristic Hasse arias, for example 'Così stupisce e cade' in *Artaserse* (1730) and 'Ogni procella infida' in *Demetrio* (1732). With some arias sung by Licomede and Nearco, the composer advances into the field of comedy, as in the amusing description of a half-domesticated lion in II, 6. (See music example 6.)

The object of this simile is, of course, Achille, whose behaviour is compared to that of a young lion controlled only by the name of his mistress (Deidamia). The seemingly naive word-painting and fluent melodiousness might be compared with some of Galuppi's arias. Beyond all the allegories and nature comparisons of Corselli's score, beyond the instrumental and vocal craftsmanship mainly reminiscent of Hasse, there is an atmospheric freshness and optimism about many of these arias that brings Metastasio's figures to pulsating life. This approach to the genre of the *dramma per musica* is an achievement shared with Pergolesi, although Corselli's melodies appear closer in style to the incipient Venetian opera buffa. However this may be, *Achille in Sciro* introduced Spanish audiences to an operatic style which was then the leading one in Europe, and the intense cultivation of Italian opera at the court of Ferdinand VI (1747–58) was partly merited by the examples of the genre which Francesco Corselli had presented to his host country.

Tragédie into *dramma per musica*

6
Apostolo Zeno's *Teuzzone* and its French models

The *dramma per musica* of the late seventeenth and early eighteenth centuries, which to a large part of the educated Italian public represented the only relevant form of literary theatre, has an ambiguous status in modern research. As may be expected, the two main ingredients of the genre – poetry and music – have been investigated quite separately by literary historians on the one hand, and by music historians on the other, and theatre historians have also added their important contribution to aspects of scenography and institutional history of 'Baroque opera'. The problem is not so much that the diverse specialists have concentrated on segments of the phenomenon only, projecting the divisions of the modern university disciplines on to the product of a humanist culture which did not yet separate the arts in this way: that is a problem with which we have to cope everywhere in historical studies, and which interdisciplinary cooperation will help solve. Rather, one must ask whether historians of either literature or music have told the full story of the *dramma per musica* even within their respective fields. When reading recent studies, one gets the impression that literary historians have not always done their best with regard to the *dramma* because they assumed it to be rather a musical subject, whereas music historians have often failed to explain the music while commenting on the presumed incoherence of the librettos. Whatever the difficulties of interpreting an allegedly 'impossible' work of art, the *dramma per musica* between Cavalli and Gluck has been a victim of avoidable misunderstandings. The failure is not only one of failing to recognize artistic merit where it exists (and there *is* good poetry before and outside Metastasio) but also one of misjudging the theatrical and dramatic feasibility of the genre as a whole.

A significant attempt to assess that feasibility, and one that was not hampered by narrow specialism, was Robert S. Freeman's excellent dissertation of 1967 which concluded by characterizing Italian opera around 1675–1725 as 'opera without drama'.[1] According to Freeman, this verdict was shared by some of the

---

1. Robert S. Freeman, *Opera without Drama: Currents of Change in Italian Opera, 1675–1725* (Ann Arbor: UMI Research Press, 1981) (Studies in Musicology, vol. 35); this is a revised version of Freeman's dissertation of 1967.

contemporaries themselves: 'While *opera seria* seems ridiculously stilted and stereotyped to many twentieth-century critics, we should remember that there were many to whom it seemed patently absurd during the 1720s and 1730s.'[2] One may quibble over the respective bias or even competence of some critics of that time, just as one might ask how many modern critics know the genre from live experience. It is more important to remember that the genre developed, in permanent struggle with its critics, into the (legitimate) form of drama which opera is for us today, and that the spoken drama of that age has not escaped similar criticism in the nineteenth and twentieth centuries. It is not just the *dramma per musica*, it is Baroque drama as a whole which deserves a new, sympathetic understanding on the basis of its own preconditions and goals.

One particular step towards such an understanding can be pointed out here: it would be the recognition of the literary status of European drama around 1700, and of the special role of the literary reform movement in Italy that was connected with the Roman Accademia dell'Arcadia and similar circles. Recent researches, above all by Piero Weiss, have opened our eyes to theoretical concepts which were held relevant for all literary theatre including opera, and to the fact that the spoken theatre, especially French 'classical' tragedy of the seventeenth century, had a formative influence on the *dramma per musica*.[3] This may well be a key not only to the theoretical understanding which authors of *drammi per musica* had of their own tasks, but also to their practical decisions. What kind of drama is actually intended when Italian librettists and composers turn French tragedies into Italian operas? Before examining the case of Zeno's libretto *Teuzzone*, we must briefly assess the situation in which most of these artists found themselves.

The libretto reformers of the period around 1700 – Domenico David, Apostolo Zeno, Girolamo Frigimelica-Roberti, Silvio Stampiglia, Pietro Pariati, Antonio Salvi and others – faced two major adversaries. One of them was the bad taste of the Seicento as they saw it: the improbabilities, immoralities, miracles, mixed metaphors and mannerisms of traditional operatic poetry. This was the adversary the reformers had taken on voluntarily, fighting together with other enlightened *letterati* in Italy and France for a return of reason and good taste to the arts. The other adversary arose from their own circles, and perhaps unexpectedly. This was the rigorism and puritanism of the most prominent members of the Accademia dell'Arcadia, such as Giovanni Maria Crescimbeni, and of other famous contemporaries, such as Ludovico Antonio Muratori. In the opinion of these arbiters of taste, the operatic genre was in itself an aberration from the true – classical – traditions of

2. Ibid., p. 255.
3. Piero Weiss, 'Teorie drammatiche e "infranciosamento": Motivi della "riforma" melodrammatica nel primo Settecento', in *Antonio Vivaldi*, ed. by L. Bianconi and G. Morelli, vol. 1, 1982, pp. 273–96; idem, 'Metastasio, Aristotle, and the Opera seria', *Journal of Musicology* 1 (1982), pp. 385–94; Italian version in *Metastasio e il mondo musicale*, ed. by M. T. Muraro (Florence: Olschki, 1986), pp. 1–12; idem, 'Neoclassical Criticism and Opera', in *Studies in the History of Music II* (New York: Broude Bros, 1984), pp. 1–30; idem, 'Baroque Opera and the Two Verisimilitudes', in *Music and Civilization: Essays in Honor of Paul Henry Lang* (New York, 1984), pp. 117–26.

tragedy. Consequently, the *dramma per musica* was the more welcome to them the closer it moved to its own annihilation.[4]

While Muratori's sharp attacks against modern operatic music were somewhat blunted by his ignorance of musical techniques, the recipes given by Crescimbeni could have been quite lethal if actually applied. He advocated the return to the aesthetic of the *favole pastorali* with their pastoral setting (i.e. without change of scenery except for *macchine*), simple conflict (*nodo semplice*), few arias and much recitative, and choruses.[5] The first two suggestions were at least extremely restrictive for the stage, and the 'simple conflict', as opposed to 'double', practically outlawed a tragedy with happy ending, because in this case the hero's fortune had to change twice in the course of the play (see also below). The last two suggestions were particularly far-reaching as they affected the business of the composer – without mentioning him. Crescimbeni is apparently convinced that a reduction in the number of arias – a process which he sees already under way in 1700, and for which he praises Zeno, among others – will benefit the expression of the affections by giving more scope to recitative. This betrays unfamiliarity with the true state of the art in 1700, when the expressivity of recitative-setting was on the wane, while that of aria-setting was rapidly growing. This tendency, in which librettists and musicians shared efforts, was indeed to outlast all the reforms: the expression of affections (and, as will be argued, of character) was to become almost entirely the task of the aria. But Crescimbeni probably thought that the affections could not be well expressed in music anyway, even in recitative: the less music there was to hinder the verbal communication, the better. As for choruses, they were being promoted by the opponents of opera, who maintained that its invention relied on the mistaken assumption that ancient dramas were sung throughout. Instead, they claimed that the ancients had no music in their dramas except for the choruses. It seemed evident by 1700 that Italian opera could not render them dramatically effective, whereas the *tragédie lyrique* succeeded with its spectacular, formalistic blend of choruses and dances. The call for choruses was, in any case, typical for those Italians who wished to limit the dramatic subject of opera to pastorals and the like.[6]

The dramaturgical restrictiveness of Crescimbeni's proposals is obvious: perhaps a private theatre such as Cardinal Ottoboni's in Rome could live on such a diet, but not a public opera house. The boredom of too much recitative – 'il tedio del

4. On these opinions, see again R. S. Freeman, *Opera without Drama*, pp. 1–54, P. Weiss, 'Teorie drammatiche', especially pp. 286ff.: 'Veramente, la riforma del melodramma era stata l'ultima preoccupazione dei trattatisti dell'Arcadia, i quali, se se ne occuparono, lo fecero piuttosto per accusar il dramma in musica di aver usurpato le scene e per augurarsi che scomparisse per sempre, lasciando il campo libero alle "vere Tragedie, e Commedie recitate senza Musica".' ('To tell the truth, the reform of opera was the least of the concerns of the theorists of the Arcadia, who occupied themselves with the *dramma per musica* – if at all – rather to accuse it of having usurped the stage and to express the hope that it would disappear for good, leaving the field to "true tragedies, and comedies recited without music".')
5. R. S. Freeman, *Opera without Drama*, pp. 13–14, quoting from Crescimbeni's *La bellezza della volgar poesia* (1700).
6. On the dramaturgical problem of choruses, see also the essay on *Tolomeo* in this volume, p. 205.

recitativo' – had been discovered already by the 1620s and has remained a problem in opera ever since. (An example is the fear of Wagner audiences of 'too much narration'.) Operagoers of the early eighteenth century – and that includes the French and English – wanted not more but less recitative. As a whole, Crescimbeni's proposals offered the *dramma per musica* the very medicine that would have killed it.

Now it is true that minor doses of the medicine could be administered with a healthy effect. Not all the pastoral melodramas were as unconvincing and boring as Pietro Ottoboni's *L'amor eroico fra pastori*, which Crescimbeni praised as a model. Zeno's own *Gl'inganni felici* of 1695 borrows the pastoral atmosphere and simple conflict for a *dramma per musica* of particular freshness and humanity.[7] Pastoral themes, and their characteristic kind of stage decoration, were popular throughout this period, and to alternate them with heroic plots was a frequent strategy of impresarios in Italy as well as abroad. Choruses and ballets in the French manner often helped attract the audiences – as can be observed in London, Hamburg or Venice – although they were dangerously expensive. Zeno's *Il Narciso* of 1697, a beautiful piece of pastoral poetry, must have had a healthy effect at least on the author's purse, as it was written on commission for the Margrave of Ansbach. But shortly afterwards, he and most of his fellow librettists must have realized that their artistic and, partly, economic future was threatened by the Arcadian restrictions. To rescue opera by reforming it became the solution advocated by Zeno and other practicians who had to make a living from the theatre.

The escape road open to them was to imitate French spoken drama. This genre, unlike the musical *tragédie lyrique*, had earned the full respect of the classicist critics and had already been accepted on the stages of aristocratic colleges in Bologna and Rome.[8] When modelled after the tragedies of Corneille, Racine and other authors of the classicist tradition, the *drammi per musica* were at least not exposed to the charges of bad taste or improbability. Thus, the model of French classical tragedy not only influenced the Italian libretto reform, it actually helped Italian opera to survive at all – at a time when its alleged degeneration had exposed it to radical, anti-operatic criticism. Several Venetian librettists before Zeno (for example Vincenzo Grimani, Adriano Morselli and Domenico David) had exploited French plays as models for their operatic plots. They had to some extent modified their approaches to dramaturgy and character. The next generation, with Zeno, Antonio Salvi, Girolamo Frigimelica-Roberti and others, increased this tendency. By 1706, Lodovico Antonio Muratori admitted that the *dramma per musica* 'triumphed' over its critics, directing his reproaches more explicitly against the music. He had little choice but to do so, since his own friend Zeno had in the meantime demonstrated that his librettos, when considered without the music, were largely free of the alleged defects.[9]

7.   See Reinhard Strohm, *Die italienische Oper im 18. Jahrhundert* (Wilhelmshaven: Heinrichshofen, 1979), pp. 30–49.
8.   For a survey of the edited translations of plays, see Luigi Ferrari, *Le traduzioni italiane del teatro tragico francese nei secoli XVII–XVIII* (Paris, 1925).
9.   See R. S. Freeman, *Opera without Drama*, pp. 22–4.

On the other hand, the librettist's personal correspondence articulates his misgivings about some of the more bothersome conventions of the *melodramma* (for example the da capo aria), which interfered with his poetic freedom. We shall also find him struggling with the operatic convention of the *lieto fine*, the happy ending which was not the norm, although by no means rare, in French drama. But Zeno's letters also show his great concern for the stage and the actors. It seems that at least with respect to dramaturgical structure, he was an author of much skill and individuality. His genuinely theatrical approach can be demonstrated when we meet one of his 'reform' librettos on its own terms: as a play, inspired by French spoken drama, and intended to have the traditional qualities of tragedy.

Il Teuzzone was premièred at the Regio Ducal Teatro of Milan in the carnival season of 1706, under the *impresa* of the brothers Antonio and Federico Piantanida. Zeno wrote the libretto most probably on commission and for money, although his dedication (which he signed and dated in Venice, 6 January 1706) to the governor of Milan, the Prince of Vaudemont, says that it was written 'per supremo comando di V. A. S.' ('at the highest request of your Lordship'). In other cases, this may imply a more personal service to the dedicatee. We know, however, from Zeno's letter to Federico Piantanida of March 1707, that after that season he and Pietro Pariati were anxiously awaiting their payment for several librettos, both revised and new, which they had written on commission for the same theatre.[10] *Il Teuzzone* of 1706 surely was such a commission as well. Zeno had not worked for Milan before. Most of the singers (who are not named in the libretto) were probably unknown to him, as were the local composers Paolo Magni (who set the first Act) and Clemente Monari (who set the second and third). *Il Teuzzone* may thus be counted among those *drammi* which, according to modern critics, paid little attention to the exigencies of the music. It was also a mercenary job, one of those which the author passes over in silence in his intense literary correspondence of those years with men such as Lodovico Antonio Muratori and Gian Gioseffo Orsi.

Nevertheless, this *dramma per musica* must have been written with some kind of literary and theatrical ambition. It is the very first opera libretto known to me with a Chinese subject, and even endeavours to bring Chinese customs and rituals on the stage. Its plot and characters are drawn from two very famous French tragedies: Jean Racine's *Bajazet* of 1672, and Thomas Corneille's *Le Comte d'Essex* of 1678.[11] A. De Carli, who noticed the strong similarities of *Il Teuzzone* with *Bajazet*, also points to analogous motives found in Thomas Corneille's *Le festin de pierre* and Racine's *Phèdre* while overlooking the link with *Le Comte d'Essex*.[12] These were all successful plays, appearing on the stage not only in France but also in Italy, where

10. Apostolo Zeno, *Lettere di Apostolo Zeno Cittadino Veneziano*, vol. 1, 2nd edn (Venice: Sansoni, 1786), pp. 418–19.
11. The editions used here are, respectively, Jean Racine, *Théâtre complet*, ed. by M. Rat (Paris: Garnier, 1960), and Pierre Corneille, *Œuvres complètes suivies des œuvres choisies de Thomas Corneille* (Paris: Firmin-Didot, 1880), pp. 1717–43.
12. A. De Carli, *L'influence du théâtre français à Bologne de la fin du XVIIe siècle à la grande revolution* (Turin: Chiantore, 1925), pp. 144–7.

at least *Le Comte d'Essex* was also printed in an Italian prose translation.[13] A closer look at Zeno's libretto may show that he did not draw on such influences to demonstrate his literary erudition and impress the private reader – no merit exists in borrowing from well-known plays – but that he aimed at theatrical effect. To this end, he employed the dramatic ideas of others as well as his own.[14]

To 'borrow' dramatic ideas – subjects, characters, scenic prototypes and so on – was of course a very common practice of the time, although perhaps more akin to the histrionic sphere of the commedia dell'arte than to erudite literature.[15] The subject of *Le Comte d'Essex* is special in that it is taken from recent history: the execution of the Earl of Essex by command of Queen Elizabeth in 1601. Popular legend or dramatic invention added a jealousy motive on Elizabeth's part; this is found already in a tragedy on the subject by La Calprenède (1632).[16] In the version by Thomas Corneille, Essex is the lover of Henriette, Duchess of Irton (a fictitious name), lady-in-waiting to the Queen. In order to save him from the effects of the Queen's jealousy once their mutual love is detected, Henriette gives up her lover and marries the Duke of Irton. Essex, a famous war-hero with popular support (this is literary invention, too), besieges the royal palace to prevent the wedding ceremony, but is caught under suspicion of high treason. It is at this point that the drama actually begins – the antecedents are narrated – and it unfolds in a series of tormenting dialogues about the Earl's fate, centering on the changes of mind of the desperate Queen and the stubborn heroism of the protagonist who refuses to ask for mercy. Henriette plays a helpless role in trying to reconcile Elizabeth and Essex; she is even forced to confess to the Queen her former relationship with the Earl, whereupon Elizabeth first breaks out in fury, then forgives (the central scene, III, 4). Although she changes her mind again, the Earl's enemies Cecily and Coban (the latter is not on stage) bring it about that he is finally led to his death while his friends are still interceding with the vacillating Queen. As Johannes Thomas observed,[17] this tragedy earned its popular success as well as professional criticism by placing all the leading characters in a lamentable position from which there is no escape: the effort to cause *attendrissement* overrides the quest for *horreur*, as the outcome is relatively certain. There is no catastrophe as required by Aristotelian theory since the hero is unhappy from beginning to end, but the faint hopes of his friends and the audience for a last-minute change of fortune are kept alive over five Acts.

Some aspects of the subject matter and of character had already occurred in Jean Racine's *Bajazet*, given in Paris six years before. Roxane, Bajazet and Atalide

13. *Il Conte d'Essex: Tragedia di Tomaso Cornelio Francese* (Bologna: Longhi, 1701).
14. Details of the following description are based on the second version of the libretto, performed in Venice in 1708 (1707 *more veneto*) with music by Antonio Lotti, which was authenticated by Zeno and printed in vol. 4 of his *Poesie drammatiche* (Venice: Pasquali, 1744), pp. 357–444. A few differences between the Milan and Venice versions will be outlined below.
15. The Essex-drama was, in fact, known in Italy also as a *scenario* for comedians: see Vittorio Viviani, *Storia del Teatro Napoletano* (Naples: Guida, 1969), p. 190.
16. Further on the history of the subject and on the various plotlines, see chapter 15 in this volume, 'The Earl of Essex', pp. 294–305.
17. Johannes Thomas, *Studien zu einer Poetik der klassischen französischen Tragödie (1673–1678)* (Frankfurt/M.: Klostermann, 1977) (Analecta Romanica, 38), pp. 230ff.

correspond rather closely to Elizabeth, Essex and Henriette, although precisely in the matter of 'character' there are striking differences as well. The same will later be observed in *Il Teuzzone*. The plotlines of the three plays are related in some ways, in others not: only very few scenes can be said to 'correspond' (in words or actions) when the plotlines of two or all three plays are aligned with each other.

The inescapable problem of deciding what are *significant* connections between individual plays, and what are merely the results of a common tradition, has probably deterred many scholars from such comparative studies in European drama. Those who have dared affirm 'borrowings' from older dramas, for example in Metastasio, have been criticized for overstating their case.[18] But comparisons are necessary, or at least useful, if one wants to understand what the author has actually done. The safest method to identify significant connections must be to compare like with like as much as possible, and I suggest that the knowledge of contemporary dramatic theory can help in this regard. The various categories or 'ingredients' from which a drama is made up, called by Pierre Corneille the 'parties intégrantes', should be examined one by one. They are, according to Corneille and the Aristotelian tradition, in descending order of importance (from left to right):

sujet	mœurs	sentiments	diction	musique	décoration
subject	ethos	pathos	diction	music	stage-sets
	character	affections	poetry		

Although some scholars tend to identify 'subject' with 'plot', this is not exactly what Aristotle or indeed Corneille meant: for them, the 'actions' or 'événements', i.e. the incidents, are a matter of course and not structurally fundamental to a play; they are indeed 'incidental'. We shall follow this suggestion and examine 'plot' only in so far as it results from, or helps explain, the more basic categories of subject, character and affections. It is advisable to concentrate at first on these more basic categories, without going into more detail, because they already demonstrate how the plays relate to each other and how Zeno's opera libretto responds to the dramatic tradition. The other three categories, in relation to which the function of music in opera also comes under scrutiny, will occupy us in the following chapter.

Bajazet and *Le Comte d'Essex* are somewhat analogous with regard to subject, or *azione principale* as Metastasio called it. Bajazet meets his death because of the jealous passion of Roxane, Essex because of that of Elizabeth. At first glance, the same seems to apply to Teuzzone and Zidiana, except that an added reversal of fortune (catastrophe) saves life and throne for Teuzzone and leads to the *lieto fine*. The two French plays lack a catastrophe in the sense that no reversal of fortunes takes place. The question arises whether Zeno's happy ending is only an action or event 'stuck on' to the plot of a tragedy, or determined by subject, character or affections and thus anchored within the dramatic structure. The latter is the case, as will be shown from the characters of Zidiana and Teuzzone: the librettist has

---

18.   On this problem, see also P. Weiss, 'Teorie drammatiche'.

5. Pierre Corneille (1606–84);
engraving by Michel Lasne.

differentiated them from their models in Racine and Thomas Corneille in order to
arrive at a satisfactory happy ending. By doing so, he complied with the theoretical
precept of tragedy, which refuses the *deus ex machina* and similar expedients such as
the sudden conversion of a villain, requiring the reversal to be dramatically 'necessary' and therefore probable (*nécessaire; vraisemblable*). Zeno's *azione principale* is
not the same as in the other two plays: it is rather 'the victory of Teuzzone's
constancy over the jealous passions and death-threats of Zidiana'.

Another question is the role of the *setting*, different in all three plays. One is
inclined to rank the Turkish, English or Chinese settings of these plays with the
category of *décoration*, implying that they have very little influence on the plot and
none on the subject or characters. *Le Comte d'Essex* is indeed a drama which could
take place in any monarchic realm, whether recent, ancient or invented.[19] With
Corneille's neutrality of setting contrasts Racine's drama, where the mysterious,
oppressive atmosphere of the Turkish *sérail* greatly enhances the tragic effect. But
this play, too, is based on allegedly true events of recent history. Racine says in the

19.   Antonio Salvi, when turning this tragedy into his opera libretto *Amore e maestà* in 1715, transferred
      the setting to ancient Persia: see chapters 8 and 9.

preface: 'Quoique le sujet de cette tragédie ne soit encore dans aucune histoire imprimée, il est pourtant très véritable. C'est une aventure arrivée dans le sérail, il n'y a pas plus de trente ans.'[20] Thus, the subject is almost sensational, and exotic enough to avoid immediate falsification. Nevertheless, Racine was subsequently criticized for having misrepresented Turkish customs – which confirms the impression that he exploited the exotic setting for purposes of character and plot according to his own imagination. *Bajazet*, despite its bold claim on historical verity, is far more *vraisemblable* than *vrai*. Zeno must have known about these controversies when he decided to remove the play to the farthest end of the world, so that his plot was sheltered from any criticism, whether in the name of truth or of verisimilitude. But he imitated Racine's sensationalism in reporting unheard-of events from exotic lands, endeavoured to add a touch of mystery, and introduced supposedly authentic Chinese customs. He explains them at length in his *argomento*, referring to a historical source. Eight different customs are quoted in the Milanese libretto of 1706, seven in the Venetian libretto of 1707 (i.e. 1708). The omitted custom is that the colour of mourning among the Chinese was white. White decorations, in fact, play a significant role in the stage version of Milan. This is clearly a case of a purely theatrical idea, which Zeno added or omitted according to the circumstances.

Another of these customs is that the Chinese emperors were not automatically succeeded by their oldest surviving heirs. This necessitates a written will of the former emperor Troncone in favour of Teuzzone, his son. Troncone's widow Zidiana, with the help of her suitors Cino and Sivenio, forges the will in her own favour. The *lieto fine* is almost guaranteed when Cino changes his mind and reveals the forgery and the true will. In such an intricate way is a supposed Chinese custom used for plot construction, even affecting the subject itself. Another custom described in the *argomento* and used in the play is the festival of the 'White Mare' on May Day. During this festival – a magnificent scene – the supporters of Teuzzone hide themselves within the wooden structure of the horse (like the Greeks at Troy) to take Zidiana and her soldiers by surprise. This action is technically not necessary for the reversal of fortunes, as Teuzzone's right to the throne is also revealed to the people by the repenting Cino. Zeno needed the scene for two purposes: first, as one of the two purely scenic effects with Chinese flavour – the other is the grand funeral of Troncone in the first Act – and secondly, to add credibility to his solution to the conflict, because otherwise the victory of good over evil would only have been brought about by the repenting villain, which might have been considered an improbability (*inverosimile*).

Unlike Racine, however, Zeno does not combine exoticism with character. None of his figures has traits like the cruelty of Roxane or the mysterious *grandeur* of Acomat. The character, or ethos, of the three leading figures is as sharply and simply defined as in *Le Comte d'Essex*. Nevertheless, our proposed distinction between pathos and ethos may clarify how Zeno again combined elements of his two models. From the point of view of the passions, the leading figures in the love

20. J. Racine, *Théâtre complet*, p. 354.

triangles of all three plays experience much the same things, although Atalide is the only one of the young lovers who also experiences jealousy. Her counterpart in the opera libretto, Zelinda, is the least tragic character and attracts almost no pity – as do the impulsive Atalide and the utterly helpless Henriette. This is mainly because Zelinda displays other means than self-sacrifice to help herself and her lover: political prudence, for example. Her ethos of 'love beyond death' is toned down to give more prominence to that of Teuzzone: glory above love and love above life. Why is Teuzzone almost a blueprint of Essex, whereas Zelinda is far less admirable or lamentable than Henriette? The answer is, probably, again the *lieto fine*, which in order to be believable requires at least one positive character to have some survival skills. Zidiana, by contrast, must be both villainous (as is Roxane) and inefficient (as is Elizabeth). This was Zeno's most difficult task. He accomplished it by emphasizing the illegitimacy of Zidiana's power (the forged will), whereas the power of Roxane is that of a Sultan's rightful *favourite*. Both women have the ethos of the usurper (neither is nobly born) and do not suffer from conflicts between their passions and their glory as does Elizabeth, whose ethos *is* glory. But Zidiana is also unsuccessful because she vacillates like Elizabeth, whereas Roxane's determination is successful in bringing about Bajazet's death as well as her own – a terrifying triumph.

In all three plays, the ethos of the three leading figures is tested not only through adverse events and villainous intrigue, but also through subtler conflicts. That the lovers conceal their understanding from the woman in power is to some extent excusable. It does remain a problem for Bajazet, who out of love for Atalide consents to dissimulate but does it badly. It is an enormous problem for Henriette, who goes as far as marrying another man to cover for Essex. Actually, it is her second such attempt, as she has previously told the Queen that Essex was in love with another woman, thus diverting the Queen's jealousy; but she feels guilty for her deception. In *Bajazet* and *Teuzzone* the dissimulation is more excusable since it deceives a villain. But Zeno divides good and evil even more sharply: unlike the sincere Roxane, whom Bajazet hesitates to deceive, Zidiana has contrived the most odious deceit herself, the forging of her husband's will. This makes the behaviour of Zelinda (and Teuzzone) so utterly excusable that, on the other hand, they risk losing the spectators' interest. They are also more successful in pursuing their own interests. In the French plays, the lovers' secret is uncovered against their will, and when they least expect it. Henriette simply has to tell the truth once the Queen generously announces that she will give up Essex and allow him to marry that 'other woman'. Atalide is forced to confess by an insidious stratagem of Roxane. Both these events are total defeats for the young heroines. Zelinda, however, succeeds in leading Zidiana by the nose until a last encounter in Teuzzone's prison cell, when victory for him is already under way: now she voluntarily reveals the secret in belated heroism.

A subtler motive, present in all three plays, is used to test the finer shadings of the *mœurs*. It could be called the 'marriage obstacle' between the hero and the woman in power. In Racine's drama, the custom of the Ottoman Sultans of never marrying their *favourites* serves Bajazet – the heir to the throne – as an excuse not to marry

Roxane. This somewhat taints his character, as it must be presumed that he would not hesitate to marry Atalide. Bajazet is punished for this falsehood, as it alerts the shrewd Roxane to the true state of things. Elizabeth is guilty of considering either a *mésalliance* with Essex or, worse, a secret love-affair. She is severely punished by losing him altogether and being exposed. Zidiana, whose marriage to Troncone had been concluded but not yet consummated when he died in battle, does not behave incorrectly when she considers marrying her stepson Teuzzone. But he, like Bajazet, holds the marriage obstacle against her to cover himself. The difference is that Teuzzone does not know Zidiana's true status and thus believes in the marriage obstacle. The contrived situation, in which both partners are fully excused, may again show how Zeno did not want to risk putting his heroes in doubt. The marriage obstacle is a motive of *bienséances* rather than ethos (as far as the two can be distinguished); we see Zeno here anxiously observe a correctness which Racine in his later plays, as well as Thomas Corneille, had all but abandoned. It may be said in general that Zeno's model for character treatment lay rather in the tragedies of Pierre Corneille (after *Le Cid*).

The desire to whitewash his heroes also forces the librettist to assemble the more interesting affections around the villainous figures. Zidiana practises deceit also in love, when she promises her hand (and the throne) to both her suitors at the same time. Two curiously choreographed arias with 'double *a parte*' arise from this. This scenic effect is also known from Thomas Corneille's comedy *Le festin de pierre* and was frequent in the *dramma per musica*. But here it is a theatrical, not a musical expedient. Almost as if excusing himself for this trivial motive, Zeno makes it work for the plot: because of the woman's double game, Cino becomes disaffected and decides to expose her fraud. Again, Zidiana is punished by her own falsehood, and the change of mind of the villain, which leads to the happy ending, is made more believable. That Cino's moral development and conflicting passions make for interesting monologues (with arias) is a welcome side-effect. Cino's rival Sivenio remains true to his villainy, and the growing jealousy between the two men – caused by Zidiana – generates further emotional situations, arias, and almost a duel. The direct models for Cino and Sivenio are the courtiers Cecily and Coban in *Le Comte d'Essex*, who are responsible for the Earl's hurried execution. But Coban does not even appear on stage, and Cecily does not cut an impressive figure. Zeno has developed these instruments of the plot into representatives of negative affections and companions of the seductive Zidiana. This also throws Teuzzone's constancy into relief.

The affections of Teuzzone and Zelinda are also developed beyond those displayed by Essex and Henriette. What Zeno loses, dramaturgically, by purifying their ethos in comparison with Bajazet and Atalide, he gains by adding situations of hope, repeated farewells, moments of happiness. This is mainly done by devoting much of the first Act to events which in the French plays are only narrated prehistory. We know from other dramas turned into operas that the musical genre thrives on direct scenic representation instead of narration. But Zeno's first Act is also needed to satisfy Aristotelian theory. It shows the death of Troncone, the (false) tears of his widow Zidiana, the original happy state of the lovers Teuzzone and

6. Jean Racine (1639–99); pen
and wash portrait by his son
Jean-Baptiste.

Zelinda, the intrigue and rise to power of Zidiana, and consequently the transformation of the rightful heir Teuzzone into an angry rebel, who must now risk his life to
regain his position. All this is theatrically very effective and balances the happy
ending. If the libretto had started with the hero already defeated or in prison (as
does *Le Comte d'Essex*, and the opening situation in *Bajazet* is not much happier),
the only reversal of fortune for the hero would be from unhappiness to happiness –
which is not admissible for a tragedy. The only way Zeno can have his *lieto fine* and
yet maintain a semblance of tragedy is a plot with a *double catastrophe* as here
(recalling, again, some plays by Pierre Corneille). The shock of seeing Teuzzone
suddenly ousted from his heritage – in a great ceremonial scene, I, 11 – has to
generate most of the audience's sympathy with the hero. It also provides him with
the negative affections of anger and hatred which Essex had already left behind
when the play began.

In our brief survey of subject, ethos and pathos of this *dramma per musica*, we have explained the analogies with its models as intentional 'borrowings' of Zeno, and the differences as intentional modifications or complications satisfying contemporary theory under the conditions of a *lieto fine*. At the same time, these modifications aimed at greater theatrical effect and diversity. *None* of Zeno's decisions requires the justification that the drama is written for music. He neither borrows from Racine where that author is at his most emotional, nor from Thomas Corneille where his figures are most lamentable (as in the various scenes with Elizabeth or Henriette). With his more anxious separation of good and evil, and his observation of the *bienséances*, Apostolo Zeno is an even more orthodox tragedist than his two forerunners. But above all, every bit of this drama is designed for presentation on stage. This must be kept in mind when the functions of poetry, music and stage decoration have to be assessed.

7
Antonio Vivaldi's setting of *Teuzzone*: dramatic speech and musical image

The French – and Aristotelian – classical tradition assigned to music the role of a mere helper of the poetic *diction*, inferior to all other ingredients of the drama except the stage decoration (see chapter 6). According to such a view of drama, music might have to express nothing but the formal elements of the poetry, as was to some extent the case in the *tragédie lyrique*. In the Italian tradition, however, music had always taken care of the *affetti* – however formalized – in recitative as well as in rhymed poetry. And poetry, even dramatic poetry, naturally accommodated itself to the sister art. Whereas the native tradition demanded that poetry and music should cooperate in the expression of the affections, the French tragedists controlled them with verbal means alone.

By imitating French spoken drama, the reform librettists around Apostolo Zeno earned the respect of their critics – as well as their own self-esteem as poets – at a high price. What was now to be the role of the music when the libretto behaved like a spoken play, complete in itself? In so far as Zeno's reform librettos functioned as convincing stage plays on the levels of subject and character, a division between dramatic structure and musical clothing would perhaps have been conceivable. Music could have resigned itself to illustrating the 'lower-ranking' dramatic ingredients – affections, poetry and perhaps stage decoration[1] – yet when a monologue which Zeno put in the mouth of his hero was a convincing expression of the dramatic situation as well as the affections, added music might be regarded as superfluous. To start with, a heroic or tragic monologue might be considered an *inverosimile* when performed as an aria.[2] As described above, Zeno's librettos are tailored to the needs of the stage and the actors: he planned his plays as a true practician of the theatre. But what tasks did he reserve for music to fulfil? Did he perhaps design his language according to its exigencies? It has sometimes been claimed that Zeno's aria texts were only pretexts to accommodate the music at the ends of scenes, but superfluous or extraneous to the dramatic discourse. On closer

---

1. Stage decoration was often musically illustrated in seventeenth-century opera, for example in pastoral scenes or in musical depictions of sea-storms, battles, ceremonies or other spectacles.
2. This problematic effect (which we might call the 'trap of verisimilitude') occupied many critics in the following decades. See P. Weiss, 'Baroque Opera and the Two Verisimilitudes'.

7. Apostolo Zeno, *Teuzzone*, music by Antonio Vivaldi (Mantua, 1719); title-page of the libretto.

inspection, however, they often fit so closely into the dramatic context that the musical settings given to them may appear superfluous. Even more importantly, the way in which Zeno's recitatives are musical has never been described. When he imitates French spoken dialogues, we may have a chance of comparing how he deviates from them to conform to the conditions of musical recitation. It may also be asked what a composer will do with Zeno's dramatic speech.

Zeno's dilemma was genuine: although an accomplished dramatic poet, he needed the musical theatre for a living, and we know that he did not intend his librettos to be performed without music.[3] Zeno's *Teuzzone* was created for, and

3. Nor did Metastasio: the various assertions that these *drammi* were successful on the stage without music were partly mere flattery (to which Metastasio succumbed), partly caused by exceptional circumstances. In the Habsburg dominions in the 1750s and 1760s, some civic theatres performed librettos by Zeno, Metastasio and others as spoken plays (alongside genuine spoken plays), because sung recitative was reserved for the Hof- and Burgtheater. See also Helga Lühning, '*Titus*'-*Vertonungen im 18. Jahrhundert: Untersuchungen zur Tradition der Opera seria von Hasse bis Mozart* (Laaber: Arno Volk – Laaber Verlag, 1983) (Analecta Musicologica, 20), p. 2, n. 4.

depends on, the musical stage. The Venetian version of carnival 1708, set by Antonio Lotti, was accepted by the poet himself for publication in his *Poesie drammatiche* of 1744. This version was given at the Teatro San Cassiano, a theatre where Zeno may have collaborated with the composer and even the singers in order to make the numerous text changes for this performance. Unfortunately, Lotti's score does not survive. (Of the Milan setting, only some arias are extant.)

The earliest extant setting of the libretto which is complete with recitatives is Antonio Vivaldi's *Teuzzone*, given at the Teatro Arciducale, Mantua, in the carnival of 1719.[4] It is not an original setting of the complete drama, but largely a pasticcio drawn from earlier arias by Vivaldi. Nevertheless, the circumstances (Vivaldi's position at the court) suggest that he tried to give his best, and the re-use of existing music – a widespread practice at the time – did not necessarily weaken the drama. Many textual alterations to the version of 1708 were necessary, of course, including the writing of parody texts. It appears that Vivaldi's libretto version of 1719 was based directly on the Venetian libretto of 1708, although several other librettos, including one of another *Teuzzone*, were used as sources for the aria texts: see table 5 (p. 137 below), which is a synopsis of Zeno's *Teuzzone* of 1708 and Vivaldi's of 1719; table 6 (p. 139 below) traces the arias of 1719 to their previous appearances. In the Mantuan version, as in several other *Teuzzone* librettos of the time, Zeno's aria texts are largely replaced by different poetry. This is to some extent a verdict on the poor singability of his verse; but more generally it reflects changes of operatic taste which had occurred between 1708 and 1719. We shall use a few examples from Vivaldi's score to investigate the contribution of music to drama, taking a case where not only the model libretto is available, reworked for the composer, but also the model tragedies, elaborated by the poet (see the previous chapter).

The role of dramatic speech is the central issue. On a linguistic and rhetorical level, the Aristotelian claim that music should be a helper of *diction* could well be found valid. Vocal music had long learned to serve rhetorical ends, and to behave almost like formalized speech itself. Musical analogies have been identified for various classes of rhetorical procedures and figures: 'figures of speech' (for example *repetitio*) as well as 'figures of thought' (for example *hyperbole, exaggeratio*).[5] Italian music around 1700 was perfectly suited to support the rhetorical structures erected in the libretto, but theatrical speech is more than rhetoric, it is also 'speech-act', and this draws our attention to the relationship between speech, music and stage character.[6] To what extent does music permit the singer of an aria or a recitative to

4. The following sources exist: a partially autograph score (*I-Tn*, Foà 33, fol. 1–142), a contemporary copy (*D-B*, N. Mus. MS 125) and an autograph copy of the sinfonia (*I-Tn*, Giordano 36, fol. 293–8). For a synopsis of the musical incipits, see Eric Cross, *The Late Operas of Antonio Vivaldi, 1727–38* (Ann Arbor: UMI research press, 1981), vol. 2, pp. 307–11. The libretto is described in Anna Laura Bellina, Bruno Brizi and Maria Grazia Pensa, *I libretti Vivaldiani: Recensione e collazione dei testimoni a stampa* (Firenze: Olschki, 1982), no. 47

5. See George J. Buelow, 'Rhetoric and Music', in *The New Grove Dictionary of Music and Musicians*, ed. by S. Sadie (London: Macmillan, 1980), vol. 15, pp. 793–803, for an introduction and further literature.

6. For the theory of 'speech-act', see J. Thomas, *Studien zu einer Poetik der klassischen französischen Tragödie*, pp. 20ff.

Table 5. Teuzzone: closed numbers in the versions of 1708 and 1719 (* = borrowed aria)

Act		Zeno, 1708			Vivaldi, 1719	
I	2	TR	Ma già vien meno	1		(Rec.acc.)
	3	ZI	Occhi, non giova il piangere	2	ZI	Alma mia fra tanti affanni (replaced by:) Al fiero mio tormento
					EG	Come suol la navicella*
	4	ZI	Dirò ad altri: mio tesoro	3	ZI	Caro adorato bene (replaced by:) Tu mio vezzoso*?
	5	SI	Puoi dar leggi da soglio	4	SI	In trono assiso*
	6	CI	L'alma godea tranquilla	5	CI	Taci per poco ancora*
	7	ZE-AR	Che amaro tormento	6	ZE-TE	Che amaro tormento (replaced by:) TE Ove giro il mesto sguardo
		ZE-TE	Mi usciria per gran diletto		ZE-TE	Lega pietoso amore
		ZE	Il mio giubilo, il mio orgoglio			
	8	CORO	Dagli Elisi ove gioite	7	CORO	Dagli Elisi ove posate
		CI-SI-TE-CORO	Avello felice			
	9	ZI	Sarai mio (lo dico a te)	8	ZI	Sarò tua regina e sposa*
	10	ZE	Salvatemi il mio sposo	9	ZE	La timida cervetta*
	11	CORO-CI-ZI	O vita o mente	10		Sinfonia
		ZI-TE-SI-CI-CORO	Alma bella		ZI-TE-SI-CI	Alma bella
		TE	Io vassallo? Io giurar fede?		TE	Come fra turbini*
	13	CI	Vassallo alle tue leggi	12	CI	Mi va scherzando in sen*
					SI	Non paventa giammai le cadute*
	15	ZE	Non si serva con mia pena	14	ZE	Ti sento, sì ti sento*
	16	AR	Amante, ch'è costante			
II	1	TE	(Rec.)		TE	Di trombe guerriere
	2	ZE	Morte vuoi? Va pur, crudele			
		TE	Addio cara. Addio, mia sposa		TE	Tornerò, pupille belle*?
	3	ZE	Fido amante – non disperi		ZE	Un'aura lusinghiera*
	7	ZE	Sì facile al tuo amor			
	8		(Rec.)		EG	La gloria del tuo sangue*
	9	ZI	Soffri costante		ZI	Ahi, che sento nel mio core (replaced by:) Vedi le mie catene*?
	11	TE	Tempo è già di armarti			
		TE	Morirò, ma la sentenza		TE	Sì, ribelle, anderò, morirò*
	12	SI	Amor che non ha ingegno		SI	(Se a un amor ch'inalza al regno)* (replaced by:) Non temer, sei giunto*
					CI	Nel suo carcere ristretto*?
	15	ZE	Penso ma mi confondo		ZE	Guarda in quest'occhi e senti*
	17	ZE	Sarà il tuo core		ZI	Ritorna a lusingarmi*?
	18	ZI	Alma amante, io vorrei pace			
III	1	AR	Per te sola il petto forte			
	2			1	CI	Quanto costi al mio riposo
		ZE	Se credi a quel bel labbro		ZE	Con palme ed allori*
	4	ZI	In te mio amore	3	ZI	Sì per regnar-sì per goder*

Table 5. Continued

Zeno, 1708   Vivaldi, 1719

5	CI	Esci di servitù	4	CI	Son fra sirti e fra procelle* (replaced by:) Son fra scogli e fra procelle
			5	SI	Base al regno e guida al trono*?
6	TE	(Rec.)		TE	Antri cupi infausti orrori
7	TE-ZE	Ferma: ascolta . . .	6		
9	TE	Prendi il core in quest'amplesso		TE	Dille ch'il viver mio (2 settings)
10	ZI	Su l'orme del furor	9	ZI	Per lacerarlo, per fulminarlo (replaced by:) Io sembro appunto*
11	ZE	Sposo amato, o tu vivrai	10	ZE	Ho nel seno un doppio ardore
12	CORO	Oggi che nacque il mondo	11	ZI-CI-SI	Liete voi, amiche trombe
15	CORO	Fermezza ha l'altezza	13	CORO	In sen della virtude.

become identified with the dramatic *persona* of the play? To what extent does music 'express' not only verbal structures and meaning but also the actions, affections, and perhaps even the character (ethos), of this *persona*? The question involves, once more, the problem of verisimilitude, because the more convincingly an actor expresses himself in musical sounds, the less probable it is that he 'is' the *persona* of the play.

Dramatic speech in opera is, first and foremost, 'recitative', or whatever its analogies are in the non-Italian traditions of musical theatre. It can also be seen as the equivalent of dialogue or monologue in the spoken theatre. Zeno's relatively faithful adherence to the subjects and, partly, to the characters and affections of the two French tragedies leads us to expect that traces of the original diction will also remain noticeable in his recitatives: there was no formal reason for him to change what the characters said. The verbal substance of his arias may be expected to be much less congruent with the texts of the model plays, because nothing really equivalent to aria-singing happens there.

As it turns out, the relationship between the texts is much more complex. Whereas Zeno treats the subject, characters and affections as an independently-minded dramatic poet, without much regard to the musical performance, the verbal matter undergoes a certain distortion. Here, he seems to be looking in both directions simultaneously: to his literary models and to his singers and composer. One of the reasons for this is, of course, that the relationship between speech and *time* is different in music; but this is not all. While, strangely enough, many of Zeno's arias inherit verbal matter from the French verse, his recitatives often seem to use different words in a different manner. The musical setting seems to add yet another twist to the transformation, and in some passages Vivaldi's setting of *Teuzzone* cuts the last threads which had connected Zeno's text with those of his predecessors. In other places, significant verbal substance survived the changes.

Table 6. Borrowed arias in *Teuzzone* 1719

The following list includes only the earlier works from which *Teuzzone* material has been derived. The source libretto is placed in round brackets if the corresponding musical version does not survive.

I	2	EG	Come suol la navicella	(*La costanza trionfante* . . . , 1716)
I	3	ZI	Tu mio vezzoso diletto sposo	(probably borrowed: 'Il mio . . .' would fit situation better)
I	4	SI	In trono assiso	(*La costanza trionfante* . . . , 1716)
I	5	CI	Taci per poco ancora	(*Tieteberga*, 1717)
I	6	TE	Ove giro il mesto guardo	(G. M. Orlandini, *Teuzzone*, Genova, S. Agostino 1712, I, 6)[7]
I	8	ZI	Sarò tua regina e sposa	(*L'incoronazione di Dario*, 1717)[8]
I	9	ZE	La timida cervetta	(*La costanza trionfante* . . . , 1716)
I	11	TE	Come fra turbini	*Arsilda* . . . , 1716: Precipitio del mio petto
I	12	CI	Mi va scherzando in sen	*L'incoronazione di Dario*, 1717
I	12	SI	Non paventa giammai	*Orlando finto pazzo*, 1714
I	14	ZE	Ti sento, sì, ti sento	(*La costanza trionfante* . . . , 1716)
II	2	TE	Tornerò, pupille belle	(G. M. Orlandini, *Teuzzone*, Genova, S. Agostino 1712, I, 6)[9]
II	3	ZE	Un'aura lusinghiera	(*La costanza trionfante* . . . , 1716)
II	8	EG	La gloria del tuo sangue	(*Tieteberga*, 1717)
II	9	ZI	Vedi le mie catene	(text perhaps from a *Griselda* opera: Orlandini, *La virtù nel cimento*, Mantua 1717?)[10]
II	11	TE	Sì, ribelle, anderò	*Orlando finto pazzo*, 1714
II	12	SI	Se un amor ch'inalza[11]	(*Tieteberga*, 1717)
II	12	SI	Non temer, sei giunto	(*Nerone fatto Cesare*, 1715)[12]
II	13	CI	Nel suo carcere ristretto	(text does not fit situation)
II	15	ZE	Guarda in quest'occhi	*Ottone in villa*, 1713[13] (music only vaguely related)
II	17	ZI	Ritorna a lusingarmi	Orlandini? *La Merope*, Bologna, 1717 (see main text and n. 10 above)
III	2	ZE	Con palme ed allori	(*Scanderbeg*, 1718)
III	3	ZI	Sì per regnar	(*Tieteberga*, 1717)
III	4	CI	Son fra sirti (1st setting)	*Arsilda* . . . , 1716 Col piacer della mia fede cfr. also RV 94
III	4	SI	Base al regno	(possibly borrowed)
III	10	ZI	Io sembro appunto	*Ottone in villa*, 1713.

7. Probably only a text borrowing.
8. I owe my knowledge of this earlier use of the aria to a kind communication from Prof. John Hill. For his computer-assisted research on verbal matches between Vivaldi arias, see John Hill, 'A Computer-based Analytical Concordance of Vivaldi's Aria Texts: First Findings and Puzzling Questions about Self-Borrowing', in *Nuovi studi vivaldiani: Edizione e Cronologia Critica delle Opere*, ed. by Antonio Fanna and Giovanni Morelli, 2 vols (Florence: Olschki, 1988), pp. 511–34.
9. Probably only a text borrowing.
10. Unlike the case of 'Ritorna a lusingarmi', the setting of 'Brami le mie catene' in Vivaldi's own *Griselda* of 1735 is musically related. Therefore, Vivaldi either borrowed in 1719 only the text, or he reused an aria which he himself had composed for Orlandini's *Griselda*.
11. Textless fragment; borrowing identifiable through further reuse in *Giustino* 1724.
12. Identification by Prof. John Hill (see above).
13. Identification by Prof. John Hill (see above).

Text example 1: Jean Racine, *Bajazet* (II, 5)

ATALIDE

Non, seigneur, Vos bontés pour une infortunée
Ont assez disputé contre la destinée.
Il vous en coûte trop pour vouloir m'épargner:

> Il faut vous rendre; il faut me quitter et régner.
>
> BAJAZET
> Vous quitter!
> ATALIDE
>   Je le veux. Je me suis consultée.

1

De mille soins jaloux jusqu'alors agitée,
Il est vrai, je n'ai pu concevoir sans effroi
Que Bajazet pût vivre et n'être plus à moi;
Et lorsque quelquefois de ma rivale heureuse
Je me représentais l'image douloureuse,
Votre mort (pardonnez aux fureurs des amants)
Ne me paraissait pas le plus grand des tourments.
Mais à mes tristes yeux votre mort préparée
Dans toute son horreur ne s'était pas montrée:
Je ne vous voyais pas, ainsi que je vous vois,
Prêt à me dire adieu pour la dernière fois.
Seigneur, je sais trop bien avec quelle constance
Vous allez de la mort affronter la présence;

> Je sais que votre cœur se fit quelques plaisirs
> De me prouver sa foi dans ses derniers soupirs;
> Mais, hélas! épargnez une âme plus timide;
> Mesurez vos malheurs aux forces d'Atalide;

2

Et ne m'exposez point aux plus vives douleurs
Qui jamais d'une amante épuisèrent les pleurs.

BAJAZET

Et que deviendrez-vous, si, dès cette journée,
Je célèbre à vos yeux ce funeste hyménée?

ATALIDE

Ne vous informez point ce que je deviendrai.
Peut-être à mon destin, seigneur, j'obéirai.
Que sais-je? A ma douleur je chercherai des charmes.
Je songerai peut-être, au milieu de mes larmes,
Qu'à vous perdre pour moi vous étiez résolu;
Que vous vivez; qu'enfin c'est moi qui l'ai voulu.

BAJAZET

Non, vous ne verrez point cette fête cruelle.

> Plus vous me commandez de vous être infidèle,
> Madame, plus je vois combien vous méritez
> De ne point obtenir ce que vous souhaitez.

3

Quoi! cet amour si tendre, et né dans notre enfance,
Dont les feux avec nous ont crû dans le silence;
Vos larmes que ma main pouvait seule arrêter;
Mes serments redoublés de ne vous point quitter:
Tout cela finirait par une perfidie!

J'épouserais, et qui? (s'il faut que je le dic)
Une esclave attachée à ses seuls intérêts,
Qui présente à mes yeux des supplices tout prêts,
Qui m'offre, ou son hymen, ou la mort infaillible;
Tandis qu'à mes périls Atalide sensible,
Et trop digne du sang qui lui donna le jour,
Veut me sacrifier jusques à son amour?
Ah! qu'au jaloux sultan ma tête soit portée,
Puisqu'il faut à ce prix qu'elle soit rachetée!

ATALIDE
Seigneur, vous pourriez vivre, et ne me point trahir.

BAJAZET
Parlez: si je le puis, je suis prêt d'obéir.

4

---

*

Apostolo Zeno, *Teuzzone* (III, 7)

ZELINDA, e TEUZZONE

ZELINDA
[A che mi astringi, amor?] Teuzzone, io vengo . . .

TEUZZONE
Zelinda . . . O Numi! Ed è pur ver, che ancora
E ti miri, e ti abbracci, anima mia?

ZELINDA
Tua più non mi chiamar. Questa si ceda
Sospirata fortuna ad altra amante;
O si ceda piuttosto alla tua vita.
Vivi, e benchè di altrui, vivi felice.

TEUZZONE
Io d'altra?

ZELINDA
       Sì: ben veggio,

1

Che il tuo cor si fa gloria
D'essermi fido ne' respiri estremi
Ma te ne assolvo. Un gran timor tel chiede.
Nulla pavento più, che la tua fede.

2

TEUZZONE
Caro mio ben quanto più m'ami infido,
Tanto meriti più, ch'io sia fedele.

3

Questo è il sol tuo comando,
Che non ha sul mio cor tutto il potere.
Perdonami un error, ch'è gloria mia.
Se non son di Zelinda, io vo' morire.

ZELINDA
Oimè! Viver potresti, e non tradirmi.

TEUZZONE
Parla. Se posso, ubbidirò.

4

Text example 2: Jean Racine, *Bajazet* (II, 5)

> ATALIDE
> La sultane vous aime; et, malgré sa colère,
> Si vous preniez, seigneur, plus de soin de lui plaire;
> Si vos soupirs daignaient lui faire pressentir
> Qu'un jour . . .   5
>
> BAJAZET
> Je vous entends: je n'y puis consentir.

Ne vous figurez point que, dans cette journée,
D'un lâche désespoir ma vertu consternée
Craigne les soins d'un trône où je pourrais monter,
Et par un prompt trépas cherche à les éviter.
J'écoute trop peut-être une imprudente audace;
Mais, sans cesse occupé des grands noms de ma race,
J'espérais que, fuyant un indigne repos,
Je prendrais quelque place entre tant de héros.
Mais, quelque ambition, quelque amour qui me brûle,
Je ne puis plus tromper une amante crédule.

En vain, pour me sauver, je vous l'aurais promis:
Et ma bouche et mes yeux du mensonge ennemis,
Peut-être, dans le temps que je voudrais lui plaire,
Feraient par leur désordre un effet tout contraire;
Et de mes froids soupirs ses regards offensés
Verraient trop que mon cœur ne les a point poussés.

O ciel! combien de fois je l'aurais éclaircie,
Si je n'eusse à sa haine exposé que ma vie;
Si je n'avais pas craint que ses soupçons jaloux
N'eussent trop aisément remonté jusqu'à vous!
Et j'irais l'abuser d'une fausse promesse!
Je me parjurerais! Et, par cette bassesse . . .
Ah! loin de m'ordonner cet indigne détour,
Si votre cœur était moins plein de son amour,
Je vous verrais, sans doute, en rougir la première.
Mais, pour vous épargner une injuste prière,

Adieu; je vais trouver Roxane de ce pas,
Et je vous quitte.

> ATALIDE
> Et moi, je ne vous quitte pas.

Venez, cruel, venez, je vais vous y conduire;
Et de tous nos secrets c'est moi qui veux l'instruire.
Puisque, malgré mes pleurs, mon amant furieux
Se fait tant de plaisirs d'expirer à mes yeux,

Roxane, malgré vous, nous joindra l'un et lautre:
Elle aura plus de soif de mon sang que du votre;
Et je pourrai donner à vos yeux effrayés
Le spectacle sanglant que vous me prépariez.

BAJAZET 6

O ciel! que faites-vous?

ATALIDE

Cruel! pouvez-vous croire
Que je sois moins que vous jalouse de ma gloire?

*

Apostolo Zeno, *Teuzzone* (III, 7)

ZELINDA
Zidiana
T'ama. Dal tuo disprezzo
Nasce il tuo rischio, e il suo furor. Se amarla 5
Non puoi, t'infingi almeno.

TEUZZONE

Finger? No: s'è viltà, manco all'onore:
Se perfidia, all'amore.
Questo non posso, e quel non deggio.

ZELINDA
Il dei,
Se l'ami, e il puoi.

TEUZZONE
Qual frutto
Trarrei da un vile inganno,
Se non morir più tardi, e con più scorno?
T'amo più di me stesso;
Ma più dell'onor mio non posso amarti.

ZELINDA

Crudel! più non si oppone
La mia pietà. Già dal tuo esempio apprendo

Com'esser forte, o disperata. Addio.
Il morir ti si affretti:

Sovra te cada il colpo:
Ma sol non cada. Alla rival feroce
Una vittima accresca anche Zelinda.

TEUZZONE

Ferma . . .
6

ZELINDA
Tu del tuo fato
Arbitro resta: io lo sarò del mio.

L'onor tu ascolta: io l'amor seguo. Addio.

TEUZZONE

Ferma: ascolta . . .

ZELINDA
Tu vuoi morte . . .

TEUZZONE
Cara vita.

ZELINDA
E morte io vo'.
a 2. Ma in te solo io morirò.

TEUZZONE
Deh! mi lascia un cor più forte.

ZELINDA
Tu non hai di te pietà.

TEUZZONE
La tua fè morir mi fa.

ZELINDA
Io pietà di me non ho.

SCENA VIII

ZIDIANA, e li suddetti.

ZIDIANA
Ti arresta.

ZELINDA

[O dei!]

ZIDIANA
Sdegna più lunghi indugi
Il destin di Teuzzone, e l'amor mio.

We shall now give a close reading to a recitative passage. It is taken from a very important scene: the dialogue between Zelinda and Teuzzone in prison (III, 7), where she tries for a last time to persuade him to give in to the advances of Zidiana, who has threatened him with death if he is unwilling. Zelinda herself will be content to give him up if this saves his life. The direct model for the dialogue is Racine's scene 5, concluding Act II, in *Bajazet* where, however, the external situation differs (it is much earlier in the play). The situation in *Le Comte d'Essex*, Act IV, scene 5 (prison scene), corresponds, but is quite differently anchored in the affections since Henriette had long given up her own claims on Essex.

In the text examples 1 and 2 (pp. 140 and 142) the encased and numbered passages of Racine's and Zeno's texts are analogous in content (straight as well as figurative), or form, or both; some lines in nos 2, 3 and 4 represent the closest approximations to Racine in Zeno's whole libretto. The striking difference in length of the two dialogues is typical for the relationship of the two works. Zeno manages entirely without the ample narrations (after nos 1 and 3, for example), the reasoning, arguing and forecasting (after nos 2, 3 and 5). Zeno rejects these detours, probably because they engage too much of the imagination. Perhaps views of the past and the future such as these (and what tearful and gruelling views they are!) seem ineffective or improper to him in recitative. Or it may be that he deliberately impoverishes the dialogue because he wants to save certain effects – for example the tender remembrance of the lovers' youth (after no. 3: 'cet amour si tendre . . .') – for arias. Not many of his aria texts pay tribute to such images, though; it is therefore likely that his reasons for rejecting them in the recitative were either dramaturgical or merely aesthetic.

No. 1

Where Zeno does borrow Racine's argument, his diction is hardly more concise, but he tends to borrow precisely the passages where the declamation seems to speed up or is interrupted. The effect of 'Vous quitter!' is partly due to the quickening of the pace; the preceding line with 'rendre . . . quitter . . . régner' is very ponderous, partly because Atalide suffers pains when speaking these words. Bajazet's reaction is an answer, not an interruption: Atalide has finished her discourse. Zeno imitates exactly this: an even longer, slow and painful discourse of Zelinda (no fewer than four full stops) leads up to 'Vivi . . . felice', which she intends to be her last words to him. The weighty repetition 'vivi . . . vivi' corresponds not in content but in form to 'Il faut . . . il faut'. Teuzzone's 'Io d'altra?' is infinitely weaker than 'Vous quitter!' By refusing to understand, he begs – with the question mark – to be instructed otherwise. Bajazet's incomprehension is absolute. Also, 'quitter' as an active verb is reduced to the weak 'di', indicating the possessive genitive, and, perhaps most importantly, 'vous' (the woman) is replaced by 'Io' (the man). We can guess what matters to Racine and what to Zeno. 'Je le veux . . .': for the serious, heroic reply of Atalide, Zelinda has a curt 'Sì', rushing on to her slightly aggressive argument (a glimpse of her character).

No. 2

The biting irony of this remark seems directed against melodramatic tragedy in general; it is a woman's rebellion against self-destructive male values, often voiced later in Metastasio. Important are the differences of tone between 'quelques plaisirs' and 'gloria', 'plus timide' and 'gran timor', 'mesurez vos malheurs' and 'nulla pavento più': the operatic diction is more extreme, also because the characters are more bluntly designed. Interestingly, Zeno seems to convert 'épargnez une âme' into 'te ne assolvo' – the irony is so much the greater when he, Teuzzone, is treated with lenience. But together with other similar alterations, Zeno's focus on the man rather than on the woman is unmistakable.

No. 3

The paradoxical and ironic relationship between 'command' and 'merit' is essentially a figure of thought, although it also involves the figure of speech

Example 7. Vivaldi, *Teuzzone* III, 6 (Mantua, 1719): recitative Zelinda, Teuzzone

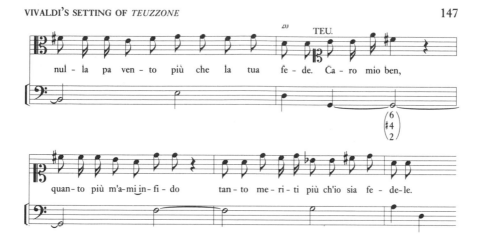

nul - la pa ven - to più che la tua fe - de. Ca - ro mio ben,

quan - to più m'a-mi in - fi - do tan - to me - ri - ti più ch'io sia fe - de-le.

'plus . . . plus' (anaphora). The second member of this parallelism divides again into two sub-members, which form the opposition of thought 'ne point obtenir . . . souhaitez'. This complex statement is simplified in Zeno, who drops the second opposition, but adds the opposition of speech 'ami infido'. This, in turn, sets up the antonymic rhyme 'infido-fedele'. It is one of those structures which Metastasio used so frequently in arias. (Thomas Corneille also emulated Racine's paradox here, in the concise but ugly-sounding line: 'Vous m'estimeriez moins, si j'osois obéir'.)

No. 4

Zeno's version of this little passage looks like a straight translation, which also preserves verbal forms such as the separated 'Parlez:'. But the substitution of 'Seigneur' with 'Oimè!' is a far-reaching change. 'Seigneur' goes almost unnoticed, whereas the exclamation (it is Zelinda's first in this dialogue) raises the tone to a more excited level. The real point is that Zeno makes Zelinda react, at once, to one word: 'morire'. Atalide, on the other hand, frightened as she must be by the forecast of Bajazet's head being carried to the jealous Sultan, totally controls her reaction. The playwright engages the spectator's horrified imagination and lets him follow Atalide's hidden emotion with sympathy – the opera librettist nails the affections down in words.

Vivaldi's recitatives for this part of the dialogue (see music example 7) are conducted on a relatively expressive level, as attested by the chromatic harmonies. But besides the harmonies, the rhythmic pace and melodic contour also invite comment. As a rule of thumb for tempo, it can be suggested that static harmonies encourage the singer to rush ahead, whereas harmonic changes (and especially chromatic changes) have a braking effect on text delivery. A series of such effects happens at the beginning, where Zelinda's opening aside, her address to Teuzzone, his surprise and outcry, are all forcefully separated by unexpected chords.

In no. 1, Zelinda actually rushes her first line, taking the harmony from Teuzzone's preceding question. This is a good use of dramatic *verosimile*: Zelinda hastily cuts short false expectations of an amorous entreaty. But she loses control in her next phrase, with the ♭ on 'sospirata', on a weak beat. This not only turns the chord into a dissonance, but also functions melodically as a *note échappée*: a 'sigh escapes her'. Two ponderous downward clauses ('amante' and 'vita') restore the slow, heroic tone. The concluding phrase 'Vivi . . . felice' has the pathetic silence, gestural contour, sharp modulation and double cadence of the most exalted manner of speaking. This felicitous setting probably took its lead from the two full stops and the doubled 'vivi'. Thus, the heritage of 'Il faut vous rendre; il faut me quitter et régner' is kept alive.

For 'Io d'altra?', Vivaldi does not use one of the common formulas for recitative questions, except for the upward gesture. While the pace is stopped with two long notes, the tying-over of the harmony seems to suggest Teuzzone's incomprehension (as it should). 'Altra', however, seems overemphasized. The point is Teuzzone's leaving of Zelinda, not what he might then do.

Zelinda's irony in no. 2 gains emphasis through dramatic pauses. The first, after 'ben veggio', keeps us all in suspense as to what she actually sees. The interruption after 'fido', when she has not told anything new as yet, is splendidly ironic: is this all she sees and wants to say? The coupling of 'ne' respiri estremi' with 'ma te n' assolvo', and the implied accelerando, somewhat obscures the words, but enhances the surprise effect (also in the harmonic evasion to b minor). Zelinda, at first hesitating and uttering only a triviality, suddenly strikes out to reach a generous, bitter 'ma te n' assolvo'. The word 'fido' also gains body, as it were. It might well be sung with an appoggiatura spanning the whole minor seventh c'-d'. Performed in this way, it could hardly sound otherwise than deeply ironic. The melody immediately regains the top register at 'respiri'. Vivaldi emphasized the 'i'-vowels here, for which high pitches would normally be avoided. It is possible, furthermore, that the return to a regular cadence on G at 'fede' retraces the steps from 'fido' to 'assolvo' which had gone astray.

Teuzzone takes all this much more seriously (no. 3). He is not ironic but simply sincere when his 'Caro mio ben . . . infido' echoes his very first 'Zelinda . . . O Numi!' The pun 'ami infido' does not mean anything to him, nor does the well-wrought conclusion of the paradox, except for the inescapable d minor cadence on 'fedele', the musical signature of this whole dialogue about tragic fidelity.

In no. 4 (music example 8) the inevitable happens: information is omitted for the sake of verbal expression. Vivaldi 'nails down' the two words 'morire' and 'Ahimé!'. 'Io vo' serves as a mere introduction; the chromatic contour really signifies the word 'morire'. But to make 'Parla' an echo of 'Ahimé' is a beautiful idea. Teuzzone takes over Zelinda's chord, in the gloomy key of c minor, repeats her pitch an octave higher, and turns the situation around by telling her to speak out – at a moment when words have just failed her.

Why has the line 'Viver potresti, e non tradirmi' been cut? When Zelinda does not announce the stratagem she has in mind, Teuzzone's expectant answer 'Se posso, ubbidirò' seems rather improbable. But Racine and Zeno are not really

Example 8. Vivaldi, *Teuzzone* III, 6 (Mantua, 1719): recitative Zelinda, Teuzzone (continued)

probable either, because Teuzzone seems too easily won over for a stratagem which does sound impossible. For Vivaldi, Zelinda's 'Ahimé' alone changes Teuzzone's mind. To have substituted this 'Ahimé' for Racine's 'Seigneur' is Zeno's greatest merit in the interest of opera here.

Similarly drastic is the end of no. 5: 't'infingi. Finger? No'. I imagine the preparatory phrase 'Zidiana t'ama . . .' as very rushed, almost ashamedly whispered into his ear, on account of the awkward chord. After the incomplete cadence at 'furor', there is a weighty series of cadential motions. 'Finger?' still sounds with the expected F major chord: has Teuzzone not yet understood? Only the actual resolve, 'No', changes the atmosphere. (What follows, however, is only standard rhetoric.).

In many recitatives of the time, harmonic surprise effects come after a chord has been taken over from the partner, but the device as used here resembles, in an ironic way, Bajazet's analogous 'Je vous entends' with which he seems to negotiate time for his resolve. (Does he really understand?) In any case, Vivaldi seems to have read Zeno's text between the lines here, partly guided by the strong similarity with 'Io d'altra?' ('Vous quitter?'). In each of these cases, the verse is broken. The harmonic break at 'No' is the strongest in the whole dialogue, and this shows an excellent perception of the drama, because Teuzzone's refusal is the turning point of the scene, at least in Zeno's version.

Whereas in Racine's scene Atalide finally succeeds in her persuasion, keeping the intrigue alive (we are in Act II there), in Zeno's the lovers move much closer to the catastrophe. Precisely speaking, they reach an impasse, a suspense duet, both asserting their willingness to die and simultaneously trying to prevent their partner from doing so. This duet, and its preparation (no. 6), is a great poetic and dramatic achievement in Zeno's libretto. In our text example 2 (p. 142) the encased two-syllable words form a climactic sequence and a framework for the dialogue. These exclamations map out the rising anticipation of catastrophe. To 'O ciel!', 'Adieu' and 'Cruel!', Zeno adds 'Ferma', as Racine adds 'venez . . . venez' – genuine *parola scenica* also for the fact that it implies movement on the stage. The duet is cut in Vivaldi's version, which jumps from 'Addio' to 'Ti arresta'. We shall understand this better when we bear in mind that Vivaldi had added an entrance arioso for Teuzzone before the beginning of our scene, where Zeno had a recitative monologue (see below). The decision is connected with the dramatic role played in Vivaldi's score by the closed numbers.

In the historical *drammi per musica* by Zeno and his generation, the greatest challenge to verisimilitude lay in the arias; although there were now fewer of them than in earlier operas, singing on stage was still deemed unlikely enough. The characters of these dramas probably never sang in real life: there was, then, no other justification for their arias than to consider them as either monologues or parts of dialogues. To give an aria the function of the monologue seems the more logical technique at first; arias are often asides, addressed to the public or to heaven, dialogues with one's own heart, or with an actually remote lover or a mute *confident*. A glance at Vivaldi's *Teuzzone* (as well as at many other operas of the time) will reveal that arias are not exclusively treated as analogies to spoken monologues. Nevertheless, there is a connection, and it justifies concentrating at first on this theatrical form.

The role of monologue in classical drama was not only to provide a lyrical break in the action, but also to establish a direct contact between the hero (or villain) and the audience. The communicative value of the monologue – speech without witnesses on stage – was vital for many plots, especially those where the villain could disclose his plans only to the public. In their quest for verisimilitude, the French often put a *confident(e)* on stage to listen to the monologue (this could be called a 'disguised monologue'); but pure monologues are quite frequent, especially in older plays.[14] They can also assume a more rhapsodic or lyrical character, a pouring out of

14.   On monologues, see Jacques Scherer, *La dramaturgie classique en France* (Paris: Nizet, 1950), pp. 245–60. An interesting contribution on an early operatic analogy is Margaret Murata, 'The Recitative Soliloquy', *JAMS* 32 (1979), pp. 45–73.

emotion, or of conflicting emotions. Finally, monologues are a favourite external form for *sentences*, the moralistic maxims often volunteered by less important characters which were considered indispensable by contemporary audiences and critics.[15]

Zeno's *Teuzzone* has eleven monologues (straight and disguised): more than either of the two model plays. Six of these are not related to monologues in the model plays. Two of these six are given to the *confident* Argonte (who has no analogy in the plays) and include 'sentence arias' (i.e. arias expressing a maxim). Two belong to the secondary character Cino whom Zeno introduced to reveal the crime and bring about the happy ending (see chapter 6); these take the form of arias in which Cino consults his bad conscience. These four monologue-arias therefore comment on the moral issues of the plot. The other new monologues are two closely matching speeches of the protagonists, directed to mute characters on stage: Teuzzone to his soldiers in II, 1; Zidiana to the guards in II, 4. They are both formal recitatives, the first of eleven lines, the second of twelve. No such symmetry of units can be observed in the model plays.

The other five monologues – those which have antecedents in the French plays – belong to the protagonists alone and express their affections. In I, 10 (end of the second stage-set) Zelinda expresses her fear of losing her spouse in the impending battle. She does this in the presence of the *confident* Argonte, but addresses the gods. The situation is equivalent to Racine's.

Bajazet I, 4 (end of I):
Atalide. (83-line dialogue with Zaïre, concluding:)
Eh bien! Zaïre, allons. Et toi, si ta justice
De deux jeunes amants veut punir l'artifice,
O ciel! si notre amour est condamné de toi,
Je suis la plus coupable, épuise tout sur moi!

Teuzzone (1708) I, 10:
Zelinda. (13-line dialogue with Argonte, concluding with the aria:)
Salvatemi il mio sposo,
Che pur è vostro dono,
O sommi Dei.
Se tor voi mi volete
Quello, in cui viva io sono,
Deh prima recidete
I giorni miei.

Vivaldi's version differs from Zeno's in so far as Argonte is a mute character, and Zelinda has a solo scene, beginning not with 'Udisti, Argonte, udisti?' but with 'Udite, Cieli, udite'. The address to the heavens is a greater *inverosimile* than in

---

15. J. Scherer, *La dramaturgie*, pp. 316–33.

Example 9. Vivaldi, *Teuzzone* I, 9: aria of Zelinda

Zeno (who had reserved the address to the gods for the brief aria): it is a *preghiera* in recitative form, as it were. It is followed by this aria:

> *Zelinda.*
> La timida cervetta,
> Che fugge il cacciator,
> Va errando per timor
> Per la foresta.
> Tal io colma d'affanni,
> In mezzo a tanti inganni
> Errando vado ognor,
> Confusa dal timor,
> Ch'il sen m'infesta.
> (See music example 9)

The proportions of dialogue and monologue in the passage from *Bajazet* preserve for Atalide's last four lines the character of a spontaneous outcry. The tension between the regular, coupled rhymes and the strong irregularities of the verse – including the enjambment in the phrase from 'Et toi' to 'O ciel!' – is exceptional even for Racine.[16]

---

16. At the same time, this is a 'pompous quatrain' – the most melodramatic type of speech in classical tragedy: see J. Scherer, *La dramaturgie*, pp. 297–302.

Zeno's aria has in common with Racine's lines that it expresses Zelinda's pathos (anxiety for her lover) in her own personified speech, although she does not actually state 'I am full of anxiety'. But here, too, the rising tension of the preceding dialogue makes the aria happen at a true emotional apex.

The da capo section (refrain) of Vivaldi's aria is a simile: Zelinda describes herself as a hind – whose timid footsteps are illustrated by the music – and here she assumes almost a narrator's pose. In the second half (stanza), she gives the explanation of this allegory, stating of herself 'I am full of grief, confused . . .'. Such a full comparison (allegory – explanation, 'qual' – 'tal') has more dramatic immediacy than a mere description of the image, because the character speaks of herself in the first person. To say 'I am anxious', however, is less convincing on the stage than to cry out anxiously or pray anxiously to the gods, and this in addition to the depersonalization produced by the simile itself.

Vivaldi may have wanted to replace Zeno's aria text with another in any case, because it was not a very good text for singing. The relative clauses of lines two and five are difficult to understand at first, and line four, with the following enjambment, sounds quite unmusical (why not simply 'se togliere volete'?). Vivaldi preferred 'La timida cervetta', partly because it scans much more nicely and regularly ('tal io colma d'affanni/in mezzo a tanti inganni' sounds particularly musical) and partly because he wanted to reuse his setting of these words, composed for his opera *La costanza trionfante* in 1716. If he was interested in the drama at all, he certainly trusted his music more than Zeno's words to express it. Whereas the borrowed text of this aria contributes nothing specific to the drama, the music contributes the image of the 'cervetta'.

In terms of the stage, the verbal description of an image is less powerful than personification: it introduces a lyrical or narrative element. Zelinda's depersonification goes so far as to suggest, at least for a moment, that she is really the contralto Teresa Mucci of Modena who is describing the character and affection of Zelinda by way of an image. But in terms of the affections, images can be powerful. Animal-similes were the great fashion of the 1710s: Pier Jacopo Martello amuses himself about them, and Vivaldi's early operas abound with them. The image of the 'cervetta' fulfils the legitimate, orthodox purpose of tragedy to cause compassion. In its early eighteenth-century form of *attendrissement*, this affection is reserved almost entirely for the spectators, and the music of the image-aria fills the gap between the affection shown on stage (Zelinda's fear) and that which the audience is supposed to feel (*attendrissement*) by presenting a sweet and lamentable little animal.

This mediatory role of music – between passions shown and passions aroused – goes far beyond that of a vehicle of the words. (One would rather say that in this case the words of the aria are a vehicle for the music.) In assuming such a more ambitious role, however, music neglects the dramatic character of Zelinda. Racine's Atalide had made herself admirable by asking heaven to destroy her, as the more guilty lover, instead of Bajazet. Zeno's Zelinda at least asked to die *before* Teuzzone – less admirably, but still conveying heroism. Vivaldi's Zelinda asks for nothing but help and pity for herself, a selfishness that is excused by her beautiful singing. The music interferes – intolerably, some would say – with the level of *ethos*. (It should be kept in mind that the *pathos* of this scene – fear – remains the same in all three cases).

Similar things happen more often in Vivaldi's opera, sometimes as a result of the composer's reuse of preexistent music. At the end of the first Act, he has a monologue for Zelinda where Zeno had a sentence aria for Argonte, a half-hearted maxim about the possibility of an excusable deceit (*inganno innocente*). By cutting Argonte's whole monologue, Vivaldi could have made the ending of the Act dramatically stronger, because it is now Zelinda who has the last monologue of the Act. She has discovered that the empress Zidiana is her rival. But unlike Zeno's text, Vivaldi's modified scene I, 14 does not deepen our sense of fear and compassion. Teresa Mucci says:

Zelinda.
Mio core, io non m'inganno. Una rivale
Scopro nella regina,
Nè mai con pace una rival si trova.
Ma non sarei sì amante,
Se non fossi gelosa. In traccia io vado
Del mio Teuzzon: lontan da' cari lacci,
Onde m'avvinse amore,
Non sa viver il core.

Ti sento, sì, ti sento
A palpitarmi in sen,
Speranza lusinghiera.
E dice al mesto cor
Qual rapido balen:
Cangierà il tuo martor,
Costante spera.

The aria is one of Vivaldi's favourite tunes, composed first for *La costanza trionfante* of 1716 and then employed in many later works, including op. X/5 (RV 434). Even apart from the fact that the status of the well-known tune may distract a knowing audience, the precious and galant tone of this aria (*sordini*, E major) interferes, this time, with Zelinda's pathos. Instead of being frightened by the discovery of a powerful and evil rival, she displays hope and tender attachment to her spouse. The 'martoro', which according to her aria will be 'changed', has hardly arisen, and she has not yet had time to react to it in the first place.

Marginally comparable is Zidiana's important monologue at the end of the second Act in Zeno. She has just received Zelinda's promise to speak for her to Teuzzone, and reacts with a mixture of fear and hope of obtaining Teuzzone's love. The situation is vaguely comparable to Roxane's solo scenes in *Bajazet* III, 7 and 8, where, however, suspicion against Atalide prevails. Roxane decides to find out the truth about her rival Atalide for herself.

Roxane. (III, 8, last lines:)
Allons, employons bien le moment qui nous reste.
Ils ont beau se cacher, l'amour le plus discret
Laisse par quelque marque échapper son secret.
Observons Bajazet; étonnons Atalide;
Et couronnons l'amant, ou perdons le perfide.

In Zeno's drama, the modification of Roxane's gloomy monologue to a relatively hopeful short recitative and aria is consistent with the goal of a *lieto fine*. The librettist preserves, however, the speech-act of Roxane's decision.

Zidiana. (II, 18:)
Seguiamla, amor. Nella prigion si vada
A prender da quel labbro
Del suo fato, e del mio gli ultimi voti.
Oh! s'egli in fine alla mia fè si rende?
Vorrei; ma non lo spero.
Troppo io sono infelice, ei troppo altero.

Alma amante, io vorrei pace,
E la chiedo a un ingrato.
A pietà pietà si renda;
O si apprenda
Crudeltà da un dispietato.

The speech-act is contained in the exhortative verbs 'allons', 'observons' etc. and 'seguiamla', 'renda', 'prenda'. Zidiana's affections seem slightly more peaceful than Roxane's, but the threat implied in her 'o si apprenda crudeltà da un dispietato' closely echoes 'perdons le perfide'. The difference between Racine and Zeno here lies in neither affection nor character, but in the diction, which produces significant allegorical nouns: 'amor', 'fato', 'voti', 'pace', and especially the rhetorical interplay between 'pietà' and 'crudeltà'.

Even this highly 'figured' and reasonably musical aria text did not satisfy Vivaldi's taste, who again substituted a simile aria, musically expressing an image and an allegory:

Ritorna a lusingarmi
La mia speranza infida,
E Amor per consolarmi
Già par che scherzi e rida,
Volando e vezzeggiando
Intorno a questo cor.
Ma poi, se ben altero,
Il pargoletto arciero
Già fugge, e lascia l'armi
A fronte del mio amor.

Little comment is needed on this almost totally Baroque piece of poetry – in dramatic terms a step backwards even over Zeno's formalized but sincere personal expression. The music, which illustrates not so much the feeling of hope as the movement of Cupid's wings, may not be by Vivaldi himself: the text occurs first, it seems, in Giuseppe Maria Orlandini's *La Merope* (Bologna, 1717); two musical sources of the aria outside Vivaldi's scores are anonymous.[17] In order to 'prepare' the borrowed Act-ending aria for Zidiana (Anna Ambreville, *virtuosa* of Modena), Vivaldi's libretto arranger simply cut the introductory recitative, so that 'Ritorna a lusingarmi' replies directly to the heartbreaking dialogue of Zelinda and Zidiana of the previous scene:

> *Zid.* Ma se m'inganni? *Zel.* Ogni pietà s'esigli.
> Sieno ancor co' suoi giorni i miei recisi.
> *Zid.* Risorgete, speranze. *Zel.* (Ahi, che promisi!)
>
> . (Aria *Zel.*) Sarà il tuo core/ Un dì contento . . .
> (Zelinda has just promised to persuade Teuzzone to accept Zidiana's hand.)

Even so, the monologues provided by Zeno's dramatic models are not always totally changed in Vivaldi's score. In the last scene of Act I of *Le Comte d'Essex*, the hero (Essex) meets the villain (Cecily) to utter veiled threats. Cecily decides on a preemptive strike, in that type of monologue which could also be called 'dialogue with himself'.

> *Comte.* (I, 3)
> Je sais que contre moi vous animez la reine,
> Peut-être à la seduire aurez-vous quelque peine;
> Et, quand j'aurai parlé, tel qui noircit ma foi
> Pour obtenir sa grâce aura besoin de moi.
>
> *Cécile, seul.*
> Agissons, il est temps; c'est trop faire l'esclave.
> Perdons un orgueilleux dont le mépris nous brave;
> Et ne balançons plus, puisqu'il faut éclater,
> A prévenir le coup qu'il cherche à nous porter.
> *Fin du premier acte.*

These are two 'pompous quatrains', and the second of them constitutes a whole solo scene for the villain.

In Zeno's *Teuzzone*, the protagonist starts off with an angry aria:

---

17.   The collection *F-Pc* X. 128 contains – anonymously – four arias from *La Merope*, including 'Ritorna'; another anonymous source of the music is the appendix to a score of Sarri's *Ginevra* (1720), *F-Pc*, D. 14296. Vivaldi set the same text differently in his *Griselda* of 1735.

Teuzzone. (II, 12)
Morirò, ma la sentenza
Soffrirò senza viltà.
Chi sa poi, che non diventi
La condanna dell'innocenza
Un supplicio dell'empietà?

The veiled threat introduced by 'Chi sa poi?' corresponds linguistically to the original 'Peut-être'. The villain, Sivenio, reacts with disguised fear in his own aria-monologue:

Sivenio. (II, 13)
Amor, che non ha ingegno,
O che non ha valor,
Non è, che un freddo amor.
Ma quando è fiamma ardente,
Caligine di mente
E gelo di timor
Si dissipa al suo ardor.

The key-word is 'timor', which Sivenio hopes to dispel in himself by acting courageously. It is also 'valor', i.e. villainy, with which Sivenio hopes to gain Zidiana's hand.

In Vivaldi's version, Teuzzone's aria is the magnificent 'Sì ribelle, anderò, morirò', a reuse of 'Anderò, volerò, griderò' as present in both his *Orlando* operas of 1714. This composition would deserve a discussion of its own; certainly the shouted character of the voice and the forceful string accompaniment are perfectly suited to Teuzzone's pathos here, if less so to his ethos. After this aria, the sequence of exits is reversed (Sivenio–Cino instead of Cino–Sivenio), so that Sivenio sings his aria to Cino who is still present, but it nevertheless corresponds to the previously quoted two monologues ('Agissons' and 'Amor', respectively). Vivaldi again substituted for Zeno's text a borrowed aria (from *Nerone fatto Cesare*, 1715):

Sivenio. (I, 12)
Non temer, sei giunto in porto,
Già sparita è la procella,
Che rubella
Il naufragio minacciò.
Ed in quella
Resti assorto
Vano orgoglio, che quel soglio
Di calcar folle tentò.
(See music example 10)

Some substance of Zeno's diction has been preserved: the concepts of fear ('temer'), which is shared between the two villains, and pride ('orgoglio'), which

Example 10. Vivaldi, *Teuzzone* II, 12: aria of Sivenio

they see in Teuzzone. The word-rhythm is much better in Vivaldi's text, with easy-flowing *ottonari* and more *piano* endings, where Zeno had two monotonous *tronco* endings in immediate succession with two-syllable words. An external image is added – stormy sea – but the threat towards Teuzzone is direct and clear. The forceful melodic contours of the bass aria are admirable in themselves; the aggressive reverberation of a pedal point suggests power and stubbornness. It is admittedly a distortion of the ethos when Sivenio now almost conveys *grandeur* like Zeno's Teuzzone, heroically defying death. His attitude is worlds away from the merely calculating audaciousness of Cecily. Vivaldi, however, liked the image of the heroic, awe-inspiring villain, and wrote some of his best bass and tenor arias for this type of character.

Common to both the Italian texts is the tendency towards abstract or allegorical speech. In Thomas Corneille's dramatic language, strong, active verbs ('animez, agissons, perdons' etc.) predominate over abstract nouns such as 'grace' and 'foi'. In Zeno's, the hero poses with strong verbs ('morirò', 'soffrirò') but also introduces the abstract qualities of 'viltà' and 'innocenza'. The villain couches his dialogue with himself in the form of a sentence aria, speaking entirely of the allegorical figure of 'Amor', who is compared to a flame. Sivenio's speech-act personifies Amor as much as it depersonifies Sivenio himself. Vivaldi's text bends the abstraction towards a nature image. It also restores the speech-act – Sivenio directly addresses a partner – and while it is irrelevant whether this partner is Cino or his own heart, the subject of his statement is a person, not an allegory. Admittedly, the images stumble over each other in this poetry: 'The storm that has just ceased will nevertheless bury the vain pride which foolishly had attempted to stamp the throne'. Despite the relative importance of verbs (but some are participles: 'sparita', 'assorto'), the aria is composed over nouns not verbs, images not actions. It is possible that this formula applies to Vivaldi's dramatic music more generally, and perhaps to other operas of the time.

In one instance, a monologue of the model play has survived through Zeno's into Vivaldi's version because it was already 'melodramatic' when spoken. This is the 'set' monologue of the imprisoned Essex, which in Zeno's libretto becomes the 'set' prison monologue. The respective position in the drama is the same, the opening of the penultimate picture.

Comte. (IV, 2)
O fortune! O grandeur! dont l'amorce flatteuse
Surprend, touche, éblouit une âme ambitieuse,
De tant d'honneurs reçus c'est donc là tout le fruit!
Un long temps les amasse, un moment les détruit.
Tout ce que le destin le plus digne d'envie
Peut attacher de gloire à la plus belle vie,
J'ai pu me le promettre, et, pour le mériter,
Il n'est projet si haut qu'on ne m'ait vu tenter;
Cependant aujourd'hui (se peut-il qu'on le croie?)
C'est sur un échafaud que la reine m'envoie!
C'est là qu'aux yeux de tous m'imputant des forfaits . . .
(*Salsbury enters.*)

Teuzzone. (III, 6: *Prigione*)
Sorte nimica! Io germe
Di Regio tralce, io d'alto Impero erede,
Quando a' miei voti a gara
Si offrian beni, piaceri, onori, e glorie,
Morir deggio innocente? e da' miei stessi
Popoli condannato?
Perdite illustri! ampie sciagure! In voi
Pur non degno impiegar gli ultimi affetti.
Tutti, tutti, o Zelinda,
Li dono a te. Voi difendete, o Numi,
Ciò che vive di me nel suo bel core,
Dall'altrui crudeltà, dal suo dolore.

There are similarities of diction: the opening exclamation and address to higher powers; the 'pregnant' nouns, rhetorical questions, pompous paradoxes ('Un long temps . . .'/'Perdite illustri . . .'). The ethos is in both cases the self-pity of a high-born, proud and inflexible man, but one who finds time to offer the audience his failed career as a moralizing example. The dissimilarities are partly those of diction:

Corneille amasses verbs (line 2), Zeno nouns (line 4); the latter also tries a melodramatic *repetitio* ('tutti, tutti'). He varies pace unexpectedly, but ends in a well-prepared rhetorical figure (opposition). Corneille forms regular quatrains, the third of which is unexpectedly cut short.[18] Furthermore, Corneille disregards *bienséance* by mentioning the 'échafaud' – a rather mercenary strategy to earn the spectators' horror and compassion – whereas Zeno credits his character with more proper verbal behaviour ('morir innocente').

The most important change is, of course, the introduction of the love element into the heroic setting. Zeno's hero subjects all his other concerns and affections to his remembrance of Zelinda, which is admirable and touching at the same time. The ethos of both heroes – honour above love and love above life – is borne out verbally.

Vivaldi has removed the whole recitative and replaced it with an 'entrance aria':

Teuzzone. (III, 6: *Prigione*)
Antri cupi, infausti orrori,
Rispondete a' miei martiri,
Se il mio ben più rivedrò?
Voi tacete?
Deh, mi dite, se sospiri
Per pietà de' miei dolori,
E contento io morirò.
(See music example 11)

Since hundreds of lovers on the Italian stage before Teuzzone had asked the winds to carry a message from or to their beloved, he may well address the walls of his prison. The *inverosimile* of the situation is only apparently greater than the addresses to 'fortune' or 'sorte' in the earlier versions: in all three texts, the address is only a rhetorical trick, furnishing an imagined dialogue partner to whom the spontaneous-sounding questions, exclamations and imperatives can be directed. And these are the verbal and conceptual forms that count. In its employment for dramatic effect (spontaneity, personification), Vivaldi's text beats the others. It is the only one where the hero actually asks his partners to do something ('rispondete'), so that his real isolation emerges in the manner of a tragic irony. The question 'Voi tacete?' is not simply rhetorical, but rather contrary to reason and therefore in Teuzzone's situation probable. Furthermore, the fictitious dialogue partner is seen to be a physical object. We have remarked on several earlier examples in which the introduction of an image weakens dramatic speech, but here the image strengthens it, because it is the scenery itself. A character who speaks to the scenery must be in a truly deplorable state of mind, and the spectator's compassion is therefore well earned. The stage set is one of 'horror': the spectators' horror may not necessarily follow, but the initial address to the 'antri cupi, infausti orrori' confronts the problem of theatrical fiction head on, as it were.

18.   This is a rhetorical figure, too (apocope). Conceivably, Corneille attempted here a verbal symbol of the execution (beheading).

Example 11. Vivaldi, *Teuzzone* III, 6: aria of Teuzzone

And so does the music. The aria is very old-fashioned for 1719 in having only voice and bass (although the latter is mysteriously reinforced by the upper strings), as well as in being brief and throughcomposed. The form of the text setting – without word repetitions – resembles a seventeenth-century *arioso* or *cavata*, although the poetry is meant to be set in da capo form, with the division after the third line. There is a single word-repetition in the music, and it is a stroke of genius: 'rispondete'. The first time, this word sounds petulant, aggressive with the largest upward leap so far, and the first animated quavers. The ostinato bass, however, uses precisely that moment to set out, again, on its stubborn circuit – like a prison guard. The voice runs after him in a desperate, distorted effort, 'rispondete a' miei martiri', trying three awkward tritone leaps almost in succession, and also losing balance over the hasty declamation in quavers. The concluding gesture 'se il mio ben più rivedrò?' in its melancholic beauty (like 'Antri cupi') is a statement of resignation rather than a question. At 'Voi tacete?' Teuzzone actually cries out at the prison walls, and they remain silent. Further on, the voice winds itself through anxious melismas (important is the high register), over an unconcerned ostinato or a dark, dead pedal point.

These are 'speech-acts' in music: the singing voice personifies or 'impersonates' the soul. And the bass impersonates the visible image of the prison, by expressing immovability through motion. The text, but to some extent also the music, conforms to a stereotype, a successful one in opera. The true provenance of the aria text cannot be determined at the moment; no earlier use in Vivaldi's operas is known. If written for *Teuzzone* of 1719, then the most remarkable departure from Zeno's text would be that the hero, far from musing about his own death or his earlier glory, longs to see his mistress, or at least to know whether she sighs for him. The point is that Zelinda appears in the very next moment in the prison cell, with an *a parte* sigh, even before Teuzzone notices her:

Zel. ('A che m'astringi, amor!'). Teuzzone, io vengo . . .
Teu. Zelinda, oh numi!
(See music example 7, p. 146 above.)

This effect is, of course, another stage trick from the bag of Venetian Baroque opera, we might say, and therefore yet another departure from the classical models we are discussing here. No: Racine, in one of the most tragic moments of *Bajazet* (III, 3, the middle of the drama), does not disdain it. In a heart-searching dialogue with her *confidente* Zaïre, Atalide concludes that Bajazet loves Roxane and that she herself should give him up for ever.

At. Il ne me verra plus.
                        Za. Madame, le voici.
                        Scène 4
Baj. C'en est fait, j'ai parlé, vous êtes obéie.

Since Zeno, in his prison scene, does not make Teuzzone mention Zelinda's absence or presence, it seems possible that Vivaldi's libretto arranger took the effect from Racine. This is speculation.

What can be said with confidence, however, is that Vivaldi and his arranger did create several theatrically convincing scenes without the help of borrowed music, either afresh or from Zeno's text. Strangely enough, many of these concern the role of the protagonist, sung by Margherita Gualandi Campioli.[19] From tables 5 and 6 (pp. 137 and 139) it can be seen where borrowed and newly composed pieces in Vivaldi's *Teuzzone* appear: it seems remarkable how unevenly Vivaldi has spread the borrowed material. The twelve or so numbers that seem to have been newly composed in 1719 (without asterisk in table 5) are mostly 'entrance arias', shorter pieces like 'Antri cupi', brief ensembles, the choruses, and some of the dramatically most indispensable numbers of the role of Teuzzone. Many of these are set *senza violini* (the so-called 'continuo arias') or, as in 'Antri cupi', with unisono accompaniment. Some are extremely simple in style and form, such as Zelinda's 'Ho nel seno un doppio ardore' (III, 12). Others use old-fashioned devices such as ostinato basses: besides 'Antri cupi', there is the beautiful *cavata* 'Quanto costi al mio riposo', with which Cino opens Act III. Also characteristic is the use of the pathetic *largo* tempo in these two ostinato arias, 'Al fiero mio tormento' (I, 2) and 'Ove giro il mesto guardo' (I, 6). The simplicity and the old-fashioned techniques (i.e. techniques with which the composer had grown up) surely saved working time. But Vivaldi's dramatic imagination is at work here. 'Ove giro il mesto guardo', bordering on the style of an accompanied recitative, has a haunting opening in superimposed, dissonant string reverberations which we also know (in more extreme versions) from the beginning of *L'inverno* and the *Siroe* aria 'Gelido in ogni vena'.[20] Another sign that Vivaldi did not substitute older arias for the mere sake of working economy are the several freshly composed pieces in the first version of the score, which he later replaced by borrowed arias. (See table 6.) One of these pieces is the highly dramatic 'Per lacerarlo', Zidiana's aria of fury in III, 9, which was replaced by the trivial 'Io sembro appunto quell'augelletto'. The rejected pieces are mostly in the simpler or old-fashioned idioms and seem to indicate a conscious wish of Vivaldi, perhaps encouraged by his Mantuan-Habsburgian environment, to preserve a taste of *il patetico* in this opera. This taste then yielded to the more *galant* idioms of arias from the Venetian operas – whether on Vivaldi's initiative alone or perhaps somebody else's, we do not know.

These more *galant* idioms strike us as the real problem in the conversion of *tragédie* into *dramma per musica*. It seems as if Racine, Corneille and their follower Zeno had all worked very well towards the goal of a tragic type of opera – the two Frenchmen by inventing melodramatic scenes and expressions, for example – but

---

19. Vivaldi seems to have had much confidence in her acting and liked composing new music for her. She had appeared in his operas *Orlando furioso* and *Orlando finto pazzo* of 1714, from which arias were borrowed in *Teuzzone*, but none was transferred either from or to her role.
20. See E. Cross, *The Late Operas*, vol. 1, p. 123, and vol. 2, ex. 71 ('Ove giro' as re-used in *L'Atenaide*); R. Strohm, *Italienische Opernarien*, music ex. 109 ('Gelido in ogni vena').

that then all this was swept away in the real world of the opera house.[21] To some
extent the conservatism of the audience and the tenacious traditions of Italian *poesia
per musica* can be made responsible for this; Marino was somehow still alive.

But the matter has another side as well. In Vivaldi's *Teuzzone* an unsettling effect
is the music's interference with the ethos of the characters. Even their pathos seems
at times unduly lightened or reversed. Perhaps paradoxically, these may be signs
that a genuine change in the Italian musical theatre was taking place. Vivaldi's
robust pictorialism is not really in conflict with his sense of drama (the latter he
demonstrates effectively in some recitative passages). It is rather an as yet immature
attempt to 'musicalize' the drama as a whole: to seize responsibility for the drama
from the poet. The 'immaturity' of the attempt can be felt in the rather chaotic
result for characters and affections in this opera. Music still needed to grow with the
new challenge: the ability to express the whole of drama could not be acquired
overnight.

21.   Freeman's verdict of 'Opera without Drama' would have to fall on Vivaldi here, not on Zeno.

8

Antonio Salvi's *Amore e maestà* and the *funesto fine* in opera

Historians and critics of opera are perhaps too convinced that opera needs and has its own history, structures and theory. A theory, or a 'poetics', of opera-writing has never really existed, and the zeal of modern scholars to reconstruct such a poetics for the works of the past seems to reflect the loss of contact with that past itself.

In Italy 300 years ago the aspiring *poeta drammatico* would have been drawn into the world of *melodramma*, if at all, by forces which might have little to do with his literary inclinations, and he would certainly not have abandoned his awareness of classical and humanist literary theories. There existed not only an authoritative poetics of tragedy – Aristotle's, of course – but also the belief that the structures of contemporary literary theatre had to conform to such classical precepts. Poets working with the *dramma per musica* were expected to observe the poetics of spoken literary theatre. By about 1700 this situation generated various forms and degrees of opera criticism, as well as attempts at libretto reform.

These criticisms and these reform attempts, however, did not evolve into a theory of opera proper, i.e. a theory which would have taken music seriously. Until the early eighteenth century, the different conditions under which dramatic poetry had to live when associated with music functioned traditionally as excuses for perceived poetic defects of the libretto. The dramatic poets, often noble *dilettanti*, spoke of their task as librettists with considerable affectation. Even Apostolo Zeno, who claimed he needed to write libretti for a living, habitually justified their 'imperfections' with the necessary concessions to music and singers. But he undoubtedly wanted a drama such as his *Teuzzone* to be measured against the same yardstick as were the model plays by Jean Racine and Thomas Corneille. Even while allowing for a happy ending, Zeno's alterations to the borrowed dramatic material tried to fulfil the same theoretical precepts as the French *tragédies* had done. Vivaldi's setting of *Teuzzone* (1719), by contrast, was an example of how a gifted dramatic composer takes the play much further down the road towards musical expression of the drama (see chapters 6 and 7, respectively). It was from that time onwards that the art, not only of setting libretti but of writing them, little by little developed into a proper discipline of its own, which it has remained until the early twentieth century. The very process in which operatic poetry learned something from spoken drama also helped to transform it into an independent genre. Whereas in the seventeenth century we have the dramatic poet who happens to deal with the musical stage and likes to disguise or excuse his involvement, the eighteenth and nineteenth centuries are the age of the professional librettist. Even if Pietro Metastasio is considered a great lyrical poet (not everyone thinks so), this talent was clearly not the one that made him a skilful librettist.

This and the following chapter will explore the emergence of a concept of the *dramma per musica* which, despite lacking a theory of its own and adhering to the Aristotelian tradition of drama, was separate and practicable on the musical stage. This concept came into being through the efforts of the opera reformers of Zeno's generation, and it has survived throughout the enlightenment era. The dominating operatic poet of that era was Metastasio; but I hope to show that he had an important forerunner in the Florentine poet Antonio Salvi (1664–1724), whose libretto *Amore e maestà* (Florence, 1715) satisfies both the classical tradition of spoken drama and the conditions of Italian operatic practice at the time. The ability to serve two masters is exactly what made, from now on, the opera libretto a unique genre.

The present chapter will deal with the external history of Salvi's libretto and with the implications of its most characteristic feature: it is a drama with a tragic ending (*funesto fine*), which was extremely unusual for Italian opera in the seventeenth and eighteenth centuries.[1] This feature plays a crucial role in the emancipation of the opera libretto from spoken drama. The next chapter will then compare Salvi's libretto in detail with its model, which is, once more, Thomas Corneille's *Le Comte d'Essex*, and will discuss the degree of its independence and the question of opera as a separate theatrical genre.

Dr Antonio Salvi of Lucignano (1664–1724) was a Florentine physician and writer. In 1699 he succeeded Cosimo Villifranchi as personal physician and court poet to Prince Ferdinando de' Medici, the famous patron of music and especially of opera. For the private performances at Ferdinando's Villa di Pratolino, Salvi contributed in 1701–10 seven *drammi per musica*, and between 1694 and 1718 he wrote or adapted about a dozen more for the civic (academic) opera houses of Florence and Livorno. He also did commissioned work for the court theatres of Reggio Emilia, Parma, Turin and Munich, and for Venetian opera houses, which occupied him mostly in the period c. 1715–24.[2] He was apparently connected with the Roman *Accademia de' Quirini* (led by Metastasio's teacher Gian Vincenzo Gravina), and provided one or two librettos for the Teatro Capranica in Rome (1711–15).[3] Salvi

---

1. The fact that French seventeenth-century opera, the *tragédie en musique*, lived up to its name and widely accepted tragic endings was not necessarily a result of its cultural association with French spoken tragedy, nor was it an emancipatory trait. Rather, this genre was strongly rooted in mytho-logical Renaissance tragedy. For a survey of the major librettists, see Cuthbert Girdlestone, *La Tragédie en musique (1673–1750) considerée comme genre littéraire* (Paris-Geneva, 1972).
2. His life and works are described in Francesco Giuntini, *I drammi per musica di Antonio Salvi: Aspetti della 'riforma' del libretto nel primo Settecento* (Bologna: Il Mulino, 1994). See also, for important details, Robert L. and Norma W. Weaver, *A Chronology of Music in the Florentine Theater, 1590–1750* (Detroit: Information Coordinators Inc., 1978), pp. 69–75 and passim.
3. See also chapter 2 in this volume, 'A context for *Griselda*', pp. 45 and 50.

was, besides Pietro Pariati, the most successful early writer of *intermezzi comici per musica*, of which we may only mention his masterpieces, *Bacocco e Serpilla* (*Il marito giuocatore e la moglie bacchettona*), Florence, c. 1712–14, and *Larinda e Vanesio* (*L'Artigiano gentiluomo*, after Molière), Florence, c. 1720. A frequent musical collaborator of the poet was Giuseppe Maria Orlandini, *maestro di capella* at the Medici court from 1713; other composers who set new librettos by him included Giacomo Antonio Perti and Alessandro Scarlatti (for Pratolino), Francesco Gasparini, Luc'Antonio Predieri and Antonio Vivaldi. The opera composer most indebted to Salvi's work was Handel, who used his librettos for his operas *Rodelinda*, *Scipione*, *Lotario*, *Sosarme*, *Ariodante*, *Arminio* and *Berenice*; Handel's acquaintance with the poet must go back to his early visits to Florence and Pratolino, 1706–9.[4]

This is not the place to present an evaluation of Salvi as an operatic poet in general.[5] Given his widespread activity as a librettist, also outside the court which employed him, he must have had a genuine interest in the musical theatre. He was a reformer of opera who positively and decisively responded to the challenge of its critics; the significance of his works for the young Pietro Metastasio still awaits investigation (see also below).

For Salvi, probably the theory and certainly the practice of the French spoken theatre was a guiding influence. He was also well aware of the Spanish theatre, and his first known libretto was derived from a Spanish model. It was *La forza compassionevole*, opera scenica (i.e. without music), Florence (Accademici Sorgenti), 1691; the play was turned into a *dramma per musica* by Salvi for the carnival of Livorno, 1694, the edition identifying the original as a *drama spagnuolo*. Similar origins are likely for his *La fortunata disperazione del principe Celimauro*, a *commedia eroica* performed in Florence in 1696.[6]

Table 7. Antonio Salvi's librettos based on French dramatic models

Astianatte (Pratolino, 1701): Jean Racine, *Andromaque*;[7]
Arminio (Pratolino, 1703): Jean-Gualbert de Campistron, *Arminius*;
Il Gran Tamerlano (Pratolino, 1706): Nicholas Pradon, *Tamerlan*;
Stratonica (Florence, 1707):[8] Thomas Corneille, *Antiochus*;
Rodelinda regina dei Longobardi (Pratolino, 1710): Pierre Corneille, *Pertharite*;
Amore e maestà (Florence, 1715): Thomas Corneille, *Le Comte d'Essex*;
Amor vince l'odio, overo Timocrate (Florence, 1715): Thomas Corneille, *Timocrate*;
Il carceriere di se stesso (Turin, 1720): Thomas Corneille, *Le geolier de soi-mesme*.[9]

---

4. See R. Strohm, 'Handel and his Italian Opera Texts', in R. Strohm, *Essays*.
5. Much of this has already been achieved in the study by F. Giuntini, *I drammi per musica di Antonio Salvi*.
6. See F. Giuntini, *I drammi per musica di Antonio Salvi*, and R. L. Weaver, *A Chronology*, pp. 170 and 177.
7. On the earliest extant setting, see Reinhard Strohm, 'An opera autograph of Francesco Gasparini?', in R. Strohm, *Essays*, pp. 106–21.
8. Details on the operas written for Florence are found in R. L. Weaver, *A Chronology*, under the respective dates.
9. Indebted not only to the model by Corneille, but also to its first libretto adaptation by Ludovico Adimari (1681).

According to the present state of research, at least eight libretti by Salvi are based on French dramas (see table 7).

Gli equivoci d'amore e d'innocenza (Venice, 1723) has traits in common with Pierre Corneille's *Don Sanche d'Aragon*, but is not directly derived from it.

Not all of the librettos in table 7 are regular *drammi per musica*. The important Tuscan tradition of *commedia per musica*, as represented by Cicognini, Moniglia, Adimari, Villifranchi and Gigli, may also have influenced Salvi in his choice of subjects, although he prefers the Spanish-French variant of the aristocratic *comédie héroïque* (a label given, for example, to *Don Sanche d'Aragon*) to the more indigenous bourgeois plots. *Amor vince l'odio*, *Il carceriere* and *Gli equivoci* correspond to the type of *comédie héroïque*. At least one other libretto by Salvi is a comedy, probably adapted from a prose comedy: *Il pazzo per politica* (Livorno, 1717). The *intermezzi* are all bourgeois comedies.

This tendency towards the comic genre in Salvi's later years is balanced by one important and successful tragedy, *Amore e maestà*. It was first given as a *tragedia per musica* in the summer season of 1715 at the Teatro del Cocomero, Florence; performances followed in Italian opera houses and abroad almost every season from 1718 onwards, mostly under the title *Arsace*. The last performance known today took place at the Teatro S. Benedetto of Venice in 1768, with music by Carlo Franchi.

In the preface to his libretto, the poet expresses an ambitious hope: 'Here is a musical tragedy, with a truly tragic ending: a novelty, as far as I am aware, without precedent, at least on the Italian stage. If it finds, as I hope, your generous appreciation, then I can be proud of having been the first to make you leave the theatre in tears, surrounded by sweet musical harmonies.'[10]

With the last, flowery sentence, Salvi may simply be repeating his – mistaken, but probably honest – belief that he had written the first musical tragedy. Or does he intend to say something more specific about the character of his creation? It would be good to know, in any case, whether he did actually achieve the described effect on his audience, and whether he was the first to do so.

One thing is certain: he was not to be the last. If there is any justice in the historiography of opera, then *Amore e maestà*, the forerunner of *Didone abbandonata* and *Catone in Utica*, must be respected as another ancestor of *Aida*, *Wozzeck* and countless other operatic tragedies, which sweeten the cathartic effect of compassion with a more expansive feeling of musical *Weltschmerz*.

Perhaps Salvi had no clear idea as yet of the dramaturgical implications of his juxtaposition of 'tears' and 'musical harmony' – but then, do we? He may also not have meant to say that the *funesto fine* of his drama and the concept of 'musical sweetness' had anything specific to do with each other. Even so, his remark is probably more than a crude assertion concerning the history of a theatrical genre. It

---

10.   'Eccoti una Tragedia in Musica, col fine veramente Tragico; Novità, per quanto è mia notizia, non più veduta, almeno sulle Scene d'Italia. Se incontrerà, come spero, il tuo gentil compatimento, mi pregierò io d'essere il primo a farti sortir dal Teatro con le lagrime, fra le dolci armoníe della Musica.'

Table 8. Tragedie per musica (with *funesto fine*) before 1730

Girolamo Frigimelica Roberti,[11] *La Rosimonda*, Venice, 1695 (music by C. F. Pollarolo)
G. Frigimelica Roberti, *Il pastore d'Anfriso (tragedia pastorale)*, Venice, 1695 (C. F. Pollarolo)
G. Frigimelica Roberti, *Il trionfo della libertà*, Venice, 1707 (Alessandro Scarlatti)
A. Salvi, *Amore e maestà (Arsace)*, Florence, 1715 (Giuseppe Maria Orlandini)
Benedetto Pasqualigo, *Ifigenia in Tauride*, Venice, 1719 (G. M. Orlandini)
Pietro Suarez, *Leucippe e Teonoe*, Venice, 1719 (Antonio Pollarolo)
Agostino Piovene, *Nerone*, Venice, 1721 (G. M. Orlandini)
B. Pasqualigo, *Giulio Flavio Crispo*, Venice, 1722 (Giovanni Maria Capelli)
Giovanni Piazzon, *Antigono tutore di Filippo*, Venice, 1724 (Giovanni Porta and Tommaso Albinoni)
Pietro Metastasio, *Didone abbandonata*, Naples, 1724 (Domenico Sarri)
Pietro Metastasio, *Catone in Utica*, Rome, 1728 (Leonardo Vinci)

seems at the same time more Aristotelian – concentrating, as it does, on the effect on the spectators – and more modern, more psychological: it identifies a culinary feeling, or even an element of seduction, in the theatrical experience of tragedy.

If it is true that opera – well beyond the confines of tragedy – conveys a sweeter and easier experience of the world, and has more 'feminine' (or, in eighteenth-century language, 'effeminate') connotations than spoken drama, this may reflect the historical moment when audiences began to become aware of such an alternative. Precisely by abandoning the musical convention of the *lieto fine* in Italian opera and embracing a tragic outcome, Salvi seems to have conquered the last bastion held by spoken drama in defiance of the musical genre.

In order to put Salvi's 'innovation' into perspective, however, we should note other early *drammi per musica* which called themselves *tragedia per musica* and had a tragic ending (see table 8).

Occasionally, Piovene's *Tamerlano*, Venice, 1711, was styled *tragedia*; Pariati's *Sesostri*, Venice, 1710, is a *tragedia di lieto fine*. Both were first set by Francesco Gasparini. A traditional tragic subject was provided with a perfunctory happy ending in Benedetto Pasqualigo's *Antigona*, Venice, 1718 (music by Orlandini).

Although the first performances of the works in table 8 mostly took place in Venice, in subsequent revivals they were distributed far and wide in Europe. For example, *Arsace* was given in London in 1721 and in the following year in Hamburg; *Nerone* followed in Hamburg in 1723. It is not a coincidence either that these two operas and *Ifigenia in Tauride* were all set to music by Orlandini, Salvi's collaborator in Florence, who almost monopolizes the genre around 1720.[12]

A tragic ending in drama can be of many kinds, and some of the librettos in the list above would not quite satisfy the concept of a 'fine veramente tragico', which

11. On the poet, see Karl Leich, *Girolamo Frigimelica Robertis Libretti: Ein Beitrag insbesondere zur Geschichte des Opernlibrettos in Venedig* (Munich: Katzbichler, 1972) (Schriften zur Musik, 26); Carlo Caruso, 'Italian Opera Libretti, 1679–1721: Universality and Flexibility of a Literary Genre', in *Alessandro Scarlatti und seine Zeit*, ed. by M. Lütolf, 1995, p. 34.

12. On his *Arsace* and *Nerone* in Hamburg, see also Reinhard Strohm, 'Die *tragedia per musica* als Repertoirestück: Zwei Hamburger Opern von G. M. Orlandini', in *Die frühdeutsche Oper*, ed. by C. Floros et al., 1981, pp. 37–54.

had to involve the unhappiness or death of the hero. For example, *Il trionfo della libertà* (with the story of Brutus, Lucretia and Tarquinius) and *Ifigenia in Tauride* ostensibly present the victory of freedom over tyranny,[13] and in *Catone in Utica* (and similarly in *Tamerlano*) the hero dies happily for his ideals.[14]

In the remaining cases, however, historical fact or approved legend dictates that the hero should become a victim of villainy, tragic error or passion, and die unhappily – even unnecessarily. In three of these genuine operatic tragedies, the victim and heroine is a woman: Rosimonda, Agrippina (in *Nerone*) and Didone. Salvi's *Amore e maestà*, whose original title deliberately hides any hero's name, occupies a pivotal position. Not only does Arsace (the Earl of Essex) die as a victim of malice, passion and his own pride, not only is his lover, Rosmiri, driven to suicide, but Statira (Queen Elizabeth), whose jealousy is her tragic error, ends up defeated and close to death. Her final solo scene, in which she curses herself and abdicates her reign, is one of the great female monologues in Italian opera of the time; its repercussions in *Didone abbandonata* are obvious, and the intrigue that leads to this ending is rather similar in each case (see also below). The later renaming of Salvi's libretto as *Arsace* oversimplifies its tragic perspective.

Despite their small number, these genuine operatic tragedies were part of the cutting edge of Italian libretto reform in the early eighteenth century. They revealed an emancipated and pessimistic spirit among the better dramatists of the day, but were soon to succumb to the political and moral euphemisms of courtly restoration (as can well be seen in Metastasio's path from *Didone abbandonata* and *Catone in Utica* to *La clemenza di Tito* and *Attilio Regolo*). The success of *Amore e maestà* in the opera houses can be linked with the early achievements of Metastasio and his singers. It is certain that the young Trapassi knew Salvi's libretto – perhaps in more than one version – and it is possible that his teacher Gravina, fundamentally an opponent of opera, recommended this one to him as an example of genuine tragedy.

Orlandini's score of 1715 does not survive; from the existing later arrangements, a rather bleak picture of his dramatic procedures emerges. Nevertheless, in many opera houses, especially abroad, the libretto was exclusively known with Orlandini's music for about a generation. The leading singers of the original production of Florence, 1715, were Francesco Bernardi *detto* Senesino (Arsace) and Margherita Durastanti (Statira). These two belcanto stars instigated the transfer of the opera to the Royal Academy of London, as Paolo Rolli attests in a letter of 18 October 1720.[15] The Florentine original was deemed unsuitable, however, without much revision, as the recitatives seemed of 'interminable' length, and there were so few *ariette* that

13.   Tyrannicide is also the theme of Frigimelica Roberti's *Mitridate Eupatore*, Venice, 1707, set to music by Alessandro Scarlatti.
14.   The latter is also the case in Metastasio's *Attilio Regolo*, derived from Nicholas Pradon's *Régulus*, as is Carlo Sigismondo Capeci's (?) reworking of a libretto by Matteo Noris, *Marco Attilio Regolo*, Rome, 1719; but the 1719 version has a happy ending.
15.   Otto Erich Deutsch, *Handel: A Documentary Biography* (London, 1955), pp. 114ff. (with a translation of Rolli's letter, erroneously reading references to Heidegger as if referring to Handel) and 122; Sesto Fassini, *Il melodramma italiano a Londra nella prima metà del settecento* (Turin, 1914), pp. 53ff. (with excerpts from the Italian original of Rolli's letter).

even Senesino had only four.[16] Rolli was commissioned to revise the libretto, and he did this 'di concerto' ('in collaboration') with the two singers. Their plan was probably to convert a number of accompagnato recitatives into arias, and insert others; also the final accompagnato scenes and aria of Durastanti were changed. Rolli and the singers encountered strong resistance from the impresario, John James Heidegger, who did not want to 'modernize' the libretto too much and whose plan involved a musical revision by the minor Venetian composer Girolamo Polani. Senesino and Durastanti got their way, however, and the opera (*Arsace*) was performed on 1 February 1721 at the Haymarket theatre, with Orlandini's music, text alterations by Rolli and fourteen additional arias by Filippo Amadei. In his dedication of the libretto to the Duke of Montague, Rolli mentions two very important aspects of this 'first' *tragedia per musica*: its change of setting from historical Great Britain to legendary Persia, and its success in three Italian centres.

'The historical subject, although changed in names and setting, is English, however, and has given rise to the first presentation of a tragedy with an entirely unhappy ending on the Italian musical stage. In Florence where the drama was created, and in Venice and Naples where it was repeated, it obtained universal applause. . . .'[17] In London, not only the protagonists Senesino and Durastanti, but also the singer of Megabise of 1715, the alto castrato Matteo Berscelli, sang his own part again.

The London *Arsace* was transferred, in turn, to the Hamburg opera house in 1722 by Johann Mattheson, who translated the recitatives into German and further arranged the opera. It is from the Hamburg production that the only early score survives. Later revivals and revisions of Orlandini's setting began in Turin in 1726, and continued throughout the 1730s in Florence, where the work was apparently looked upon with patriotic pride. It was probably Orlandini who in 1725 arranged also *Didone abbandonata* for the Florentine Pergola theatre, reinforcing a link with the 'next generation' of musical tragedies. Metastasio's libretto had also been set in that same carnival by Albinoni for the Teatro S. Cassiano, Venice. The Teatro Regio of Turin selected, in the seasons of 1726 and 1727, three of its four operas from this stylistic sphere: in 1726 Salvi's *Publio Cornelio Scipione* (set by G. A. Giay) was followed by Orlandini's *Arsace*; in 1727 Sarri's *Didone abbandonata* (with alterations) and Orlandini's *Antigona* were presented.

Similarly important, at least for the Italian development, were three other settings. The second production of the drama, titled *Arsace*, was given in the carnival of 1718 at the Teatro S. Giovanni Grisostomo in Venice with music by Michelangelo Gasparini; repeats followed in Modena, 1719, Padua, 1722, and Vicenza, 1731. The Venetian production had an extraordinarily splendid cast, with Nicolino Grimaldi (Arsace), Marianna Benti (Statira), Faustina Bordoni (Rosmiri)

16. Correctly: five. The 1715 libretto has a total of 33 closed numbers – by no means a low figure for this period.
17. S. Fassini, *Il melodramma*, p. 54: 'Il soggetto storico, benché cangiato di nomi e sito, è però inglese, ed à prestato il motivo di porre per la prima volta su'l teatro musicale italiano una tragedia di fine totalmente funesto. In Firenze dove questo drama nacque, ed in Venezia e Napoli dove fu trasportato, incontrò l'universale compiacimento. . . .'

and Antonio Bernacchi (Mitrane). These particular singers could all be said to be ideally suited to their roles as Salvi had conceived them, even in terms of age and physical appearance.

It is no surprise that, again, the leading singers of this production seem to have taken the work elsewhere: Benti and Grimaldi reappeared as Statira and Arsace in Domenico Sarri's setting, performed in Naples in December 1718. This had apparently been planned as a particularly splendid occasion to celebrate the Austrian Viceroy Wirich Daun and his wife, Barbara von Herbstein (the libretto is dedicated to the latter). There was a splendid prologue, as usually presented in Naples in gala performances staged at the Palazzo Reale (it is not clear why this particular opera was presented only at the Teatro S. Bartolomeo, or else why no libretto mentioning the palace performance was printed). The interesting thing is that the prologue 'in Heaven', acted by Venus and Vulcan, was inserted into the first scene, not prefixed to it, and was introduced as a 'play in the play'. These mythological *intermedii* (*sic*), ostensibly performed to celebrate the wedding of Rosmiri and Mitrane in the presence of Statira, are then interrupted by the first dramatic events: Artabano rushes in to report Arsace's revolt. The comic characters Morante and Merilla, when meeting later for their first *scena buffa*, tease each other with the roles previously played as Vulcan and Venus. The addition of *scene buffe* followed Neapolitan conventions and should not be regarded as a criticism of the tragic ending, which was maintained. The libretto preface ('Cortese lettore . . .'), signed by the impresario Nicola Serino, reaffirms Salvi's claim that this is the first 'tragedia in musica col fine veramente tragico'. It also implicitly refers to the Venetian production as its model, and justifies an alteration for which it is indebted to that version:

In another theatre, the ending was partly modified to avoid a totally tragic outcome; also in the present version, the director has taken on the hard task of changing some arias and extending or shortening several recitatives, whilst on the other hand the *buffo* roles had to be added.[18]

The alteration of the tragic ending concerns the suicide of Rosmiri, who is here made to survive the poison, comforted by Megabise. The words of Statira's last aria are also altered to resemble more closely a conventional *ombra* aria ('Vieni, Arsace, ah dove sei?').[19] The wording of the preface seems to suggest that the modifications were undertaken with reluctance, or at least that they were requested from outside. This becomes quite evident in the next adaptation, that of the Teatro Alibert in Rome, carnival 1720, where the tragic ending is actually eliminated. The opera, given as *Amore e maestà* again, was composed by Francesco Gasparini (whose house was then frequented by Pietro Metastasio, who apparently intended to marry his

18. '. . . Vi è stato in altro Teatro in qualche parte variato il fine, per non renderlo totalmente funesto; come ancora in questo con non poca pena di chi l'ha diretto vi si sono variate alcune Arie, et accresciuti, o diminuiti alcuni Recitativi, come altresì vi si sono dovuto ponere le parti Buffe . . .'.
19. The score and libretto have been edited in facsimile by Howard M. Brown in *Italian Opera, 1640–1770* (New York: Garland Inc., 1978), vols 22 and 53.

daughter). The owner-impresario of the theatre, Conte Antonio d'Alibert, dedicated the libretto to James Francis Stuart, pretender to the British throne
('Giacomo III'), who was a well-known patron of opera in Rome at the time. His
ancestor James I Stuart had, ironically, inherited the British crown from Elizabeth
Tudor in 1603, just two years after the alleged events of *Le Comte d'Essex*, where the
anticipation of the Queen's unhappy death is the main theme of the tragic ending.
Alibert shows his awareness of this circumstance in his *argomento*: 'The subject
matter of this opera, although it is taken from a historical event which happened in
a European capital, and although it has been presented as such with the proper
names of its true protagonists on the French stage by the famous Corneille, was
nevertheless for good reasons transferred by the Italian author, no less famous than
the other, to the Persian court.'[20] (We shall come back to this transfer of the setting.)
The éloge for Salvi is cleverly inflated by presenting him as Thomas Corneille's
equal but omitting the latter's Christian name, so that the even more famous 'Pierre'
could be inferred.

This time, the unknown libretto arranger – presumably one of the many Academic poets in Rome – makes it perfectly clear that he altered Salvi's tragedy against
his wishes and literary judgement. After narrating the plot, his *argomento* concludes:

> Such was the ending of this most noble tragedy, which two writers had drafted
> with such understanding of the good taste of the learned, that to alter any of it
> would surely be temerity. But the spirit of the carnival season, and the inclina-
> tions of the one who wants it filled with pleasurable rather than lamentable
> matters, must serve as an excuse for the decision to conclude it with a happy
> ending – the invention that Mitrane, moved by Arsace's generosity, saves him,
> deceiving Artabano, and then conducts him alive to Statira who in the end
> marries him, whilst Rosmiri remains with Mitrane. The person who has carried
> out this idea as best as he could, did this under the constraint of his obedience to
> the one who commanded it; and yet he apologizes more than anyone else for it,
> admitting that his error is too bold.[21]

I suggest that these lines illustrate a tension between the Arcadian (or Quirinian)
litterati and their patrons and audiences, at least in Rome but probably also in
Florence and Venice. Surely, death and destruction shown in historical plots have

---

20. '. . . L'Argomento di quest'opera, ancorche sia preso da un fatto Istorico successo in una Regia di
    Europa, e tale l'habbia esposto co' i nomi proprii de' personaggi veri, sulle Scene Francesi il famoso
    Cornelio, fu nondimeno per saggi motivi dall'Autore Italiano, non meno celebre dell'altro,
    trasportato alla corte di Persia . . .'.
21. '. . . Tale era il fine di questa nobilissima Tragedia trattata da due penne Maestre con metodo sì
    adattato al buon gusto degli eruditi; che non può negarsi essere stata temerità, il mutarla in alcuna
    parte; Ma il costume del tempo Carnevalesco, & il genio di chi desidera in esso oggetti piacevoli, e
    non lacrimosi, servirà di scusa alla risoluzione presa di farla terminare con fine lieto, fingendo che
    Mitrane mosso dalla generosità di Arsace lo salvi, ingannando Artabano, e poi lo conduca vivo a
    Statira, che a lui finalmente si sposa, restando a Mitrane Rosmiri. Chi ha eseguito nel miglior
    modo che ha saputo questo pensiero, lo ha fatto, costretto dall'obedienza che doveva a chi glie
    lo ha comandato; e però ne chiede più d'ogn'altro il perdono, confessando per troppo ardito il suo
    fallo.'

a disquieting, possibly enlightening effect. If treated according to the precept of verisimilitude and with a minimum of historical truth (or even realism), the tragic ending ties the spectator down to the wrongs of this world, forcing him to think politically.[22] Furthermore, there is the tension between the 'erudite' dramatic poet and the spectators who want nothing but entertainment: the same constellation can already be observed in earlier Venetian operatic debates, for example on the occasion of *Mitridate Eupatore* by Frigimelica-Roberti and Alessandro Scarlatti in 1707.[23]

These tensions were avoided, it seems, by Metastasio in his first independent opera libretto a few years later in Naples. *Didone abbandonata*, the subject of which was chosen because of its tragic ending, owes its existence largely to the influence of the primadonna Marianna Benti-Bulgarelli, and to the poet's and her enlightened Austrian patrons. This circumstance provides the first of several analogies with the Neapolitan production of *Arsace* in 1718 (of which Metastasio must have known at least through Marianna). The poet himself forges much closer links between his *Didone abbandonata* written for the carnival of 1724 and the opera of 1718.

By 1724 the *scene buffe* have become genuine *intermezzi comici* (*L'impresario delle isole Canarie*), thus freeing the actual drama of comic servants. At the same time, Metastasio's intermezzi take up the idea of the 'play within the play', because the buffoonists Dorina and Nibbio are professionals of (serious) opera and thus correspond to Merilla and Morante who in *Arsace* sang serious arias in the roles of Venus and Vulcan.[24] The two roles of the *Arsace* prologue are themselves symbolically connected with Aeneas (son of Venus) and with Dido's death in the fire (the element of Vulcanus). Their prologue 'in Heaven' is transformed in 1724 into a *licenza* at the end which literally clears away the clouds of Dido's tragic suicide in the flames of Carthage, with the splendid appearance of the Temple of Neptune in the blue sky.

Let us now consider the tragic ending itself, made inevitable by a conflict of passion and glory. This conflict between passion and ethos is the principal subject matter of both dramas, and in Salvi's it also provides the title. First of all, both librettos entrust the full dramatic weight of the final scene(s) to the primadonna and protagonist alone. Operas or plays ending in soliloquies (laments) existed before,[25] but in *Amore e maestà* and *Didone abbandonata* the scenic situation exactly matches the psychic condition: Statira (Elizabeth), who has lost her lover and her friends, is

22. Ulderico Rolandi, *Il libretto per musica attraverso i tempi* (Rome, 1951), p. 147, makes the interesting suggestion that the ecclesiastical censors in the papal states were more hostile to tragic operas than the authorities elsewhere.

23. See Roberto Pagano, Lino Bianchi and Giancarlo Rostirolla, *Alessandro Scarlatti* (Turin: ERI, 1972), pp. 185–9.

24. The impresario motive is borrowed, most probably, from Girolamo Gigli's *La Dirindina*, Rome, 1715.

25. See also Wolfgang Osthoff, 'Zur musikalischen Tradition der tragischen Gattung im italienischen Theater (16.–18. Jahrhundert)', in *Studien zur Tradition in der Musik: Festschrift Kurt von Fischer zum 60. Geburtstag*, ed. by Hans Heinrich Eggebrecht and Max Lütolf (Munich: Katzbichler, 1973), pp. 121–43, especially pp. 132ff. with a discussion of Sarri's monologues for *Didone* of 1724.

also *abbandonata*. (She is not alone on stage; as in *Le Comte d'Essex*, her helpless courtiers are present but cannot reach her.) The two figures surely have a common ancestry.[26] Both women are also losing their realms, an immensely significant aspect of the plot on the level of ethos. Dido as well as Elizabeth desperately try to assert their *gloire* while saving their love, and end up losing both. Already Metastasio's first aria for Didone states programmatically: 'Son regina e sono amante', asserting that she alone will dispose of her heart as well as her throne. One of Salvi's alterations in comparison with Thomas Corneille is the intrigue that the main villain and traitor, Artabano (Coban), wants to marry Statira (Elizabeth) himself, thus becoming king. This corresponds to the ploy of Metastasio's Jarba: the villain is after the Queen's hand as well as her realm. Not only is the self-determination of a woman at stake in these libretti, but the legitimacy of the female succession in general, which is why the 'heretic' reign of Elizabeth I had been an embarrassment to the Catholic monarchies. Her closest counterpart, Queen Christina of Sweden, converted and abdicated – which was what the Catholic party would have hoped from Elizabeth, too, at least after she had taken such leave of her senses as to fall in love. Christina's conversion was to spiritual love. Against this background, Dido's catastrophe, although often seen on the Renaissance and Baroque stage, receives a new moral and political connotation in Metastasio. The Queen, who sins against her ethos (*gloire*), is punished by also losing the object of her affections. In Salvi's tragedy there is obviously the question of the other victim, Arsace. Statira demands and receives almost as much sympathy as the rebellious Earl, but her collapse on stage inspires more terror. Thus the actual victim, Arsace, in the end takes second place to the spiritual victim, i.e. to the one who has become guilty of forgetting herself. This modification of the well-known story paved the way for Metastasio's *Didone*.

It could be claimed that Salvi gives sharper edges to the *sujet*. The very fact that the Dido subject was half-legendary and more traditional (and by no means always developed entirely tragically) makes Metastasio's version a safer choice than a political tragedy. And the tradition of the Dido subject suggests that she goes mad (as in Busenello's *Didone delirante*), which takes the political sting out of her suicide. Salvi has to maintain historical verisimilitude and therefore cannot pretend that Elizabeth/Statira is out of her mind. The line with which she begins the final monologue, 'Furie che m'agitate', is a tribute to conventions not really developed in the scene itself.

Salvi, too, pays tribute to conservative influences by transferring the *setting* of his libretto from recent English (Christian although Protestant) to ancient Persian (pagan and barbarian) history. This transfer, and the stereotypical 'Persian' names chosen for the characters, make them and the plot 'unverifiable', in a way similar to Zeno's transfer of *Bajazet* to ancient China. But Salvi could not have disguised his sources. The historical events underlying his version were widely known, and the

26. Patrick J. Smith, *The Tenth Muse: A Historical Study of the Opera Libretto* (London, 1971), pp. 61 and 78, interestingly connects the final monologues of Metastasio's *Didone* and Quinault's *Armide* (1686). In that case, too, a realm is destroyed.

attention of the reader was drawn to them in many libretto prefaces.[27] Quite differently from Zeno's approach, Salvi makes his dependence on the original so clear that he deprives himself of the opportunity to change the plot – and, what is more, the ethos – of his characters. His transfer of the setting is a trivial change by comparison with that fidelity. What he intends may be a political domestication of the plot, and an opportunity (not an obligation) to have colourful oriental stage-sets and costumes. Nevertheless, by choosing an artificial setting for a well-known story, the dramatist also gives profile to the structure of the intrigue and the interests involved. His characters are quasi-allegories of the tragic story, relatively unencumbered by the literary traditions of this particular plot.

Finally, we should remember that the vast majority of the opera librettos which in this period were derived from French *tragédies* had their original tragic endings changed into happy ones. It has become a commonplace to expect opera to end happily. Is this the result of its very essence as a genre? Is there a theory of opera which can formulate a reason why opera has to have a *lieto fine*? Salvi's operation in *Amore e maestà* forgoes, with the *lieto fine*, one of the most frequent, traditional excuses of librettists for the 'imperfections' of their dramas. In fact, he does not acknowledge any 'imperfections'; the Roman arranger of his text in 1720 testifies to the libretto's reputation as a genuine, even *nobilissima, tragedia*. As shown in chapter 6, Zeno's alterations to the subjet and ethos of his characters in *Teuzzone* were necessary to achieve a *lieto fine*. The Queen, for example, had to become a villain, and one of the ordinary villains had to repent. But it remained uncertain, in turn, why the happy ending was actually deemed necessary. In *Amore e maestà*, the musical performance remains the only a priori difference from the French model, since the guidelines of Aristotelian drama are fully accepted. An excuse with the exigencies of the music is, however, spurned by Salvi, except for the transfer of setting. If his libretto is found to diverge from its model in important dramaturgical elements – and this will be the subject of the next chapter – then we shall have to seek the reason not in the music as such, nor in an aesthetic convention, but in the emerging status of the opera libretto as a dramatic genre in its own right.

27. In London, for example, *Arsace* was given almost simultaneously with the play by John Banks, *The unhappy favourite*, a version of the Essex story also inspired by Thomas Corneille.

9
Amore e maestà: the emancipation of an opera libretto

It is well worth questioning whether the opposition 'opera/drama' is of a quality that transcends the history of the respective manifestations. Perhaps opera is a concept that was not given by nature – as many writers on opera seem to believe– but by history. A better knowledge of the transfers from drama to opera in the Baroque period – in addition to similar studies in the late eighteenth- and nine-teenth-century theatre – may help us to outline the 'essence' of opera as a theatrical genre in its own right. Antonio Salvi is a promising author for such studies. The following investigation compares, once more, Salvi's libretto with its model, Thomas Corneille's tragedy *Le Comte d'Essex* of 1678.

Amore e maestà and *Le Comte d'Essex* are more similar to each other than were Apostolo Zeno's *Teuzzone* and its French models, discussed in chapters 6 and 7. Nevertheless, there are changes of characters, setting, scenic structure, stage-sets, actions and diction. Salvi's libretto preface, the beginning of which we have consid-ered earlier,[1] acknowledges its model as well as the alterations:

> The subject is the same as has been presented on the French stage by the famous Thomas Corneille, under the title of the Count of Essex; but since the tragedy has to serve the music, the cast, and the Italian stage, I rather decided to set the scene in Persia, diminish the number of roles, vary the stage-sets, introduce varied actions, and greatly change the piece with respect to the original. I have, however, preserved the characters of the principal roles, made the catastrophe more fatal and tightened the succession of events. . . .[2]

These interesting assertions of the author can guide us to the recognition of the different levels on which the libretto deviates from the spoken play.

---

1. See p. 168 above.
2. 'Il soggetto è l'istesso che già espose sulle scene di Francia il famoso Tommaso Cornelio, sotto il nome del Conte d' Essex; ma dovendo questa [sc. Tragedia] servire alla Musica, alla Compagnia, ed al Teatro Italiano, m'è convenuto fingere la Scena in Persia, scemare il numero degli Attori, variar lo Scenario, far comparire varie azioni; ed alterarla molto dal suo Originale. Ho però conservato i caratteri de' principali Personaggi, e resa la catastrofe più funesta, e più spessi gl'incidenti; . . . .'

The first sentence (until 'original'), which lists a series of changes, still recalls the older habit of librettists who excused themselves for their 'shortcomings' with the operatic conventions – despite the fact that this librettist does not admit any shortcomings. But how 'music, cast and Italian stage' can have caused the particular changes that were made in this case is still to be determined.

The second sentence, by contrast, seems to refer to the similarities with the model that remain. Making the catastrophe more fatal and tightening the course of events are presented not as changes but as enhancements of the inherent tendencies of the subject, or indeed of Corneille's tragedy. This may indicate that Salvi saw himself as writing in the same dramatic genre.

We shall discuss the various dramaturgical elements mentioned in Salvi's preface one by one, but begin with a tabulated overview of the characters (table 9) and stage-sets (table 10).

Table 9 immediately shows how the hierarchical structure of the cast is preserved, notwithstanding the cutting of one role (Crommer speaks only once in Corneille). The reduction of roles brings their number to six and thus conforms to conventions of casting ('compagnia') in Italian opera. A note on Salvi's names for his *personaggi* may be in order. Although none of them is actually unknown in the Italian libretto tradition (and some are actually historical, at least that of Statira), they all allude to their French models in a hidden manner. 'Mitrane', for example, has four letters in common with 'Irton', 'Artabano' four with 'Coban', 'Statira' four with 'Élisabeth'. 'Arsace' recalls the sound of 'Essex'; and even 'Rosmiri' retains one syllable of 'Henriette'. This game with partial anagrams[3] has probably no deeper meaning beyond showing that the characters in Persian garb are more similar to the original English ones than may at first appear.

The opera libretto carries the statement 'La scena si finge in Persepoli Metropoli della Persia' ('The scene is set in Persepolis, capital of Persia'). The replacement of a modern British with a supposedly ancient Persian courtly setting is one of the changes which the poet attributes to the requirements of 'la musica, la compagnia e del teatro italiano'. Particular reasons have already been suggested in the previous

Table 9. Characters

Le Comte d'Essex	*Amore e maestà*
Thomas Corneille (1678)	Antonio Salvi (1715)
Élisabeth, reine d'Angleterre	Statira, regina di Persia
Henriette, Duchesse d'Irton, aimée du comte d'Essex	Rosmiri, principessa, sposa di Mitrane
Le Comte d'Essex	Arsace, supremo generale del regno
Le Comte de Salsbury, ami du comte d'Essex	Megabise, amico di Arsace
Cécile, enemi du comte d'Essex	Mitrane, principe Persiano
Tilney, confident d'Élisabeth	Artabano, consigliere della regina
Crommer, capitaine des gardes	–

3. Also played by Metastasio when he alludes, in his *L'Olimpiade*, to the characters' names of the model, Zeno's *Gl'inganni felici*.

Table 10. Scenes and stage-sets[4]	
Le Comte d'Essex	*Amore e maestà*
	'a' I, 1–3 Sala reale addobbata per le nozze di Rosmiri e Mitrane
I, 1–3	'b' I, 6–9 Piazza di Persepoli avanti la Regia
II, 1–8	'c' I, 10–13 Camera Reale
–	'd' II, 1–6 Salone del consiglio con trono
–	'e' II, 7–9 Giardinetto dell'appartamento di Rosmiri
III, 1–4	'f' II, 10–14 Anticamera con tavolino
	da scrivere, e sedie
–	'g' III, 1–2 Cortil Regio
IV, 1–5	'h' III, 3–5 Prigione
V, 1–8	'i' III, 6–13 Giardino Reale

chapter; they included the greater freedom from historical restraints, and possibly the greater appeal of colourful scenography afforded by a more exotic setting.

Our further discussion will operate with a distinction between 'corresponding' and 'non-corresponding' scenic units in the two plays, as shown in table 10. Salvi's scenic units 'b', 'c', 'f', 'h' and 'i' correspond to units of the model (i.e., its five Acts); the others do not correspond.

Few individual scenes of the model are bypassed altogether: most of the French play is reflected in the adaptation. When compared with the model, there is also little reshuffling of individual scenes (as defined by entrances); the librettist follows the order of scenes of the model in each unit, but then inserts totally new scenic units like larger building-blocks. These are the non-corresponding scenic units 'a', 'd', 'e' and 'g'. Only slight modifications of the other, corresponding scenic units result from these insertions.

Corneille has five Acts and Salvi three, divided into nine scenic units (3 × 3). Five of these correspond to the original five Acts; the added four units are symmetrically distributed over the three Acts (1–2–1). The nine scenic units 'a'–'i' coincide with Salvi's stage sets. French tragedy, of course, did not traditionally work with changeable scenery (*mutazioni di scena*), whereas Italian opera always did. The varied stage-sets are, then, an alteration resulting directly from the traditions of 'the Italian stage' ('il Teatro Italiano'). I suspect, however, that Salvi specifically mentioned the matter because his individual selection of stage-sets had to do with changes of the plot.

The main characters

As has been suggested in chapter 6, *Le Comte d'Essex* aims at a more sentimental variant of the Aristotelian effects of fear and compassion. *Attendrissement* is caused in this play not so much by the events, nor even by the fluctuating passions, as by a basic, unchanging constellation of interests and values among the leading

---

4. The letters 'a', etc., denoting scenic units (stage-sets), will be quoted throughout this study to distinguish Salvi's Act and scene numbers from Corneille's.

8. *Le comte d'Essex*, painting by Nicolas Lancret representing Act V, scene 6 of the play by
Thomas Corneille: Tilney reports the execution of Essex to Élisabeth and Henriette.

characters: Élisabeth, Comte, Duchesse. The tragedy is static also in not producing
a reversal of fortune (catastrophe). The main opponents, Elizabeth and the Earl,
miss every single opportunity to avert the dreaded outcome. Particularly ineffectual
is the Queen: when in the central scene III, 4 ('f' II, 13) she is told the secret of
Henriette's earlier relationship with the Earl, she refrains from punishing her rival
and, while forgiving the lovers, fails to find any means of rescuing them. It is as if
the revelation could just as well not have happened.

The three leading characters and the relationships between them are the layer of
the play which Salvi did not modify, i.e. he judged them to be suitable for 'la
musica, la compagnia, e il Teatro Italiano'. It was probably his decision to accept the
funesto fine which enabled him to follow the French model with regard to character.

The Queen's dilemma between love and glory (pathos and ethos) is straightforward. It is not actually a tragic dilemma: for her, the two values ought not to be of
the same rank at all. She predictably subordinates her love to her glory when she
insists on the Earl's apology before pardoning him, while giving up her claims on his
person. After having given in to passion with 'il y va de ma vie' (III, 2), she says to
Salsbury immediately afterwards (III, 3):

'Mais je dois à l'état encor plus qu'à moi-même'

and then to Henriette (III, 4):

'Il y va de ma gloire, il faut qu'il cède.'

Nevertheless, even the insistence on her status and her decision to forgive – *gloire* above *amour* – are, in the end, strangely coloured by passion. When the Earl obstinately refuses to ask for pardon, insisting on *his* honour, the Queen reconciles herself to his death in a state of mind that might be called utter jealousy (V, 1; and V, 5, when she admits it to Henriette). Her pursuit of glory is tainted by love and jealousy. Salvi has fully accepted this 'psychological' dilemma:[5] his title *Amore e maestà* emphasizes not only the pathos-ethos conflict but their pernicious inter-mingling in the character of the Queen.

The relationship between the Queen and Essex is a direct competition about honour and glory – because he, too, ranks his honour above everything. But after his revolt aimed at preventing Henriette's wedding – an act of passion which is exploited against him by his enemies – his and the Queen's glories cannot be reconciled any longer. In contrast to her, the Earl does not need to overcome any internal conflict, but is crushed as a result of his ill-considered revolt.

The justice done to both by the tragic outcome is, in his case, a punishment for his blind action, whereas his system of values remains intact and he can die happily. The Queen, on the other hand, remains alive but is punished with remorse and desperation as her passions have tainted her integrity.

Henriette contrasts with both the other main characters by lacking any respect for glory. Her highest value is love, for which she sacrifices everything else. Her wedding – an act of self-sacrifice – is intended to save the Earl's life, which is unfortunately what he is least interested in. Thus he has reason to reproach her even for hastening his death: by withdrawing herself and so making him wish to die. Henriette's dilemma is the only one in the play that is purely tragic: she cannot fulfil one duty (towards the Earl's life and wellbeing) without offending the other (towards his love). The conflict between the lovers is unchanging: his greatest value is glory, hers love. To him, love is only a passion; to her, a status. This constella-tion epitomizes the conflicts of many opera libretti of the time where one character exhibits this particular attitude towards love and so comes into conflict with all the others.

When Salvi adopts this characterization for his figure of Rosmiri, he furnishes his libretto with a trait which, in hindsight, might be called 'typically operatic'. But the observation that operas usually cast a woman in the role of the self-sacrificing lover and victim, and the resulting suspicion that the 'nature of opera' includes a sexist

---

5. 'Psychological' only by analogy, of course, with modern theories which claim that human motivations are naturally 'impure' and mixed, whereas the rationalist epoch believed in pure motivations.

element, that opera is itself an agent of gender discrimination,[6] might be tempered by a look at its historical intertwinement with the spoken theatre and the rest of our literary traditions.

Whereas this characterization of Rosmiri comes, indeed, straight from the French model, there are some remarkable traits on the level of plot which the librettist has invented for her. First, she becomes a much more tragic heroine than was Henriette. She commits suicide at the end, accusing the Queen of having murdered Arsace ('i' III, 10). Both her suicide and her accusation are violent denials of the value of 'glory'; it is as if Rosmiri were trampling *maestà* under her feet after it has destroyed *amore*. The scene is a net addition by Salvi and gives the performer of Rosmiri extra weight in the drama.

Secondly, she has added solo scenes at the end of Act II ('f' II, 14) and in the middle of Act III ('h' III, 5). In these cases at least, a scenic structure which we may justly consider 'melodramatic' is utilized for a more heroic presentation of the woman. Whereas in Corneille's Act IV Henriette has fainted and is being taken care of, in Act III of the libretto Rosmiri awakes alone and resolves to do her utmost to save her lover. The content of the final scene of Act II is very similar. Arsace is given an 'operatic' Act-ending solo as well, though not as a net addition to the model: Salvi's solo scene 'c' I, 13 is based on a 'pompous quatrain' of the model in II, 8 (see also below).

While recognizing the librettist's essential fidelity to his model in the portrayal of the main characters, we note the different weighting he gives to their scenic relationships. Thus, he omits some dialogues between them. One of these is II, 7, a dialogue between the Earl and Henriette which almost doubles their first argument in I, 2 (analysed below). Another is II, 2, where the Queen and Henriette treat each other amicably since the secret of the lovers is still undisclosed.[7] Salvi also cuts V, 5, where Elizabeth is given a last opportunity to express her remorse; instead, he adds Rosmiri's accusation against her ('i' III, 10).

In the libretto, the Queen and the hero meet twice more often than in the play: in 'd' II, 3 (a non-corresponding scenic unit) and in 'f' II, 12, where Statira and Arsace repeat their previously-held argument (of 'c' I, 11), again without success.

The overall result of these changes is that Statira meets Rosmiri fewer times than in the play, but Arsace more often; the lovers meet more rarely. This accentuates the feeling of conflict in the whole drama. The dialogues are, on the whole, more aggressive or at least fruitless, and usually shorter. Considering also that Salvi eliminated two deliberative scenes between the Queen and her confidant Tilney, only partly redistributing their contents among other scenes, we can refer his claim to have 'tightened the succession of events' to this aspect of the scenic structure: his

6. See, for example, Cathérine Clement, *Opera, or the Undoing of Women*, with a foreword by Susan McClary (University of Minnesota Press, 1988).
7. A faint reflection of this omitted dialogue may be found in Salvi's non-corresponding scene 'a' I, 1, where the Queen speaks amicably to Rosmiri.

version of the tragedy is tighter because less amicable or conversational dialogue happens between the main characters.

The secondary characters

Salvi's most significant change to the drama lies in the role of Mitrane. This figure, like Cécile, occupies prime position among the villains, at least in terms of scenic appearance. But Salvi has given him a much more complex role by collapsing the absent figure of Henriette's husband, the Duke of Irton, and the primary villain into one character. Two entirely new scenic units deal with Rosmiri's and Mitrane's marriage. The first, 'a', shows the wedding itself and provides a ceremonial opening to the *dramma per musica*. The second, 'e', is in central position and essentially shows a matrimonial conflict. The jealous Mitrane forces Rosmiri to confess her love for Arsace. She, in turn, warns him not to insist on possessing her heart, too, after she has given him everything else.

'e' II, 8
Rosmiri.
La mia destra, il mio seno,
Il mio volto, il mio onore, e la mia Fede,
Tutto è tuo, fuor che il cor, ma s'ancor questo
Con la morte d'Arsace
Aspiri a posseder, perdi anco il resto.

Molto vuoi, troppo mi chiedi,
Tutto brami, e nulla avrai.
Quanto è mio, tutto possiedi
Fuor che 'l cor, ch'altrui donai.

If he is going to destroy Arsace, he will lose her entirely. This is what happens in the end: Mitrane succumbs to his jealousy and contrives Arsace's death; Rosmiri takes her own life. The last dialogue between the spouses, therefore, echoes the central scene:

'i' III, 10
Rosmiri.
. . . troppo volesti
Con la morte d'Arsace,
E per troppo voler, tutto perdesti.

Mitrane's late remorse ('tardo rimorso', 'i' III, 9) is partly a reflection of his concern over Rosmiri; his final accusations against the Queen and his punishment – which derive from the play (Cécile V, 4) but are greatly expanded and exaggerated

– now appear to be triggered by the failure of his marriage. They are, in a sense, the revenge of Rosmiri's offended love. The marriage theme, new in Salvi's adaptation, may have been drawn from models within the Italian libretto tradition – but this must remain an open question at present.[8]

Mitrane is really a 'mixed character'. He starts feeling remorse for his villainy at the beginning of Act III. At that point his doubts are allayed by Artabano, but at the very end Mitrane's conversion is complete – too late to save either his wife's or his rival's life. On the whole, the character of Mitrane adds moral and emotional tension to the plot. With this figure, Antonio Salvi has compounded a typically 'Baroque' structure – the struggle of pathos and ethos, love and glory – with a more modern, almost 'psychological' conflict of love, hatred, exploitation and jealousy between spouses.

It seems worth asking in what respects *Amore e maestà* was imitated by the Essex dramas of the Romantic era, written by François Ancelot and by the librettists Romani and Cammarano.[9] Ancelot reproduces two specific traits which distinguish Salvi's libretto from its predecessors: at the beginning there is a ceremony or happy wedding scene, at the end a long monologue for the despairing Queen. We have already linked this 'operatic' ending with the final monologue of Metastasio's *Didone abbandonata*. The dramaturgical stereotype of a final solo for the primadonna has since become an ingredient of the opera tradition. Salvi introduced it in the history of this subject by expanding the few, dry words spoken by Corneille's Elizabeth into a long and passionate discourse. But is it for that reason an operatic trait? Ancelot, for his spoken tragedy, seized upon it. His followers Romani and Cammarano differed: the former had no use for the monologue at all; the latter retained its dramatic impact and overall length but added a chorus. Donizetti's music makes this concluding scene a great moment for a great singer. Nevertheless, the idea of a final tragic monologue for the protagonist is not specific to one theatrical genre.

Returning to Thomas Corneille: his minor characters underwent extensive reworking in Salvi's adaptation. This was a result of the changes in the figure of Mitrane. Although he represents Corneille's Cécile, his other 'engagements' on stage in the scenes with Rosmiri force him to give up some of Cécile's activities – otherwise he would be dominating the play altogether. For this reason, the librettist has awarded stage presence to a second villain, Artabano. He corresponds to Corneille's Coban, who pulls the strings of the revolt against Elizabeth, but does not personally appear on stage (a particularly mischievous trick?). Salvi's Artabano has an added motivation to plot against Arsace: he himself wants to marry the Queen in order to gain the throne. Thus, the two villains are symmetrically arranged as Arsace's rivals in love as well as in politics – another manifestation of the title *Amore e maestà*.

8.   The terms in which the spouses confront each other in the quoted scene 'e' II, 8 – the almost cynical separation of 'heart', 'hand', 'body', 'honour' and the verbal enumeration itself in which they are couched – sound exploitative to us. At the same time, this is the rhetorical language of many Baroque opera librettos. To what extent does this higher-pitched rhetoric in the Italian linguistic context send a different moral and social message?

9.   See chapter 15 in this volume, 'The Earl of Essex', pp. 301–5.

Artabano's stage appearances are to some extent taken over from the scenes for Cécile. This also affects the plot and the intrigue: Artabano, not Mitrane, is the one who presents the forged evidence against Arsace (a letter of treason) in 'd' II, 2 (Cécile in II, 3). Furthermore, in 'f' II, 10 Artabano briefly takes on Cécile's function (II, 1). In 'c' I, 12 he is allowed to arrest Arsace, a task given by Corneille to the subordinate Crommer, whose only speaking appearance this was (II, 3). Artabano's other appearances, however, arise out of a doubling of the villain's role in Salvi's version. He either makes Mitrane and Artabano appear as a pair where Corneille had only Cécile (in 'f' and 'i') or he gives them newly-invented scenes in which they appear together with other characters or converse among themselves (in the non-corresponding units 'a', 'd' and 'g'). In the latter cases, they have successive exits ending in a solo scene.

In particular, the sequence 'd' II, 2–4, in the courtroom, shows the villains together in charge of events, since they are Arsace's appointed judges. Their conspiracy appears thus all the more dangerous; Statira gives up much of her leading role in 'd' II, 4 (for example, at 'volta le spalle'). The dramaturgical advantages of having a pair of villains instead of a single person lie in the general parallelism of the plot, as well as in the provision with dialogue scenes when the traitors can discuss and so disclose their plans without improbability. Salvi adds or retains soliloquies in addition to this: for example, Mitrane retains Cécile's monologue 'Agissons, il est temps' (I, 3) as 'Perdasi l'orgoglioso' ('b' I, 9: see below).

The pair of villains, one of whom is morally 'mixed' and repents at the end, is surely reminiscent of Zeno's *Teuzzone*. Strikingly similar is the portrayal of the worse of the two, Sivenio/Artabano, as a dark warrior-figure. Cino's repentance, on the other hand, had been instrumental in achieving Zeno's *lieto fine*. It is no coincidence that the later revisions of Salvi's libretto, where the *funesto fine* is modified (1718) or overturned (1720), effect this change on the basis of Mitrane's repentance.

Conversely to the case of the villains, Corneille had operated with two confidants whom Salvi collapses into one. Salsbury, friend of the Earl, and Tilney, confidant of the Queen, are both replaced by Megabise, who takes on many of their functions of advisers, mediators and messengers. To balance this double employ for Megabise, he is excused from many scenes which Tilney spends with the Queen. In Corneille's Act II he is permanently on stage with her; and he accompanies her for parts of Acts III and V as well. The libretto either eliminates his presence altogether or places a monologue for the Queen before her dialogue with Megabise. Such monologues arise in 'c' I, 10, 'f' II, 11 and 'i' III, 6; all are labelled 'Statira poi Megabise'. Nevertheless, the difference from the original is small, since in any case Elizabeth opens these scenes with a solo *tirade* to her confidant, i.e. with a 'disguised monologue'.[10] Thus, while generating more dialogue material for the villains (and retaining the only self-revealing monologue, 'Perdasi l'orgoglioso'), Salvi has transformed some dialogues (or disguised monologues) for the Queen into actual

10. In two of these scenes (I, 10 and III, 6), the libretto of 1715 has entrance arias for Statira, both of which were omitted in performance.

Table 11. Secondary characters

Le Comte d'Essex	Amore e maestà	
		(function of characters)
Salsbury		(*good; on stage*)
>	Megabise	
Tilney		
>	Mitrane	(*bad; on stage*)
Cécile		
>	Artabano	
Crommer		
Coban		(*bad; not on stage*)

monologues. This emphasizes, I believe, an overall hierarchical structure by isolating the protagonist and her inner conflict.

For the secondary characters, the transfer of material from Corneille to Salvi – character traits as well as actually spoken text – may be represented as in table 11. Megabise takes over functions and characteristics from both Salsbury and Tilney, Mitrane from Tilney and Cécile (crossing the border from good to bad), and Artabano from Cécile, Crommer and Coban (also acting out some of Coban's invisible role).

Stage-sets

To 'vary the stage-sets' and 'introduce varied actions' was one of Salvi's major aims in adapting the drama. He created several scenic units which had no correspondence in the original ('a', 'd', 'e' and 'g'; see table 10). These provided him with opportunities to change character and plot, especially in the Rosmiri-Mitrane and Mitrane-Artabano scenes. This was helped, of course, by the stage-sets which suggested varying places of action.

As often in opera librettos of the time, the unity of place is stretched but not transgressed – because all the sets represent places fitting the general designation given in the 1715 libretto: 'The stage is set in Persepolis, capital of Persia'. Even so, four scenographies (in units 'c', 'e', 'f' and 'i') have no strict connection with the historical placement and serve only to diversify the visual aspect: one of them ('e') is the garden of Rosmiri's apartments. Such a generically royal *ambiente* will have been varied by scenographers in revivals, perhaps emphasizing or de-emphasizing characteristic Persian imagery. The other three of these sets occur in scenic units corresponding to Corneille's Acts II, III and V and are generically labelled 'Camera Reale', 'Anticamera con tavolino da scrivere, e sedie' and 'Giardino Reale', respectively. The units 'b' and 'g' are similarly unspecific, but are outdoor sets suitably serving as backgrounds for military actions or their discussion. Of these units, 'b' corresponds to Corneille (Act I), the other not. The sets mentioned so far could well be called 'generic'.

Of a different kind are the sets for the *prison scene* ('h'), which corresponds to Corneille's Act IV, and the *wedding scene* ('a'), added by Salvi. These are necessary, functional environments for a specific dramatic action or situation built into the plot. Nevertheless, these actions or situations are stereotyped in Baroque drama or opera; the sets can therefore be classified as 'functional' and 'stereotypical'.

Only one unit, added by Salvi, characterizes the individual plot of this drama, i.e. it is at the same time 'functional' and 'characteristic': the courtroom scene ('d'). The extent to which the librettist has expanded the few references to legal practice given in Corneille seems significant (see also below). In the libretto, the courtroom scene conveys a realistic and contemporary, even comedy-related atmosphere. Satire and criticism of legal practice were mainstays of contemporary comedy, Italian and French.

Taken as a whole, the stage-sets are chosen and distributed in a hierarchical, symmetrical fashion, with one of the three 'functional' sets in each Act, and with the two outdoor sets in Acts I and III. The royal interiors occupy the tail-ends of each Act as a result of the total disposition of the corresponding scenic units. Of the non-corresponding scenic units, 'e' occupies a central position in the opera. This puts into focus both the subject of the unit – the marriage of Rosmiri and Mitrane – and, potentially, the stage-set of her private 'Persian' gardens.

Scenic structure and arias

'Scenic units' are not only contained within individual stage-sets, but also defined by the much-discussed *liaison des scènes*, a convention according to which the stage should be empty as rarely as possible. Very often one character remains on stage when another leaves. There are two basic types of *liaison*: a 'static' type, in which the same character remains on stage throughout the unit while others enter and exit, and a 'dynamic' or 'chain'-type, where all the characters leave one after the other.

The 'dynamic' type can be presumed to be more interesting, but more difficult to achieve dramaturgically. The French tradition, with its vague definition of actual place, and absence of *mutazioni di scena*, could tolerate potential conflicts between probability and 'Aristotelian' unity of place. In an opera with changing sets and thus more individually defined places, however, the 'dynamic' type of *liaison* often conflicts with probability – such as when three, four or more characters all happen to meet successively in the same private apartments. Comedy is close at hand in this case.

By 1715 Italian opera had long crystallized the convention of the exit aria, by which the person who sings the aria must leave. In this convention, the 'static' type of *liaison* would long deny the exit aria to the very person who is staying on for several scenes, and therefore presumably of high status or important to the plot. (To achieve the *liaison* merely by keeping confidants or servants on stage was doubtless frowned upon.) If used, the 'static' type of *liaison* will at least make the final exit aria of its dominating character a dramatic climax to the whole scenic unit. On the whole, the 'dynamic' type is more suitable to the *dramma per musica*.

If we compare the appearances of all the characters in Salvi's corresponding scenic units ('b', 'c', 'f', 'h' and 'i'), we can see how he has achieved a reasonable variety of exits even where his model offered only a 'static' *liaison*, but has avoided crass improbability or implied change of place. He has also provided much opportunity for exit arias (indicated in the following tables 12, a–e, with *).[11]

Table 12a. Unit 'b'

Le Comte d'Essex			Amore e maestà	
I, 1–3			I, 6–9	
Co.	Sa.		Ars.	Meg.*
Co.	Du.		Ars.	Ros.*
Co.		Cé.	Ars.*	Mit.
		Cé. *seul*		Mit. *solo**

This 'static' unit has been reproduced faithfully; it dramatically ends with the unexpected departure of the hero, to leave the villain alone for the climactic conclusion, when he discloses his plans to the audience. Salvi did this probably also because he was impressed by Cécile's pompous quatrain 'Agissons, il est temps'.[12] It seems to have been easy for him, with some repetition of verbal matter, to turn a total of only eight lines of Corneille into three components: an exit aria for Arsace ('Je sais que contre moi vous animez la reine' – 'Tanta pace ha il reo nel seno'), a recitative for Mitrane *solo* ('Agissons, il est temps, c'est trop faire l'esclave; Perdons un orgueilleux . . .' – 'Perdasi l'orgoglioso'), and an exit aria for Mitrane ('Quel torrente, ch'orgoglioso').

Table 12b. Unit 'c'

Le Comte d'Essex					Amore e maestà	
II, 1–8					I, 10–13	
El.	Ti.				Sta. *poi* Meg.*	
El.	Ti.	Du.			(omitted)	
El.	Ti.	Du.	Cé.		"	
El.	Du.				"	
El.	Ti.	Du.				
				>	Sta.* *poi* Ars.	
El.	Ti.	Du.	Co.			
		Du.	Co.		(omitted)	
			Co.	Cr.	Ars.*poi* Art.*	
					Ars.**solo*	

From this 'static' sequence around the Queen, Salvi has cut the scenes (2–4 and 7) involving Henriette, but retained 5 and 6 from which only her part was cut. Two

---

11. Abbreviations: El. = Élisabeth, Co. = Comte, Du. = Duchesse (Henriette), Ti. = Tilney, Sa. = Salsbury, Cé. = Cécile, Cr. = Crommer; Sta. = Statira, Ars. = Arsace, Ros. = Rosmiri, Meg. = Megabise, Mit. = Mitrane, Art. = Artabano.
12. See chapter 7 above, p. 156.

scenes with Tilney (1 and 5) have been transformed into short monologues preceding a dialogue scene, with the typical direction 'Statira *then* Megabise' (Sta. *poi* Meg.). A similar construction opens I, 12 (Ars. *poi* Art.). This last section of the unit is particularly interesting. Artabano takes over Crommer's task of arresting Arsace, but has his part expanded to include an exit aria. Arsace's final *solo* scene is developed from the concluding 'pompous quatrain' of the model ('Vous avez dans vos mains'), with which the hero proudly reacts to his arrest.

Salvi has made this unit more 'dynamic' by letting Statira dominate the first, Arsace the second half in almost symmetrical fashion. The encounter of the two in I, 11 is the pivot, and its opening solo of Statira the high point of drama, showing her anxious anticipation while she sees him approach. Any observant composer will have set these lines as accompanied recitative:

'Ahi vista! Ecco l'ingrato; io gelo ed ardo;
Tremo per lui, egli esulta . . .'

The lines are close to the original text of the corresponding scene 5:

'Qu'il entre. Quels combats troublent déjà mon âme!'

Table 12c. Unit 'f'				
Le Comte d'Essex				*Amore e maestà*
III, 1–4				II, 10–14
El.	Ti.	Cé.		Sta. Art.*
El.	Ti.			
			>	Sta. *poi* Meg.*
El.	Sa.			
(absent)				Sta. *poi* Ars.*
El.	Du.			Sta.* *poi* Ros.
				Ros. *sola**

As already mentioned, the second encounter of Statira and Arsace, in this unit (II, 12), is an insertion by Salvi. It adds visual interest and is relevant to the 'varied actions', as the hero appears in chains (*incatenato*). He gets an opportunity to throw his sword at her feet when rejecting his pardon. Again, Corneille has furnished a 'static' sequence with the Queen as its only centre – which Salvi has preserved this time. And yet, with a last twist he gives Rosmiri the final exit with a *scena ed aria–* she decides to rescue Arsace at all costs. This solo scene, already mentioned for its importance for character and plot, is also structurally without precedent in Corneille.

It is a 'static' unit, to which the Earl is central because he is in prison and thus bound to remain on stage. Nevertheless, Salvi has given it some variety and a twist again. Corneille lets the Earl say the last words of the scene, asking the guards to take care of the fainted Duchess, while he himself is led to the scaffold (oh terror and pity!). Salvi gives Rosmiri a solo scene after she has revived:

Table 12d. Unit 'h'

Le Comte d'Essex IV, 1–6				Amore e maestà III, 3–5
Co.	Ti.			(omitted)
Co.	*seul*			
			>	Ars. *poi* Meg.*
Co.	Sa.			
Co.	Sa.	Du.		
			>	Ars.* Ros.
Co.	Du.	Cr.		
				Ros.* *sola*

'Ah, crudeli, fermate:
Dove, ahi lassa, guidate
La mia vita, il mio cor, l'Idolo mio?
. . .'

and the concluding aria:

'A morir senza di me
No'l permette la mia Fé . . .'.

It is rarely recognized how much dramatists cared for the dramaturgical implications of prison scenes. In this case, Arsace *leaves* the dungeon to go to his death; Rosmiri stays behind and wakes up in a prison which is now empty for the most horrible of reasons. This seems a remarkable way of creating drama out of an empty stage-set.

Table 12e. Unit 'i'

Le Comte d'Essex V, 1–8				Amore e maestà III, 6–13
El.	Ti.			Sta. *poi* Meg.
El.	Ti.	Du.		
			>	Sta. Meg. (*parte*) Ros.
El.		Du.		
El.		Du.	Cé	Sta. Ros. Mit. Art.
El.		Du.		
			>	Sta. Meg. Ros. (*parte*) Mit.
El.	Ti.	Du.		
(absent)				*detti*, and Ros. (returning)*
El.	Ti.			Sta. *poi* Meg.
El.	Ti.	Sa.		Sta. Meg. Mit.
				Sta. *sola**

The last unit is irregular in Salvi's libretto and in opera generally, as it has only two exit arias: one for the dying Rosmiri (she leaves in III, 9 to take poison, and returns in the next scene dying), and the other for the despairing Statira. An entrance aria for Statira in III, 6 was printed but not performed.

Here, Salvi cannot help but retain the 'static' structure; he has to focus on the Queen as the catastrophe unfolds before her eyes. Are his alterations, however, the result of operatic traditions or conventions? They may have initiated some conventions, such as the final monologue for the protagonist, discussed above, but I submit that this and also the other changes of scenic structure have genuinely dramatic goals and are not due to the 'Italian theatre', the cast, or indeed the music.

'Varie azioni'

In his preface, the librettist tells us that he has introduced 'varied actions' – a surprisingly blunt statement. Did the original contain no actions? Almost all the *évènements* of *Le Comte d'Essex* happen off-stage, except for the Earl's arrest (II, 8). Genuine stage action was largely expendable in French classical drama, though rarely lacking altogether. The actions added by Salvi go surely beyond those generally seen on the French stage of his time. They were also connected with his stage-sets. We can accept as *azioni* the following types of events:

    1. Scenic units 'a' and 'd' are stage ceremonies (wedding, trial), during which there is at least some movement on stage by the chorus (in 'a') or other non-speaking characters ('cavalieri e dame'; 'satrapi e guardie', respectively).

    2. Some stage directions call for the speaking partners to make active or aggressive gestures or movements that go deliberately beyond expected or reasonable behaviour. Most of these actions serve to underscore the dialogue, and their dramatic impact depends much on the style of the acting. Some would fit an Italian *scena di forza*, as described by contemporary writers. Here are several examples.

II, 3: Sta. 'volta le spalle' . . . Mit. 's'alza, e le dà il foglio di Dario' . . . Ars. 'Straccia, e calpesta il foglio' . . . Sta. 'Scende dal trono'.

II, 12: Sta. *poi* Ars. *incatenato, e guardie* . . . Sta. 'gli rende la spada' . . . Ars. 'le getta la spada a'piedi'.

II, 13: Sta. 'getta la penna'.

III, 4: Ros. 'cava uno stiletto per ferirsi, Arsace glielo toglie e lo getta' . . . 'Entrano Soldati nella prigione' . . . Ros. 'si sviene. Arsace la posa sopra d'un sasso.'[13]

    3. Rosmiri's successful suicide in III, 10 is a different matter, as it is a structural alteration to the plot itself. Even so, it adds purely scenic movement as well: Rosmiri rushes off-stage, where she takes poison; she returns dying, collapses on stage and is carried off.

    4. Other traits introduced into the plot, which increase the general level of activity on stage, are the following:

'b' I, 6 – which presents not a debate about the Earl's failed assault on the palace as

---

13. II, 3: Sta. 'turns her back to him' . . . Mit. 'stands up, and gives her the letter from Dario' . . . Ars. 'tears the letter into pieces and tramples on it' . . . Sta. 'descends from the throne'. II, 12: Sta., then Ars. in chains, with guards . . . Sta. 'returns the sword to him' . . . Ars. 'throws the sword at her feet.' II, 13: Sta. 'throws the pen away'. III, 4: Ros. 'pulls out a dagger, to stab herself; Ars. takes it off her and throws it away' . . . 'Soldiers enter the prison' . . . Ros. 'faints. Ars. lays her down on a rock.'

does the model, but its actual calling off: 'Arsace con spada nuda e seguito da armati, tenuto per mano da Megabise'. Arsace later asks his followers (*popolo*) to disperse; and I, 7 – where Mitrane overhears the dialogue between Arsace and Rosmiri.

Perhaps some of these *azioni* were chosen because they were more ingrained in the Italian opera tradition. But we cannot reasonably claim that they make the libretto cross the supposed borderline between drama and opera. Some of them were well known in the spoken theatre, of course; the eavesdropping by the jealous husband belongs rather to the vocabulary of comedy. Salvi's version seems, if anything, to blur the pure tragic style of the play rather than to transgress the boundaries of spoken drama altogether.

Dramaturgical balance

In the scenes corresponding with the model, the librettist had varied the exits to obtain exit arias for more characters, and at the same time to create more variety of stage appearances while preserving the *liaisons*. The added, non-corresponding scenes, on the other hand, seem to be intended to strike a dramaturgical balance.

To start with, their 'aria count' completes the total in a significant way: Statira has three arias in the corresponding scenes, three in the non-corresponding ones (3/3); Rosmiri 4/2, Arsace 4/1; Mitrane 1/4; Megabise 4/1 and Artabano 2/3. Thus, the new scenes give much opportunity for aria-singing to the villains, and help 'decentralize' the drama away from the leading roles.

Distributed over the nine scenic units, Salvi has created the following scene-ending arias (see table 13).

Table 13. Scene-ending arias

'a': Sta. Ros. Mit. Art. *solo*
'b': Meg. Ros. Ars. Mit. *solo*
'c': Meg. Sta. Art. Ars. *solo*
'd': Sta. (non-exit) Sta. Ars. Art. Mit. *solo*
'e': Meg. Ros. Mit. *solo*
'f': Art. Meg. Ars. Sta. Ros. *sola*
'g': Mit. Art. *solo*
'h': Meg. Ars. Ros. *sola*
'i': Ros. Sta. *sola*

The surprising number of solo scenes – one at the end of each scenic unit – seems characteristic for Antonio Salvi at this stage of his career. As has been shown, some of these solo scenes are developed from 'pompous quatrains', spoken alone, in Corneille; more of them, however, are introduced for purposes of plot and characterization. Thus, the nascent operatic stereotype of *scena ed aria* seems to arise here from the librettist's confrontation with his French model, albeit a critical confrontation.

Salvi was concerned not only with a balanced distribution of arias. A sign of his full adherence to the precepts of the French theatre is his planning of the actual stage appearances, i.e. dialogue participation of the characters. Even after considerable modifications of Corneille's dramaturgy, the libretto strikes a new, hierarchically ordered balance when we consider scenic units. The stage appearances of the characters are distributed as shown in table 14.

Table 14. Characters' appearances	
Le Comte d'Essex (Acts)	*Amore e maestà* (scenic units)
El. II, III, V (total 3)	Sta. a, c, d, f, i (total 5)
Du. I, II, III, IV, V (total 5)	Ros. a, b, e, f, h, i (total 6)
Co. I, II, IV (total 3)	Ars. b, c, d, f, h (total 5)
Cé. I, II, III, V (total 4)	Mit. a, b, d, e, g, i (total 6)
Ti. II, III, IV, V (total 4)	Meg. a, b, c, e, f, h, i (total 7)
Sa. I, IIII, IV, V (total 4)	Art. a, c, d, g, i (total 5).

One should not expect the number of appearances to match the rank of a role. On the contrary, subordinate figures are seen rather often (without, sometimes, being really 'seen'); the French and the Italian texts agree on this point (Tilney – Megabise). The interesting aspect of stage appearance in both dramas is the game about absences and reappearances. To give some examples: in Corneille, both the Earl and Elizabeth open one Act after they have been absent for the whole previous one. Elizabeth together with Tilney opens Act II (II, 1), which is the first appearance in the play for both of them, and the Queen also opens Act V after having been absent from IV. The Earl dominates Act IV which he also opens, whereas in III and V all characters *except him* are on stage. It may be surprising to discover that the Earl and the Queen coincide in one Act only: II.

In the planning of the libretto, analogous calculations have taken place. Arsace is absent from units 'a', 'e', 'g' and 'i'; in 'a' and 'i' (first and last), all characters but him are seen on stage. He, in turn, dominates 'b' and 'h', which he also opens in a dramatic fashion (I, 6 'con spada nuda'; III, 3 with prison monologue 'Un palco infame a me?').

Rosmiri is absent from 'c' and 'd' but then dominates 'e', opening it (II, 7) with Megabise who had been absent from the preceding unit, too. Statira opens 'c' (I, 10), 'f' (II, 10) and 'i' (III, 6), after she had been absent from the respective preceding units. In 'c' and 'i', she has initial monologues. Mitrane opens Act Two ('d') after his absence from unit 'c', and Act Three ('g') with an important monologue (remorse), after 'f' had presented everybody but him.

Whereas Henriette is seen in all five of Corneille's Acts, Rosmiri's stage appearances are brought in line with those of the other characters. Here, Salvi had to restore a balance, because he had given Rosmiri and Mitrane such an important secondary conflict. He excised the appearance of Henriette/Rosmiri from Corneille's Act II ('c') , and both appearances of Cécile/ Mitrane from Acts II ('c') and III ('f'). (See also tables 12b and 12c above.)

Another interesting structure could be shown to exist in the balanced and partly symmetrical patterns of stage encounters; for example, the appearances/encounters of Statira and Arsace are exactly symmetrical.

Diction

Finally, there is a global statement apparently covering everything else: 'alterarla molto', i. e. the tragedy has been greatly altered. This may have to be read in a specific sense, too – probably as indicating actual changes of the dialogue (*diction*). This aspect of the comparison can be touched upon only briefly here (for an extended discussion of a parallel case see chapter 7 above). There is almost no scene where Salvi reproduces the original dialogue throughout in its succession of argument and counterargument. In many cases, however, he takes over more than one argument or *concetto* from the original scene, combining them with new material or omitting other original material. Textual analogies like these occur almost exclusively in corresponding scenes, whereas the non-corresponding scenes are mostly freely invented. In some corresponding scenes, Salvi's diction closely reflects Corneille's, and approaches the status of a translation:

> *Le Comte d'Essex* (V, 4)
> *Élisabeth.*
> Approchez: qu'avez-vous fait du comte?
> On le mène à la mort, m'a-t-on dit.
> *Cécile.*
> Son trépas
> Importe à vôtre gloire ainsi qu'à vos états.

> *Amore e maestà* 'i' (III, 8)
> *Statira.*
> Artabano, Mitrane,
> Che faceste d'Arsace?
> *Artabano.*
> Quanto il giusto chiedea,
> L'interesse del Regno, e la tua pace.

Even here, a lesser element of communication is omitted (line 2); what counts is the reproduction of argument and counterargument (of 'ideas') in their original conceptual status and order.

More often, Salvi's discourse reorders or revaluates the ideas. The following passage involves, significantly, an aria as well.

> *Le Comte d'Essex* (I, 2)
> *Comte.*
> Cet amour où mon coeur tout entier s'abandonne . . .
> *Duchesse.*
> Comte, n'y pensez plus, ma gloire vous l'ordonne.
> Le refus d'un hymen par la reine arrêté
> Eût de nôtre secret trahi la sûreté.
> L'orage est violent; pour calmer sa furie,   5

Contraignez ce grand cœur, c'est moi qui vous en prie;
Et, quand le mien pour vous soupire encor tout bas,
Souvenez-vous de moi, mais ne me voyez pas.
Un penchant si flatteur . . . Adieu: je m'embarrasse;
Et Cécile qui vient me faut quitter la place.   10

Amore e maestà 'b' (I, 7)
Arsace.
Pensi tu che 'l mio core
Possa cangiare affetti, e possa . . .
Rosmiri.
                  Addio,
Se più t'ascolto, ahi lassa!
Me stessa, e 'l mio dover pongo in obblio.
Arsace.
Così mi lasci ingrata   5
Nè vuoi ch'io t'ami più?

Arsace.
Amami pur se vuoi,
Ma sia l'amar virtù,
Per non mirar mai più questi miei rai;
Tra dolci sospir tuoi   10
Getta un sospir per me,
Ma non cercar mercè che non l'avrai.

The common ideas are: 1. his total devotion (lines 1/1–2)–not expressed, however, in the same terms; 2. that she orders him not to see her again (lines 2, 6, 8/7–
9, 12); 3. that she fears to lose her countenance (lines 9/3–4). These ideas do not
appear in the same order and are interspersed with other arguments individual to
each text (lines 3–5, 10/5–6). Additionally, there is the common idea or image of
the 'hidden sighs' (lines 7/10–11): but in Corneille, they are hers, in Salvi his! (This
has also to do with the character of the aria, on which see below.)

    The announcement of Cécile's arrival (line 10) is a dramaturgical convention
typical of the French tradition and is omitted by Salvi, although it is by no means
unknown in Italian librettos. It seems to me that the leading or generative idea of the
passage is the concise rhetorical opposition 'Souvenez-vous de moi, mais ne me
voyez pas', which becomes inflated to

'Amami pur se vuoi,
Ma sia l'amar virtù,
Per non mirar mai più questi miei rai.'[14]

14. 'Per mai vedermi più' would have been more effective but probably too wooden in sound; the term
    'virtù', albeit a shadow of 'contraignez ce grand cœur', may have crept into Salvi's aria text for
    reasons of sound and rhyme as well.

It is the concept of loving self-sacrifice around which the passage revolves; it breathes all the tenderness and self-pity of this sentimental love-story as a whole. Corneille's diction is at a high point here, despite the rather sobering, tactical argumentation in lines 3–5. Salvi omits this point and concentrates on the emotional interest, but his diction is not at its best. No doubt both authors intended the same effect on the audience: *attendrissement*.

Conclusion

The points that have been made may suffice to attempt a conclusion. Antonio Salvi's *Amore e maestà* has become a very different tragedy from Thomas Corneille's *Le Comte d'Essex*. In addition to generic and stylistic divergences (stage-sets, stage-action so on), the individual dramaturgical structure is largely remodelled. It is equally true that those components which a dramatist of the period would have considered as primary – subject, plot, and the ethos of the leading characters – have been maintained. These components include, of course, the tragic ending.

In using Salvi's libretto preface as a guide to the understanding of his modifications, we paid special attention to those changes which, according to him, had been necessary for the sake of 'the music, the cast, and the Italian stage'. There were, for example, the stage-sets, the provision of exits convenient for aria-singing, the reduction in the number of characters. Nevertheless, none of these changes cancelled or even damaged the play's credibility as a tragic drama. We do not have to claim that *Amore e maestà* could have been performed without music (I do not believe it could, though many plays were written for the reading public) when asserting that Salvi's alterations did not cross the borderlines of spoken tragedy as a genre. What he did can be summarized thus:

1. He preserved the dramaturgical conventions of the classical tradition of spoken theatre: for example, the *liaison des scènes*, the hierarchical arrangement of characters, the particular conventions of monologue and dialogue, of Aristotelian unities, and so forth.

2. Where 'music, cast and Italian stage' necessitated adjustments, he re-balanced the drama in such a way as to satisfy these demands as well, without breaking any rule.

3. He did alter elements of plot, character and scenic structure, for example around Rosmiri and Mitrane, or in the matter of solo scenes, but these changes were obviously intended to make the tragedy more convincing as a drama, or to give more exciting parts to individual characters, such as Mitrane. Several of the changes were intended to strengthen the main lines of Corneille's plot, for example the conflict between the Queen and Arsace. Thus, Salvi may even have attempted to correct his predecessor – he certainly did not succumb to the demands of a diverging genre.

4. There is also an element of modernization, still within the realm of spoken tragedy. Around 1715, increased stage action, and certain elements of high comedy (such as the motive of the jealous husband), would have been expected from French tragedies, too.

9. A performance of Antonio Salvi's *Arsace*, music by Francesco Feo, Teatro Regio, Turin, 1740; painting by Pietro Domenico Olivero.

If some of Salvi's changes (such as final solo scenes) suggest that he fulfilled the 'typical requirements' of opera as a theatrical genre, then we should ask by what time such elements had actually started to characterize opera rather than drama – if they ever did. Perhaps Salvi's librettos (among which there are several other adaptations) stood at the beginning of a differentiation of opera and drama in these dramaturgical matters. More research into the dramaturgy of seventeenth-century Italian opera is surely needed to clear up this point. But on the basis of the comparisons presented in the four parts of this study, it may well be doubted whether 'drama' and 'opera' did, in that period, constitute two essentially different theatrical genres. It seems much more likely that specific, datable historical processes – such as the libretto-writing of Zeno, Salvi and their successors – helped gradually to differentiate them. We may claim that the respective essences of 'opera' and 'drama' were not given by nature, but were man-made.

Theory and practice

10
Tolomeo: Handel's opera and the rules of tragedy

The drama of Handel's time

Although historians of the Baroque stage and critics of today's Handel opera performances usually address different audiences, I should like to encourage a dialogue. Our historical research may become really worthwhile at that point where we experience its effect – stimulating or deadening as it may be – on the artistic practice of our own day. Conversely, the legitimacy of today's Handel performances might remain questionable as long as the historical subject itself is not called into question. No doubt our common aim is not so much the promotion of certain products or fashions as the endeavour to make this artistic heritage our own through living interpretation and reception.

What we call 'Baroque opera' will become better understood only when it is acknowledged to be a part of Baroque theatre. Opera research has to open itself up towards general theatre studies and social history. To escape the ghetto of purely musicological opera research, it is not sufficient to specialize also in other individual sectors such as scenographies or libretti, although the information flowing from those particular fields is in itself highly valuable; beyond that, we have to reconstitute the great context of ideas in which opera then existed. Part of this context was the intellectual tradition, to be discussed here, of the rules of literary drama in the seventeenth and early eighteenth centuries.

The wide gap between the views of drama in Handel's time and in ours is already indicated by the concept of rules in drama. 'Regular drama' or 'regular tragedy' was the literary drama which conformed to classical, especially Aristotelian, rules, and to the models provided by French seventeenth-century tragedy. It respected the principles of verisimilitude and necessity in the imitation of nature. It was, typically, tragedy, since for comedy no classical rules could be adduced. It became, particularly in England and Germany, the literary drama we associate with bourgeois reforms and enlightenment. The efforts of playwrights and critics to develop a high-level literary drama that was emancipated from histrionic and improvisatory traditions (Vienna's 'Hans Wurst' and Italy's commedia dell'arte, among others) were related to aspects of intellectual and social emancipation in Germany, Italy and England, for example with Johann Christoph Gottsched

(1700–66) and his school,[1] with Carlo Goldoni or Joseph Addison. Above all, the debates concerning classicist theories of drama promoted the development of special and national genre traditions, not excluding the genre of opera. The discussion about national traditions began well before 1700 with the reactions of the erudite Bolognese Gian Gioseffo Orsi to Nicolas Boileau-Despreaux's influential *L'Art poétique* of 1674. Of the subsequent developments, only two may be emphasized here: first, the quarrel about French and Italian operatic and musical styles, conducted, among others, by Charles Saint-Évremond (1685), François Raguenet (1702), apparently Nicola Haym (1709) and finally Johann Mattheson.[2] Second, we may think of the careers of significant actors and theorists of the theatre, for example Orsi's student Luigi Riccoboni ('Lelio'), who failed to convert the Italians to regular tragedy but continued to propose his reformist theories in his writings and performances. In 1713 he performed in Modena the tragedy *Merope* written by his friend and patron Marchese Scipione Maffei, contributing to a revival of Italian literary tragedy. Two years before, the librettist Apostolo Zeno had a homonymous *dramma per musica* performed in a Venetian opera house, with music by Francesco Gasparini, and not without later complaints that the musicians had disfigured the dramatic text.[3] With the names of Riccoboni, Maffei, Zeno and Gasparini, we have probably arrived at the centre of the problems concerning opera and literary drama at that time.

This chapter first outlines the consequences for opera arising from the reformist tendencies of the literary theatre around 1700–40. Then there follows a sketch of those tendencies as they manifested themselves in a typical Handel libretto, and a brief inquiry into Handel's reaction to them. With these preliminary remarks I hope at least to establish the main question: what was the relationship between Handel's operas, operatic reform, and regular literary tragedy?

Six potential conflicts of opera with the rules of tragedy

1. The main conflict arose, of course, from the singing of arias. Singing on stage is reputed to be *improbable* in classicist theory (it contradicts Nature), especially in tragedy, which prefers heroic and historical plots and characters. In Italian opera

1. On him, see chapter 4 in this volume, especially pp. 81–6.
2. For several of these authors, see Robert S. Freeman, *Opera without Drama: Currents of Change in Italian Opera, 1675–1725* (Ann Arbor: UMI Research Press, 1981) (Studies in Musicology, vol. 35), pp. 1–54; Piero Weiss, 'Teorie drammatiche e "infranciosamento": Motivi della "riforma" melodrammatica nel primo Settecento', in *Antonio Vivaldi*, ed. by L. Bianconi and G. Morelli, vol. 1, 1982, pp. 273–96; Lowell Lindgren, 'The Accomplishments of the Learned and Ingenious Nicola Francesco Haym (1678–1729)', *Studi Musicali* 16 (1987), pp. 247–380. Mattheson's views are found in his journal *Critica musica* (Hamburg, 1722ff.), and his *Die neueste Untersuchung der Singspiele* (Hamburg, 1744).
3. See Sergio Martinotti, 'Un nuovo incontro con Apostolo Zeno', *Chigiana* 25 (nuova serie no. 5) (1968), pp. 81–98. On Maffei, see also Laura Sannia Nowé, 'Una voce sul melodramma nelle discussioni del primo settecento (S. Maffei)', in *Metastasio e il melodramma*, ed. by E. Sala Di Felice and L. Sannia Nowé, 1985, pp. 247–70.

the 'reform' librettos of the period around 1700, by increasingly adopting such plots, created a contradiction: according to the theory, gods and shepherds were allowed to sing arias, but Alexander or Julius Caesar was not.[4] This type of problem had already surfaced a century earlier: orthodox Aristotelians, judging from the viewpoint of verisimilitude, condemned not only singing but even speaking in verse on the tragic stage.[5] The official interpreters of classicist theory, as far as they commented on opera at all, requested the return to mythological plots, supranatural actions and pastoral idylls, where the requirement of verisimilitude was not so pronounced.[6] Many opera librettists, however, among them Apostolo Zeno, Silvio Stampiglia, Antonio Salvi and others, attempted to present historical heroes on the operatic stage without infringing the laws of verisimilitude. Contemporary critics such as Lodovico Antonio Muratori, Joseph Addison and Johann Christoph Gottsched made fun of these coloratura warriors, just as the modern spectator might experience the occasional bewilderment at them.

Conventional musicology and literary criticism have established as a ground rule of opera seria the division between 'aria=emotion' and 'recitative=action'. It is claimed that this basic distinction, fully established in the librettos of Pietro Metastasio, enabled opera seria to resolve the conflict between dramatic verisimilitude and musical spectacle. But already the initial problem – the conflict with verisimilitude caused by an increasing taste for heroic, historical and even realistic subjects in the years c. 1680–1720 – was such that a simplistic dramaturgical formula would not have solved it. If it were true that the arias had to express only emotion and the recitative only action, then the arias would now have become less important in opera, and recitative more important, if Julius Caesar and Alexander the Great were to be presented under the precepts of verisimilitude. Unlike Tirsi and Clori of the pastoral dramas, these heroes presumably had more use for action than for emotion! The opposite happened, however: in the heroic-historical 'reform' librettos of a Zeno or Salvi, the arias, while being reduced in number, were charged with a much greater significance in the drama, often appearing as dramaturgical turning points. The purpose of these arias was much more comprehensive and more dramatic than is possible under the formula 'aria=emotion, recitative=action'. The increase in importance, textual as well as musical, of the da capo aria in this period was more in agreement than in conflict with literary reform ideas.

A close reading of the libretti of Zeno and his contemporaries, followed perhaps by comparisons with their literary dramatic sources, might sharpen our perception

4. Model discussions of this issue are found in Piero Weiss, 'Baroque Opera and the Two Verisimilitudes', in *Music and Civilization: Essays in Honor of Paul Henry Lang* (New York, 1984), pp. 117–26, and idem, 'Neoclassical Criticism and Opera', in *Studies in the History of Music II* (New York: Broude Bros., 1984), pp. 1–30.
5. Thus Paolo Beni (Padua, 1600) said of poets whose characters spoke in verse: 'Ut . . . non Naturam Ducem sequantur isti: non decorum aut verosimile tueantur: sed a Natura discedant . . .' ('So that . . . these people do not follow Nature as their guide, nor protect the *decorum* nor the *verosimile*, but diverge from Nature'). Quoted after P. Weiss, 'Neoclassical Criticism', p. 5, n. 8.
6. For example Giovanni Maria Crescimbeni, the mentor of the Roman Accademia dell'Arcadia, in his *La Bellezza della Volgar Poesia*, quoted by R. S. Freeman, *Opera without Drama*, pp. 21–2.

of the dramaturgical role of the arias. In fact, many da capo arias will turn out to be actual parts of the monologue or dialogue, serving the action and carrying the weight of dramatic communication between the dramatis personae, or the actor and the audience.[7] Metastasio was well acquainted with this function of the arias. In his writings and letters, he did not – to my knowledge – approach the problem of verisimilitude from a principle of strict division between actions and emotions. The suspected improbability which occurred when ordinary communication on stage was accomplished by singing instead of speaking could not simply be removed by communicating feelings rather than thought.

Metastasio made theoretical attempts to legitimize the presence of arias in tragedy by means of their alleged classical ancestry in the strophic choral songs.[8] In his own *drammi per musica*, however, he practised varied kinds of aria functions, inherited from the dramaturgical vocabulary of classicist literary drama: deliberative monologue, part of dialogue, oration, sermon or reproach, sentence and so on. As can be expected, the most problematic type was that of an aria addressing a partner on stage (henceforth referred to as 'dialogue aria'). A monologue expressing popular wisdom or a popular sentence, on the other hand, was directly modelled on monologues in the spoken theatre and thus quite compatible with dramatic theory. Metastasio's frequent 'sentence arias' (which in themselves contradict the interpretation of the arias as expressing only emotions) can in fact be judged as evidence of the 'undramatic' character of opera seria only if we adopt the clichés of the nineteenth and twentieth centuries, not the dramatic principles of the seventeenth and eighteenth.

The essential concept is that of a separation between form and content. The aria in a 'reform libretto' was formally isolated from its context just as the Greek *stasima* had been – this could not be helped. Its content, however, had to carry whatever communication was required by the drama at that point, within the boundaries of necessity and verisimilitude. According to this formula, Julius Caesar and Alexander were just as welcome to sing as was Orpheus or Apollo, as long as their words in the aria conformed to their characters, thoughts, feelings and the dramatic situation. This compromise, although rejected by theatre reformers such as Addison or Gottsched, helped to bring about a greatly expanded dramatic role for the music of the arias, which was now invited to support verisimilitude, instead of

7. See chapters 7 and 9 in this volume, on monologues, dialogues and arias.
8. He objected at least once to a proposal to perform his *drammi per musica* as spoken plays, omitting the arias. In a letter of 7 May 1767 to Daniel Schiebeler concerning such a plan, he mentions the obstacle of the 'sistema teatrale' (i.e. the Viennese theatre regulations), and only briefly sketches, for lack of time, how the arias are legitimate successors of the choruses in the classical tragedies. See Paolo Gallarati, 'Zeno e Metastasio tra melodramma e tragedia', in *Metastasio e il melodramma*, ed. by E. Sala di Felice and L. Sannia Nowé, 1985, p. 97 and n. 12; Piero Weiss, 'Metastasio, Aristotle, and the Opera seria', *Journal of Musicology* 1 (1982), pp. 385–94, especially pp. 388–9. Also Ranieri de' Calzabigi, in his *Dissertazione . . . su le Poesie Drammatiche del Signor Abate Pietro Metastasio*, vol. 1 (Paris, 1755), justifies the arias with reference to the ancient choral stanzas, which neither he nor Metastasio would have considered as mere expressions of feelings.

being judged its enemy. When Handel's aria settings are found to 'dramatize' their texts by assuming communicative and scenic functions not even intended by the poet, then this may well be considered an extension of the principle of verisimilitude into the musical score. In such cases, music declares itself responsible for the drama to a degree which the poets had not originally envisaged.

2. The singing not only of arias but also of choruses falls under the suspicion of improbability or unnaturalness in a historic-heroic drama, unless of course the choral passages are ostensibly rehearsed choruses which would be sung even in real life. It would be rewarding to investigate how in Metastasio's dramas, for example, the fiction of real choral singing is usually still maintained, often with the aid of considerable artifice. His choruses are, furthermore, habitually linked to dance, march or other collective movements on stage; they appear in the context of ritual ceremonies or political mass-scenes. Even the choice of subject or setting of a libretto may be related to the question whether choruses will be required.[9] Such respect for the principle of verisimilitude is common to Metastasio and other poets of his time. Two items, however, must be distinguished from choruses. The first are simple choral acclamations by the people, usually celebrating a victorious ruler ('viva, viva' etc.). In a 'regular' drama, the common people are deemed to be uneducated and incapable of artistic singing. Acclamations prescribed in a libretto were normally not set to music but shouted from behind the stage. Secondly, the final tutti or *coro* of an opera score,[10] which was usually performed by all the dramatis personae, was an exception to the rule of verisimilitude by virtue of being almost an afterthought of the dramatic presentation itself, addressed to the audience. Often it included an explicit or implicit homage to the prince who was present in the auditorium; this homage could also be elaborated to form a short scenic item called *licenza* – the 'farewell' of the actors to their patron. Handel does not have *licenze*, but his final tuttis often have the character of a homage, particularly in view of their length, complexity and musical similarity with French dance-types, which in turn can be understood as complimenting royalty. Those dramatis personae who have lost their lives in the plot of the opera are usually required to join in the singing of the final tutti.

3. The most important scenic and dramaturgical element which had separated seventeenth-century opera from the principle of verisimilitude was the supranatural: gods and ghosts on stage, flying carriages and machines, monsters, transformations, speaking tombs or statues, falling mountains. The call for an end to all this was occasionally answered in the simplest possible way, when in an eighteenth-century revival a Baroque libretto was deprived of its *deus ex machina* or

9. Choruses are frequent in connection with ancient Greek subjects, or plots relating to other ancient or exotic civilizations. Algarotti, Calzabigi and Gluck inclined towards archaic operatic subjects as part of their tendency to revive the use of choruses.

10. In the librettos, it is more often labelled 'tutti'. In the scores – where also the term 'aria' was used for the final number in the seventeenth century – the term 'coro' probably warned the conductor that several singers had to be accompanied.

underworld scene. There were, on the other hand, librettists who tried to create regular dramas while maintaining a close interest in the metaphysical, for example Pietro Pariati in his *Arianna e Teseo* (1714).[11] We may also mention Handel here. His *Orlando* (1733) is often quoted together with the early 'magic' operas, *Rinaldo* (1711) and *Amadigi* (1714),[12] and in fact it contains a sorcerer and magic events like those operas. Nevertheless, the educated audience of *Orlando* will not have missed the point when in the opening *accompagnato* the magician declares with grand gesture that the stars are but 'beautiful obscurities' from which nothing can be read. These words, added to the libretto for Handel's setting in London, must be heard as an at least ostensible homage to reason.

It would be worth a study of its own to illustrate how much the librettists of the eighteenth century endeavoured to exploit the mysterious and magical, as transmitted by history and legend, while eschewing conflicts with verisimilitude. Generally it may be stated that opera often transported the magic or religious subject matter contained in many traditional plots on to the plane of antiquarianism and romantic archaism, for example in the treatment of oracles, ancient treaties and inscriptions, or to the level of the symbolism of ancient buildings and works of art. As for the *deus ex machina*, whose function is to rescue the hero in the last minute, he can be secularized into a real prince who changes his tyrannic mind in the last moment. This case often also implies a second manoeuvre in favour of verisimilitude: the change of mind which triggers the final 'catastrophe' or peripety has to be rationally motivated, i.e. it cannot occur without the knowledge of the audience or just by divine inspiration. One of the most convincing solutions is to gather all the characters on stage in the last scene, imploring the tyrant for mercy and making him finally yield.

4. A conflict between opera and regular drama was furthermore inescapable in matters of scenography and stagecraft. Here we encounter the famous three 'Aristotelian' unities, on which only a few words can be said.[13] The fundamental problem in our context is the principle of the unity of *place*, which is not really traceable to Aristotle, but has occupied the minds of operatic poets the most. Why? The availability of movable scenery in Italy towards the end of the sixteenth century, which allowed for the visual experience of a change of location, made opera from its very beginning a paradigm of the disunity of place. Even today, opera is expected to gratify the spectator with changeable sets, possibly connected with spectacular sights and a musical *couleur locale*. Paradoxically, the spectacular tendency grew in Italy at the same time as classical dramatic theory gained influence. The conflict was sharpened, once again, by the increase of historical subjects in opera around 1700,

11.   See Giovanna Gronda, 'Varianti di un mito classico nella librettistica settecentesca', in *I vicini di Mozart*, ed. by M. T. Muraro and D. Bryant (Florence: Olschki, 1989), pp. 3–18, and eadem, 'Das Arianna-Libretto und seine Vorlagen', in *Gattungskonventionen der Händel-Oper: Bericht über die Symposien 1990 und 1991*, ed. by Hans Joachim Marx (Laaber, 1992) (Veröffentlichungen der Internationalen Händel-Akademie, vol. 4), pp. 139–57.

12.   See Winton Dean, *Handel and the Opera Seria* (Berkeley and Los Angeles: University of California Press, 1969), pp. 89–97.

13.   See also P. Weiss, 'Baroque Opera', and idem, 'Neoclassical criticism'.

because where historical verisimilitude reigns, improbable and rapid changes of location in the dramatic plot can hardly be tolerated. This applied even more to opera plots based on French spoken tragedies, where even imagined changes of scenery or place had been excluded. A play such as Racine's *Bajazet* goes so far as to thematicize the unity of place (the enclosure of the *serail*), bordering on the claustrophobic. The poet's Italian imitator, Apostolo Zeno, did not dare adopt this theme in his librettos.

As for the other 'unities', that of action can only benefit from the unity of place. Several librettists, however, yielded to the temptation of employing sudden changes of place to support the impression of a unity of time, by presenting certain scenes which supposedly happened 'elsewhere, but simultaneously'. In this way, abrupt changes of scenery could be made to suggest simultaneity of more than one action, and furthermore to condense several actions into the same time-frame. A form of compromise between theory and practice in these respects, initiated long before Metastasio and eloquently defended by him,[14] was a liberally understood unity of place. The location of a drama was defined as a capital city or residence of a ruler, of which varied aspects were shown in turn: hall, chamber, garden, dungeon, harbour and so forth. Thus the operatic stage also reflected the social *ambiente* of the genre itself. These stereotypical stage-sets could be made more contrasting by emphasizing social differences, as between royal private chambers on the one hand and the courtyards or corridors (*gallerie*) of a palace on the other. Individualized sets were frequent as well, and they often conformed to historical verity or verisimilitude when, for example, well-known architectural monuments or works of art were shown on stage. Many scenographers were accustomed, in their 'real life' profession of architects, to imitating historical monuments such as the Roman Pantheon. Some patrons and theatre architects of the early eighteenth century, however, especially in Rome, aimed at a noble simplicity, limiting themselves to a few related stage-sets that could be transformed into each other. Open-air scenes were preferred for this procedure, as the pastoral world was the paradigm of simplicity. The libretto model for Handel's *Tolomeo* (see below) comes from this circle: it is a drama which takes place entirely outdoors, in varying locations of a large wood near a palace. Its scenography very closely observes the principles of unity.

An important dramaturgical principle – albeit not a strict rule – was that of the *liaison des scènes* (scene-connection) in classical spoken drama.[15] It prevented the stage from being empty between one scene and the next, since one or more characters always had to remain to meet the next entrant. This principle, too, existed in a potential triangular conflict with the law of verisimilitude and the unity of place. For the more unified a suggested place is, the more improbable it is that many characters of the drama would meet there in strict succession according to the *liaison*

14. See his 'Estratto dell'arte poetica d'Aristotile e considerazioni su la medesima' (1773), in P. Metastasio, *Tutte le opere*, vol. 2 (Milan, 1965), pp. 957–1117.
15. Pierre Corneille, 'Trois discours sur le poème dramatique (1660)', in P. Corneille, *Œuvres complètes*, vol. iii, ed. by Georges Couton (Paris: Gallimard, 1987), p. 177: 'ce n'est pas qu'un ornement, et non pas une règle'.

des scènes, one person always encountering another who happened to be there earlier. (Unless, of course, this place is a prison during visiting hours.) There were relaxations of the principle, the so-called *liaisons de fuite* and *de recherche*, where the preceding partner would have recently disappeared, but these techniques did not mitigate the main restriction. On the other hand, the principle of *liaison* was not valid across a change of stage-set, because it would be improbable if the same character we have just seen in one location were suddenly present in another. Operatic practice, which favours scene changes, tended to use a relative disunity of place as a means to maintain some sort of *liaison* and dramatic verisimilitude. A typical solution was to maintain the *liaison* during the scenes belonging to one stage-set ('royal chamber', for example), but to let only some of the characters appear there, for example the members of that court. The next stage-set ('military camp under the walls of the city', for example) could then show all the members of the opposing party. Heroic-historical opera therefore came to favour a tableau-like grouping of scenes in larger units, driven by the rule of verisimilitude.

5. As well as the principle of verisimilitude, which already in Aristotle is flanked by that of 'necessity', tragedy also aimed at purity of genre and formal regularity. Concerning the latter, some theorists absolutely required a tragedy to have five acts, and prescribed where sections such as protasis, epitasis and so on had to be placed.[16] Operas in five acts were the rule in France; in Italy they are found mostly around 1680–1720 in connection with pastoral, tragic or classical Greek subjects. These cases can usually be interpreted as imitations of regular spoken tragedies rather than of French operas.[17] Aristotle had only emphasized that a drama had to have a beginning, a middle and an end – which could be taken as an endorsement of the three-act tradition in Italy.

More important for opera were the questions regarding the mixture of tragic and comic genres, and the necessity of intrigue and catastrophe. Contemporary writers including Metastasio[18] credited Apostolo Zeno with the achievement of having purged the *dramma per musica* of the mixture of tragic and comic elements. The circumstances of this process of purgation (Venice, 1706) might have to do with vested interests as well, for example those of intermezzi performers.[19] The mixture of genres affected, to some extent, the unity of action and potentially those of place and time, but the important question here was that of *decorum*. The definition of tragedy implied ethical as well as social superiority; the comic element in drama was not simply something ridiculous but also stood for the socially inferior. In seventeenth-century opera, audiences habitually laughed at the stupidity of servant characters. For comedy, there was the Aristotelian definition as a genre of 'contemporary and ordinary' personages, which in Italian opera was observed relatively

---

16. See P. Weiss, 'Neoclassical Criticism'.
17. Handel's *Teseo*, derived from a French operatic model (Quinault's and Lully's *Thesée*), is an example to the contrary.
18. Letter to Angelo Fabroni, 7 December 1767; quoted in R. S. Freeman, *Opera without Drama*, p. 65.
19. See Reinhard Strohm, 'Aspetti sociali dell'opera italiana del primo Settecento', *Musica/Realtà* 2 (1981), pp. 117–41.

faithfully. A play identified as *commedia* would not normally have a historical or heroic subject, nor indeed a classical or mythological one. Whether it was also 'comic' in the modern sense of the word could be a different question. By contrast, the *dramma per musica* of Zeno and his contemporaries, which rejects ordinary, contemporary characters and events, in this respect emulated regular tragedy.[20] It is therefore slightly alarming when modern critics praise such a *dramma per musica* – perhaps one set by Handel – for offering a mixture of tragic and comic elements. It must in any case be assumed that a modern concept of what is comic would be involved here. As for Handel and his time, the almost total absence of ordinary and contemporary characters from his plots should speak for itself.

Even in the period of its greatest assimilation to spoken tragedy, Italian opera did not give up its convention of the *lieto fine*, despite the fact that operas with a *funesto fine* were more frequent in the period c. 1690–c. 1730 than before or after.[21] Few commentators of the time would have considered a happy ending in opera an 'irregularity', and it in any case occurs quite often in French tragedies. All the same, a regular tragedy had to arouse terror and pity in the spectator (see also below), which required that at least one character, who enjoyed the spectators' sympathy, had to be thrown into misery. But the intrigue against this hero could fail and its perpetrator be punished, allowing for a happy ending without neglecting the effects of pity and fear. Tragic heroes and heroines were, in a sense, more indispensable than tragic actions: the personalization of the tragic was a dramaturgical principle of spoken drama which opera has successfully absorbed to make it one of its own major characteristics.

When, however, a hero was to be made unhappy and later happy again, the distribution of happiness and unhappiness among the characters had to be reversed twice in the plot, which was called 'double catastrophe'. It had to be matched, also in order to avoid improbability, by a double intrigue (*doppio intreccio*). This combination could complicate the action enormously. Some writers, for example the theorists of the Arcadian Academy headed by Crescimbeni, objected to such complexity on behalf of verisimilitude and simplicity, preferring a single *intreccio* and catastrophe. As a result, another triangular conflict arose, this time between the ideals of *lieto fine*, purity of genre and simplicity: a drama where the hero is not made unfortunate is not a tragedy; a drama where the hero remains unfortunate has no *lieto fine* as required by opera; a drama where the hero is made first unfortunate and then fortunate again offends simplicity. The last-named variant was considered the least of the evils by opera librettists of the time, and this is the main reason why their plots often strike us as excessively complicated. An alternative solution was to present the hero in an unhappy state right at the outset, and later rescue him from

20. Whether it is 'comic' in the modern sense may be a different question as well. The famous *aperçu* of Francesco De Sanctis that Metastasio's *dramma* is 'a superficie tragico, a fondo comico' ('superficially tragic, inherently comic') seems misleading if not actually wrong to me.
21. See Reinhard Strohm, 'Die *tragedia per musica* als Repertoirestück: Zwei Hamburger Opern von G. M. Orlandini', in *Die frühdeutsche Oper*, ed. by C. Floros et al., pp. 37–54, and chapter 8 in this volume.

that condition; but according to some legislators of drama, a play where the only reversal of fortune leads from bad to good was not a tragedy but a comedy.

6. All this rationalist game with abstract conceptualizations of the world and human nature was underpinned, however, by an idealist and moralist attitude in general. The seventeenth and eighteenth centuries regarded the theatre as a moral institution, which was not allowed to cease educating and morally improving the spectator. The main goal of a regular drama was not to offend good manners – also called *decorum* or *bienséances* – but to confirm their validity. The aesthetic effect of simplicity and regularity was in itself a *decorum*, since morally and socially elevated personalities allegedly also spoke more elegantly.[22] The importance of good manners on stage also implied the characters' appearance and deportment, their observance of courteous rituals and their appreciation of social values. Among the last, *honour* occupied the highest rank according to unanimous opinion. In each of these respects, the *dramma per musica* was able to equal literary drama even without reform operations. For example, it was an obvious thought to express aristocratic civility through the skilful observance of certain poetic-musical forms, and this was even compatible with verisimilitude. Beyond that, however, there was the Aristotelian idea of 'catharsis' (purification) through the arousal, in the spectator, of fear of the wicked and sympathy for the good. It gave the theatre an ethical purpose, one almost comparable to socially established laws. This created an aesthetic difficulty. What had good and bad, right and wrong to do with music? How were they supposed to be presented to the senses? Today, literary scholars emphasize that the Aristotelian 'reception nexus' (*Wirkungszusammenhang*) – i.e. the ethical function – is intrinsic to the concept of tragedy of this period:[23] in opera, too, the role of *decorum* must not be be underestimated. To understand this may help to bridge the gap between the appreciation of Baroque theatre by its contemporaries and by us. But we have to keep in mind the fluctuations of the concept of *decorum* in the eighteenth century. The concept varied from a strictly ethical view of the purposes of tragedy to the purely social-aesthetic principle of not offending the tastes of the aristocratic spectators.

The role of *decorum* was integral to the dramaturgical practice of the time and was often coupled with the pursuit of verisimilitude: for example, when critics considered it 'unlikely' that high-ranking personages might indulge in base feelings or intentions. In the famous *Querelle du Cid* concerning Pierre Corneille's play (from which Handel's *Flavio* is partly derived), critics mingled their objections to its unorthodox ending with reproaches concerning the play's morality: a princess could not have any further dealings with the murderer of her father, as this would have been immoral and 'therefore' improbable. In other words, those characters for whom the spectator has sympathy cannot voluntarily offend the *decorum*. It is from this point of view that the real infringements of *decorum* in *Flavio* might be correctly identified and interpreted.

22.   This conviction characterizes classicist poetics, for example Nicolas Boileau-Despreaux's *L'art poétique* of 1674.

23.   See, for example, Hans-Jürgen Schings, 'Consolatio Philosophiae', in *Deutsche Dramentheorien I*, ed. by Reinhold Grimm, 3rd edn (Wiesbaden: Athenaion, 1980), pp. 19–55, especially pp. 21–2.

Handel's *Tolomeo*

If we were to interpret the *dramma per musica* of Handel's time according to the contemporary principles of verisimilitude and *decorum*, we might come closer to what the composer and indeed his audiences saw in these dramas. One of the most interesting questions concerns the development of theatrical aesthetics in the London opera productions of the time, and consequently Handel's share in the unfolding of classicist influences on the Italian *dramma per musica*.

For reasons of space, only one *dramma per musica* can be used as an example here. I have chosen *Tolomeo re d'Egitto*, the opera produced by Nicola Haym and Handel in 1728, for two reasons. First, some hypotheses which I expressed on the origin and the artistic significance of Handel's *Orlando*[24] may profitably be examined again from the angle of *Tolomeo*, because my suggestion seems to have gained credibility that the two operas were planned together and that the demise of the Royal Academy of Music (1728) only delayed an already envisaged creation of *Orlando*.[25] Secondly, there is the question of a stylistic reorientation within the opera reform itself. As has been elucidated by Elena Sala di Felice, the poetry of the *dramma per musica* around 1720–40 reflects two different reformist tendencies. An older one, influenced by French models and represented by Zeno, derives catharsis from an equilibrium between the punishment of the wicked and the rewarding of the good; a younger one, which is the tendency of Metastasio, reduces Aristotelian terror to a minimum and presents infringements of the *decorum* as only temporary aberrations.[26] The majority of Handel's operas of the Royal Academy period (1720–8) can without any difficulty be seen as reflecting the former tendency: a heroic-historic orientation, which endeavours to demonstrate the punishment of evil and the triumph of righteousness as drastically as possible. In its choice of dramatic subjects, and partly in the literary style of its libretti, this tendency differed from that of the Italian faction of the Royal Academy, documented in Giuseppe Riva's letters to Lodovico Antonio Muratori of 5 September and 3 October 1725.[27] With the last operas of the Academy, however – the settings of Metastasio's *Siroe re di Persia* and Capeci's *Tolomeo* – the tide seems to turn: is it possible that here a step towards a more galant, classicist type of opera was undertaken? Admittedly, *Siroe* is a very old-fashioned drama for Metastasio, with an almost biblical plot approximating to

24. Reinhard Strohm, 'Comic Traditions in Handel's *Orlando*', in R. Strohm, *Essays on Handel*, pp. 249–67.
25. Not only did both libretto models originate in the same Roman season (1711) and were produced for the same theatre by the same artists, but both librettos also seem to have reached London together, possibly on behalf of Haym who, as Lowell Lindgren has noted, owned them both. See Ellen T. Harris, *The Librettos of Handel's Operas*, facs. edn with introductions, 13 vols (New York: Garland, Inc., 1989), vol. 7, pp. xii–xvi. (I am by no means of the opinion that *Orlando* is a comic opera, as Harris reads me on p. xv.)
26. Elena Sala Di Felice, 'Virtù e felicità alla corte di Vienna', in *Metastasio e il melodramma*, ed. by E. Sala Di Felice and L. Sannia Nowé, pp. 55–87.
27. See Hans Dieter Clausen, 'Der Einfluß der Komponisten auf die Librettowahl der Royal Academy of Music (1720–1729)', in *Zur Dramaturgie der Barockoper: Bericht über die Symposien 1992 und 1993*, ed. by Hans Joachim Marx (Laaber, 1994) (Veröffentlichungen der Internationalen Händel-Akademie, vol. 5), pp. 55–72.

Zeno's taste. Or does Handel now eschew the reform, seeking pastoral, meta-physical or spectacular effects around this time? According to Ellen T. Harris, this was exactly what Handel did in the years from 1732, whereas in the operas of the years 1726–32 she sees the rise of a new interest in scenography and in Metastasio.[28] Obstacles to this interpretation are, on the one hand, the libretto of *Admeto* (1727) with its high Baroque underworld scenery and mythical cast, and on the other, *Tolomeo* with its refined Arcadian simplicity of stage-set and drama. The choice of the 1711 libretto version was surely a judgment of taste – but of a taste that needs to be described and evaluated. Let us investigate the authors' intentions by exam-ining, comparatively, both the London libretto of 1728 and the Roman model of 1711[29] – always in relation to verisimilitude and *decorum* as the guiding principles of the reform. The deviations from these principles might indicate the direction in which Handel was moving.

As with *Orlando* (albeit for different reasons), it is an open question whether *Tolomeo, re d'Egitto* is actually a pastoral opera. Whereas in *Orlando* several thematic layers are compounded and the pastoral element rivals the heroic-ethical and the romantic-magical, *Tolomeo* as a whole has a unified pastoral setting, which is used by all the characters in their different ways, by some only as a disguise. It may be asked, on the other hand, whether the main intrigue, which is courtly and dynastic, has anything to do with pastoral legend.

The antecedents of the plot of *Tolomeo* are narrated, in the model libretto of 1711, with a long Latin quotation from Justin, book 39. Cleopatra, Queen of Egypt, has persecuted her son and co-regent Ptolemy with excessive hatred, partly because she fears that after his marriage to Seleuce an heir will finally deprive her of her power. She has also instigated Ptolemy's younger brother Alexander against him. Ptolemy flees, in disguise, to Cyprus, where he appears in pastoral garb as Osmino. But he has lost Seleuce in a shipwreck. She, however, independently finds her way to Cyprus, where she passes herself off as the shepherdess Delia. The king of the island, Araspe, and his sister Elisa live in a 'pleasant country estate near the sea'; there all the characters of the play arrive simultaneously, including also Dorisbe in the habit of the shepherdess Clori, who had once been loved but then abandoned by Araspe. (This role was cut in 1728.) This tying of the knot in itself demonstrates some care for the unities of place, time and action.

Table 15 reports all the stage remarks and aria incipits of the opera in both versions of *Tolomeo*, serving as an anthology of linguistic-dramaturgical elements of the work which might help us determine the attitude of the authors towards opera reform and the rules of tragedy.

At first glance, not much in this dramaturgy seems compatible with verisimili-tude. But a more subtle view may be required, especially as regards the variants between the two versions. What does play a role in both of them is a conscious handling of the *decorum*.

28.   E. T. Harris, *The Librettos*, p. vii.
29.   On the latter, see R. Strohm, *Essays on Handel*, pp. 58–9.

Table 15. Carlo Sigismondo Capeci, *Tolomeo re d'Egitto*: verisimilitude and *decorum*
Abbreviations:
Tol. = Tolomeo, Sel. = Seleuce, Ales. = Alessandro, El. = Elisa, Ar. = Araspe, Dor. =
Dorisbe. I a etc.: unity of stage-set. *Italics*: sung texts. –: absent. E.: entrance aria.[30]

1711	1728
Ia Campagna alle rive del mare	**Campagna alle rive del mare**
Tol. solo *Rendimi o crudo fato*	
(invokes fate; non exit)	
Tol. *Cielo ingiusto*	*Cielo ingiusto*
(invokes heaven; has rescued Ales. from the sea;	
Ales. has fainted)	
El. *Voglio adorar ma chi?*	–
(also in presence of unconscious Ales.)	
Ales. (a parte) *Non lo dirò col labro*	*Non lo dirò col labro*
(already in love; a parte saves decorum)	
–	El. sola *Quell'onda che si frange*
	(nature simile/monologue)
Ib Campagna con villa deliziosa	Campagna con villa deliziosa
d'Araspe	d'Araspe
Sel. sola *Amor, tu che lo fai*	–
(non exit; enter Ar. Dor.)	(Ar. himself, not Dor., announces
	arrival of Ales.)
Ar. *Vezzosi lumi*	–
(forthright love-declaration)	
Sel. *È un grave martire*	Sel. sola *Mi volgo ad ogni fronda*
(expresses sympathy)	(addresses Nature and Cupid)
Dor. sola *Alma avezza a pene e affanni*	–
(Ar.'s quick return motivated)	
Dor. *La tortorella*	–
(nature simile and hint to partner)	
Ar. Ales. a 2 *Verdi piagge selve amene*	–
(addressing Nature)	
Ic Campagna con veduta di capanne	**(still I b: break of liaison)**
pastorali	
–	El. *Se talor miri un fior*
	(nature simile: instructs Tol.)
El. *Addio direbbe il cor*	–
(a parte saves decorum)	
Tol. solo *Tiranni miei pensieri*	*Tiranni miei pensieri* (abridged)
(sleep aria: no break of liaison as sleeping	
Tol. remains on stage)	
Sel. *Non più stelle non più*	Sel. *Fonti amiche aure leggiere*
(invokes stars, in presence of sleeping Tol.)	(invokes Nature)
(Ar. enters, observes Sel.'s indiscretion)	
Ar. *Respira almeno un poco*	*Respira almeno un poco*
(addresses own heart; a parte)	
Tol. solo *Torna sol per un momento*	*Torna sol per un momento*
(invokes shadow)	
IIa Campagna con villa deliziosa	**Campagna con villa deliziosa**
E.Ales. solo *Sempre qui chiara e tranquilla*	–
(El. enters)	

30. Entrance arias are sung by a character who is just appearing on stage. (The Italian nomenclature of
the time was different, calling these *arie d'uscita* and the exit arias *arie d'entrata*.)

Table 15. Continued

Ales. *Quella fiamma che m'accende* (love–declaration) (El. then Tol.)	–
–	E. El. *Voi dolci aurette al cor* (invokes Nature; Tol. interrupts)
(Ar. enters; El. Tol. exeunt together, motivated)	(Ar.Tol. exeunt singly, unmotivated)
Ar. *Pensieri che dite* (addresses own thoughts)	–
–	El. sola *Quant'è felice* (nature simile, monologue) (break of liaison)
(non exit) Ar. *Destrier che spinto al corso* (nature simile = threat)	–
Dor. *Vorrei vendicarmi* (non exit)	–
Sel. Dor. a 2 *Ma quando mai* (interrogate each other)	–
Sel. sola *Non son le pene mie* (sentence aria)	Sel. sola *Aure portate* (invokes Nature)
(surprised by El. and Tol.) Tol. *Non prezzo il tuo dono* (*rebukes El.*)	Tol. *Se un solo è quel core*
El. sola *Sù sù mio core* (non exit; Ales. enters)	–
El. *Il mio core non apprezza* (instructs Ales.: badly)	*Il mio core non apprezza*
Ales. solo *Pur sento, oh Dio che l'alma* (true monologue expressing feelings)	–
(non exit)	(exit)
Dor. sola *Dolce speranza* (invokes Hope)	–
IIb Bosco Sel. *Son qual cerva sitibonda*	**Bosco**
Tol. Sel. a 2 *Ditemi dov'è* (unintentional hide-and-seek) (Ar. enters)	E. Sel. Tol. a 2 *Dite che fa dov'è*
Ar. *Piangi pur ma non sperare* (declares revenge to Tol.)	*Piangi pur ma non sperare*
Sel. Tol. a 2 *Empia man ci divide* ('Farewell forever')	Sel. Tol. a 2 *Se il cor ti perde*
IIIa Campagna con villa E. Ar. *Sono idee d'un alma stolta* (denies higher justice) (El. enters)	**Cabinetti . . . di Araspe** –
–	– (Ales. then Ar.) E. Ales. solo *Se l'interno pur vedono* (hopes for higher justice)
Ar. *Per giungere a chi s'ama* (command)	Ar. *Sarò giusto e non tiranno* (false self-justification) (break of liaison)
(Sel. enters) El. *Voglio amore, o pur vendetta* (threatens Sel.) (Tol. enters)	(Sel. El. enter) *Voglio amore, o pur vendetta*

Table 15. Continued

Sel. *Hai vinto sì crudele*	Sel. *Senza il suo bene*
(accuses Tol.; non exit)	(appeases Tol. with nature simile)
(Sel. Tol. take another farewell)	(Sel. exit)
El. sola *Io voglio vendicarmi*	El. *Ti pentirai crudel*
(threatens in monologue)	(threatens Tol.)
–	Tol. solo *Son qual rocca percossa*
	(nature simile; monologue)
(break of liaison)	
(Ales. then Ar.: =1728 IIIa)	
Ales. *Se l'interno pur vedono*	
Ar. *Sarò giusto e non tiranno*	(see above)
(non exit; Dor. enters)	
Dor. *Tra l'erbe e tra fiori*	–
(fakes belief in Ar.'s deceit)	
(Bosco: Rec. Ales. 'In questa più remota parte del bosco')	IIIb Bosco
Ales. solo *So che sperare*	–
(true emotional monologue)	
(Ales. frees Sel., then exit)	
Sel. sola *Stelle vi credo o no*	Sel. sola *Torni omai la pace*
(invokes stars)	(addresses Hope)
(break of liaison)	
Tol. solo Rec. and A. *Stille amare*	*Stille amare*
(addresses poison drops and drinks)	
(El. interrupts Tol.)	(tutti enter)
Tol. *Io moro ahi lasso io moro* (faints)	–
El. *Cielo ingiusto ma il cielo non fù*	
(invokes heaven, repents)	
(tutti enter)	
(Ar. attempts suicide; Dor. reveals her identity, forgives him)	–
(Sel., believed dead, enters; general forgiving and reconciliation)	
Sel. *E sol m'è gradita* (addressing Tol.)	Tol. Sel. a 2. *Tutta contenta or gode*
Sel. *Lieto giorno*	Coro. *Applauda ognuno*
(moral: renunciation enhances honour)	(call for general rejoicing).

In the first unit (Ia), both Capeci and Haym carefully motivate all the singing, making every aria situation appear as an unobserved monologue. The four arias are either invocations of higher forces, and almost prayers, or they are asides (sung *a parte*) and therefore deliberately concealed from the partner on stage. This technique generally characterizes the authors' intentions. Although the rules of tragedy forbid it as improbable that somebody should address a partner on stage with an aria in the course of ordinary communication ('dialogue aria'), plenty of situations can be created where singing is legitimate, because either it is not directed to someone on stage (true monologue) or is addressed to higher beings (prayer, invocation), or addressed to a partner who cannot hear because he is unconscious or asleep (apparent monologue). This, of course, is a form of casuistry that we may consider comical, but the game about dramatic rules – if that is what it is – goes much further, involving more serious concerns.

At the end of Ia, Haym and Handel create an effective dramatic exit with Elisa's solo 'Quell'onda che si frange'. In contrast to Tolomeo's 'Cielo ingiusto', this aria is a true monologue, such as may even occur in spoken dramas. Thus a dramaturgical convention is being exploited which Capeci had still eschewed in this first unit. The definition as a monologue applies to the verbal form of the aria, whereas its subject is rather a 'dialogue with Nature', to be used more often in both opera libretti.

With his discreet *a parte* aria, Alessandro has already given us to understand that he respects the rules of *decorum*. Araspe, however, who enters in unit Ib, does the opposite by declaring to 'Delia' his feelings suddenly and openly. He infringes both *decorum* and verisimilitude. His aria was cut in 1728. Further on, Haym largely avoids 'dialogue arias' employed for direct communication with a partner. On the other hand, the deletion of the role of Dorisbe makes his dramaturgy improbable when Araspe has to interrupt himself to announce the arrival of Alessandro.

Seleuce's 'È un grave martire' is a legitimate song because she disguises her communication to the partner as a commonplace. Such sentiments are acceptably expressed in song and verse. Haym, however, who seems dissatisfied with this legitimation, turns the scene into a soliloquy. As indicated by the words 'Mi *volgo* ad ogni fronda', Seleuce turns her previous deliberative monologue about nature into an address to Nature and to Cupid. Nor does Capeci miss the opportunity to address Nature in this unit, offering the duet 'Verdi piagge'.

Instead of Dorisbe's 'La tortorella', a nature simile directed to a partner, Haym has Elisa's 'Se talor miri un fior'. In both cases the dialogue situation seems tolerable because there is a didactic intention which may be allowed to be clad in verse and melody.

In 1728 the second and third stage-sets were amalgamated; in other words, set Ic with the shepherds' huts was omitted. Since there is no longer a change of scenery after Seleuce's aria 'Mi volgo', the result is a break of the *liaison*. Towards the end of the Act, both versions manage to avoid improbability only with some effort. 'Tiranni miei pensieri', the aria in which Tolomeo falls asleep, is set by Handel only until the halfway-point and without Da Capo, which in itself is a concession to verisimilitude. The sleeping Tolomeo (disguised as the shepherd Osmino) now remains alone on stage, providing a *liaison des scènes* to link up with Seleuce's entrance, despite the fact that she does not initially notice him. This makes her aria a disguised monologue, as in the first unit. For the purposes of the *liaison*, therefore, Tolomeo is taken seriously as a character on stage, whereas when it comes to legitimizing an aria as a monologue, he does not count! This may also point to a reason why, in seventeenth-century opera, sleep-, ghost- and ombra-scenes were so popular. When you address a shadow or someone who is asleep, he does not count as a real dialogue partner, and you may, with verisimilitude, sing just as well as speak.

The moment that Seleuce approaches the sleeping Osmino, to confirm a hope that he is really her husband Tolomeo, she is interrupted by Araspe who accuses her of indecency. This is unjustified, since her hope has turned out to be true. From her point of view, then, Seleuce has not committed an indecency, but Araspe does not know this: the *decorum* is shown to be relative. The same happens to verisimilitude with Araspe's 'Respira almeno'. Albeit in Tolomeo's presence, he sings an aside, recognizable by the fact that he addresses his own heart. For Araspe himself, no improbability occurs, although Tolomeo might wonder what Araspe is murmuring. Such casuistic approaches to *decorum* and verisimilitude are found throughout the drama.

Act II opens in both versions with entrance arias which, according to tradition, comment on the new scene (IIa): Capeci's Alessandro speaks about nature, Haym's Elisa addresses Nature. Of the five dialogue arias placed in this Act by Capeci, Haym has retained three ('Il mio core', 'Piangi pur', and 'Se un solo' with altered words); of the two duets, in which the partners address each other, he has left one ('Se il cor ti perde', also with changed words). The scene between Seleuce and Tolomeo in the woods (IIb) conforms to a mannerist stereotype. Just as they keep losing each other almost throughout the drama, they are unable to find each other between the big trees of this wood, so that their vocal parts remain, subjectively speaking, monologues. Handel, however, has combined their monologues into an involuntary musical duet, driving the game with verisimilitude to an extreme. This game is only fully understandable when its rule is known that sung dialogue was to be avoided as much as possible.

In Act III, Capeci offers as many as seven dialogue arias. A separate interpretation applies to the triumphal conclusion with two arias by Seleuce, who is found to be alive after all. In such a situation, musical effusion seems completely appropriate. Nevertheless, Haym and Handel transform even these dialogue arias into a love duet and a final tutti, respectively. Of Capeci's other dialogue arias, Araspe has two, and Elisa, Seleuce and Dorisbe each have one. All these arias present *negative* aspects or show an outright breach of *decorum*. Araspe reveals himself as a villain, intending to kill Tolomeo, with his dialogue arias 'Per giungere a chi s'ama' and 'Sarò giusto', only the second of which is kept by Haym. Elisa has similar aspirations in 'Voglio amore, o pur vendetta'. Haym has given her an additional accusatory aria ('Ti pentirai crudel') in a dialogue situation. Dorisbe deceives Araspe with 'Tra l'erbe', and even the virtuous Seleuce reproaches Tolomeo with 'Hai vinto, sì, crudele'. These words are toned down a little by Haym, who introduces a nature simile ('Senza il suo bene la tortorella'). This image of the enamoured dove is dramaturgically and linguistically analogous to Dorisbe's eliminated aria 'La tortorella' in Act I. Haym and Handel, in fact, do not have the slightest objection to simile arias, although scholars influenced by the aforementioned nineteenth-century clichés have sometimes condemned them as undramatic or un-Handelian. In the context of 1728, one of their functions is, again, to make singing on stage acceptable.

The observation that dialogue arias and *decorum* are linked could be followed further back into Acts I and II. It appears that the characters avoid dialogue arias to about the extent that they respect social conventions. Monologue arias are more easily justified than dialogue arias. But they, too, know stronger and weaker forms of legitimacy. 'Invocation of higher beings' is by far the preferred type, in Haym's as well as Capeci's libretto. Tolomeo, the protagonist, seems always free to sing arias when he is alone and in extreme situations, for example in the scene when he is forced to drink poison. The ritual and lyrical invocation of higher powers – among them even the bitter drops of poison ('Stille amare') – is a specialty of both Tolomeo and Seleuce. These leading characters are close to God and Nature, and their emotional outbursts tend to be acceptable whether probable or not. Admittedly, this statement could be simplified to the formula that arias equal emotions. It is possible that *all* kinds of legitimation of aria-singing – which furthermore include sentence aria, disguised monologue, unconscious partner, aside, and others – are hierarchically ordered in *Tolomeo* in such a way as to give the greatest legitimacy (and thus opportunity) of aria-singing to the heroes, a lesser one to Alessandro and Elisa, and the smallest one to the villain Araspe.

I believe that Haym's rearrangement of scenes in Act III is of paramount significance. It obviously relates to the introduction of the only indoor stage-set ('Cabinetti di Araspe', IIIa), by which the beautiful uniformity and simplicity of the 1711 version is disrupted. This unique scene, and its opening position in the Act, draws the spectator's attention to Alessandro's opening monologue aria 'Se l'interno pur vedono i numi', by which he reveals himself as a deeply righteous person. His words allude to an 'internal' sphere in himself, so that the scenery becomes a symbol for the soul itself. Capeci had offered, in this passage, the negative 'creed' of the villain ('Sono idee d'un alma stolta'), eliminated by Haym. But in both versions, Alessandro's positive 'creed' is followed on the heels by Araspe's self-revealing aria, 'Sarò giusto', in which he falsely maintains his righteousness. This diametrical opposition forms a unit which is separated from the following by a break of *liaison*.[31]

Before the next scenic unit ('Bosco', IIIb), Tolomeo's simile aria 'Son qual rocca' is inserted, the most elaborate maritime tableau of the opera. The aria alludes to Tolomeo's earlier shipwreck and to Seleuce, whom he believes dead. It also emphasizes his constancy in the face of his own death. But the final rescue is near – also because much of Capeci's text has been cut – despite the imminence of death and destruction. The ensuing change of scene and break of the *liaison* accentuate the drastic contradictions between constancy and fear of death.

In the last scenic unit, Seleuce is rescued by the magnanimous Alessandro, without Tolomeo's knowledge. After the solo 'Stille amare', in which Tolomeo believes that his brother wants him dead, Capeci makes him faint (again), in order to play the game about verisimilitude for a last time: in the presence of the unconscious Tolomeo, Elisa's aria ('Cielo ingiusto') is classifiable as a monologue, and yet a break of the *liaison* is avoided. In this aria, Elisa repents her misdeeds. Haym and Handel have eliminated the scene; Elisa's conversion is only mentioned later. The

---

31.   Such a separation is also intended in Capeci's version, with a break preceding these two arias; but Dorisbe appears in this sequence as well.

final solution – with the tutti on stage – breaks loose over Tolomeo as he (consciously) expects his death: not a fragile *liaison* but the major peripety of fortune in the drama, and from bad to good, of course

The drama seems to be recreated by Haym and Handel in such a way as to make the final solution erupt, so to speak, from the vigorous oscillations of the scenic units throughout Act III. The significant events are dramaturgically accentuated; the main turn of events can be identified as 'the revelation of Alessandro's inner goodness', for it is he who rescues the constant couple Tolomeo and Seleuce. The role of *decorum* is enhanced to bring about the peripety, and a conventional or playful observance of the rules of tragedy has acquired dramatic power. This is apparently connected with the function of the pastoral sphere. For Capeci, the pastoral stage is 'a place of good manners', 'a pleasant abode of virtuous people'. Haym and Handel ultimately break out of the pastoral sphere – also dramaturgically – to identify a drama of the souls and their deeper morality. The same indeed happens in *Orlando*. This more intimate blending of play and ethos distinguishes Handel's opera from the poetics of both Capeci and Metastasio.

11
Arianna in Creta: musical dramaturgy

The following essay is an attempt to evaluate the music of Handel's *Arianna in Creta* (1734) as a part of the drama; it therefore raises the question of the work's 'musical dramaturgy'. The first section offers a few basic notions regarding dramaturgical conventions of operatic music in Handel's time, adducing musical examples from the opera. The second section considers aspects of the dramaturgical structure of Handel's score.

To avoid any misunderstanding, 'dramaturgy' is taken here to mean quite simply and traditionally 'the art, or instruction in the art, of creating and performing a drama'.[1] The term 'musical dramaturgy', however, does more than simply extend this definition to mean 'the art, or instruction in the art, of creating and performing a musical drama'. Rather, the term would suggest that the music may in itself be a constituent of the drama.[2] If this is accepted, some far-reaching consequences arise: for example, the idea that musical means (it remains to be seen which) may be employed in an opera to support not a musical but rather a dramatic structure; or the idea that a musical score may be subject to the same methods of interpretation as a literary drama, whose 'form' (structure) and 'content' (communication) would now have to be sought in the sounds rather than the words.

The assumption that music per se carries a dramatically decisive weight in opera may initially seem to be a more helpful strategy for analyses of nineteenth- and twentieth-century works than for the study of Handel's operas. Nevertheless, since promising strategies of interpretation are otherwise few, let us proceed on the assumption that a Handelian musical dramaturgy does exist, even if distinct from that of later ages. The 'musical dramaturgy' to be discussed here would concern the *contribution* of music to drama or, better still, the *integration* of music into the textual-scenic-gestural presentation of a drama.

In order to avoid being misled by Classic-Romantic dramaturgical aesthetics, we may wish to concentrate on those aspects which eighteenth-century opera had

---

1. Carl Dahlhaus, 'What is a Musical Drama?', *Cambridge Opera Journal* I, no. 2 (1989), p. 1.
2. Such a formula is proposed, with reference to nineteenth-century Italian opera, in C. Dahlhaus, 'Drammaturgia dell'opera italiana', in *Storia dell'opera italiana*, ed. by L. Bianconi and G. Pestelli, vol. 6, 1988, p. 79.

inherited from the previous century and which were not transmitted further. Three aspects seem worth mentioning.

1. The most neglected aspect of the dramaturgical aesthetics of the eighteenth century is, I believe, the classical theory of drama. The Aristotelian Poetics were constantly invoked – whether approvingly or not – by the protagonists of dramatic literature throughout the seventeenth and eighteenth centuries. The most important concepts of that theory should become a basic resource for criticism and research in opera history of this period.

For example, we might pay attention to the classical six components of drama (which Pierre Corneille labelled *parties intégrantes*): subject, ethos, pathos, speech, music and stage decoration.[3] They were regarded as a hierarchy in which music was ranked beneath speech, almost like its servant. The historical development of opera, however, has progressively revaluated the contribution of music. Music that was being sought for opera had to be capable of portraying not only speech but also feelings, and even of expressing ethos and ultimately the dramatic subject itself. Handel and his contemporaries crossed the borderline into a culture in which all the *parties intégrantes* might present a potential challenge to the composer and performer. Not that these challenges were perceived everywhere and without differentiation, and surely not in isolation from each other. Arias or ensembles that represented the affections (pathos) could be intermingled with others dedicated to the status (ethos) of a character – for example the royal honour, rather than the affections, of a prince. Of course, the musical setting of an aria could reflect different *parties intégrantes* at the same time, or conflicts between them, as for example a conflict between love and honour. In Arianna's concluding aria of the first Act of our opera, the affections of 'sdegno' and 'amore' are at war with each other. Each of them is identified with a musical sign heard in the pronunciation of the respective word: 'sdegno' is expressed by a bare, dismissive downward leap, 'amore' by a semitone-step downwards which can be expressively ornamented. The musical substance of the aria, however, is otherwise dominated by the metaphor of 'guerra'; the music describes an allegory, not an affective state of mind. Handel's time was, in fact, still very interested in the musical portrayal of allegorical concepts – for example the Baroque *topos* of the 'chains' of love, to mention just one.

Even the lowest-ranking dramatic component of our hierarchy, stage decoration, is occasionally a subject worthy of musical elaboration. In the first scene of *Arianna in Creta*, a marble tablet suddenly falls to the ground, breaking into pieces; Cupids fly up from it, holding olive branches. This event is musically depicted by a short *sinfonia* which begins with downward scales and ends with ascending figurations like flapping wings. (See music example 12.)

A glance at the theory of musical *inventiones* developed by the opera composer Johann David Heinichen might show, in any case, how rich a palette of musical expression was accessible on this basis.[4]

---

3. For details, see chapter 1, pp. 17–18, and chapter 6, p. 127, in this volume.
4. Johann David Heinichen, *Der Generalbaß in der Komposition* (Dresden, 1728), introduction.

Example 12. Handel, *Arianna in Creta* I, 1 (London, 1734): sinfonia

La lapide ove sono scolpiti li patti d'Atene cade e s'infrange.

Quattro Amorini con ghirlande e rami d'olivo nelle mani volano per aria.

2. The name of Heinichen in itself testifies to a contemporary appreciation of *rhetoric* which influenced not only the theory but also the practice of opera composition.[5] To put it briefly: rhetoric, allegory and emblematics provided connections between intellectual and sensual experiences. They were, so to speak, the glue of communication in the theatre. Allegory, for example, assigns to a verbal figure (e.g. 'being in love') a visual image (e.g. 'a flickering flame') which can then be represented by flickering musical figurations. In this way, music can figuratively express the concept of being in love.[6] In *Arianna in Creta*, Handel chooses this allegorical connection in Alceste's aria 'Non ha difesa'. (See music example 13.)

Critics ought to know about such connections, otherwise they may not realize that among the various verbal figures of this aria text, that of 'being in love' is the one singled out for allegorical presentation. In the case of this aria it is clear, because the key metaphor, 'fiamma d'amore', is pronounced in the aria text itself. In other cases such a key is missing and has to be deduced from the general conventions of

5.   On Heinichen and rhetorics, see George J. Buelow, 'The *Loci topici* and Affect in Late Baroque Music: Heinichen's Practical Demonstration', *The Music Review* 27 (1966), pp. 161–76.
6.   For a brilliant explication of this principle, see Reinhold Kubik, *Händels Rinaldo: Geschichte, Werk, Wirkung* (Neuhausen-Stuttgart: Hänssler, 1982), pp. 218–26.

Example 13. Handel, *Arianna in Creta* II, 4: aria of Alceste

Example 14. Handel, *Arianna in Creta* II, 5: aria of Arianna

the time. This process of deduction may in itself be one of the listeners' reactions intended by the composer.

To give another example: in Arianna's aria 'So che non è più mio', the beginning of the middle section achieves great rhetorical effect through an *apostrophe* which suddenly addresses the gods and the allegorical character of Fidelity: 'Numi del ciel ch'invoco! Fede da lui tradita!' Apostrophe was a well-known rhetorical device – ancient orators used it in court when suddenly calling up an opponent or an absent person or god, to bear witness to what had just been said – which because of its relative emphasis had to be used judiciously. In the present aria text, the figure has a very strong effect due to its isolation. This helps us understand the special harmonic and rhythmic treatment Handel has reserved for the passage – the abrupt beginning with the unprecedented key of Ab major and the soloistic anticipation of the beat (*rubato* entry) by the voice, which escapes from the instrumental accompaniment, as it were, to invoke the protector gods in extreme despair. (See music example 14.)

Incidentally, we may note that apostrophe and other so-called 'figures of speech', which are not always discussed in the familiar studies of musical rhetoric, are generally more important for musical composition than the so-called 'figures of thought', which include, above all, the various types of metaphor.

3. With all due caution, I may touch upon a third area which I still hope to explore more thoroughly. On the Baroque stage, gesture and stage direction might have been just as influential for music as was rhetoric, if we take the above suggestions seriously. Eighteenth-century stage acting is known to us through numerous sources including printed treatises; there is no reason to presume that opera composers had no knowledge of it. On the contrary, they might even have communicated regularly about it with the singers, although the stage rehearsals in opera were usually directed by the librettist (a 'director' in the modern sense did not yet exist in opera). It seems fair to speculate that musical composition in some way reflected or even suggested gestures, movements or positions on stage. In music example 14, the isolated eb″ at the beginning might be considered the written equivalent of a gesture of hand or arm. If contemporary rules are applied, the figure of apostrophe inherent in the passage would be matched by an upward stretching-out of the right hand.

In Dene Barnett's highly significant study of eighteenth-century acting,[7] it is striking that the rules governing the musical stage are not presented as being in any way different from those of spoken drama. The sources themselves, although they sometimes differentiate by genre, do suggest a homogenous tradition. Even the differentiation between the performance of recitatives and arias, which of course reproduces, on a smaller scale, the contrast between spoken and sung drama, is for Barnett only a gradual one. It would be fortunate indeed for opera research and criticism if the possible influence of contemporary principles of acting and gesture on dramatic music were to be systematically explored. First steps were undertaken in 1987 by Stefan Kunze, who limited himself to illustrative and instrumental music, i.e. to links between composition and scenography.[8] Another step might be proposed here.

With the help of contemporary sources, Dene Barnett has reconstructed an eighteenth-century convention of classifying gestures in the three categories of 'indicative', 'imitative' and 'expressive': a classification that might fruitfully be applied also to their musical expression. For example, 'Numi del ciel ch'invoco!' (as quoted above) would have to be accompanied by an 'indicative' gesture, by pointing out what is being addressed: 'numi del cielo'. In operas of Handel's time, personal

---

7. Dene Barnett, *The Art of Gesture: The Practices and Principles of Eighteenth-Century Acting* (Heidelberg: Winter, 1987). On 'Acting in Opera', see particularly pp. 15–16. According to Barnett, stage action and oratory were intimately connected, above all in pedagogical practice. Also Joachim Eisenschmidt, *Die szenische Darstellung der Opern Händels auf der Londoner Bühne seiner Zeit* (Wolfenbüttel and Berlin, 1940), of course uses treatises on spoken drama.
8. Stefan Kunze, 'Szenische Aspekte in Händels Opernmusik', in *Händel auf dem Theater: Bericht über die Symposien der Internationalen Händel-Akademie Karlsruhe 1986 und 1987*, ed. by Hans Joachim Marx (Laaber, 1988) (Veröffentlichungen der Internationalen Händel-Akademie, vol. 2), pp. 181–92.

10. Franciscus Lang, *Dissertatio de actione scenica* (Augsburg, 1727): figures showing indicative (*left*) and expressive (*right*) gestures.

pronouns such as 'tu', 'io', indications of place such as 'dove?', là, 'fuori', meta-phorical place-names such as 'cielo', 'terra', 'patria' are strikingly often singled out rhythmically or melodically as verbal units of their own, as if their musical pronun-ciation had to support a certain indicative gesture. This is just as true for arias as for recitatives, or rather more so; often the musical setting seems to aid the gestural emphasis on a certain word.

'Imitative' gestures – as, for example, the drawing of waves in the air – are closely analogous to musically-imitative 'figures'. It needs to be investigated whether the composers' decisions in favour of such 'figures' were in any sense influenced by acting conventions. This would open another path towards the explanation of musical text-setting. 'Expressive' gestures mostly translate abstract notions into spatial symbols, as when upright, stretched-out palms signify 'rejection'. These spatial symbols can occasionally be expressed by musically imitative 'figures', for example when falling or rising melodies represent rejection or acceptance. In such a case, where the music has recourse to a spatial image, the musical 'gesture' is not expressive but imitative. On the other hand, expression can be derived more usually from the musical structure itself, as when expressive emphasis is achieved through the choice of key, tempo, amount of dissonance, and so on. These technical devices have no extramusical significance by themselves, but they derive it from the semantic conventions of the musical art. This is analogous to the use of numerous 'expressive' gestures, for example the wringing of hands as a sign of grief: the gesture as such does not mean anything, but on the stage it customarily accompanies the portrayal of grief.

To sum up, we may envisage the following approximate classification for the musical expression as compared with the gestural-scenic one:

– Indicative-declamatory music, analogous to indicative gestures: isolation and demonstration of, above all, the verbal structure and its recitation on stage;
– imitative-illustrative music, analogous to imitative gestures: translation of concepts into visual metaphors, for which musical analogies are available;
– expressive music, partly analogous to expressive gestures: either recourse to the imitation of spatial metaphors, or the use of semantic conventions attached to abstract musical devices.

Here is an example of a motive by Handel that can be understood as gestural in two ways. In Tauride's aria 'Mirami altero in volto', the composer isolates the first word both rhythmically and melodically from what follows.[9]

Example 15. Handel, *Arianna in Creta* I, 2: aria of Tauride

First, the musical isolation of the word 'Mirami' corresponds to an indicative gesture, which visualizes apostrophe and imperative by pointing out the partner who is addressed, and nailing him to the spot: 'It is you I am talking to!' Secondly, this partner is an opponent, even a mortal enemy. Handel expresses this feeling with an energetic downward move, surely corresponding to the rule that downward-pointing hand gestures can signify refusal and contempt. (Further downward moves follow at 'altero in volto'.) Thus the musical motive of 'Mirami' implies an indicative as well as an expressive gesture, most probably that of a hand stretched forward with the index finger pointing half downward. Although Tauride, who is singing, requests his opponent to fix his gaze on him (Tauride), in Handel's interpretation he must not point towards himself. In that case, he would have to sing a self-confidently ascending motive.

The second section of this essay may now consider the dramaturgical structure of *Arianna in Creta*, as Handel has defined it by his musical composition. Has he

9. So much indeed that 'altero' incorrectly appears to refer to 'volto' rather than to the addressee, Teseo.

created such a structure at all? The strongest argument in favour of this hypothesis would be the identification of musical structures (for example, an overall key-scheme) which make sense on condition that they are viewed in the context of the drama, or of musical signs (for example certain repeated motives) whose significance can be recognized when they are seen as part of a dramaturgical plan. To put it briefly: if the drama explains something in the music that does not seem to have a specifically musical *raison d'être*, it is legitimate to assume that the composer had a dramaturgical intention.

The key structure of *Arianna in Creta*, as designed in Handel's original composition (see table 16),[10] would not make much sense if it were viewed only as a linear succession of musical numbers.

Table 16. Aria keys in *Arianna in Creta*[11]

a) gathered along the scale (*downwards*):

	(major sixth)
minor keys	e d c b a g
	(minor sixth)
major keys	B♭ A G F E E♭ D

(C major does not occur)

b) articulating the three Acts:

Ouverture	First Act	Second Act	Third Act
d/D	>A	F >a	B♭ >D

c) assignation to characters along scale (*downwards*):

Arianna	c B♭ a G
Teseo	A G F E D
Tauride	G F E D
Alceste	B♭ g/G E♭
Carilda	a/A e/E
Minos	b

The straightforward succession of aria keys in the opera disappoints expectations of variety and balance. In section a) of the table, however, the purely musical fact may seem worth noticing that the minor keys fill the major sixth E–G, the major keys the minor sixth B♭–D, whereas C major does not occur at all. This structure may become interesting if a dramaturgical reason can be supplied. As section b) of

---

10. The following analysis is based on the original version of the opera as reconstructed in Reinhold Kubik's forthcoming edition for the *Hallische Händel-Ausgabe*. This version is dramaturgically and musically superior to the version actually performed in 1734. See also Reinhold Kubik, 'Die Fassungen von *Arianna in Creta* HWV 32: Überlegungen zum Werkbegriff der Opera seria', in *Gattungskonventionen der Händel-Oper: Bericht über die Symposien 1990 und 1991*, ed. by Hans Joachim Marx (Laaber, 1992) (Veröffentlichungen der Internationalen Händel-Akademie, vol. 4), pp. 159–70.

11. Minor keys are indicated by lower case letters.

the table shows, the beginning and end of the opera converge on d minor/D major. More interesting analogies begin to appear when the dramaturgically decisive final arias in Acts I and II, as well as the openings of Acts II and III, are considered.[12] Arianna's two arias concluding Acts I and II contrast in mode but share the degree of A which is the dominant of the final D; the total progression of Acts II and III is each time a major third, rising to the dominant A and final D, respectively. The degrees of F and B♭ employed in this succession may be regarded as 'strategical' keys. It is notable that Handel's libretto version *differs* from those used in earlier settings by beginning Act II with a great programmatic monologue for Teseo – set in F major – and by ending this Act with a solo scene of the imprisoned Arianna, in a minor.[13]

The dramaturgical reason for the distribution of aria keys becomes clearest when their assignation to the dramatis personae is compared with their distribution along the scale (section c). Teseo and Arianna share a seventh-scale (counting downwards) from C to D, in which only G major is employed twice. The second pair of characters fills the fifth-scale B♭ to E♭ chromatically and in alternation, whereby Carilda has the 'hard' keys, Alceste the 'soft' ones; the tonal relationship of their keys is chromatic, that of Arianna and Teseo diatonic. Minos extends Carilda's circle of hard keys to b minor; Tauride only copies Teseo's keys. The characters show preferences for certain modes and collections of keys; for example, Carilda and Minos have mostly hard keys in the minor mode, Alceste predominantly soft keys in the major mode; Teseo and Tauride cultivate only the major mode, Arianna mixes both modes.

Keys and modes are only one of the many musical means of expression which Handel has apparently distributed dramaturgically. The arias of the second pair lend themselves to a parallel arrangement in two 'quartets', with regard also to their tempi, time signatures and genre character: see table 17.

Compare the variety and balance of Carilda's metres with the three 6/8-signatures for Alceste (draft version), or the four different dance types employed by Carilda. They may provide an explanation for Tauride's e minor gavotte which he sings as he threatens Carilda with force ('Che se fiera poi mi nieghi', II, 11). With the dance character he is trying to gain her confidence, but the key usurps her constancy, as expressed in her aria in e minor, 'Quel cor che adora'.

The origins and revisions of an opera score can provide relevant clues as to its musical dramaturgy, since compositional choices can sometimes be compared with their alternatives. This is very much the case with *Arianna in Creta*. As an example, let us consider the question of what Handel dramaturgically intended with Alceste's aria 'Par che voglia il ciel sereno' and with the final number, 'Bella sorge la speranza'.

---

12. Act II opens with an accompagnato recitative, Act III with a sinfonia.
13. Concerning libretto versions of *Arianna*, see Giovanna Gronda, 'Le peripezie di un libretto', in *La carriera di un librettista: Pietro Pariati da Reggio di Lombardia*, ed. by Giovanna Gronda (Bologna: Il Mulino, 1990), pp. 289–737, and eadem, 'Das Arianna-Libretto und seine Vorlagen', in *Gattungskonventionen der Händel-Oper: Bericht über die Symposien 1990 und 1991*, ed. by Hans Joachim Marx (Laaber, 1992) (Veröffentlichungen der Internationalen Händel-Akademie, vol. 4), pp. 139–57.

Table 17. The two aria 'quartets' of Carilda and Alceste

Act	Carilda	Alceste
I	'Dille che nel mio seno' a Andante 3/4 [minuet-sarabande]	
		'Talor d'oscuro velo' B♭ Andante 6/8 [?]
	'Quel cor che adora' e Allegro 6/8 [passepied]	
II		'Non ha difesa' G Andante Allegro C [concerto]
	'Narrargli allor saprei' E Allegro C [bourrée]	
		'Son qual stanco pellegrino' g Andante 6/8 [siciliano]
III	'Un tenero pensiero' A Allegro C [gigue]	
		'Par che voglia il ciel sereno' E♭ Andante Allegro 3/4 [polonaise] (draft version of aria: 'Lusinghiera nel mio seno' E♭ Andante Allegro 6/8 [?])[14]

In place of Alceste's aria (III, 2), Handel had found in Leonardo Leo's libretto of 1729 the text 'Lusinghiera nel mio seno/ Bella sorge la speranza'. He had set it for Alceste to the music now sung by Teseo as the final number of the opera, 'Bella sorge la speranza', although originally in E♭ major instead of Teseo's D major. (This alone may show how aria keys can depend on dramaturgical conditions such as their position in the drama as a whole.) When transferring the aria, Handel or his librettist simply switched the first two text lines. The words describe a nature simile as do two of the other three arias sung by Alceste: the feeling of hope arising in his heart is compared to an atmospheric image, almost a Fata Morgana, which 'rises' ('sorge'). Interestingly, several other libretto versions have meteorological similes in this place, for example Porpora's version of 1727 ('Quando spunta in ciel l'aurora') and the Florentine libretto of 1728 ('Quel basso vapore'). The libretto of 1721, which was known to Handel, does not have a nature simile but contrasts 'speranza' and 'timore'. In Pariati's original libretto of 1715, Carilda and Alceste sing a duet

---

14. For the draft version of this aria, to be distinguished from the (later) 'original version' of the opera as a whole, see the next paragraphs.

Example 16. Handel, *Arianna in Creta* III, scena ultima: aria of Teseo

about hope, the nature simile 'Tanto brama il fior l'aurora'. Dawn (aurora) is a symbol of hope also in Handel's opera, in Alceste's aria 'Talor d'oscuro velo' (B♭ major) in Act I. A close neighbour of the aria in III, 2 is the opening sinfonia of Act III, in B♭ major. Carilda's intervening aria, in which she encourages Alceste's love for the first time, uses the sharply contrasting A major; but this is the dominant key to the opera's final D, whereas the sinfonia's B♭ major forms the dominant to Alceste's E♭ aria. There appears to be a parallel structure of two 'V–I' progressions towards a happy ending.

Handel then decided to give Alceste's aria to Teseo and to place it at the end of the opera, because the music already sounded 'final' enough; since it now concluded the whole drama and not only Alceste's personal story, it had to be transposed to the more general final key of D major. The main melody of the aria vividly presents the 'rising' of Hope. (See music example 16.)

There are precedents in the opera for the musical motive of ascending and descending motions, for example in the fugal theme of the overture (see below). It has been suggested that Handel's theme of 'Bella sorge la speranza' is borrowed from Giuseppe Vignati.[15] This composer's aria theme ('Sciolta dal lido'), however, has only the descending, not the ascending motion. An individual trait in Handel's setting is, furthermore, its initially note-repeating but then contrapuntal bass, and

---

15.   John H. Roberts, 'Handel and Charles Jennens's Italian opera manuscripts', in *Music and Theatre: Essays in Honour of Winton Dean*, ed. by Nigel Fortune (Cambridge: Cambridge University Press, 1987), p. 195.

the sliding descent in parallel tenths, b. 4–5. The leap from the tonic upwards, followed by a stepwise, sliding descent (such as here in the bass, b. 3–4), can be found also in the aria 'Dille che nel mio seno' (I, 3; B-section), in the duet 'Bell'idolo amato' (I, 11, in the original version described here) and in the minuet of the overture (top voice and bass, often in imitation or parallel tenths, as in b. 10–13). This D major minuet generally impresses with its melodic contours. Further on, a particularly beautiful motion of ascent and descent is designed in Alceste's meteorological 'Hope'-aria 'Talor d'oscuro velo' (I 6; this text comes from the 1729 libretto as well), where also the metre and tempo resemble those of 'Bella sorge'. To these various images of motion we may add the perhaps most significant one: the violin figuration of ascending pairs of semiquavers, each of which drops by a third or fourth, as in b. 5 of 'Bella sorge' (music example 16). This figuration, which probably depicts rising or fluttering hope, recurs in Alceste's aria 'Non ha difesa' (music example 13), where it refers to the flickering flames of love.

The same figure also characterizes the little sinfonia of Act I (music example 12), which accompanies the crash of the marble tablet and the flying Cupids. This sinfonia was composed as an afterthought (it is added in the autograph in a space originally left free) and thus probably derives its main figuration from the idea of 'ascending' or 'flying up', which Handel had already elaborated in 'Bella sorge la speranza'.

We can now see that this coherent motivic imagery, which is of the 'imitative' kind and uses spatial gestures, also applies to Handel's replacement aria for Alceste, 'Par che voglia il ciel sereno'. (See music example 17.) When the *secondo uomo*, Alceste, had lost his greatest aria to the protagonist (and the following tutti), Handel composed a new aria for him, also in E♭ major and initially even with the same words. During the writing of the A-section, the text was changed, so that Handel's autograph of the aria (fol. 61v–62v) begins with the words 'Lusinghiera nel mio seno' but ends underlaid with 'Par che voglia il ciel sereno'. Table 18 shows how the new words reiterate the imagery of 'Bella sorge' and use closely related verbal figures.

A form of verbal bridge between 'Par che voglia' and 'Bella sorge' is provided by the intervening duet 'Mira adesso questo seno' (III, 7) which, like the final tutti, equally addresses satisfied hope and the reconciled heart. Much of this verbal coherence is due to the Italian rhyme-words, which is not a trivial coincidence, since rhymes are musical and rhetorical elements of speech, as well as serving communication. As for the contents of the texts, they are enriched in 'Par che voglia' by the image of the serene sky (also addressed by Alceste elsewhere), and the meteorological motive is preserved in the image of 'rischiarar' (lighting up, dawn).

The music of the new aria certainly expresses the spatial gestures of descent and ascent, which should count as fundamental dramaturgical elements, and in addition, a contrapuntal opposition of 'above' and 'below', which in the opera is musically realized in just this one aria by 'linear polyphony' with many implied suspensions (for example, b. 8–9). The triple metre interestingly creates irregularities of the parallel voice-leading here: the two implied upper voices of b. 8–9 might be compared with the counterpoint between voice and bass in b. 4 of 'Bella sorge'.

Example 17. Handel, *Arianna in Creta* III, 2: aria of Alceste

Table 18. Repetition of verbal imagery in different texts

'Par che voglia'	'Mira adesso' (duet)	'Bella sorge'
ciel sereno	seno / più sereno	sorge . . . seno
afflitta l'alma		prova l'alma
palma		calma
fido amante cor		crede il fido cor
speme // timor	amore // tormento	speranza // dolor

I am inclined to interpret the violin figure (six semiquavers) in b. 3 etc. as a joyfully ascending 'rocket' which illustrates Alceste's rising spirits. By choosing a moderately fast 3/4-metre for this aria, Handel has increased the rhythmic variety of Alceste's arias and also connected it with Carilda's first aria and the minuet of the overture – a link hitherto not present in the composition. What is its dramaturgical significance?

Whenever Handel composed the overture, he has given it a good amount of internal contrast and coherence.[16] (See music example 18.) The opening imitation of the Grave presents two upwards motions within the d minor triad, traversing the

---

16.   Handel often composed the overture first; the last items to be composed in *Arianna in Creta* were, according to the evidence of the autograph, the little sinfonia in Act I and the aria 'Par che voglia'.

Example 18. Handel, *Arianna in Creta*: ouverture (grave-allegro)

Example 19. Handel, *Arianna in Creta* II, 14: aria of Minos

fifth and then the fourth. The Allegro combines the two basic motives within the
fugal theme (*dux*) alone, beginning with the ascending fourth followed by the fifth,
this time descending. The *comes*, entering at the lower fifth, replaces the fourth by
an ascending fifth again (later fugal entries always happen at the octave, however);
thus the head-motives of Grave and Allegro appear switched between *dux* and
comes. Also significant is the 'Dorian' (a minor) sound in the *comes* entry, which in
turn will be answered by E major later on. A striking subsidiary motive of the
Allegro is a slow, chromatic ascent in crotchets, of the kind that in operas of the time
might be associated with the feeling of toil or grief, corresponding perhaps to an
'expressive gesture'. The compositional style of the movement as a whole recalls
ancient, severe fugal idioms, quite comparable to the style of the aria 'Se ti
condanno' (II, 14), in which Minos, the Judge of the Dead, condemns his own
daughter to death – in b minor! The fugal theme of that aria is an ascending fifth,
too, immediately answered by the fourth and thus clearly referring to the very first
bar of the opera and to the overture in general. (See music example 19.)

The minuet, while taking over the most important melodic motives of the movements in d minor, unexpectedly converts them into D major and gives them galant,
placid and song-like contours. (The effect is almost comparable to the entry of the
maggiore in J. S. Bach's d minor violin ciacona.) The theme now begins with the
rising fourth a'–d" and then fills the lower fifth with ornamented steps in the

Example 20. Handel, *Arianna in Creta*: ouverture (minuet)

following three bars. (See music example 20.) The minuet offers many further allusions to the ascending and descending motions of all the numbers discussed so far; there is in addition a slow, chromatic ascent in its middle section which tends towards b minor.

In Carilda's first aria, 'Dille che nel mio seno', the unfortunate young hostage is introduced as a proud Athenian woman who does not fear death – but she conceals that she is hopelessly in love with Theseus. The choice of the minuet-metre (containing elements of a sarabande, as often with Handel's noble characters) and of the key of a minor is by now dramaturgically transparent. (See music example 21.) We have already cited the upward-leap followed by a sliding descent at the beginning of the B-section ('Io lieta moro'). In other passages, too, the aria is characterized by dignity and grace, which nevertheless must be maintained through some slow, chromatic ascents and descents. It does seem a surprise that in this serious aria the melodic contour of the beginning exactly shadows that of the D major minuet (see arrows in music examples 20 and 21).

Example 21. Handel, *Arianna in Creta* I, 3: aria of Carilda

It may be suggested that the keystone of the whole construction of this opera is the little sinfonia of the first scene, composed later. The tablet which suddenly crashes down contains the ancient treaty, so dreadful for Athens, requesting the delivery of hostages for the Minotaur every seven years. The Cupids, however, who fly up holding olive branches, with their fluttering wings (violin figurations), symbolize the hope for a victory of love and peace, which is explicitly stated in the final number. The ancient treaty is associated with the fugal technique, the minor mode, with Minos and his status as a Judge of the Dead, and with Carilda's and Arianna's misfortune. Hope, love and human dignity are associated with the minuet, D major, the rising and fluttering motions. These contrasts interact in ever varied constellations in the various numbers of the opera, so that often the dark or negative elements also yield a glimpse of the positive. (This happens, for example, in Arianna's aria 'Se nel bosco resta solo' at the end of Act II, which connects the key of a minor and darkness with the minuet rhythm.) The general formula of the opera might be expressed in terms of a musical enlightenment: minuet overcomes fugue.

Handel is not a philosopher but a dramatist. He does not stop at 'expressive' symbolisms or abstractions (such as key characteristics) but transforms the dramatic content as much as possible into allegories, and these in turn into visual-spatial gestures. For this reason, the little episode with the tablets is the turning point, as it were, of the drama: the tablet does not simply break, but crashes *down*, and the Cupids with the olive branches do not simply appear, but fly *up*.

We have already sketched an interpretation of the opera as a whole without even discussing its two main characters, Teseo and Arianna. To find out in what other ways the musical dramaturgy of *Arianna in Creta* may be determined by the protagonists would require at least another essay. One important connection may already be pointed out: of all the arias, Arianna's in a minor, 'Se nel bosco resta solo', is closest in character to a minuet. In Handel's original version, discussed here, this aria follows like an immediate reaction to the fugal aria 'Se ti condanno,/ giusta vendetta', which is Minos's sentence. Thus the second Act perhaps ends with a confirmation of the general formula just proposed, 'minuet overcomes fugue': a statement about civilization which is actually very characteristic of Handel.

12
Sinfonia and drama in opera seria

The character, and perhaps the artistic merit, of an opera overture is often judged by the way in which it is musically integrated with the opera that follows. This integration, in turn, is predominantly sought in the overture's and the opera's thematic content, a criterion that suits Classic-Romantic instrumental music. Instrumental forms of earlier periods, such as the overture and sinfonia of the earlier eighteenth century, are often less dependent for their form and character on specific individual themes: circular reasoning thus leads to the conclusion that they were *not* usually integrated with their respective operas.

It is indeed widely believed that musical correspondence, or integration, of overture and opera was not practised before the so-called Gluckian reform. Gluck's famous admonition, in his preface to *Alceste* (1769), that the overture 'ought to prepare the spectators for the dramatic subject that is to be performed, and ought to be, so to speak, its *argomento*',[1] has been interpreted as a watershed between the abstract Baroque sinfonia or overture consisting of little more than festive noise, and the Classic-Romantic overture that is thematically integrated with the opera (which implies its being thematically constructed).

In this contribution, evidence will be adduced to suggest that the task of 'tying the overture to the opera in mood and theme'[2] was more widely accepted by opera composers in the early part of that century than is often believed. At first, however, a possible misunderstanding of Gluck must be ruled out. He did not mean to recommend that the overture-*argomento* be identifiable with specific musical themes or motives; it would be hard to prove this to be the case even in *Alceste*. Furthermore, Gluck's and Calzabigi's recommendations to opera composers published in this famous preface are derived (as already observed by Alfred Einstein) from a long tradition of thinking about operatic reform. The mentor of both men, Francesco Algarotti, had similarly lamented the monotonous noise of current opera sinfonias, and their musical separation from the following drama. Such an abstract

1. My translation, from the Italian given in Giorgio Pestelli, *L'età di Mozart e Beethoven* (Turin: EdT, 1979), p. 289.
2. Nicholas Temperley, 'Overture', *The New Grove Dictionary of Music and Musicians*, ed. by S. Sadie (London: Macmillan, 1980), vol. 14, p. 34.

independent sinfonia, he says, is as inadequate as a preface (*esordio*) of a poetic work that presents nothing but clichés suitable for any kind of *orazione*.[3] It appears that Gluck's recommendation differs little from Algarotti's except by replacing *esordio* with *argomento*. Both these terms, to be sure, belong to the traditional vocabulary of literary rhetoric and poetics.

A well-known article by Daniel Heartz likens the function of the overture of Mozart's *La clemenza di Tito* to that of a dramatic *argument* in Gluck's sense, i.e. to a summary of antecedents and main elements of the drama such as a poet would offer to introduce a dramatic work.[4] One of the characteristics of Mozart's overture highlighted in Heartz's study is the emphasis on tonal, not only thematic, relationships with the opera. Another, equally significant for the following discussion, is 'Mozart's practice of tying the overture together with the end of the opera, a not unnatural consequence of their having been written within a short time of each other'.[5]

Heartz does not have to make explicit that those elements of the Titus drama, which in his hearing have had a generative influence on the overture, are by no means simply 'the plot'. There is both more and less to the integration overture-opera in this case than, for example, in Weber's or Wagner's overtures.[6] There is less of a tangible identity of themes, and therefore less reference to identifiable situations in the drama, but more multiple cross-referencing with motivic patterns or harmonic progressions that appear to represent the morals and passions of the leading characters (Sesto and Vitellia). There is also, surely, the generic unity provided by musical clichés denoting the Holy Roman/Roman Imperial setting: trumpets and drums, fanfares, C major, unisono slide figures in the strings, dotted rhythms. Most of these devices would fit any symphonic or operatic work alluding to grandeur and rulership, of course. But how this array of semantically stereotyped elements prevails, in both the overture and the finale of *La clemenza di Tito*, over the passions of hatred, anguish and guilt as represented by the rival flat keys and minor modes, results from a process of individualization. It is as predictable dramaturgically as it is musically individual and powerful. In this opera seria, the harmonic-thematic resolution of the overture predicts, like a symphonic oracle, the dénouement of the drama.

If we can describe the relationship between a Classical overture and its opera in terms borrowed from the literary poetics (*argomento*) or rhetoric (*esordio*) of the previous (Baroque) era, then poetics and rhetoric might also contribute to a better understanding of the opera introductions of that era itself. Can the Baroque opera sinfonia in general have been expected to function as an *argomento*?

3. 'Saggio sopra l'opera in musica', in F. Algarotti, *Scritti*, ed. by Giovanni Da Pozzo (Bari: Laterza, 1963), p. 159.
4. Daniel Heartz, 'Mozart's Overture to *Titus* as Dramatic Argument', *Musical Quarterly* 64 (1978), pp. 29–49.
5. Ibid., p. 30.
6. Thematic integration in works of that period came increasingly in conflict with symphonic forms. See Reinhard Strohm, 'Gedanken zu Wagners Opernouvertüren', in *Wagnerliteratur-Wagnerforschung*, ed. by Carl Dahlhaus and Egon Voss (Mainz: Schott, 1985), pp. 69–84.

The 'argument' was, in the seventeenth and eighteenth centuries, familiar to theatregoers as a printed introduction to the subject matter of a drama or opera libretto.[7] It was not a preface, nor necessarily a synopsis of the plot; more often the author concentrated on the prehistory of the action in order to prepare the spectator for basic conflicts and constellations between the characters. Rarely did an *argomento* give away the turning points of the dramatic intrigue. Sometimes it mentioned them, but only in a roundabout way. When listening to the music, the opera audience could experience a marvellous analogy between overture and 'argument', brought about by the semantic ambiguity of instrumental music itself: even where the overture appeared to tell the outcome of the drama, the feeling of suspense did not collapse, because the orchestral statements remained enigmatic.

Just as Algarotti's *esordio* was a fixed part of a literary work according to the tradition of rhetoric, so the practice of the *argomento* was rooted in the classicist (Aristotelian) poetics of drama, which through the French Classical theatre so strongly influenced Italian opera of the early eighteenth century. The classicist poetics was well known to dramatists and reflected in such commentaries as Pierre Corneille's *Trois discours sur le poème dramatique* (1660) or Metastasio's *Estratto dell'arte poetica d'Aristotile e considerazioni su la medesima* (1773).[8] One of the most fundamental rules established by Aristotle – although less debated in the eighteenth century than the notorious three unities – was the distinction of a tragedy into six ingredients or 'inherent parts' (Corneille: *parties intégrantes*; Metastasio: *parti di qualità*). They were, in descending order of importance:

Sujet (*soggetto*) or *azione* (also *azione principale*);
Moeurs (*costumi*);
Sentiments (*sentenza*);
Diction (*discorso*);
Musique (*musica*);
Décoration (*decorazione*).[9]
(The last two elements were often quoted in reverse order.)

Now it is in the *argomento* of a drama that a playwright or librettist should explain the major issue, i.e. the subject (*soggetto*) or the main action (*azione principale*), although he will rarely give a detailed account of the whole 'plot', which is not the same thing in any case. He may, furthermore, summarize the characters' *moeurs*, or (Aristotle's term) *ethos*, and he may even hint at some of the passions they are going to experience and express – *sentiments*, *sentenza*,[10] *pathos* – but without giving a full account of these fleeting conditions.

---

7. Much of what follows could be confirmed by the brilliant *argomenti* of the leading eighteenth-century librettist, so seldom read today, Metastasio.
8. Pietro Metastasio, *Tutte le opere*, vol. 2, 2nd edn, pp. 957–1117.
9. See also chapter 6 in this volume, pp. 127–8.
10. Strange as it may sound, the Italian word for 'passion' here is *sentenza*, not *sentimento*, as explained by Metastasio in the *Estratto*, p. 1029.

This usage alone might shed new light on the role of the sinfonia in opera seria. If, in considering eighteenth-century *drammi per musica*, we cannot find that any of the thematic material of the arias is announced in the opening sinfonia, this may simply mean that none of it is deemed fundamental or general enough for such a cardinal position in the musico–dramatic discourse. What we are tempted to hear as perfunctory, cheerful noise[11] could have been intended by the composer as relating to subject or morals rather than to affections or plot. The sinfonia which seems to refer only to itself may rather refer to the drama all wrapped up in one single concept. As regards the subject matter of the average opera seria, stereotypes loom so large in any case that orchestral pieces illustrating them can hardly be expected to have much individuality.

It was probably welcome to classicist critics that the orchestral introduction, by sounding celebratory and conventional, could reflect the contemporary setting in which operas were performed. To the Aristotelian, tragedy is a ceremonial reenactment or celebration of heroic deeds and fortunes of the past. It is something people *do with the past*. The orchestral music that announces such a theatrical reenactment, i.e. an opera, is already part of the celebratory act itself. The frequent allusions to dance in Baroque sinfonias and overtures often anticipate the royal (and real) dances at the ends of Acts or of the whole opera; dance and ceremony are ritual actions naturally associated with Classical and classicist drama.

Let us also consider the state of the instrumental language of that period. Musical means such as key, mode, instrumentation, metres, characteristic rhythms, dance patterns, large-scale form and temporal disposition were used by composers to individualize truly 'abstract' genres such as sonatas. They could just as well become vehicles of dramatic meaning and integration in sinfonias, in preference to thematic-motivic material. It should of course be kept in mind that the three-movement form of the sinfonia, which was still around in the 1770s, calls for strategies of interpretation different from those of the more concentrated one-movement form.

We have now cast our net so wide that we should be able to catch some dramatic meaning in the following random examples of early eighteenth-century sinfonias. We shall discover more that is dramatically relevant or individual than we may have bargained for: there will even be thematic integration and pre-announcements of specific motives. The Gluckian watershed should not worry us. All that is needed to understand these earlier compositions might be to give up nineteenth-century aesthetic prejudices.

Giovanni Battista Pergolesi's sinfonia to *Adriano in Siria* (1734)[12] can hardly escape the verdict of conventionality: no dramatic content, no connection with the opera, just stereotyped instrumental formulae seem to characterize this orchestral piece.

11.   Much – although not all – of the sinfonia of Gluck's *Orfeo* might fall under this verdict.
12.   Giovanni Battista Pergolesi, *Adriano in Siria*, ed. by Dale Monson (New York and Milan: Pendragon Press, 1986) (Pergolesi, *Complete Works*, ed. by B. S. Brook, F. Degrada and H. Hucke, vol. 3).

Were we to find a connection with Metastasio's drama even in such a work, uncomfortable questions about the uses of musical convention might arise. Here is a suggestion.

According to Metastasio's *argomento*, the drama accomplishes a development: that of Hadrian from an emperor freshly elevated by the troops to an emperor worthy of his glory. His virtue which had 'fallen asleep' is awakened: he becomes a victor over himself.[13] This event in Hadrian's personal development is surely the 'principal action' of the work. It was a suitable *sujet* – from the poet's point of view – to honour the emperor who had commissioned the libretto. The other elements of the drama which the *argomento* quotes are significant because they help this main event to come about. They are partly ethical characteristics – Osroa's ferocity, Farnaspe's innocence, Sabina's tolerance – and partly fleeting passions such as Hadrian's own 'amorous doubts' and Emirena's anxieties. What should we expect the composer to do with this menu of *parties intégrantes*?

The first scene actually presents the Roman troops acclaiming Hadrian as emperor in a chorus, which constitutes the first step in the main action. After Hadrian's reply, the first stanza of the chorus is sung da capo. Pergolesi's score[14] uses an abridged version of the libretto: the chorus is not notated but the 'sinfonia' is to be repeated, surely because the sinfonia, or part of it, is suitable music to illustrate the ceremonial acclamation and the main *sujet*. Now, Pergolesi's sinfonia as a whole has in common with the *end* of the opera at least the key, D major, and most probably also a connection with the emperorship of Hadrian, because the finale (with horns instead of trumpets) is another chorus of the soldiers in D major, 'May Augustus's name be heard up to the ether'. Even without the support of motivic-thematic connections, it must be legitimate to relate the sinfonia to the *sujet*, especially the first Allegro movement. I suggest that its excited runs in quavers through all the stringed instruments, succeeding each other in quasi-fugal imitation, are a simile of the approaching troops who hasten to greet the new emperor. The key, the trumpets and the general heroic tone of the movement confirm the stereotype of rulership. The Allegro would thus present, in order to announce the subject matter, Hadrian's elevation, which is the immediate prehistory of the opening scene. In the Andante, a G major melody expectedly introduces soft, charming and sentimental traits appropriate to the passive and loving character of Emirena

13. 'Era in Antiochia Adriano, e già vincitore de' Parti, quando fu sollevato all'Impero.' There follows the description of the events, historical and otherwise; the author concludes: 'Le dubbiezze di Cesare fra l'amore per la principessa de' Parti e la violenza dell'obbligo che lo richiama a Sabina, la virtuosa tolleranza di questa, le insidie del feroce Osroa, delle quali cade la colpa sull'innocente Farnaspe, e le smanie d'Emirena ne' pericoli or del padre, or dell'amante ed or di se medesima, sono i moti fra' quali a poco a poco si riscuote l'addormentata virtù d'Adriano, che, vincitore alfine della propria passione, rende il regno al nemico, la consorte al rivale, il cuore a Sabina e la sua gloria a se stesso.' Metastasio, *Tutte le opere*, vol. 1, 2nd edn, p. 529. The *argomento* of Pergolesi's libretto is identical in the quoted passages.

14. Giovanni Battista Pergolesi, *Adriano in Siria*, ed. by Dale Monson (New York and Milan: Pendragon Press, 1986) (Pergolesi, *Complete Works*, ed. by Barry S. Brook, Francesco Degrada and Helmut Hucke, vol. 3).

11. Antonio Galli Bibiena, 'Gran Piazza d'Antiochia', stage design for *Adriano in Siria*, I, 1, Vienna, 1732?, with titles of subsequent stage-sets.

(but not to her plight and passion); the sextuplets correspond to the triplets of her first, presentational aria 'Prigioniera abbandonata'.[15] The final movement is predictably a minuet, with trumpets again and in D major. The minuet represents, as so often, a combination of festal celebration and high-ranking etiquette. Interestingly, in Pergolesi's abridged version of the first scene the repeat of the sinfonia overlaps with the appearance of the Parthian heroes Farnaspe and Osroa, who approach with their train across a bridge.[16] This dramaturgical cut may not be entirely fortuitous, but planned to give the minuet the function of linking, like a bridge, the Roman imperial company with the equally dignified and heroic Parthian princes.[17] In

15. I say more on this aria, and on the relationship between aria conventions and dramaturgy, in 'Auf der Suche nach dem Drama im "Dramma per musica": Die Bedeutung der französischen Tragödie', in *De Musica et Cantu: Studien zur Geschichte der Kirchenmusik und Oper Helmut Hucke zum 60. Geburtstag*, ed. by Peter Cahn and Ann-Katrin Heimer (Hildesheim: Olms, 1993), pp. 481–93.

16. 'Replicandosi la sinfonia, passano il ponte Farnaspe ed Osroa col seguito . . .'. Pergolesi, *Adriano in Siria*, Act I, scene 1. A stage design by Antonio Galli Bibiena for this very scene, presumably in its original Viennese production (1732, with music by Antonio Caldara), is reproduced as illustration no. 11 above.

17. It also seems acceptable to repeat, as a recent recording does, the minuet from the sinfonia alone, or even to perform it as a chorus of soldiers and courtiers with the words given by Metastasio.

operas of the time, dance movements including minuets quite consistently allude to exotic or pastoral characters or themes. In a contemporary performance, the Parthians would be immediately recognizable by their exotic costume; the scenery would depict the Eastern metropolis of Antioch, a 'setting' which is here so important to the subject that it is part of Metastasio's title. To illustrate the 'setting' of a drama was another purpose for which dance movements were often used allusively. If these guesses are correct, then Pergolesi's sinfonia not only announces the main *sujet* centering on Hadrian and his deserved emperorship, but also refers to the ethos and dignity of other main characters and even to the 'setting'. It does not replace the *argomento*, but shadows it. We could perceive the three-movement discourse as saying, with a telling amplification of Metastasio's title: 'Adriano – ed Emirena – in Siria'.

Some years ago I offered a brief characterization of Johann Adolf Hasse's sinfonia for his *Siroe re di Persia* (Bologna, 1733).[18] The relationship between sinfonia and opera appears, in this case, as a network of a few selected musical parameters that appear in varied combinations. For example, the sinfonia's main key, G major, also ends the opera and is its most frequently employed key. The tempo and metre of the first movement, fast and common time, recur at strategic points in arias, sometimes connected with G major, sometimes not. The last movement is a fast minuet or passepied (3/8), resembling the final G major *coro* ('I suoi nemici affetti'). But the first aria of the opera, King Cosroe's blustering reprimand of his son, 'Se il mio paterno amore', is a fast minuet (3/8) in B♭ major, and his even more threatening aria in the second Act, 'Tu di pietà mi spogli', is in a fast 3/8 metre and in G major again. Are we invited to perceive a connection between Cosroe's doomed kingdom and fast 3/8? The middle movement of the sinfonia deviates in tempo and metre (Lento, 3/4) but not in key, although it starts ambiguously, more as if in D major. The sarabande type of a slow triple metre (Lento, 3/8) recurs in the opera only once: for the first aria sung by a female character, 'Ancor io penai d'amore'. Emira's nostalgic aria, in D major, has an alternating section (G major, fast duple metre), to illustrate her aggressions, too. It is possible to hear this section as corresponding to the first movement of the sinfonia, and therefore the whole self-presentational aria of the primadonna as an inversion and exaggeration of the first two movements of the sinfonia. The subject of the drama is, in fact, the deadly revenge planned by Emira against the guilty but not villainous Cosroe, which is finally overcome by her love for Siroe who becomes king in place of his father.

Some more expressive items to be found along the path of the drama, such as the traitor Medarse's simile-arias and Cosroe's ombra-arias, are not reflected in the sinfonia. Nor are most of the numbers given to the title-role, the immaculate Siroe,

18. R. Strohm, *Die italienische Oper*, p. 204; see Johann Adolf Hasse, *Siroe re di Persia*, facs. edn, in *Italian Opera, 1640–1770*, ed. by H. M. Brown and E. Weimer (New York and London: Garland Publishing, Inc., 1977ff.), vol. 33.

whose varying states of mind and lamentable fate appealed to many composers. This may be seen as a solution typical for Hasse, whose stylistic decisions tend to keep to the middle of the road, and whose selection of musical parameters within an opera can be very economical. But by denying the more extreme elements of the action a place in the musical *argomento*, and by referring to the main subject as it unfolds between the only two characters of mixed ethos, Hasse also decided in favour of a classicist dramaturgy. He combined the stereotypical building materials of his work in a carefully balanced unity, in which the one rare or 'individual' element of the score, the sarabande type, is allowed to form a semantic link between the sinfonia and the opera.

To consider here the sinfonia of Leonardo Vinci's *Didone abbandonata* (Rome, January 1726)[19] means exposing my case to the most serious objection: that of the alleged interchangeability of opera sinfonias in this period. The problem is closely related, of course, to that of aria transfers and text parodies. The *Didone* sinfonia served *in toto* as the introduction to Vinci's opera *Astianatte* (Naples, autumn 1725); its last movement also concluded the sinfonia for his *Siroe, re di Persia* (Venice, February 1726). Vinci cannot have 'integrated' his sinfonia equally well with all three operas, even assuming that this was his intention. Significantly, he also made double use of some of the arias heard in these three operas, each time employing parody texts; undeniably some of these texts fit the music better than others.

We should question the traditional view that operatic music has to be totally stereotyped and abstract to be suitable for such transfers. Could it not be that in at least one of these transfers the individualized character of the original work was successfully transplanted, even gaining a new meaning from its new artistic context? So much of the meaning of music is contextual in any case. It could be, furthermore, that some combinations of sinfonia and opera were more cogent than others, just as some aria texts fitted the music better than others – a variation that can have arisen quite naturally from fluctuations of circumstance, artistic intention, and capability.

In circumstances investigated elsewhere,[20] it is likely that Leonardo Vinci, when composing the score of *Didone* for the carnival of 1726 in Rome, decided to use some of the music already in *Astianatte*, given in Naples in the autumn season of 1725. Since *Siroe* was scheduled for the carnival of 1726, too, but in Venice, he was able to divert some pieces to that performance as well, significantly reducing his total workload. The sources of the operas seem reliable enough to assure us that these transfers were the composer's own intention. As a result (and in addition to a few musical borrowings from even earlier operas), *Didone* shares four arias with *Astianatte* and two with *Siroe* ; the latter two works also share two arias. Details of the text setting strongly suggest that three of these six arias in *Didone* were originally

19. Leonardo Vinci, *Didone abbandonata*, facs. edn, in *Italian Opera, 1640–1770*, ed. by H. M. Brown and E. Weimer, vol. 29.
20. R. Strohm, *Die italienische Oper*, pp. 172–81. An English version is in R. Strohm, *Essays*, pp. 213–19.

composed for this opera, all on words by Metastasio: 'Fra lo splendor del trono' (sung by Jarba in Act I), 'Ardi per me fedele', and 'L'augelletto in lacci stretto' (both sung by Selene in Act II). These three settings fit their dramatic cirumstances perfectly: they were composed for *Didone* and then transferred and fitted with new texts. In the other three cases, the original contexts are in the other operas.

To give caution its due, we cannot be certain that transfers of sinfonias or parts thereof were made for the same reasons and with the same results as those affecting arias. Nevertheless, it is important that Vinci's dramaturgy did allocate a specific 'home' to the aria music, rather than providing passe-partout compositions.

The sinfonias of all three operas are in F major, but none of the operas gives particular preference to that key or ends in it. A feature of the first and third sinfonia movements is the use of *trombini* (so styled in most sources) in F; the score of *Siroe*, in the concordant third movement, calls the same parts *corni*. The first movement of the *Didone/Astianatte* sinfonia is characterized by an attack of fanfares in the strings in dotted rhythms, followed by very energetic violin figurations, and repercussions of pedal-point harmonies. In a later episode, the two violins have complementary semiquaver figurations. I suggest that these, and the dotted rhythms, link up with solos sung by Enea, communicating both his royal status and his agitated mind, for example in his opening accompagnato-arioso 'Dovrei . . . ma nò . . .'. This piece begins in F major and ends in B♭ – just as does the first Act, and indeed the whole opera, if the sinfonia is considered part of it. Of Enea's other arias, all but one have either poignant dotted rhythms or energetic violin figurations or both, comparable to the first movement of the sinfonia:

'Quando saprai chi sono' (G major, Act I, scene 10, a *ciacona*; the subject of the words is Enea's royal status),
'Se resto sul lido' (ending the first Act, in B♭),
'Vedi nel mio perdono' (F major, Act II, Scene 8), and
'A trionfar mi chiama' (F major, Act III, Scene 8; referring to Enea's mission).

Of these, the last-named has no dotted rhythms but features two *corni da caccia* in F, and a texture most closely related to a stereotypical first movement of a sinfonia. Very similar violin figurations also occur in Jarba's 'Chiamami pur così' (F major, Act II, scene 17): Jarba asserts his power against Didone, who has just called him a barbarian. All these arias are in duple metre (fast and slow). The only other aria for Enea, 'Vivi superbo e regna' (C major, Act III, scene 1), seems to speak of Enea's royal attitude (ethos) of *superbia*, but in fact refers, contemptuously, to that of Jarba. Although it has a few traits recalling the other numbers, it is Enea's only aria in triple metre (fast 3/8).

An open-scene sinfonia occurs near the beginning of the third Act, just before the traitor Jarba tries to attack Enea with his soldiers. The dotted rhythms and fanfares in D major, shared between strings and two *trombe* in D, refer to Enea not to Jarba.

In *Astianatte* there are only two arias that resemble the first movement either by key and metre or by typical figurations and texture. The closer match is found in

Pirro's remonstrating 'Ti calpesto o crudo fato' (Act I, scene 11), in F major with 2 *corni da caccia*. Pirro is in this drama the half-barbarous king who threatens the honour of Andromaca and the life of her son Astianatte. Parallels between the *Didone* and *Andromaca* dramas have been drawn.[21]

The second movement of the sinfonia is somewhat unusual for Vinci with its totally serious tone; it begins with a Corellian string of suspensions and adds diminished-seventh chords and a pathos-laden fermata. It is in d minor, Largo, and in a sarabande-like 3/4 metre. The only corresponding piece in the opera is the very last number, Didone's cavatina 'Va crescendo il mio tormento', in d minor, Largo and 3/8.[22] The Corellian suspensions are the second idea of the ritornello.

The slow movement of the *Siroe* sinfonia is – quite comparably – in d minor, Adagio and 3/4, making more use of repetitive violin figuration. No aria in that opera corresponds to it, however, except perhaps Emira's 'Ancor io penai d'amore' (g minor, slow, 3/8), which seems no surprise given the significance of that aria also in Hasse's setting of the libretto (see above). In Vinci's *Astianatte*, it is again the *prima donna* who matches the tone of the slow sinfonia movement with a single aria: the first Act's cavatina 'Un tuo vezzo amato figlio' (d minor, Largo, 3/8), where she starts to pour out her grief but is interrupted.

In *Didone abbandonata*, the second movement ends or is interrupted on a domi-nant fermata (as is Didone's cavatina 'Va crescendo'). But it leads into a fast dance movement in 6/8 – a gigue-forlana – with a few dotted rhythms. It is easy to relate this piece to Selene's 'L'augelletto in lacci stretto' (Andante, 6/8), particularly for its tied-over notes and scalic motives, which are relevant to the imagery of the words. Slightly looser connections seem to exist with Didone's more assertive first aria, 'Son regina e sono amante' (fast 3/8, Act I, scene 5), whereas Jarba's self-presentation 'Son quel fiume che gonfio d'umori' (Presto, 3/8, Act I, scene 13) is, by comparison, too agitated. Its figurations would even resemble the first sinfonia-movement if turned into duple metre. All these three arias are in C major.

Selene's aria has been secondarily employed in *Astianatte* as 'Io non vi credo, pupille belle' of Oreste (Act II, scene 10). No aria in *Siroe* matches this type of music (Medarse's 'Deggio a te del giorno i rai', Act II, scene 6, is too slow), demonstrating that the movement did not originate for that opera.

It is probably transparent that the three composers Pergolesi, Hasse and Vinci have similar conceptions of an opera sinfonia. What they all want to express is a generalized image of the most important subject matter and characters of the drama, hierarchically differentiated. The first movement presents the royal and male subject, the second a suffering female or a conflict with her or within her, and the third catches a glimpse of further characters and their backgrounds (pastoral, or otherwise diversified from the main subject). If the functions of the three move-

---

21.   Ettore Paratore, 'L'*Andromaque* del Racine e la *Didone abbandonata* del Metastasio', in *Scritti in onore di Luigi Ronga* (Milan: Ricciardi, 1973), pp. 515–47. Additional results might have been obtained by considering Antonio Salvi's libretto version *Astianatte*, which is also the one set by Vinci.

22.   The fact of the tempo equivalence of the crotchet and quaver in these particular instances must be demonstrated elsewhere. For more on the music of the cavatina, see R. Strohm, *Die italienische Oper*, pp. 172–81.

ments were to be identified with dramaturgical terms, the first would be dedicated to the *soggetto* and the *ethos* of the leading character(s), the second to *pathos* and probably also *ethos* of the *prima donna*, and the third would mix *soggetto* and perhaps aspects of setting, *decorazione*; it might have a physical connection with the beginning of the drama itself. The first and last arias of certain characters, the beginnings and ends of Acts as well as of the opera, will be consciously placed to respond to the sinfonia. Quasi-correspondences with similar vocabulary in other parts of the drama may attempt to mislead us; but Vinci's Jarba is shown by the structure of the whole opera to be a false king. Pergolesi's first movement illustrates an event – a tableau – not actually seen but implied in the poet's *argomento*. Hasse demonstrates his interpretation of the *soggetto* by alluding to the real dramatic conflict of guilt and royalty, rather than the pathetic title hero; he also highlights the conflicts *within* his leading characters Cosroe and Emira. All three composers make use of the structures of the operas themselves to balance and explicate the instrumental introductions. All three sinfonias, stereotyped as they may be, somehow reflect their composer's interpretations of the dramas in terms of traditional dramatic theory.

At this point it might be argued that our three 'Neapolitan' composers, who presumably learned from each other,[23] were developing a pre-Classical approach to writing opera sinfonias which was really characteristic of a later age. The true Baroque sinfonia and overture would not yet show such reformist traits. As for the overture (the use of the French form was widespread for Italian opera introductions, especially in centres outside Italy), I hope to illustrate the problem at some other time. As for the writing of sinfonias, let us consider an example by the antipode of the Neapolitans in matters of contemporary opera, Antonio Vivaldi.

Vivaldi's *Giustino*, performed in Rome in the carnival of 1724, is a work that stands outside the Neapolitan and Metastasian sphere of influence: not exactly in terms of time and place, but quite decidedly in terms of music and dramaturgy. It is almost a fairy-tale opera, overlong, anti-rational, with all the trimmings of the Venetian Seicento.[24] Nevertheless, the *argomento* of the libretto, arranged by an unknown hand (A. M. Lucchini?) from Beregan and Pariati, stresses the conventional *soggetto* of honour and glory at imperial courts:

> At the time when the Empress Arianna, widow of Zenone, elevated Anastasio to the Empire, Vitaliano the Younger moved from Asia Minor with a powerful army, and having triumphantly crossed the Bosphorus, laid siege to Constantinople. At the same time, Giustino, having left behind his plough, got up to fight for the Greek Emperor, and having captured Vitaliano, merited coronation with the Imperial laurels. Over these given facts is the present drama constructed.[25]

23.   Hasse and Vinci both lived in Naples in 1724–9, and Pergolesi may even have studied there with Vinci around 1729.
24.   Antonio Vivaldi, *Giustino*, ed. by Reinhard Strohm, 2 vols (Milan: Ricordi, 1991) (Istituto Italiano Antonio Vivaldi).
25.   'Nel tempo, che l'Imperadrice Arianna Vedova di Zenone inalzò all'Impero Anastasio, si mosse dall'Asia minore con poderoso Esercito Vitaliano Juniore, e passato trionfante il Bosforo Tracio assediò Costantinopoli. Nello stesso tempo, Giustino lasciato l'Aratro andò à militare à favore del Greco Imperatore, e fatto prigioniero Vitaliano, meritò d'esser coronato coll'Alloro Imperiale. Sopra gl'antecedenti fatti è tessuto il presente Dramma.'

248

Example 22. Vivaldi, *Giustino* (Rome, 1724):
  a. sinfonia (allegro)
  b. aria of Anastasio

Already the verbal shape of this *argomento* implies that not so much the well-known tale of a peasant made emperor as the double success of an imperial couple triumphing over adversity, and of virtue rewarded with laurels, forms the *azione principale* of this libretto.

The sinfonia of the opera, written for strings only, has the three movements: C major, fast, common time; c minor, Andante e piano, 3/8; C major, Allegro, 3/8. Several actual motives of the sinfonia recur in the opera, sometimes literally. The noisy and assertive first movement presents two repetitive motivic groups which also appear in two arias of the Emperor Anastasio. One of them, a striking unisono-motive (not, by the way, a musical stereotype of opera seria), links the sinfonia with Anastasio's first aria, 'Un vostro sguardo' (Act I, scene 2), which expresses love as well as military prowess. Anastasio says that the lovely glances of his wife Arianna will help him protect her from the enemy Vitaliano who intends to capture her. The motive underscores the words 'più forza avrà'. (See music example 22.)

Of the emperor's other, more indirectly related arias, his most imperial is 'Verdi lauri, cingetemi il crine'. It introduces a scene of triumph exactly in the middle of the opera (C major, Act II, scene 9). Anastasio has the role of the *primo uomo*, although the opera's title names the 'actual' dramatic hero Giustino.

The second movement of the sinfonia takes much of its music from the *prima donna* Arianna's last aria, 'La cervetta timidetta' (Act III, scene 7) which is in B♭ but displays a strange leaning towards c minor. It expresses Arianna's anxiousness and longing for her husband Anastasio. (See music example 23.) Also in Act I, Arianna has a significant love-aria in c minor.

The last movement is an energetic passepied whose bouncy, rustic triplet figures seem reflected in Leocasta's first aria of the opera, 'Nacque al bosco e nacque al prato' (Act I, scene 6). (See music example 24.)

But here, the *seconda donna* Leocasta really speaks of Giustino: having just been rescued by him from a wild monster, she imagines the young peasant as a wild

Example 23. Antonio Vivaldi, *Giustino* (Rome, 1724)

   a. Sinfonia (andante), b. 26-9
   h Sinfonia (andante), b. 41-3
   c. III, 7: aria of Arianna, b. 19-25
   d. III, 7: aria of Arianna, b. 37-9

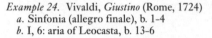

Example 24. Vivaldi, *Giustino* (Rome, 1724)
  a. Sinfonia (allegro finale), b. 1–4
  b. I, 6: aria of Leocasta, b. 13–6

flower blossoming in the courtly lifestyle to which she is going to introduce him (like *My Fair Lady* in reverse). Thus her aria uses the minuet characteristics also to describe *him* – and to refer to courtly etiquette. The composer's decision to let this aria respond to the minuet-like last movement of the sinfonia links courtly dance, pastoral imagery and the portrayal of the two secondary but still very important characters whose love will be crowned in the end. Nevertheless, the two have to share the third movement of the sinfonia, whereas Anastasio and Arianna each have one full movement to themselves.

The minuet-like ending of the sinfonia leads into a magnificent opening tableau where Arianna is seen crowning Anastasio, to the sound of celebratory soli and chorus in minuet patterns (A major, 3/8). The end of the opera witnesses the second coronation: of Giustino as co-emperor, and of his newly-acquired bride, Leocasta. The final *coro*, 'Doppo i nembi e le procelle', is a complex minuet-chaconne in 3/4 and C major, with a contrasting middle section in c minor, sung by Arianna and Giustino. The tonal layout thus matches that of the sinfonia, corroborating the association of the imperial couple with C major and c minor, respectively. And the solo–chorus structure of the opening coronation minuet is also mirrored here.

Source studies show that Vivaldi wrote the sinfonia originally for this opera, although borrowings from a wide variety of previous works form the backbone of the rest of his score. (They include the opening theme of *La primavera* – also employed here with dramatic significance – and, in fact, the finale or some version of it.)[26] It is also certain that he composed 'La cervetta timidetta' as an afterthought

26. For details on these cross-relations, which also involve instrumental concertos, see A. Vivaldi, *Giustino*, ed. by R. Strohm, text volume, pp. 24–8. A full account of the compilation of the autograph is found ibid., pp. 73–83.

when the opera was almost completed – to replace a different, borrowed aria – and that he only *afterwards* wrote the sinfonia. It is as if the sinfonia had been intended to impress the final mark of unity on the whole opera. Vivaldi does not shun direct thematic references, but he also relies on structural connections – by analogy and symmetry, for example. Like any other opera composer of the period, he works with stereotypical musical ideas such as triplets, unisonos, major-minor contrasts; but he achieves semantic relevance with exactly this musical vocabulary. And finally, his sinfonia represents a dramaturgical choice as did those of the Neapolitan composers, especially Hasse's. In Vivaldi's interpretation, it is not the ascent of the peasant Giustino as such – the dramatic 'plot' and its hero – that is chosen for emphasis through the sinfonia, but the notion of imperial glory, doubly preserved through bravery and love. Thus the sinfonia sides with the emphasis of the *argomento* and, in a sense, against that of the opera's title. In any case, such a musical introduction has to be viewed against the title and *argomento* of the drama to reveal its true function – and against the structural counterparts in the music of the opera itself.

Themes and dreams

13
Handel's *Ariodante*: Scotland and Arcadia

What kind of opera is *Ariodante*? What is its significance for Handel's artistic development and for opera history in general?[1]

Ariodante, composed between 12 August and 24 October 1734 and premièred on 5 January 1735 at the Covent Garden Theatre, is distinguished from Handel's preceding operas, but linked to *Alcina* (1735), by such traits as a partially English cast, the use of chorus and ballet, and purportedly other scenic, dramaturgical or musical 'innovations'. In addition, its libretto shares with those of *Alcina* and *Orlando* (1733) descent from a famous non-dramatic source, Lodovico Ariosto's epic poem *Orlando furioso*, which, however, provided only an indirect model, whereas the direct model was another opera libretto.

Scholars have often interpreted the 'innovations' of *Ariodante* as deviations from a perceived norm or set of norms governing opera seria (i.e. *dramma per musica*). This led almost inevitably to the conclusion that Handel achieved a compositional-dramaturgical 'progress' with his Covent Garden operas, because the norms from which an artist deviates are traditionally regarded as a regressive, non-artistic constraint.

It is quite probable, however, that the norms of opera seria in the form as described by musicologists, i.e. as an artistic consensus, did not exist in the early eighteenth century. They seem rather to be rationalizations formulated by later generations. Furthermore, even if these norms must be taken seriously as ideas, they were only parts of a larger whole, consisting of literary, musical and other tendencies and traditions, and of practical necessities of various sorts. A musical work which did not satisfy certain expectations, for example because it mixed pastoral and heroic elements, might have fulfilled others. For Handel, this might have meant that he could exchange one artistic orientation for another without thereby attempting a musical or dramaturgical 'progress'.

As is known, Handel moved in the summer of 1734 from the King's Theatre in the Haymarket to the Covent Garden Theatre, managed by John Rich. In this way,

---

1. The questions posed here concerning the status and significance of *Ariodante* were stimulated by its absence from Carl Dahlhaus et al. (eds), *Pipers Enzyklopädie des Musiktheaters*, vol. 2 (München-Zürich: Piper, 1987).

he got access to the resources of this theatre, which already since 1733 had included a chorus[2] and a ballet troupe. The latter was led by the famous ballerina Marie Sallé, who continued to dance in the Covent Garden performances of 1734–5, not only in Handel's operas.[3] His own productions of this season comprised the newly composed operas *Ariodante* (HWV 33) and *Alcina* (HWV 34), a revision of his *Il pastor fido* (HWV 8c) with ,the added prologue *Terpsicore* (HWV 8b), a slightly altered revival of his *Arianna in Creta* (HWV 32) and the newly arranged pasticcio from his own earlier works, *Oreste* (HWV A 11). Ballets were performed in all these productions, and choruses in all except *Oreste*. Most of the works had a conspicuous pastoral element in scenery and drama.

The reorientation of the musical-dramaturgical means in these stage works by Handel also concerned the vocal soloists. In this season, he employed for the first time more native than Italian singers, surely (and perhaps exclusively) in order to save money. The use of a chorus on stage, on the other hand, was not a new feature, as already the wedding serenata *Il Parnasso in festa* (HWV 73), premièred at the Haymarket on 13 March 1734, had contained choruses. Handel had also inserted choruses into the revivals of *Il pastor fido* of May–June 1734, likewise performed at the Haymarket. This was publicly noted at the time.[4] We may assume, furthermore, that relatively ambitious stagecraft had been employed in the 1733–4 season, for example in *Arianna*.[5] The revival, in May 1734, of a Handel opera based on Guarini's arch-pastoral marks an emphasis on the pastoral taste which was quite unrelated to the subsequent change of theatres; it had rather been prepared by the revivals and new versions of *Acis and Galatea* in the years 1732–4. Ellen T. Harris, whose aim it was to present Handel's interest in the pastoral as a general, ever-increasing tendency of his career, believes that the pastoral potential of the model libretto of *Ariodante* might well have determined the composer in favour of this drama in the first place, instead of being suggested only by the stage possibilities of Covent Garden.[6] It is indeed probable for reasons of working economy that *Ariodante* had already been planned during the 1733–4 season. Handel seems to have known the model libretto, Antonio Salvi's *Ginevra, principessa di Scozia* of 1708, since at least 1720, when he used an aria text from that libretto ('O scemami

2. See Bernd Baselt, 'Thematisch-systematisches Verzeichnis: Bühnenwerke', in *Händel-Handbuch*, 4 vols, ed. by Kuratorium der Georg-Friedrich-Händel-Stiftung, vol. 1 (Leipzig: VEB Deutscher Verlag für Musik, 1978), p. 408.
3. For details, see Sarah Y. McCleave, 'Dance in Handel's Italian Operas: The Collaboration with Marie Sallé', unpubl. PhD diss. (University of London King's College, 1993), ch. 1.
4. The *Daily Journal* of 18 May and 1 June 1734 announced the imminent performances each time with the remark: '. . . an opera called *Pastor Fido*, composed by Mr. Handel, intermixed with choruses. The scenery after a particular manner.' See B. Baselt, 'Thematisch-systematisches Verzeichnis', in *Händel-Handbuch*, vol. 1, p. 241.
5. The financial situation of this season is described in Judith Milhous, 'Händel und die Londoner Theaterverhältnisse im Jahre 1734', in *Gattungskonventionen der Händel-Oper: Berichte über die Symposien der Internationalen Händelakademie Karlsruhe 1990 und 1991*, ed. by Hans Joachim Marx (Laaber, 1992), pp. 117–37, especially 131–3. For *Arianna in Creta* and its stagecraft, see also the contributions by Giovanna Gronda, Reinhold Kubik and Reinhard Strohm in the same volume, the last one being translated and reprinted as chapter 11 in this volume.
6. Ellen T. Harris, *Handel and the Pastoral Tradition* (London, 1980), pp. 250–1.

il diletto') in his *Radamisto*. There is also no trace of any alternative opera plan for 1734–5 which *Ariodante* might have ousted when the move to Covent Garden materialized. Admittedly the roles of Dalinda and Lurcanio were transposed in the score of the first and second Acts to suit different voice ranges, but the change of theatre is not the only possible explanation for this revision, and if it was the reason, this would at least prove that the first two Acts had been composed before the new cast at Covent Garden was determined.[7] In any case, the novel features of *Ariodante* do seem to owe more to an aesthetic reorientation on Handel's part than a sudden change of material conditions.

Signs of an aesthetic reorientation might be discovered in the rarely noted fact that *Ariodante* does not contain a single musical borrowing from earlier works by Handel.[8] At the same time, however, Handel produced *Oreste*, a musical drama consisting almost entirely of his own earlier compositions. This pasticcio of his own works, in turn, contrasts with his performances of no less than three pasticci with other composers' music in the season of 1733–4.[9] And, in the area of libretto and dramatic subject, the character of *Ariodante* as a chivalric and pastoral play with 'romantic' ingredients – a description requiring verification – would seem to contrast sharply with the classicist-rationalist character of *Oreste*, emphasized by Bernd Baselt.[10]

How real, therefore, was the artistic change in 1734? Clearly we should not confine Handel's artistic development or creative tendency – if such a thing existed at all – within the limits of a specific genre or taste. Rather, he would have tried to enrich his creative development through continuous change, emulating ever different genres and tastes. This general attitude may also be found within a single work, *Ariodante*.

It is precisely because of its stylistic complexity that the opera has been subject to such diverging classifications in the Handel literature, whether as pastoral, ballet opera, Ariosto opera, French-influenced opera, or yet others. Where these genre definitions have been applied too strictly and unambiguously, the work has defied them.

Winton Dean, to mention a more cautious interpreter first, groups the work with his category of 'anti-heroic' operas, but does not classify it as such; he rather stresses the general human intelligibility of the plot and of the characters' motivations. He reads *Ariodante* as a combination of humanism, irony and Romanticism that is

---

7. The original voice ranges of Lurcanio and Dalinda – soprano and contralto, respectively – might still have been intended for Scalzi and Durastanti, and thus in 1733–4. Alternatively, these roles could already have been composed for Cecilia Young (pants' role) and Maria Rosa Negri, to be engaged at Covent Garden. When John Beard (tenor) then became available for the role of Lurcanio, Handel gave Cecilia Young the part of Dalinda, dropping Negri.

8. Regarding other composers, only one borrowing from Keiser is cited in B. Baselt, 'Thematisch-systematisches Verzeichnis', in *Händel-Handbuch*, vol. 1, p. 409. Two further 'allusions' to other composers will be mentioned below.

9. See Reinhard Strohm, 'Handel's Pasticci', in R. Strohm, *Essays*, pp. 164–211, especially pp. 182–96.

10. G. F. Handel, *Oreste*, ed. by Bernd Baselt (Kassel, etc.: Bärenreiter, 1991) (*Hallische Händel-Ausgabe*, series ii, vol. 1), pp. xiv–xv.

ultimately owed to Ariosto's poem.[11] According to Dean, the changes in Handel's artistic strategy in this Covent Garden season were fortuitous, occasioned only by the forced departure from the Haymarket, although they did lead to such superb creations as *Ariodante* and *Alcina*.[12]

Ellen T. Harris rejects the idea of a sudden change, emphasizing the gradual increase of the pastoral taste in the revival of *Il pastor fido*, 1734, and the preceding operas *Orlando* and *Arianna*.[13] She, too, remarks on the connections between the three so-called 'Ariosto operas', *Orlando, Ariodante* and *Alcina*. The result of this influence she sees in a loosening of the opera seria conventions, accepting in this regard the thesis of an artistic 'progress'.[14] There is surely a need to review the relationship between Handel's operas and the literary tradition.

Other scholars identify artistic change in *Ariodante* alone; Paul Henry Lang, for example, claims to hear the first 'neo-Neapolitan' influences in the music and interprets the ballets as demonstrating the influence of modern French dance (Rameau).[15] More recent studies, however, have linked the ballets to older French models with which they can also be compared musically.[16] Bernd Baselt calls *Ariodante* and *Alcina,* together with *Terpsicore*, 'Ballet Operas', apparently implying that they belong to a different genre from that of Handel's other operas.[17] Sabine Henze-Döhring takes an even more radical view, asserting that Marie Sallé was strongly influenced by the English dancer and dance historian John Weaver, and relating the ballets in *Ariodante* to this model.[18] In this context, she places not only the allegorical ballet-pantomime of the second Act, but also the large, pastoral and festive scenes with choruses and ballet in the first and third Acts, without elaborating on the differences between them. Certainly these ballets and choruses at the ends of Acts, the likes of which Handel had not used since *Admeto*, constitute the most striking theatrical 'innovation' of the opera.

11. Winton Dean, *Handel and the Opera Seria* (Berkeley and Los Angeles: University of California Press, 1969), pp. 102–3.
12. Ibid., p. 27 ('makeshift policy') and p. 142: 'In all four of his opera productions in the Covent Garden season of 1734/1735 (revivals of *Il Pastor Fido* and *Arianna*, and the newly composed *Ariodante* and *Alcina*) Handel made considerable use of chorus and ballet. This was the accidental result of his move to Covent Garden, where a ballet had already been engaged, but he took characteristic advantage of the opportunity.'
13. E. T. Harris, *Handel and the Pastoral Tradition*, pp. 227–9.
14. Ellen T. Harris, *The Librettos of Handel's Operas*, facs. edn with introductions, 13 vols (New York: Garland , Inc., 1989), vol. 13, pp. vii–xi.
15. Paul Henry Lang, *George Frederic Handel* (New York, 1960), pp. 251 and 636.
16. Hellmuth Christian Wolff, 'Händel und Frankreich', *Händel–Jahrbuch* 32 (1986), pp. 115–24; Herbert Schneider, 'Händel und die französische Theatermusik in ihren dramatisch-szenischen Belangen', *Händel–Jahrbuch* 37 (1991), pp. 103–20. On these contributions, see below.
17. B. Baselt, 'Thematisch-systematisches Verzeichnis', in *Händel-Handbuch*, vol. 1, pp. 396–421. Incidentally, the genre titles found in Handel's original libretti deserve more consideration. They may be consulted in E. T. Harris, *The Librettos*: most of the bilingual librettos have 'dramma (per musica)' in the Italian title, and 'opera' in the English title, the latter being replaced by 'drama' from *Poro* to *Orlando*. The titles given in *Händel-Handbuch*, vol. 1, do not always match those of the librettos.
18. Sabine Henze-Döhring, 'Zur Gattungstradition von Händels "Ariodante"', in *Gattungskonventionen*, ed. by H. J. Marx, 1992, pp. 39–62.

The ballets

The last scene of Act I, scene 12, has a new stage-set which was not present in the libretto model: 'Valle deliziosa'. Ariodante and Ginevra meet in this pleasurable place to celebrate their betrothal. After an introductory sinfonia in pastoral style, they sing a duet ('Se rinasce nel mio cor') in *tempo di gavotta*. It is repeated by a chorus of 'ninfe, pastori e pastorelle' who then dance to the same music, played as the first segment of a dance suite. No action takes place in this scene that is required for the understanding of the dramatic plot. In any case, another pastoral set ('Giardino Reale') had gone immediately before.

At the end of Act II – in scene 10 – Ginevra, having completed her desperate aria, 'Il mio crudel martoro', sinks into an exhausted sleep. It seems that at this point there followed a ballet pantomime comprising the following segments: 'Entrée des songes agréables – Entrée des songes funestes – Entrée des songes agréables effrayés – Combat des songes funestes et agréables'. The music, however, has been removed from the autograph score and was apparently later copied into the conducting score of *Alcina*. This pantomime is followed by a six-bar *recitativo accompagnato* ('Che vidi? oh Dei!') of the frightened Ginevra. Several musical sources contain here, perhaps as an alternative, the short dance sequence 'Entrée de' Mori–Rondeau'.

In the *scena ultima* (Act III, scene 13) a new stage-set, 'Salone Reale', is shown. It features an elevated balcony from which flights of stairs descend. All the characters except Polinesso, plus 'Dame e Cavalieri', sing two short choruses; between these, the ladies and cavaliers perform a ballet. The last dance movement is musically identical with the second chorus. The musical accompaniment is supported by an on-stage orchestra seated on the balcony.

Marie Sallé, who created these ballets, is said to have brought to her dance performances in London, 1733–5, a novel and particularly expressive acting style, which seems to have aroused some opposition as well. Conceivably she was encouraged by the model of the English ballet-master John Weaver. For the ballets performed (or at least prepared) by Sallé and her troupe, Handel has composed more than a dozen different musical movements. But how significant was their novelty, and their position in the context of the opera?

It should be noted that in all three dance scenes, the vocal soloists are present and take part in the performances, in contrast to the mere ballet-divertissements which were added to many operas of the time. Although in the scene concluding Act II Ginevra is mostly passive, this ballet has a much stronger dramatic function than the others, as it presents a characterizing dance which allegorically relates to the main conflict of the drama. In Act I, by comparison, a dramatically superfluous pastoral scene has been added; in Act III, a stereotyped final scene has been further elaborated with the use of chorus and ballet, reconnecting the dramatic performance to the reality of the auditorium as was usual in seventeenth-century opera.

Sarah McCleave has investigated all the known sources for Handel's collaboration with Sallé (documents, scores, librettos, iconographic material), concluding that this collaboration is important for our understanding of *Ariodante*; she characterizes the resulting overall layout of the dances as a novel combination of French,

English and Italian elements.[19] To her, the extant source material does not suggest a significant influence of John Weaver, particularly when Sallé's own productions of the 1733–4 season are considered.

Unfortunately, we cannot establish with certainty what part of the ballets was actually performed in 1735. There are no choreographical sources. In contrast to the conventional opinion that the ballets of Acts I and II were added later by the composer and are thus less significant for the interpretation of the opera as a whole, McCleave concludes from a letter by Handel of 27 August 1734 that he had by then agreed to have ballets. In fact, the first Act of the autograph score, on which he was then working, contains his reference to a ballet, written at the time of composition.[20] This reference was cancelled at some later stage. Similarly, the ballet pantomime of Act II, which had been sketched or written out in full in the original layer of the autograph, was later removed and partly copied into *Alcina*. Only the dances of Act III are not completely eliminated. The libretto of 1735 mentions the dances of Acts I and III, but not of Act II. Taking all the extant musical sources, including the non-autograph ones, into consideration, it must be doubted that all the dance movements available today were performed in January 1735. But it is almost certain that the composer was envisaging the ballet ingredient at an early stage. In the second Act, it is still unclear whether the ballet pantomime of the *Songes agréables et funestes* was performed, or the shorter sequence *Entrée de' Mori – Rondeau*. If the latter, Handel could be said to have stepped back from an innovation, since the *Entrée de' Mori*, a grotesque dance, would appear less connected with the action. McCleave has proposed, however, to relate this piece to the allegory of jealousy and to attribute a symbolic meaning even to the concluding rondeau.[21] It is worth noting here that the idea of the good and bad dreams may derive from a passage (Act II, scene 7) in Salvi's libretto of 1708, where Ginevra, exhausted, tells of her bad dreams of the previous night. This recitative passage is cut in Handel's libretto version.

More than one researcher has related the dances to French prototypes. Hellmuth Christian Wolff has been able to cite a *Ballet des songes funestes et agréables* in Lully's ballet *Le Triomphe de l'Amour* (1681); Herbert Schneider offers a comparison of the final scene in Act II of *Ariodante* with Lully's *Atys*.[22] These forerunners do show that for the most strongly characterizing dance-scene in *Ariodante* there existed a tradition accessible to Handel and, in part, to his audience. Schneider also identifies convincing parallels in earlier French opera for the scene with ballet and chorus at the end of Act I.

19.   S. McCleave, 'Dance in Handel's Italian Operas' (n. 3 above).
20.   The description of the autograph in *Händel-Handbuch*, vol. 1, p. 408, is misleading in this respect.
21.   Sarah Y. McCleave, 'Handel's Ariodante: a study of performance issues relating to Baroque dance in London Opere serie', in *Ariodante Papers, collected at the International Workshop Conference, London 1993*, ed. by R. Strohm (in preparation).
22.   See H. C. Wolff, 'Händel und Frankreich' (n. 16 above), p. 199, and H. Schneider, 'Händel und die französische Theatermusik' (n. 16 above), pp. 107–17. Schneider deviates from the consensus of Handel scholarship in so far as he assumes that all the extant dance movements of Act II were performed in 1735.

These connections with the French tradition, formally close as they are, do not prove that Marie Sallé could not have presented essentially novel creations in the fields of choreography, expression and dancing technique. But as regards the evaluation of the opera itself, two other questions need to be addressed. First, if Sallé was aiming at innovations here, what role did Handel play in them? The formal layout and the musical style of his ballet compositions would have suited entirely traditional operatic dances: in other words, Handel did not change his musical style because of Marie Sallé. The dance sequence in Act I, headed by the *tempo di gavotta* 'Se rinasce nel mio cor', is textually and musically akin to the final number of *Orlando*, the *bourrée* 'Trionfa oggi il mio cor'. The third sequence, likewise, can be compared with other Handelian *finali*, for example of *Arianna in Creta*, from which it could appear to be developed by the mere addition of instrumental dance movements.

Secondly, how far is it correct to consider *Ariodante* a special case because it offered, or intended to offer, French ballets within the drama? For Henze-Döhring, it is certain that the opera was unique: with a scene like the pastoral tableau of Act I, Handel 'departed for good from the genre of *dramma per musica* of Italian provenance, conceiving an opera for which, as a genre, he had no models to rely upon'.[23] If this were true, then Pietro Metastasio would also have departed for good from the genre of the *dramma per musica* when writing his pastoral and mythological scenes with choruses in *L'Olimpiade* (1733) and *Achille in Sciro* (1736). Not to mention Antonio Vivaldi, whose *Dorilla in Tempe* contains three pastoral scenes, integrated into the drama, with choruses and dances; the ballet music is partly extant in the score (Venice, 1734). And not to mention other Venetian operas, or a tradition such as the Italian opera in Vienna, where the protagonists often shared scenes with dancers. To be sure, we are comparing these examples with the pastoral tableau of Handel's Act I, not the dream pantomime of Act II.

A scene by Metastasio which integrates dance and chorus into the action had been used by Handel himself a year before: Act II, scene 2 of *Semiramide riconosciuta*, as set to music by Leonardo Vinci. When Handel arranged this scene for his pasticcio opera of the same title late in 1733, he eliminated both the stage direction calling for a ballet and the chorus, although this happened in two separate phases of arrangement.[24] The scenic situation is a courtly banquet with festive music and *ballarini*,[25] which, however, is then disturbed by upsetting events. Just as in the first Act of *Ariodante*, this scene celebrates a betrothal.

Celebratory scenes with choruses and dances were not only compatible with the genre of the *dramma per musica*, they constituted a broad tradition within this framework. The whole development of the *dramma per musica* is somehow situated

23. S. Henze-Döhring, 'Zur Gattungstradition', p. 43: '. . . trennte sich der Bearbeiter endgültig von der Gattung des Dramma per musica italienischer Provenienz und konzipierte eine Oper, für die er sich *als Gattung* auf keinerlei Vorbilder beziehen konnte'.
24. See R. Strohm, *Essays*, p. 186.
25. Thus the direction in the first collected edition of the poet's works (Venice: Bettinelli, 1733 etc.): see Metastasio, *Tutte le opere*, vol. 1, 2nd edn, p. 1424; the edition of 1780 (Paris: Hérissant) eliminates the *ballarini*.

in a magnetic field between the poles of the Baroque pastoral and of the classicist, heroic drama. This may briefly be explained.

The Baroque tradition regards music and feast as sisters, not only in reality but also on stage. When, for example, weddings or other joyful celebrations are shown in a drama, on-stage music is often used to enhance the directness and thus verisimilitude of the action. (Late examples of this principle can be found in *Don Giovanni* and even in *Rigoletto*.) Such festive scenes in opera are frequently embedded in pastoral surroundings or are given some type of *couleur locale*, because light-hearted celebrations with dance-music were considered typical rituals of rural or exotic communities: a belief reflected in countless 'village weddings' and similar genre scenes of mainstream theatre and opera, up to the cinema of the 1990s. In earlier periods, the presentation of festal scenes could in itself generate the minimum of action required for such operatic genres as the *favola pastorale* (seventeenth century), the *dramma pastorale per musica* (c. 1650–1780), the *azione* or *festa teatrale* (eighteenth century), as well as the French *opéra-ballet* and *comédie-ballet*.[26] Choruses and ballets are by no means absent from Italian comic opera: the *dramma giocoso per musica* (after 1740), and before that the Neapolitan *commedia per musica*, make frequent use of them for rural or mythological-pastoral festivities and rituals.[27]

The *dramma per musica*, as it developed in the later seventeenth century under the influence of the French *tragédie* (spoken) and *tragédie lyrique* (sung), often lacked, because of its heroic-historical subject matter, a *couleur locale* or a pastoral playground. Such ingredients could of course be inserted as required. For example, a Baroque stereotype was the 'gardeners' ballet', since even a heroic and tragic plot was usually located in a palace sheltered from real life by a buffer zone of gardens and gardeners. Whether in the impresario productions or at court, operatic practice allowed the unpredictable insertion of pastoral scenes, choruses and ballet *entrées* in almost any plot. Unfortunately, few ballet scores survive, and the librettos after c. 1700 usually lack descriptions of the *entrées*.[28] Italian opera ballets of this period do not normally have vocal solos; choruses and instrumental pieces are played separately, although sometimes within the same scene. While Italian and French dancing styles were distinguished by many observers of the time, French operatic dancing exerted a strong – albeit not uncontested – influence on Italy. To what extent it influenced the music of Italian opera is one of the many thorny questions addressed by Kathleen Kuzmick Hansell,[29] but we can take it for granted that the

26. As, for example, in André Campra's *Le carneval de Venise* (Paris, 1699).
27. A good example is *La festa de Bacco* by Francesco Antonio Tullio, music by Leonardo Vinci (Naples, 1722 and 1732), where pastoral, myth and suburban realism are intermingled.
28. The mere presence of dances in Venetian operas after 1700 is recorded (not entirely accurately) in the catalogue of Taddeo Wiel, *I teatri musicali veneziani del settecento* (Venice, 1897), repr. ed. by R. Strohm (Leipzig: Peters, 1979).
29. Kathleen Kuzmick Hansell, 'Il ballo teatrale e l'opera italiana', in *Storia dell'Opera Italiana*, ed. by L. Bianconi and G. Pestelli, vol. 5 (Turin: EdT, 1988), pp. 175–306, especially pp. 182–97 concerning this period. The author emphasizes the neglect of the role of ballets in the *dramma per musica* of the time, noting the lack of extant musical sources. She does not mention that the manuscripts of Viennese court operas often contain the ballet music. There are also more Italian sources than is sometimes believed. See also the following note.

French pastoral ballet scene, in the manner of Lully's *tragédies lyriques*, enjoyed an increasing popularity inside and outside Italy, particularly at the great court operas. Typical forms of Italian opera in Germany, which influenced Handel's attitude towards the whole operatic tradition, comprised French-inspired ballets, as seen for example in his *Almira*.

Kathleen Kuzmick Hansell's hypothesis, that the development of the reformed *dramma per musica* during the two decades from about 1700 to 1720 progressively eliminated the *balli* from the dramatic context, can be mitigated by a fair number of witnesses to the contrary.[30] Nevertheless, these examples usually turn out to be indebted to older traditions, so that her view of the development remains essentially acceptable. The libretto reformers, including, for example, Apostolo Zeno, rejected not only the comic scenes but also the ballets as improbable and impure admixtures to the dramatic genre.

To return to *Ariodante*: the use of ballets in this opera, even in the forms and to the extent originally planned by Handel, is consistent with the traditions of the Italian *dramma per musica*, particularly if its earlier history in Germany is taken into account. Like so many alleged innovations of Handel, this one is an element surviving from the seventeenth-century tradition. Furthermore, the dream panto-mime of the second Act and its probably symbolic substitute (*Entrée de' Mori*) are traditional types, although they have so far been found only in French operas. Handel probably planned them himself, as the idea of Ginevra's bad dreams may have come from Salvi's libretto. The special art of Marie Sallé is unfortunately not documented in any detail in the surviving sources. This might have been the case, had her artistic conception tallied with Handel's own in major respects. But it seems that his idea of the opera as a whole went so much beyond the dance aspect that he could happily omit one or another *entrée* when the material conditions were unfavourable.

Ariosto – pastoral and ethos

The suggestion of Ellen T. Harris that Handel acted by design when deriving three of his operas from the famous *Orlando furioso* – highly esteemed in England – and that he wished to exploit its pastoral potentials, in particular, is attractive.[31] Lodovico Ariosto is, after all, mentioned by name in all three librettos.

Just as in the case of Handel's *Orlando*, however, it was not the Renaissance epic itself that engendered Handel's drama but a libretto adaptation coming from the circle of the Accademia dell'Arcadia of the early years of the eighteenth century

---

30. Here are a few examples of *drammi per musica* with ballets integrated into the action, which Handel probably knew: *Giulio Cesare in Egitto*, Sartorio, Venice, 1677 (Acts I and II); *Muzio Scevola*, G. Bononcini, Vienna, 1710; *Porsena*, Lotti, Venice, 1712; *Proserpina rapita*, C. F. Pollarolo, Rome, 1713 (Charles Jennens owned a score); *Teofane*, Lotti, Dresden, 1719 (Acts I and II; in II there is also a *macchina*); *Scipione*, Predieri, Rome, 1724; *Adelaide*, Orlandini, Venice, 1729; *Scipione in Cartagine Nuova*, Giacomelli, Piacenza, 1730; *Dorilla in Tempe*, Vivaldi, Venice, 1734.
31. E. T. Harris, *The Librettos of Handel's Operas*, vol. 13, pp. vii–xi.

12. Faustina Bordoni as
Ginevra in *Ariodante*,
music by C.F. Pollarolo,
Venice, 1716, caricature
by Antonio Maria
Zanetti.

which, in turn, had a considerable ancestry of *Ariodante* dramatizations. Among
them was Shakespeare's *Much Ado About Nothing*; the first libretto arrangement of
the subject (a serious one) had originated in 1655.[32] However important the name of
Ariosto may have been to Handel's audience, he relied on the operatic tradition for
the actual selection of plot elements, and also for their musical and dramaturgical
interpretation. His dramaturgy, in particular, was indebted to the poetic concepts of
the reformist *dramma per musica* of his own lifetime. Had Handel chosen an
Ariodante arrangement by a different librettist, for example that of Grazzini (1690),
it might be possible to doubt whether he was really interested in that version or
whether he needed it only as a bridge to Ariosto. But in the case of Antonio Salvi,
the librettist most often chosen by him – and for operas as divergent as *Rodelinda*,

32. See Emilie Dahnk-Baroffio, 'Zur Stoffgeschichte des *Ariodante*', *Händel-Jahrbuch* 6 (1960), pp.
    151–61; Lucia Mencaroni, 'La "Ginevra principessa di Scozia" nell'opera del primo settecento',
    unpubl. diss., laurea in lettere (Rome, Università degli Studi 'La Sapienza', 1990).

Sosarme and *Berenice* – his interest in the dramatic content and dramaturgical form of the libretto of 1708 seems assured.[33] By deciding for Salvi, the composer opens up his version of the play to the influence of French tragedy and the so-called 'regular drama', as well as to the social norms and the linguistic culture of the Roman and Florentine aristocracy, which he knew at first hand.[34] It has also been suggested with good reason that Handel studied more than one musical setting of Salvi's text, including for example Carlo Francesco Pollarolo's of 1716/18.[35] He might not have done this, had he not been interested in Salvi's dramatization.

The poet's linguistic and dramaturgical efforts, and Handel's reactions to them, form a subject on its own which I hope to describe another time, but the questions concerning the pastoral element and the ethos of *Ariodante* belong in the present context because it could be argued that they were prefigured in Ariosto and that their integration was new in opera.

According to Ellen T. Harris, Handel's London variant of the *dramma per musica* is connected with the tradition of the German pastoral, which unfolded more or less independently of Italy. This theory, which has been debated and sometimes rejected, has the one advantage that it emphasizes Handel's inclination to cultivate relatively old traditions of his art. Nevertheless, besides the German and the French pastoral traditions in the theatre, an Italian variant did play a role for him: Harris herself notes the significant parallels in the plots of *Ariodante* and G. B. Guarini's *Il pastor fido*.[36] Other scholars too are certain of the significance of the pastoral sphere for *Ariodante*. For Winton Dean, the score reflects, among other things, Handel's 'intense love for the countryside, which goes far beyond the demands of the pastoral convention'.[37] We should not forget, of course, that the number of actual outdoor stage-sets in the opera (five of a total of nine) is smaller than in other Handel operas with a more conventionally pastoral character. *Orlando*, for example, has no indoor set at all (only a temple in the last scene), *Tolomeo* has only one *intérieur*, *Atalanta* is a pastoral play with outdoor scenes only, and so is, of course, *Il pastor fido*.

Ariodante adheres to this ostensible, scenographic type of pastoral, as it were, only in the second half of the first Act, mentioned above. The second stage-set ('Giardino reale') provides an opportunity to address Nature in the entrance aria 'Qui d'amor nel suo linguaggio/parla il rio, l'erbetta e'l faggio' in particularly conventionalized poetry. Handel's beautiful Eb-Major setting is subtly reminiscent

33. Reinhard Strohm, 'Handel and his Italian Opera Texts', in R. Strohm, *Essays on Handel*, pp. 34–79, especially pp. 69–70. For another libretto version which he may have consulted (Venice, 1733), see E. T. Harris, *The Librettos of Handel's Operas*, vol. 13, p. xviii.
34. This context has been studied in some detail in Francesco Giuntini, *I drammi per musica di Antonio Salvi: Aspetti della 'riforma' del libretto nel primo Settecento* (Bologna: Il Mulino, 1994), pp. 9–54.
35. See Olga Termini, 'From *Ariodante* to *Ariodante*', in Carlo Francesco Pollarolo, *Ariodante* (Venice, 1718), facs. edn, ed. by O. Termini (Milan, 1986) (Drammaturgia Musicale Veneta, vol. 13), pp. ix–lxxiv; L. Mencaroni, 'La Ginevra' (n. 32 above), with an evaluation of the musical connections between the settings of Pollarolo and Handel. A surprising thematic borrowing – albeit in melodic inversion – from Pollarolo's setting is discussed in Reinhard Strohm, 'Händel und Italien – ein intellektuelles Abenteuer', *Göttinger Händel-Beiträge* 5 (1993), pp. 5–43, especially pp. 37–41.
36. E. T. Harris, *Handel and the Pastoral Tradition*, p. 252.
37. W. Dean, *Handel and the Opera Seria*, p. 103.

of pastoral solos in Alessandro Scarlatti's *Griselda* of 1721 ('Mi rivedi, o selva ombrosa'; 'Finirà, barbara sorte'). Similarly, the introductory sinfonia of the following set ('Valle deliziosa') seems to share musical material with Vivaldi's pastoral scene in *Giustino* of 1724 ('Bel ristoro de' mortali'). In *Alcina*, on the other hand, green Nature has been thematicized by Handel much more importantly. The whole opera, and the famous aria 'Verdi prati' in particular, expresses his personal sympathy with the mortality of natural beauty. This beauty, however, turns out to be manipulated by evil forces. In *Ariodante* the locations 'Night', 'Wood' and 'Seashore' are shown to be full of dangers for personal happiness. A 'Romantic' self-identification with Nature can hardly be found in either of the two operas of 1735.

What might be worth investigating in these operas, however, is a more ethical motif: the articulation of a pastoral nostalgia which longs to get away from courtly etiquette, whether in a pastoral location or through a certain type of behaviour. Such motifs do exist in *Ariodante*, I suggest. Already the literary tradition as mediated by Antonio Salvi had drawn direct connections between a pastoral 'lifestyle' – including, for example, the *incognito* – and the existential conflicts of morality and love. In this drama the link is constituted above all through the *tertium comparationis*, or the allegory, of light and eyesight.

I believe that this link is present in all three 'Ariosto' operas by Handel, supporting the idea of their artistic congruence. In all three works we find a conflict at first. Orlando has to learn to overcome his jealousy when he is excluded from the pastoral love idyll inhabited by Angelica and Medoro. Ruggiero, seduced by the loveliness of Alcina and her enchanted island, must find his way back to the true love and fidelity of Bradamante. (When he has realized this, he sings – only in Handel's version – the farewell aria 'Verdi prati'.) *Ariodante* begins with a happy young couple whose betrothal is fittingly celebrated by shepherds and nymphs in a 'delightful vale'. This *ambiente* yields, in the second Act, to night and treacherous moonlight; a short time later, deceit and jealousy have driven the lovers to the brink of desperation. Ariodante is seen in a dark wood, attempting to kill himself by jumping into the sea; brigands threaten Dalinda's life. Ginevra has been sentenced to death for unchastity, as commanded by a 'cruel and disgusting law of the Scottish kingdom' (*Orlando furioso*, iv, 59). How could all this have happened?

When narrating the story of Polinesso's fraudulent pantomime with Dalinda in Ginevra's clothes, Ariosto says that Ariodante could 'clearly recognize' her clothes in the moonlight (v, 49). This light was obviously insufficient for Ariodante to recognize her face as well, and he should therefore not have trusted his eyes. In this and other passages Salvi's libretto makes reference to the following motifs: eyesight, sun and moon, truth and falsehood, light and darkness. These motifs are even emphasized by Handel's music – for example with the special sinfonia at the beginning of the second Act, which depicts the moonlight or moonrise. As soon as Ariodante has caught a glimpse of the truth, he accuses his eyes of betraying him ('Cieca notte, infidi sguardi': III, 1). Handel's setting of this aria, in c minor, has an overwhelming gestural impact. It is as if Ariodante were looking into an abyss.

The protagonist's initial reliance on the testimony of his eyes – a naïve attitude he shares with his brother Lurcanio, and in a sense with all primitive societies – is being questioned and criticized by Ariosto and Salvi. It is not, of course, the eyesight that lies, but the mind which interprets it. Thus the reversal of fortunes towards a happy ending is made possible only when the testimony of the eyes is correctly reinterpreted.

This decisive moment[38] happens when Ariodante, believed to be dead but present in full harness on the tournament pitch, opens his visor ('alza la visiera'). All those present recognize him immediately when they see his face (!); Lurcanio and the King accept his presence as a champion of Ginevra as proof of her innocence. Already the verbal structure ('opens his visor') symbolically interprets the final solution and the victory of innocence as the correction of a type of blindness. The fates of Ariodante, Ginevra and Polinesso are decided in a 'moment [*Augenblick*] of truth'. Salvi's version of the plot concentrates the *dénouement*, in which the fortunes of the protagonists are reversed, on this one moment, a *catastrophe* in the sense of the Aristotelian-classicist poetics. Of the traditional dramaturgical means towards that end, he particularly uses that of agnition.

In order to bring about this situation, Ariosto had already focused his conflict on the ritual of a 'trial by mortal combat', which is won by the enlightened hero Rinaldo. Such trials, based on the belief in God's personal intervention in human justice, were considered primitive by humanism and enlightenment, but the rural people in the legendary Scotland of this story still believe more in the truth of visual signs than of truthful words. In Ariosto's fable, however, the Scots are learning how much one's vision can be deceived (perhaps also because so far north there is not enough light in the sky?). Besides, the fable demonstrates how God's hand can yet interact with human endeavour to restore the truth – although unpredictably and sometimes at the last minute. This moral of the story, reminiscent of medieval mystery plays, was important in the context of the *dramma per musica* as well. Its dramaturgical realization, 'rescue at the last minute', suited the needs of the librettist Antonio Salvi, as it helped him to concentrate, operatically, the Aristotelian *catastrophe* and *catharsis* in a single moment.

The opera librettist furthermore seizes the opportunity to surround the moment of truth with spectacular scenery. This scene is the tournament pitch ('steccato') in the central square of the royal city of Edinburgh, populated by knights and ordinary people: definitely an instance of *couleur locale*. The final sequence of the drama is articulated in sharp scenic contrasts: the public square is followed by a room in the palace serving as Ginevra's prison, and this, in turn, by the huge palace hall with flights of stairs, musicians' balcony and company of dancers. (This last set is absent in Salvi's libretto, but probably at least the back prospect was opened at that point.) These scenographies, too, may have been intended to confirm the prejudice that Scotland was an underdeveloped pastoral community. The same country generates beautiful gardens, vales, shepherdesses and betrothal dances, on the one hand, and

---

38. The German word for 'moment', 'Augenblick', suitably describes the event.

dark crimes, patriarchal laws and bloody rituals of justice, on the other: pleasant as well as funereal dreams. This whole assembly of motifs is compatible with the portrayal of Scotland in the clichés of Romantic opera.

But the enlightened librettist had at the same time to solve his ethical question. The world of the Baroque pastoral was by no means beyond good and evil. 'Noble simplicity' in the theatre – as advocated by François Raguenet (1702) – was a battle won against evil forces. Giovanni Battista Guarini's *Il pastor fido* (1585) was essentially concerned with innocence and guilt, betrayal and the revelation of truth. The Italian libretto reformers influenced by the Accademia dell'Arcadia were interested in an ethical dimension of the pastoral world, as they were striving to demonstrate the moral dignity of the musical divertissement called 'opera'.[39] In certain pastoral libretti by Apostolo Zeno (*Griselda*, for example), good and evil are more in conflict than in some spoken tragedies. Antonio Salvi places fidelity and honour in relative contrast to the pastoral world, but the 'rural behaviour', which needs enlightenment and correction, is not actually evil, it is only an obstacle to be overcome. On the other hand, whereas Ariosto had not introduced a definitely evil character – Polinesso is driven by love, not ambition – Salvi has totally blackened Polinesso's behaviour, so that his death would be less frightening to the spectators; at the same time, the virtue of the others is illustrated more brightly. Dalinda, the accomplice of Polinesso's treachery, is exonerated – because of love – in order to meet the demands of *decorum* on the modern stage.[40]

With these adjustments, the librettist of course removed much of the fairy-tale atmosphere and the narrative generosity of the original poem. His attempt to tighten the epic story into a moral drama ultimately created one-dimensional, passive protagonists. Handel surely realized that Ariodante was the first of his opera heroes who does not have to overcome either an enemy or himself to win princess and throne. He just needs to subject himself to the trials and learn from his mistakes. (He resembles the somewhat lame character of Ruggiero, who in the end easily destroys Alcina's realm with borrowed magic – after the battle has raged between the sorceress and Bradamante.) Ginevra, too, is an innocent victim but not in conflict with herself nor even plagued by self-doubts.

Was Handel interested, then, in a loosening of the dramatic-ethical grip of the *dramma per musica*? Did he welcome the clichés and the slightly unheroic characters? Was this perhaps connected with his use of entertainments such as choruses and dances? My conclusion centres on the observation that Handel did select Salvi's version of the story of *Ariodante*, rejecting others. This was an arrangement of Ariosto's plot which risked dramatic conviction in order to give sharper profile to

39. A prime example of this effort is Pietro Ottoboni's *dramma pastorale L'amore eroico fra pastori* (Rome, 1696).
40. Antonio Salvi, in his libretto preface of 1708, explains: 'Ho caricato alquanto il Carattere scellerato di Polinesso Duca d'Albania, facendolo operare per interesse, e per ambizione, non già per amore, perchè nella di lui morte senta meno di orrore l'Audienza, e perchè maggiormente spicchi la Virtù degli altri Personaggi . . .' and: 'Io mi son preso licenza di purgare il costume di Dalinda, per farla un Personaggio più riguardevole, e perchè nel nostro secolo non sarebbe comparso in Scena senza biasmo.'

the contrast between guilt and innocence than the Ariostean tradition had provided. Quite similarly, in *Orlando* and its twin opera *Tolomeo* Handel had attempted to demonstrate the relevance of good and evil, of true and false, precisely in the pastoral environment.[41] With these works, Handel took the side of the reformers and moralists within the tradition of the *dramma per musica*. In contrast to other proponents of this tendency, however, and as a superior artist, he also allowed himself in *Ariodante* the divertissements of choruses, dances, *couleur locale* and pastoral atmosphere. Not only were these welcome tools to diversify the effect of the performances, but they also served to deepen, in the sense of an enlightened dramaturgy, the feeling of contrast and *catharsis*.

41. See, respectively, 'Comic traditions in Handel's *Orlando*', in R. Strohm, *Essays*, pp. 249–69, and chapter 10, on Handel's *Tolomeo*, in the present volume.

14

Rulers and states in Hasse's
drammi per musica

I

Princes and rulers, political and military power, states and nations, were among the most significant themes Italian opera seria was expected to address. Their investigation has to involve both text and music, and may tell us something about the interactions between music and drama. As a basis for the following preliminary discussion, I have selected a few examples from the thirty or so *drammi per musica* set by Johann Adolf Hasse (1699–1783) which celebrate or illustrate institutionalized power. My aim is not to paint a comprehensive panorama of this subject matter in Hasse's operas, but to shed more light on the ways in which it could be expressed. This was partly a question of individual artistic choices, although the creators of operas were limited as well as inspired by the developing ideologies of the day.[1]

Opera history is often viewed as a set of functional relationships between its contributory arts, for example music and drama (as in *dramma per musica*), or scene, music and text, and so forth. The individual arts in themselves – poetry, music and scene – are regarded as mere contributory 'systems', with no history of their own.[2] But in opera, the 'collaboration between the arts' (the expression recalls Baroque allegories) is expressive as well as functional: it is a semantic effort. In order to understand this collaboration, we should be looking more closely at the vocabularies available to each of the contributing arts, and at the subject matter that is communicated. In a phrase such as 'the *galant* style of Johann Adolf Hasse's arias corresponds to the enlightened sentiments expressed by Pietro Metastasio's poetry', the concepts of '*galant* style' and 'enlightened sentiments' must be considered as prob-

1. Political ideologies in Metastasio's *drammi per musica* have been discussed by Elena Sala Di Felice, 'L'arbitro dei destini: Ideologia e drammaturgia in Metastasio', in E. Sala Di Felice, *Metastasio*, pp. 149–68; Giuseppe Giarrizzo, 'L'ideologia di Metastasio tra cartesianismo e illuminismo', in *Metastasio*, ed. by Accademia Nazionale dei Lincei, pp. 43–77; and Jacques Joly, 'Un'ideologia del sovrano virtuoso', in J. Joly, *Dagli Elisi all'Inferno*, pp. 84–94. The present essay, while indebted to some of the observations of Jacques Joly, does not presume to emulate any of these writings; but it is the first attempt – as far as I know – to identify a specifically musical dimension of the subject.
2. This is essentially the thesis of Erik Fischer, *Zur Problematik der Opernstruktur: Das künstlerische System und seine Krisis im 20. Jahrhundert* (Wiesbaden: Steiner, 1982) (Beihefte zum Archiv für Musikwissenschaft, vol. 20).

lematic; if they are not critically differentiatcd, the meaning of 'corresponds' also remains obscure. The most dangerous myth is that of an unchangeable, strictly-defined functional relationship. The differentiations in the expressive fabric of the Metastasio-Hasse operas – vastly underrated by historians – may need to be appreciated work by work and case by case. They may be found to include divergence or non-correspondence.

Opera cannot automatically be expected to be able to convey political or philosophical ideas. A presumption that this is not feasible applies to Metastasio and Hasse. The *dramma per musica* of their century developed under the eyes of literary reformers and other critics, many of whom regarded the problems of opera as generic and inborn. Starting with immutable definitions of 'music' and 'drama', which ascribed (or prescribed) beauty and ignorance to the former, necessity and ethos to the latter, these critics regarded opera seria at best (aesthetically) as a mésalliance of rationality and irrationality, an impossible art-form, and at worst (politically) as a wrecker of social messages and obstacle to human improvement. This view has influenced modern interpretations until at least the 1980s. Enrico Fubini is one of the historians who think of music as categorically superficial, beautiful and 'evasive', i.e. non-political.[3] He assigns it an indifferent or negative role when combined with the 'complete' concept of enlightenment drama. Pietro Metastasio is described by him – and by others – as somebody who was happy to demonstrate with his texts nothing more than the *cantabilità* of a drama, however political his subjects may have been.[4] Fubini repeats the well-known allegation – prefigured already in Lodovico Antonio Muratori[5] – that enlightened drama 'degenerated' through the influence of music to form a belcanto island of courtly escapism:

> But the degeneration was already contained *in nuce* in the genre of opera itself, from its very first appearance: music inevitably corroded its dramatic aspirations from its roots; it encroached on it as an element of disturbance, as a certain feeling, unexplainable under the light of reason, and unacceptable on the theatrical stage.[6]

As regards Fubini's political argument (the charge of 'evasion'), political intentionality contributed to the difficulties of opera seria precisely because it was not avoided. That the relationship between music and humanistic or ideological content was a precarious one is of course undeniable and will be demonstrated here in more

3. Enrico Fubini, 'Razionalità e irrazionalità in Metastasio', in *Metastasio e il melodramma*, ed. by Elena Sala di Felice and Laura Sannia Nowé (Padua: Liviana editrice, 1985), pp. 39–53.
4. Ibid., p. 49. This view is essentially related to that of Robert S. Freeman, *Opera without Drama: Currents of Change in Italian Opera, 1675–1725* (Ann Arbor: UMI Research Press, 1981).
5. See R. S. Freeman, *Opera without Drama*, pp. 22–32.
6. 'Ma la degenerazione in fondo era già contenuta *in nuce* nello stesso genere melodrammatico sin dal suo primo apparire: la musica ne corrodeva irremediabilmente alle radici le sue aspirazioni teatrali drammatiche, s'insinuava nella sua compagine come elemento di turbamento, come un *non so che* di inspiegabile coi lumi della ragione, di inammissibile sulla scena di teatro.' (Fubini, 'Razionalità', p. 42.)

detail. As for the aesthetic charge (the indifference of music to enlightenment drama), the idea of a 'degeneration' process of Italian drama through music does not seem a wise judgment when we consider how thin the tradition of spoken drama in Baroque Italy was. If we look at the process from the musical side, the reverse seems to have happened: music did not weaken drama, but drama strengthened music. The rationalist and heroic ideals of classicist drama, introduced into the *dramma per musica* well after its establishment in the seventeenth century, forced the musical tradition to change. It was the influence of drama, among other influences, which stimulated music of this period to become rhetorical and 'imitative' as never before. Above all, we must not underrate the effects of the metaphoric power of music. In the course of the eighteenth century, the capacities of dramatic music outgrew the demands of classicist poetics and enlightened absolutism; while never being entirely able to satisfy the ideals of necessity, ethos and *imitazione della natura*, music gradually learned to say what dramatists had never dreamed of saying. Eighteenth-century critics such as Francesco Algarotti who complained about the evasive character and the sensual superficialities of Italian operas often also describe what was universally desired: more musical participation in the drama, more appeal to the deeper levels of consciousness and morality.[7] The dramatization of music and musicalization of drama that took place went well beyond the earlier rationalist forms of 'collaboration'. All the major achievements of the genre, among them Hasse's *drammi per musica*, somehow took part in this spiralling transformation.[8]

II

Rulers and states were not only important subject matter but also the main organizers of the *dramma per musica*. The display of their glory on the operatic stage was itself considered an undertaking worthy of praise. The task of the creative and performing artists in opera was to communicate glorious 'facts' in glorious forms. But the conditions for this communication changed.

The monarchic or aristocratic self-display in courtly opera of the seventeenth century could be said to have required 'translation' rather than formulation. For example, the ancient heroes Alexander, Scipio, Julius Caesar and so on served with the whole of their transmitted histories (*fabulae*) as images of the modern ruler. Because they were idols, their strengths and weaknesses could be displayed in unbroken succession, sometimes to the brink of ridicule. The common denominator of the various virtues of monarchs was power. In the arts it was apostrophized as 'glory', however different the ways in which it had been achieved. Operatic idolatry was, like the 'heroic style' in general, a traditional part of the musical and scenographic vocabularies. It was usually allowed to be naive and direct.

7. 'Saggio sopra l'opera in musica', 2nd edn (1763), in Francesco Algarotti, *Scritti*, ed. by Giovanni Da Pozzo (Bari: Laterza, 1963).
8. The *dramma per musica* was a reform genre which advanced identification with values through music and, when this led to contradictions, had to reform itself to the point of becoming unrecognizable. See also chapter 1 in this volume.

Opera seria under 'enlightened absolutism' developed more selective and subtle modes of communicating the standard virtues of the ruler (while at the same time banning the humorous or occasionally satirical traits of older operas). The virtue of magnanimity might be disguised at first, overshadowed by inglorious passions, to reappear as the climax or catastrophe of a conflict. Alternatively, military exploits could be made to yield to more intimate concerns of rulership when a battle scene was followed by a sentimental aria. Such integration of message and dramaturgical technique often also modified the transmitted *fabula*. The artistic challenge to present the themes of power and glory in ever newer dramaturgies also gradually promoted new formulations. Eighteenth-century princes on the stage distinguished themselves not only by personal integrity and generosity, but also by their respect for human issues or even for 'human rights', appreciation of nature and its laws, and patronage of 'the arts'. These endeavours were presented as part of their global responsibility for their subjects and the well-being of their lands. This was the age when the administrative machinery of the state was extended to the areas of justice, trade and industry, education, environment and entertainment, which in the preceding centuries had largely been private, dynastic toys, or controlled by the Church. Court music and opera likewise developed from the status of a princely entertainment into that of a government programme.

This development was reflected on the operatic stage itself. Seventeenth-century princes, when not posing as warriors and rulers, appeared in the operas as poets, painters, musicians, gardeners, Olympic athletes, travellers to Venice, and of course shepherds, but privately and *incogniti*. 'Enlightened' opera, on the other hand, celebrated monarchies where the arts flourished, happiness in human pursuits and enjoyment of nature were possible: happiness and enjoyment even for the common people. Royal *incognito* status, still occasionally shown on stage, was only an awkward state of transition, before the superior responsibilities of rulership were taken on. Before the eighteenth century, the pastoral playground had been available only to princes: now the princes in opera were those who could complain that they were denied the state of simple shepherds. Their shepherd status was reduced to the care of their human flock.

Hasse's earliest Italian opera was *Sesostrate*, given in Naples for the young arch-duchess Maria Theresa's birthday on 13 May 1726.[9] It is very similar in subject and plot to Metastasio's *Il re pastore*, commissioned in 1751 by Maria Theresa as Empress.[10] Both works illustrate the contrast between the pastoral world and that of the courts. The early opera, however, does not make an issue of the born ruler's morality and duty, but presents her changing fate as a demonstration of the power of Fortune. The first aria, 'Lascia i boschi in abbandono:/vieni al trono' (I, 1), calls upon a royal child to grow up and govern. The subject of dynastic succession appears as a fairy-tale or children's lesson; the fact that this is the first aria stresses the point. The protagonist, obeying the call, takes leave from the woods and his

9. For sources of Hasse's earlier operas, see R. Strohm, *Italienische Opernarien*, vol. 2, pp. 172–82.
10. The reason may be a common descent from Silvio Stampiglia's *Abdolomino* (Vienna, 1709).

beloved Timareta (I, 3): 'Farewell, I am departing, it's true, but all my thoughts remain with the woods, streams and meadows. I am yours , beloved eyes, and if my path leads to the throne, for you, my love, I shall always be a shepherd.'[11]

Hasse's aria settings in this opera reflect the pastoral idea mostly in two traditional ways. Several of them are graceful minuets sung by characters destined to rule, but longing to be shepherds, as in Timareta's 'Se m'accosto al bel ruscello' (I, 4) or Berenice's 'Lascia ai boschi, al praticello' (I, 7). Others are simile arias painting a nature image, as in 'Passagier che in selva oscura' (II, 3), 'Arboscel, che in verde prato' (I, 15) or 'Come foco che cresce col vento' (III, 10). 'Se m'accosto' combines minuet rhythm with tone-painting for 'ruscello' in the accompaniment.

Timareta's aria 'Ti sospiro, o bella e cara/libertà de' boschi miei' (II, 13) belongs to neither of these categories. It is in g minor, Allegro cantabile, duple metre, in a modern style, quite appropriate to the growing association of nature and *libertà* in sentimental literature of those years,[12] and of course foreshadowing Metastasio's Argene in *L'Olimpiade*. On the other hand, Sesostrate's farewell to the woods, just mentioned (I, 3), has the conventional traits of the pathetic sarabande: g minor, slow and staccato, 3/4 metre. There may well be a differentiation of genders: the actual ruler conforms to conventions much older than the ideas women can indulge in. As musical metaphors, the two arias work so well because they are in the same key and can thus be heard as dialectically related.

In the heroic dramas *Gerone tiranno di Siracusa* (1727) and *Attalo* (1728), the imagery predictably develops darker colours, mainly among the simile arias (for example in 'Dal nero Flegetonte', *Gerone* III, 9). These operas have predominantly royal characters, good and bad; the issues connected with rulership – war, pride, envy, glory, betrayal – are distributed over different characters. The tyrant Gerone (tenor) has 'modern' feelings in the passepied-like aria 'Sta diviso in petto il core' (II, 1) but finally insists on heroic power in an extreme *aria patetica* in Grave tempo (III, 11).[13] In *Attalo*, the final solo of the royal protagonist (soprano) is articulated as a heroic *accompagnato* ('Col brando in pugno'), followed by a large simile aria which, surprisingly, articulates distress and loneliness ('Peregrin che in erma arena').

Hasse, of course, was still exploring traditional vocabulary as well. The libretto of *Tigrane* (1729), by an anonymous arranger following Francesco Silvani, offered him the figure of Mitridate (tenor), a tyrant and overpowering father whose control over other people's affections is justified by his 'glory' and physical courage. The young hero Tigrane (soprano), as an image of acceptable rulership, is occupied with love and with bravery towards a hostile fate. Hasse seems to stress the distinction. Tigrane's heroic aria 'Del mio fato ad onta e scorno,/mi vedrai morir da grande' (II, 3) perhaps expresses horror rather than heroism; this emphasis seems confirmed

---

11. 'Addio, mi parto, è vero,/ma tutto il mio pensiero/resta col bosco e'l rio, col praticello./Vostro, mie luci, io sono,/e'l piè s'io porto al trono,/sempre per te, ben mio, son pastorello.'
12. See the comments on Rolli's 'Solitario bosco ombroso', and Hasse's setting of it, in Reinhard Strohm, 'Hasse, Scarlatti, Rolli', *Analecta Musicologica* 15 (1975), pp. 220–57.
13. 'Se torbido aspetto/di Parca sdegnata/la falce spietata/mi mostra o minaccia,/non fa ch'io soggiaccia/a tema o viltà'.

Example 25. Hasse, *Tigrane* (Naples, 1729)
   a. I, 1: aria of Mitridate
   b. III, 8: aria of Mitridate

a. **Allegro e spiritoso**

(Coronato il crin d'alloro

b. **Allegro**

(Al nume del mio sdegno

when the final *ombra* scene of the primadonna, lamenting Tigrane's expected death ('Parte, parte Tigrane . . . Presso all'onde d'Acheronte': III, 11), is given the greatest musical weight in the opera. A surprising compositional choice, on the other hand, is the close musical similarity between Mitridate's two most contrasted arias. The first displays his glory in a victory celebration, as well as his magnanimity towards the victorious Tigrane (I, 1),[14] the second his increasingly weakened rage and death-threats against Tigrane, now discovered to be his mortal enemy (III, 8).[15] Both arias belong to the same heroic D major-Allegro stereotype with excited semiquaver figurations, the figurations themselves being quite similar. (See music example 25.)

The reference to the gods and to sacrifice in the revenge aria was perhaps seen by Hasse as analogous to the ceremonial context of the first aria. Mitridate's rage of a cruel father against his daughter ('Ti guardo e con iscorno': II, 13) is expressed in one of those furious c minor flights which Hasse often used for desperate affections in the early works. Overall, the music presents a one-sided image of rulership as an exercise of physical power, and seems to deny the monarch admirable qualities even where possible. Not that this necessarily represents a moral point of view. The facts of rulership, as governed by supernatural forces and uncontrollable passions, are portrayed in a fatalistic manner. The long path from a concrete, naive to an abstract, sentimental presentation of state and ruler has not really been entered yet.

In Hasse's setting of Metastasio's *Ezio* (Naples, autumn 1730), the Emperor Valentiniano unsuccessfully competes for the audience's sympathy with the hero

14. 'Coronato il crin d'alloro,/vieni al trono che accrescesti,/se il mio Regno difendesti,/chiedi e tutto avrai da me'.
15. 'Al nume del mio regno,/per far che non s'adiri,/saranno i tuoi sospiri/gl'incensi ch'offrirò'.

who is a commoner. But Valentiniano is by no means a tyrant (as his model, Nero in Racine's *Britannicus*, undoubtedly and traditionally is). The poet aims to create a subtler kind of tension between power and morality: this Emperor is not bad but only weak.

As regards Hasse's activities in 1730, a crucial year of his career, the composition of *Artaserse*, performed in Venice in February, was his first encounter with a Metastasian libretto. This drama was new, and Hasse shared with Vinci the privilege of being its first composer. *Ezio*, however, had been written in 1728, and perhaps this libretto conveyed a more traditional image to Hasse.[16] It is no surprise that his Neapolitan setting of *Ezio* resembles in many respects the Neapolitan *Tigrane*, rather than the Venetian *Artaserse*.

Ezio begins with the same scenic situation as does *Tigrane* – reception of the successful leader of the troops by a grateful monarch – and goes through the same type of anxieties, involving a hero believed to be dead and a monarch driven by unjust fury. But the positive sides of power are displayed as well, and Hasse's music accepts them. The opening scene with a military march and subsequent Imperial speech ('Se tu la reggi al volo': I, 3) bears no musical hints of mistrust or tyranny. The final arias of Ezio and Varo, both sung in sympathy with the Emperor, are cheerful and happily illustrative. It is more significant that Ezio, in the heroic-martial outburst 'Se fedele mi brama il regnante' (I, 11: A major, Allegro), musically ignores the finer points of jealousy against the Emperor, which Metastasio has expanded in this scene. The poet has also given Valentiniano no fewer than three arias showing weak affections: anger in 'So chi t'accese' (I, 9), love in 'Vi fida lo sposo' (II, 3) and fear in 'Per tutto il timore' (III, 3). Hasse has expressed these without any reference to the Imperial character, ignoring the contrasting concept of 'vi fida il regnante' in the second aria. These straightforwardly scenic and affect-related presentations contrast with the philosophical statements in Onoria's 'Quanto mai felici siete' (I, 7) and Varo's sentence aria 'Nasce al bosco in rozza cuna' (II, 8). The first of these is a new, incredibly efficient formulation of the *topos* of a princess envying the life of shepherds, set by Hasse as a royal minuet, but with a pastoral immediacy as if this desired state had already materialized. The second expresses an old-fashioned soldier's commonplace wisdom about rulers and states being controlled by the goddess Fortune. The archaic image of Fortune's wheel and the fall of the mighty is combined with the more fashionable pastoral topic, to the point of suggesting a rotation of fortunes between the woods and the thrones.[17] Such fairy-tale material is hardly meant to convey the poet's opinion at this point, in a drama which demonstrates how easily a ruler can be persuaded by a traitor to act against his own interests. Hasse, however, is happy with the words. He concentrates on the external imagery – high and low status, Fortune's lofty wings ('aure') and the blows of fate.

16.   Hasse's *Arminio*, performed in Milan on 28 August 1730, used an old libretto by Antonio Salvi (Pratolino, 1703). It had a highly political subject which might also have interested us here, but most of the music is lost.
17.   Probably the aria also alludes to Pietro Pariati's text 'Nacque al bosco e nacque al prato' in *Giustino* (Bologna, 1711).

Thus it is left to a single aria, Valentiniano's 'Che mi giova impero, o soglio' which follows the main tragic confrontation at the end of the second Act, to raise the problem of power. In this aria Metastasio perhaps for the first time portrays the self-doubts of a prince, and credits him with the possibility of self-improvement through reflection. What is more, the aria explicitly denies the responsibility of the allegorically personalized passions: 'What is the use of reign and throne, when I do not want to leave my worries behind, when I nourish my own tyrants in the affections of my heart? That I am unhappy in this world is my own fault, I know that: it is not the fault of Hatred, it is not the fault of Love.'[18] In Hasse's setting, this aria-text has been replaced by new words, 'Amare e mirare, partirsi infedele', and the music for these is a straightforward love-song.

Hasse's setting of *Ezio* may be charged with a musical evasion of the problems of power and rulership which interested Metastasio in this libretto. After the splendour of the opening ceremony, the music is not further concerned with physical power. Nor does it suggest any conflict or tension within or about rulership. Conceivably, the Neapolitan authorities prevented any emphasis on such delicate political themes as expressed in 'Che mi giova', but it is doubtful whether Hasse would at this point have had the musical vocabulary or the wish to express them.

Pietro Metastasio habitually developed and improved motives from his own earlier dramas in the later ones. In *Ezio* the political motive of the conspiracy of Massimo – derived from Thomas Corneille's *Maximien* and other sources – is overshadowed by the rivalry between the Emperor and the hero for Fulvia's hand. The primadonna is torn between love and duty. In *Artaserse* (Rome, 1730) the conspiracy motive is placed in a much better dramaturgical focus. Arbace owes loyalty to his guilty father, Artabano, as well as to his friend and sovereign, Artaserse. He is torn between duty and duty. The concentration on the three male characters, and the placement of love relationships at the margins of this conflict, makes *Artaserse* a potentially more political drama. But while Metastasio's arias already indulge exclusively in the passions aroused by personal relationships, not in concepts of power, glory or loyalty, Hasse's setting goes even further in that direction. Several arias were inserted for Hasse by Giovanni Boldini, perhaps to please the singers.[19] Artaserse's very moving plea 'Deh respirar lasciatemi' (I, 11), which exposes the prince's anxiety and irresolution, is omitted in the Venetian libretto. The central scene of the drama (II, 11), in which the guilty Artabano sentences his own innocent son to death to protect himself, ends in a highly emotional farewell-aria of the faithful Arbace ('Per quel paterno amplesso'), but its second part does refer to political duties: 'I go to die happily, if Persia's fate can be reconciled through me.'[20] This element is suppressed in Hasse's setting. A stereotypical scene of stately

18. 'Che mi giova impero e soglio,/s'io non voglio uscir d'affanni,/s'io nutrisco i miei tiranni/negli affetti del mio cor?/Che infelice al mondo io sia,/lo conosco, è colpa mia;/non è colpa dello sdegno,/non è colpa dell'amor.'
19. Of these, 'Pallido il sole', 'Lascia cadermi in volto' and 'Parto qual pastorello' became favourites of the century.
20. 'Vado a morir beato,/se della Persia il fato/tutto si sfoga in me'. There are some minor verbal changes in Hasse's version. All Metastasio quotations in this essay are taken from Pietro Metastasio, *Tutte le opere*, ed. by Bruno Brunelli, vol. 1, 2nd edn (Milan: Mondadori, 1953).

character is the ceremony of the oath of allegiance at the end of the drama. Hasse carefully articulates the ritual prayer with the repeated accompagnato recitative 'Lucido Dio'. The final chorus 'Giusto re, la Persia adora' also has some musical weight. But these moments in the *scena ultima* are not significant enough to overshadow the musical impact of what is really the focal number of the opera, the preceding famous duet of the lovers, 'Tu vuoi ch'io viva, o cara'.

III

Just as Metastasio regularly returned to earlier dramatic motives, so Hasse revived his earlier operas, often improving them. In his Dresden years (1733–63), he created new versions for many of his earlier Metastasio settings, and most of these revisions adhered more closely to the poet's original texts. This was not a question of performance circumstances alone, since Hasse also removed non-Metastasian traits from works given in Dresden first and then repeated elsewhere. For example, *Alessandro nell'Indie* as performed in Venice in 1736 and 1738 was much closer to Metastasio's drama than the Dresden *Cleofide* of 1731. The revisions made for Warsaw show a similar tendency, of course. Only the Dresden revision of *Artaserse* in 1740 does not exactly belong to this category: the non-Metastasian substitute arias were almost all retained.[21] Nevertheless, 'Deh respirar' was inserted in an attractively passionate setting.[22]

The artistic intentions behind the practice of opera revisions in this period have rarely been investigated if at all noticed.[23] Let us assume that revisions often aimed at achieving fresh theatrical conviction through a new division of labour between poetry, music and performer. For example, the availability of a strong new singer in a tyrant's role might have encouraged the authors to 'build up' that role with more aggressive or heroic arias. But at the same time, the views of the composer and librettist of how to express a certain subject matter must in themselves have developed, and thus shifted the balance achieved in an earlier collaboration.

Metastasio's dramatic choices developed in some clearly identifiable directions. Around 1728–32 the poet cultivated and developed an image of enlightened rulership characterized by the aria-*topos* of 'Che mi giova impero e soglio' (*Ezio*, 1728): the recognition by a monarch that power will not sort out the problems of his own heart. Metastasio increasingly combined this idea with the question of innate versus externally obtained rulership, expressed by another aria-*topos*, 'Alma grande e nata al regno' (*Demetrio*, 1731): 'The great soul, born to reign, casts some ray or

21. The version has been described in the pioneering study of Oscar G. T. Sonneck, 'Die drei Fassungen des Hasseschen *Artaserse*', *Sammelbände der Internationalen Musikgesellschaft* 14 (1912–13), pp. 226–42. See also Frederick L. Millner, *The Operas of Johann Adolf Hasse* (Ann Arbor: UMI research press, 1979), passim, for this and other revisions.
22. It is possible that this aria setting had already originated in 1730, as its text is found in the *Artaserse* libretti of Lucca, autumn 1730 (music attributed to Hasse), and Milan, carnival 1731.
23. Technical aspects of the revisions are aptly described in F. Millner, *The Operas*, and Helga Lühning, '*Titus*'-Vertonungen im 18. Jahrhundert: Untersuchungen zur Tradition der Opera seria von Hasse bis Mozart* (Laaber Verlag, 1983) (Analecta Musicologica, 20). For textual revisions, see Reinhard Wiesend, 'Metastasios Revisionen eigener Dramen und die Situation der Opernmusik in den 1750er Jahren', *Archiv für Musikwissenschaft* 40 (1983), pp. 255–75.

signal of its oppressed majesty even in the remotest woods: just as a fire in a sheltered place never ceases to cast a light; just as a noble river does not go in a narrow bed.'[24] In other words, he demonstrated how the mighty and powerful a) have no reason to enjoy the responsibility of rulership, and b) are either a priori qualified for it by their innermost nature, or are unfit to rule. Thus, instead of the wheel of Fortune, with its unpredictable effects on the ups and downs of political careers, superior laws of nature and humanity identify the true monarch. Rulership attains a higher sort of dignity and merit. In many librettos, this superiority is illustrated through conflicts with other, rivalling values – love, family bonds, acquired power or military might. In particular, it is contrasted with the pastoral nostalgia for personal peace and enjoyment, which is almost always incompatible with rulership.

Demetrio, Metastasio's first libretto for Vienna (1731), is a striking (and strikingly successful) example of an opera libretto demonstrating these ideas. The hero and heir to the throne, himself ignorant of his royal status, cannot but appear qualified for the throne by his natural virtue, self-denial, heroism and noble behaviour. And his rival Olinto, an awkward young man, exposes the weakness of inherited nobility by insisting on his mere status against the inner qualities of a supposed shepherd. The heroine Cleonice, apparently destined to rule (but in reality the descendant of a usurper), 'qualifies' for the throne by acquiring these same qualities, one of which is the ability to sacrifice private emotions to the *raison d'état*. Cleonice at first complains, in an aria of the 'Che mi giova'-type, that the throne is useless for her if it restricts her personal happiness ('Se libera non sono,/se ho da servir nel trono,/ non curo di regnar, l'impero io sdegno': I, 8), but as she overcomes this nostalgia she finally gains her legitimate status. The motive is repeated in *Adriano in Siria* (1732): Adriano, elected Roman Emperor while in Siria, grows into his new duties by renouncing illegitimate love for a Parthian princess.

These dramas demonstrate the ideal of self-conquest in a ruler. On the other hand, intrinsically weak princes and tyrants such as Jarba, Cosroe, Valentiniano no longer appear in them. The moral ambiguity of dictatorship (Cesare) is avoided; deception of the people to benefit the dynasty (Semiramide) is rendered unnecessary. The subjects of enlightened realms have become their beneficiaries; evil and treason disappear as the foundation of these younger realms unfolds in the opera plots. The remaining mortal conflicts in the dramas after *Ezio* are often caused by ancient feuds and prejudices surfacing in members of the older generation, some of whom are barbarians (Massimo, Ircano, Poro, Timagene, Artabano, Osroa), and they are of course all resolved. It is as if Metastasio had anchored all these plots in that same historical moment when opposition to enlightened rulers was supposedly dying out.[25] His preferred solution to dramatic conflicts became the correction of

---

24. Mitrane, I, 6: 'Alma grande e nata al regno/fra le selve ancor tramanda/qualche raggio, qualche segno/ dell'oppressa maestà:/come il foco in chiuso loco/tutto mai non cela il lume;/come stretto in picciol letto/nobil fiume andar non sà.'
25. This is confirmed even by the special case of *Issipile* (1732), where ancient feuds threaten the happiness of a whole community as well as its ruling family.

misguided behaviour and the removal of misunderstandings. This separated him, as Elena Sala Di Felice has brilliantly shown, from Apostolo Zeno and an older dramatic tradition which had favoured just retribution and the punishment of the villains.[26] But the price to pay for such generalized happiness – or removal of mortal enemies – was, at least for the privileged individuals, often the sacrifice of love and individual happiness. The strictures of the *raison d'état* affected the rulers more than the subjects.

In the 1730s Hasse received commissions to set these new dramas, as well as others, characterized by more old-fashioned ideas about rulership. In addition, he frequently had to revise his own earlier settings of both dramatic varieties. This task was complicated. To develop new musical answers to an essentially new interpretation of the subject matter, at the same time as doing justice to earlier or more old-fashioned presentations of it, was perhaps impossible. Hasse clearly tended towards compromise. His scores for Metastasio's *Demetrio* (Venice, carnival 1732) and for Zeno's *Cajo Fabricio* (Rome, carnival 1732) were only moderately responsive to the contrasting political ideas of their authors, almost obliterating the difference between them. Both operas were hugely successful as musical settings, full of showpieces for singers. The ideology of *Demetrio*, as described here, is not really expressed in Hasse's music. He provides Mitrane's 'Alma grande e nata al regno' (see above) with illustrative music about the rise and fall of the mighty, and gives it a pastoral dance character. In fact, the music is derived from 'Nasce al bosco in rozza cuna' in *Ezio* (I, 8). Thus the composer's willingness to respond to the related theme is certain. But the large distance between Mitrane's enlightened view ('True nobility is given by nature, whatever the circumstances') and Varo's political superstition ('Goddess Fortune turns her wheel around') is eliminated. Olinto's problematic or ironic aria 'Che mi giova l'onor della cuna' (see above) is omitted. Fenicio's aria 'Giusti Dei, da voi non chiede' (III, 8), which expresses the old man's absolute devotion to the well-being of the dynasty, is set as an old-fashioned minuet in a demonstratively simple and gentle style. In this aria and in 'Alma grande', Hasse still relies on a semantic code operating with dance-types: slow minuet for royalty but also innocence; sarabande for pathos; gigue and passepied for pastoral or exotic subjects, and so on. In the Dresden revision of *Demetrio* (1740), 'Giusti Dei' as well as 'Alma grande' received new, majestic music: the former in a *Maestoso* setting in 3/4 metre, the latter in a march-like *alla breve* metre. 'Che mi giova' was now set: as an excited Allegro assai in duple metre, depicting youthful anger.[27]

Apostolo Zeno's *Cajo Fabricio* has a plot demonstrating Roman republican severity, symbolized in the paternal hero, and contrasted with the monarchy of Pyrrhus. Hasse's music, when expressing the darker sides of this conflict between the hopes of young lovers and the law of the republic, is very effective, generally more diversified than that of *Demetrio*. The musical intensity is, of course, greatest in the simile arias and love-songs. But Zeno avoids dramatic or sentence arias more

26.   Elena Sala Di Felice, 'Virtù e felicità alla corte di Vienna', in *Metastasio e il melodramma*, ed. by E. Sala Di Felice and L. Sannia Nowé, 1985, pp. 55–87.
27.   On the revision of *Demetrio*, see F. Millner, *The Operas*, pp. 133–40.

than does Metastasio, and thus the musical emotions and the political plotline develop in almost complete separation. Musical correspondences between *Cajo Fabricio* and other Hasse scores further compromise the expression of subject matter. For example, the opening aria 'In così lieto giorno', which announces a stately celebration, has the same energetic music as the opening aria of *Demetrio*, 'Di quell'ingiusto sdegno', where Olinto complains about Cleonice's coolness towards him. Sestia's 'Il trono, il regno,/che m'offre in dono' (I, 5) speaks only of aroused emotions, and Pirro's peace offer to Rome, 'Reca la pace in dono' (I, 8), paints the effects of peace as a pastoral-royal minuet, when in fact two conflicting political ideologies are at stake. Hasse revised *Cajo Fabricio* for Dresden as early as 1734, and thus it is no surprise that very little was changed.

In 1733 Hasse composed *Siroe re di Persia*, Metastasio's most retrospective libretto (written in 1726).[28] Here, all characters except the protagonist are involved in intrigue and lust for power, and the solution to the mortal conflict is achieved by deceiving the deceivers. The villain Medarse is musically privileged with four arias of the greatest intensity: two grandiose nature similes and two arias of great emotional warmth, where the character's falsehood is not reflected in the music. The ruler, Cosroe, is treated almost like the tyrant Mitridate in *Tigrane*, with three arias that are musically coherent, obliterating the positive or ambiguous sides of his character. One aria ('Fra sdegni ed amore') depicts his impotent rage. In addition, however, Cosroe has the famous *ombra*-aria 'Gelido in ogni vena', which gives an awesome depth to the fate of this misguided ruler. Hasse's musical imagery, a *perpetuum mobile* of running blood, seems to mythicize this character altogether. The semantic mode of this music is Baroque, allegorical.[29] There is also an aria text of the 'Che mi giova'-type. It is sung by the heroine Emira before she attempts to murder the king ('Non vi piacque ingiusti dei, ch'io nascessi pastorella') and is set in emphatic and energetic declamation. The outdated political statement of the soldier Arasse, 'Al tuo sangue io son crudele', who recommends tyrannical retribution rather than generosity, has been cut and replaced by a love-song in minuet rhythm ('Io sento amore in petto').

Hasse revised this opera at least once, for the performance in Warsaw in 1763, and there may have been an earlier revision for Naples, 1747, the sources of which seem to be lost. The Warsaw revision has been described in detail by Millner,[30] but the circumstances forcing the composer to restrict innovation (an attack of gout, among others) have perhaps been exaggerated. At the outset of the opera, a more positive statement about the figure of the monarch is made than anything in the 1733 version: the first, programmatic aria of Cosroe, 'Se il mio paterno amore' (I, 1),

---

28. Some of my earlier thoughts on this opera are assembled in Reinhard Strohm, *Die italienische Oper im 18. Jahrhundert* (Wilhelmshaven: Heinrichshofen, 1979) (Taschenbücher zur Musikwissenschaft, vol. 25), pp. 198–211.
29. On the compositional characteristics of this piece, see Helga Lühning, 'Cosroes Verzweiflung', in *Colloquium 'Johann Adolf Hasse und die Musik seiner Zeit' (Siena, 1983)*, ed. by Friedrich Lippmann (Laaber, 1987) (*Analecta Musicologica*, vol. 25), pp. 79–130.
30. F. Millner, *The Operas*, pp. 152–69. It seems that the score in *I–Vnm*, MS IV 575, might represent an intermediate version, perhaps the one given in Naples.

Example 26. Hasse, *Ezio* II, 8 (Dresden, 1755): aria of Varo

now has stately and authoritative music (C major, Andante maestoso), whereas the 1733 setting of the same words had portrayed the king as a threatening despot. It also seems that the expansion of the part of Arasse, apparently made for a good new singer, served to strengthen an affirmative view of power and *raison d'état*. Both the restored 'Al tuo sangue' and the inserted original aria 'Se pugnar non sai col fato' are settings of heroic vigour.[31] But in any case, this view of power still appears old-fashioned: what was evasion in 1733 has now become unenlightened affirmation.

Apparently similar conclusions might be drawn from Hasse's second setting of *Ezio*, given in Dresden in 1755, which has entirely new music in the arias. Heroic arias are more frequent here than in the 1730 opera, and of the formerly omitted texts with political significance, at least one is now set, 'Che mi giova impero e soglio' (II, 14). There is also increased orchestral pomp for the victory celebration in the first scene, followed by the dramatic, contrapuntal gesticulation of 'Se tu la reggi al volo' (I, 2); and there is a new setting of Varo's archaic opinions, 'Nasce al bosco in rozza cuna' (II,8), which employs naive, allegorical tone-painting. (See music example 26.)

The effort put into the exquisite orchestration of this aria, and the freely–chosen compositional emphasis of placing huge coloraturas on words such as 'regno' and

31.   F. Millner, *The Operas*, pp. 156–7, relates these changes to the new singer of Arasse, Antonio Pio
       Fabri. I wonder whether the new Arasse arias originated in 1763.

Example 27. Hasse, *Ezio* II, 14: aria of Valentiniano

'dominar', seem typical for Hasse's second setting of the drama. There is more direct musical affirmation of physical power than in the first setting. Also Valentiniano's 'Che mi giova', which concludes the second Act, receives an apparently pompous, self-confident setting, surprisingly contradicting the meaning of the words. (See music example 27.)

The B-section of this aria, however, pronounces the words 'che infedele al mondo io sia' in an appropriately timid mood (g minor, Allegretto, 3/8), so that the overall balance of the aria is closer to Metastasio's thinking than might at first appear. Hasse used these discrete Andantinos and Allegrettos in minuet rhythm and minor mode more and more often as middle sections of arias, formalizing a psychological tension which in the words was usually expressed more simultaneously. The choice of expressing conflicting thoughts by contrapuntal tension between voice and bass-line was less natural for him than, for example, for Handel or Graun. Ezio's rebellion against the ruler, 'Se fedele mi brama il regnante' (I, 11), has new music in the same ebullient mood as the old one, but with superior orchestrational means. Valentiniano's aria 'Vi fida lo sposo' (II, 3) is a wonderful character painting, combining grand gestures and anxious syncopations in a most natural manner; and finally, Onoria's 'Quanto mai felici siete' (I, 7), with its explicit longing for a shepherdess's life, is a beautiful depiction of this distant dream. Thus the opera as a whole does live up to its subject matter. If music is evasive here, it seems to illustrate precisely that evasion which is impossible; the conflict between these arias demonstrating power, confidence, anxiety and desire in the hearts of princes is as unresolved as is the human reality itself.

IV

It was perhaps Metastasio rather than Hasse who could not live with contradictions of this kind. Let us retrace the steps of his career as a 'political' dramatist. After *Adriano in Siria*, the two *drammi per musica* of 1733 constitute a major break.

Neither *L'Olimpiade* nor *Demofoonte* takes a position about rulers or states, although the latter employs the motives of tyranny and dynastic succession. It seems indicative of the fate of opera seria as a whole that these two profoundly humanistic librettos have become Metastasio's most acclaimed works with contemporary and later critics, whereas contemporary performance statistics slightly favour *Artaserse* and *Alessandro nell'Indie*. If the relative freedom from ideological content in the works of 1733 unchained the author's poetic inspiration, the courtly opera houses still preferred the heroic dramas.[32]

In 1734, however, Metastasio perfects his ideal image of the enlightened ruler with *La clemenza di Tito*. This drama involves an extremely well-considered revision of the idea of the monarch's self-conquest, already tried in *Alessandro* and *Adriano*. *Artaserse*, too, provided a precedent with the complication through friendship between prince and conspirator, except that there the supposed traitor was innocent, now he is guilty.

Ruling and obtaining glory is becoming harder. Power and love are in conflict in the wedding opera for Maria Theresa, *Achille in Sciro* (1736), with a particularly ample depiction of the natural qualities in a young prince. In a more serious mood, the laws of the state as distinct from those of the dynasty surface in *Ciro riconosciuto* (1736). This heir to the throne brought up in the woods turns out to possess superior wisdom and justice, so that the goals of pastoral nostalgia can be directly identified with the common good, as proclaimed in the final chorus: 'Leave your woods behind, Cyrus, come to the throne. Come to the throne, our love. Exchange your simple sheepshed for a palace, your humble rod for a sceptre; you will rule a different flock, and be a shepherd even as a king.'[33] The idea constituting *Il re pastore* of 1751 is fully developed here: the identity of 'pastoral', i.e. natural, goodness, and of rulership for the benefit of the common good is absolute. Metastasio was less successful with his attempt, in *Temistocle* (1736), to revise the ruler-subject conflicts displayed in *Ezio*, a failure which may have motivated him to avoid political themes again in *Zenobia* (1740). This, in turn, may have added a motivation to come forward with his most explicit political statement in *Attilio Regolo* (1740), a tragedy which Metastasio declared to be his preferred work, although not necessarily his best.[34] This probably meant that he was, at some stage, aware of having overstretched dramaturgical and poetic form in favour of a political idea. As in earlier works, the idea of *Attilio Regolo* is, of course, the prevalence of the common good over private happiness, but this time the task of self-conquest and sacrifice falls upon a republican leader and his family. Although Attilio is shown in one scene (II, 7) as fighting for his self-control, his is not only a personal, individual but a public achievement. All are affected by it; it is a national event. There is also a greater presence of 'the state' in the scenic fabric itself. Not by coincidence, the early scenes of the libretto

32. For some critical reactions, see the notes in P. Metastasio, *Tutte le opere*, vol. 1, 2nd edn, pp. 1496–7.
33. 'Le tue selve in abbandono/lascia, o Ciro, e vieni al trono;/vieni al trono, o nostro amor./Cambia in soglio il rozzo ovile,/in real la verga umile;/darai legge ad altro gregge;/anche re, sarai pastor.'
34. P. Metastasio, *Tutte le opere*, p. 1505.

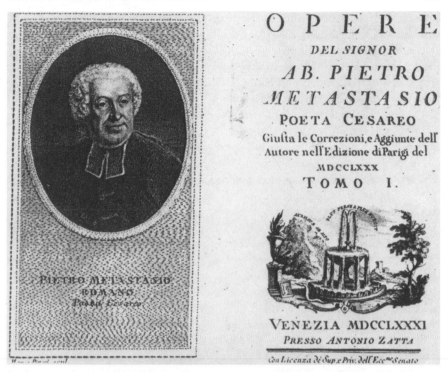

13. Pietro Metastasio, *Opere* (Venice, 1781); frontispiece and title-page of volume I.

contain the most realistic presentation of a state bureaucracy in Metastasio's *œuvre*. Unlike some earlier works such as *Demetrio*, with its passing satires of state rituals (I, 1 and I, 7–8), the difficulties experienced with the Roman administrative machinery by Attilia and by Attilio himself taste of real-life experiences that could have been undergone in Vienna. In I, 3, Attilia even decides to invoke 'popolar soccorso', being severely disappointed by the hostile or absent government.

The drama is full of allusions to the new perspective of a popular consensus in politics; the main content of the *commun bene* is repeatedly defined as *libertà*. While *Attilio Regolo* seems rather isolated in Metastasio's career, partly because of its performance history (the opera, composed by Hasse, could not be performed until 1750 because of the wars; later settings remained few), he especially returned to its themes in *Il trionfo di Clelia* (1762), where similar heroism is ascribed to a Roman republican woman and her companions. Although written so much later, it was obviously intended as a match to *Attilio Regolo*. The work is imbued with the idea of collective sacrifice for liberty and common happiness. It certainly anticipates nationalist dramas on Roman subjects. Like *Attilio Regolo*, it was set originally by Hasse but similarly avoided by most other composers, perhaps partly because it places excessive weight on the dialogue, whether for political and philosophical debate or for inspired speeches. Most of the aria texts are, for Metastasio, dry or contorted. Some theatricality is regained, in comparison with *Attilio Regolo*, through spectacular actions and scenography. Metastasio's letter to Hasse concerning (and concerned about) the accompagnato recitatives in *Attilio Regolo* have often been discussed;[35] scholars seem to agree that the composer, in following the advice of the poet, did not do himself justice. It remains to be seen whether Hasse was able to raise his recitative composition in *Il trionfo di Clelia* to the rhetorical and ideological level which the poet obviously required.

In *La clemenza di Tito* there is a balance which *Attilio Regolo* then upsets. On the long path from *ragione di stato* to *commun bene*, here is the point where Metastasio concentrates all the virtues in the soul of a single person, and resolves all the conflicts within a single mind. The individual ruler and the machinery of political power are in utter conflict: not only does Tito resent his privileged position, having to sacrifice his personal feelings, he has to act against the judgment of all – by pardoning Sesto – in order to achieve his glory. The core of Tito's suffering is his isolation from other human beings. It is expressed in the first of the two famous monologues (III, 4: 'È pur di chi regna/infelice il destino!'), where the soul-searching Emperor blends the 'Che mi giova'- and 'Alma grande'-topics into one complaint: that of having to fear his own friends. This sentiment is also expressed in an aria, 'Ah se fosse intorno al trono' (I, 9): the composer's greatest chance of capturing the messages of the drama in music lay here.

Hasse came to compose this work for an isolated *scrittura* (commission): it was given under the title of *Tito Vespasiano ovvero La clemenza di Tito* as the opening performance of the Teatro del Sole, Pesaro, 24 September 1735. In the libretto dedication the *impresari* describe the opera as 'one of the most sumptuous dramas ever heard' ('uno de' più sontuosi drammi, che siensi mai sentiti') – for its poetry, music and singers. Faustina sang the *prima donna* role of Vitellia. The Hasses lived in Venice from autumn 1734 and remained there throughout 1735. In the whole period between late 1734 and carnival 1736, when *Alessandro nell'Indie* (the revised version of *Cleofide*) was given in Venice, Hasse does not seem to have written music for any other opera.

The near contemporaneity of his work on *Alessandro* and *Tito*, and the fresh renown of both libretti, may well have stimulated Hasse's awareness of their common theme. Not only the issue of princely magnanimity, but also the obstacles to such virtue are similarly treated. In both dramas, these obstacles are partly private affections, such as Alexander's feelings for Cleofide or Tito's friendship for Sesto, and partly wider political considerations, such as the danger of not punishing the traitors. This personal moment distinguishes the two libretti from *Artaserse* or *Ezio*, where the political offence can be forgiven as soon as the innocence of the main suspect is established (in the climactic final scenes). It also distinguishes them

35. See, most recently, Sabine Henze-Döhring, 'Die *Attilio Regolo*-Vertonungen Hasses und Jommellis – ein Vergleich', in *Colloquium 'Johann Adolf Hasse und die Musik seiner Zeit' (Siena, 1983)*, pp. 131–55; Wolfgang Osthoff, '*Attilio Regolo*: Metastasios musikdramatische Konzeptionen und Hasses Ausführung', in *Dresdener Operntraditionen* (Dresden, 1986), pp. 147–73.

from the main source for *La clemenza di Tito*, Pierre Corneille's *tragédie Cinna* and its Italian sequel, Carlo Sigismondo Capeci's *La clemenza d'Augusto* (1697). The motivation for Vitellia's conspiracy is a combination of that of Livia (in *Cinna*), who is inspired by dynastic vendetta, and of Hermione in Racine's *Andromaque* (1675), with the psychological motive of offended feminine pride. *Ezio* and *Artaserse*, on the other hand, share the motive of family bonds bridging both sides of the political conflict (Valentiniano-Onoria, Poro-Erissena, Arbace-Semira, Artaserse-Mandane, Sesto-Servilia are all brother-sister pairs). Concerning a different side of the subject, scenic display of power and peaceful rulership was not much developed by Metastasio before his Viennese libretti; *Tito*, with its two stately scenes and choruses, was Hasse's first Metastasian drama that required such ingredients. Again, the most elaborate political ceremonial before *Tito* had been tried out in the last stage-set of *Alessandro*.

The Pesaro setting of the opera, of which very little music has so far been found, was followed by a revision for Dresden in 1738; a final version was prepared for Naples in 1759.[36] Some of the extant sources may well refer to the several other performances which took place in the intervening time. In general, however, we have an early setting, slightly differentiated in several performance versions, and a late one, with a considerable amount of musical changes.

Example 28. Hasse, *La clemenza di Tito* I, 5 (Pesaro, 1735?): aria of Tito

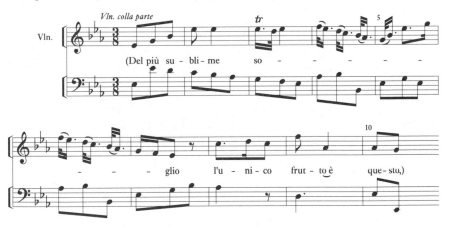

Few of Hasse's monarchs before Tito had had to sing as many as three programmatic arias directly concerned with their own status. The first of these in the opera is 'Del più sublime soglio' (I, 5). The emperor despises all the privileges of rulership except one – the chance of doing good to his subjects. The problem of Hasse's

36.   See F. Millner, *The Operas*, pp. 169–88 (musical sources mentioned on pp. 292 n. 56, 383 and 390), and H. Lühning, '*Titus*'-*Vertonungen*, pp. 133–92, for detailed discussions of the revisions.

approach to the subject matter is highlighted by the different music given to these words in 1735/1738 and 1759. The early setting of the aria was welcomed by Johann Adolph Scheibe in 1745: 'Majesty shows itself in the opening, and then a very perceptive melody makes clear what the poet wished to say with the words "l'unico frutto è questo".'[37] The triadic ascent and the wide coloratura on 'soglio' are heroic gestures, but they are, typically, under the control of a passepied-rhythm which may imply a gentle or *galant* musical character. (See music example 28.)

The 1759 setting, however, abandons this balance: its triplet ornaments, staccato-repercussions in the bass, and fluttering pairs of semiquavers in the voice are entirely playful. (See music example 29.)

Example 29. Hasse, *La clemenza di Tito* I, 5 (Naples, 1759): aria of Tito

This setting is a 'parody' of Hasse's music for 'So ch'è fanciullo Amore' in his *Olimpiade* of 1756 (II, 7): 'I know, Cupid is a child interested only in playing, who does not like to converse with old age. He indulges in little games and gets tired of rigour. Respect and freedom are not easily reconciled.'[38] The B-section of Hasse's aria continues the playfulness but also describes 'rigour' with the minor mode and chromaticism. Thus Hasse's semantic choice in *La clemenza di Tito* is to present the emperor as an innocent child who prefers to do those gentle things which the traditions of rulership deny him. An evasion? Perhaps, but one which the music deliberately expresses, not one to which it unwittingly contributes.

As Millner has established, the score of 1759 contains as many as twelve parody settings taken from Hasse's operas *Olimpiade* (1756), *Il re pastore* (1755) and *Ezio*

37. 'Die Majestät zeiget sich sonderlich im Anfange, und giebt uns durch eine sehr scharfsinnige Tonfolge zu erkennen, was der Poet unter den Worten "L'unico frutto è questo" sagen will.' Johann Adolph Scheibe, *Critischer Musicus* (Leipzig, 1745), pp. 779–80, quoted after F. Millner, *The Operas*, p. 307 n. 9.
38. 'So ch'è fanciullo Amore,/né conversar gli piace/con la canuta età./Di scherzi ei si compiace;/si stanca del rigore:/e stan di rado in pace/rispetto e libertà.'

14. Giovanni Carlo Galli Bibiena, stage design for Metastasio's *La clemenza di Tito*, I, 5, music by Antonio Mazzoni, Teatro del Tejo, Lisbon, 1755.

(1755);[39] but we should beware of the hasty conclusion that Hasse only wanted to save time by filling up his score with some recent music. Not all parodies replaced particularly original music, in any case. The 1759 setting of Publio's 'Tardi s'avvede/del tradimento' (III, 1) was taken from *Olimpiade* ('Nò, la speranza/più non m'alletta'). The old setting had been an altered version of a rather cheerful aria that had originated in Hasse's serenata *Enea in Caonia* (1727), to the words 'Se, qual tu sei,/qui son sì belle' (I, 1), and had been sung in his *Euristeo* (1732) with the words 'Che mi giova esser regnante' (III, 6)! Since Publio's maxim is that innocent people are usually too credulous, implying that Tito's goodness itself is the cause of his difficulties, the connection may seem justified. Hasse replaced this music with a slightly more agitated setting, in which Publio seems to 'lose hope' (as does Argene, who also calls for vengeance), so that the maxim is reduced to a private emotion.

There is also new music which enhances and strengthens the expressive fabric. The choruses accompanying the state ceremony in I, 5 ('Serbate o Dei custodi') is recomposed in the same (passepied-) metre, but given vast instrumental splendour through the use of a double orchestra, forming a serene panorama of peace and collective happiness – perhaps a hint of that newer Metastasian idea of the *commun bene*. Sesto's great farewell-aria 'Se mai senti spirarti sul volto' (II, 15) is musically

39. F. Millner, *The Operas*, pp. 174–5.

Example 30. Hasse, *La clemenza di Tito* I, 9 (Naples, 1759): aria of Tito

emancipated from the pretty minuet-tune of 1738, which it only recalls in the B-section. Tito's two great monologues in the third Act are newly set, with more emphasis on changing affections. But little of the new music refers to the main dramatic subject.

Tito's second aria, 'Ah, se fosse intorno al trono' (I, 9), illustrates the plight of the ruler who has no sincere friends any more. The two settings of 1738 and 1759 express the same tension – the responsibility for a 'vasto impero', the anxiety of being betrayed – with approximately the same means, especially the combination of large gestures and chromaticism. The music chosen for 1759, however, was first used for the words 'Il nocchier che si figura' in *Ezio* (I, 5). It was there sung in a solo scene by the traitor Massimo, who compared his evil plans to a sea-voyage into the unknown, hoping that the unpredictable goddess Fortune would assist him. The common image of the two arias is the fear of the unknown, the vast sea, the danger; Fortune is reinstated in her influence on realms and rulers. The villain Massimo and the best of all Emperors share the same *condition humaine*. (See music example 30.)

At the same time, the melodic-rhythmic type of 'Il nocchier' closely resembles the marching self-confidence of Valentiniano's 'Che mi giova Impero, e soglio' in *Ezio* (II, 15; see music example 27). The apparent contradiction of words and music in this aria, mentioned above, is now further explained: Hasse's affirmative

Example 31. Hasse, *La clemenza di Tito* III, 8 (Naples, 1759): aria of Tito
    a. Da capo section
    b. Middle section

marching tune really portrays false confidence, a threatened status; it is whistling in the dark.

Tito's greatest aria – and the last musical document of his victory over himself – is 'Se all'Impero, amici Dei (III, 8): 'If the realm, protector gods, requires severity from my heart, either take the realm from me, or give me a different heart.'[40] Expressed here is a type of bargain with the protector gods, offered from a position of newly gained strength through self-conquest.[41] Tito is truly master of the

40.   'Se all'Impero, amici Dei,/necessario è un cor severo,/o togliete a me l'Impero,/o a me date un altro cor.'

41.   For a precedent in Corneille's *Cinna*, see P. Metastasio, *Tutte le opere*, vol. 1, 2nd edn, p. 1501 n. 20.

situation – as demonstrated by the *maestoso* march with trumpets and timpani that accompanies him – but the composer also considers the possibility of 'a different heart' with a strikingly divergent, graceful phrase for 'un altro cor'. (See music example 31a.)

It goes unnoticed that the difference as intended by the poet would mean severity, not grace. In the much more reserved B–section (3/8), strange tutti fanfares blast into a quest for true fidelity, probably to remind the searching soul of cold Imperial realities. (See music example 31b.)

The music of this aria had been composed to the words 'Voi, che fausti ognor donate' of Alessandro in *Il re pastore* (III, 7), where the divergent phrase in the A-section expressed 'anche i moti del mio cor', opposing them to Imperial laurels. The B-section of that text speaks only of luminous glory: I suggest that a critical differentiation has occurred in the fitting of this music to the new, more ambivalent words. The sense of Tito's words exactly matches that of another aria in *Il re pastore*, the obviously programmatic 'So, che pastor son io' (I, 2). It is sung by the shepherd Aminta, who does not wish to exchange his lowly status for 'a thousand realms', unless heaven gives him 'different thoughts'. But Hasse portrays him as if he were already in charge of those realms – they appear in his grandiloquent coloraturas – and also emphasizes a change of style at 'different thoughts' ('altri pensieri'). That this other aria was not chosen to supply the music for 'Se all'Impero' may simply be a question of the non-matching text metre. But the musical differences between the shepherd Aminta, the conqueror Alessandro (in *Il re pastore*) and the enlightened Tito appear altogether small. What matters is that the 'difference' between ruling and human feelings, between state action and the searching heart, is maintained in all these settings, and seems even accentuated in the last of them, 'Se all'Impero, amici Dei'.

Two concluding remarks seem possible. The first is that there was, despite stylistic changes, a relative consistency in Hasse's musical language – a certain reliance on rhythmic or metric stereotypes of dance and march, a habit of emphasizing keywords through coloraturas, an inclination to use chromaticism for generalized expression – but this is not evidence for an unchanging view of the contents of his operas. His consistency provides, on the contrary, a matrix by which shifts in semantic accentuation or formulation become identifiable, not only for the modern critic but perhaps also for the assiduous contemporary public. The second remark is that these undeniable shifts in formulation did not move in the same direction as did Metastasio's. Hasse's treatment of rulers and states, starting in the pre-Metastasian phase with naive-allegorical, negative or simply indifferent representations of power, later occasionally acquires more positive, majestic and serene colours. But finally he concentrates on portrayals of the ruler as an individual, in conflict with the demands of the state. His music often remains allegorical, and only exceptionally endorses, perhaps, the abstract ideal of a *commun bene*. It paints evasion and nostalgia more convincingly than power and self-confidence. Even the goodness of Tito is musically likened to the innocence of a child in the dark woods. This attitude, which is partly determined but not completely dictated by the state of the musical language of the mid-eighteenth century, becomes a counterweight to

Metastasio's escalating trust in total happiness under enlightened governments. That rulers are only human after all, and that states are a dire necessity, was a truth Metastasio increasingly denied, probably against his will. Hasse continued to say it for him.

15

The Earl of Essex, *servitore di due padrone*

Possibly the last opera seria on the story of the Earl of Essex, Donizetti's *tragedia lirica* of 1837,[1] was also the first to reveal his name. Ever since Robert Devereux,[2] first Earl of Essex, had met his death in the Tower in February 1601, his life and personality had become the spoils of historians, dramatists, journalists, novelists and librettists in at least five languages. A sensational political event, so recent and yet so unexplained, could not easily be ignored by the literary world of this period. An autobiographical *Défense* written by Devereux himself (1599) was reprinted several times posthumously. As early as 1607, French readers satisfied their curiosity with an anonymous *Histoire de la vie et mort* of the Earl. The first dramatization was apparently the *tragédie Le Comte d'Essex*, by Gautier de Costes, seigneur de la Calprenède, which was published in Paris in 1639, but first acted already in 1632. This drama will be discussed below. Its contemporary is the Castilian play *El Conde de Sex* by Antonio Coello, first performed at the Real Palacio of Madrid on 10 November 1633 and printed in 1638.[3] In this work, the tragic – historical – outcome is reached by a completely invented path of courtly intrigue: the Earl sacrifices himself for his fiancée Blanca, whose failed assassination plot against the Queen he refuses to betray.

The great success of the seventeenth century was the anonymous romance *The Secret History of the Most Renown'd Queen Elizabeth and Earl of Essex*, published in many editions, first in English about 1650, then in an even more widely-circulated French translation. From this piece of tabloid journalism *ante litteram*, John Banks derived his tragedy *The Unhappy Favourite: or The Earl of Essex*, London, 1682.

1. Libretto by Salvadore Cammarano, performed at the Teatro San Carlo, Naples, 28 October 1837. I have used an apparently unaltered reprint of the libretto published for the Teatro Rè, Milan, *quaresima*, 1838, and the libretto and piano-vocal score of the work as reprinted by the Donizetti Society (London: Egret House, 1975). On the work, see also William Ashbrook, *Donizetti and his Operas* (Cambridge: Cambridge University Press, 1986), pp. 400–9; Winton Dean, 'Donizetti's Serious Operas', *Proceedings of the Royal Musical Association* 100 (1973–4), pp. 123–41.
2. Not 'D'Evreux' as given in Franca Cella, *Indagini sulle fonti francesi dei libretti di Gaetano Donizetti* (Milan, 1966) (Contributi dell'Istituto di Filologia Moderna, Serie francese, vol. 4), pp. 517–18.
3. See Emilio Cotarelo y Mori, 'Dramáticos del siglo XVII: Don Antonio Coello', *Boletín de la Real Academia Española* 5 (1918), pp. 550–600, especially pp. 574–84. The play was reprinted many times afterwards, often under the title *Dar la vida por su dama, la tragedia más lastimosa del Conde de Sex*.

The play was still performed at Drury Lane under Handel's and Heidegger's noses and survived well into David Garrick's time, in adaptations by James Ralph (1731), Henry Brooke (1750, probably in collaboration with Garrick) and Henry Jones (1753).[4] Banks had also been influenced by Thomas Corneille's tragedy of 1678, *Le Comte d'Essex*, seen by some as the masterwork of this prolific playwright and librettist, whose fame has naturally been overshadowed by that of his brother Pierre.[5] *Le Comte d'Essex* was on the stage in several countries until the mid-eighteenth century and is cited, for example, in Lessing's writings about German spoken tragedy.[6] Around 1700 an Essex *scenario* for the commedia dell'arte, derived from Thomas Corneille, is said to have been in circulation.[7] At least two operatic ballets are recorded under the title *Il conte di Essex*: one by Domenico Ricciardi, performed with an *Adriano in Siria* at the Teatro S. Benedetto, Venice, in 1780, the other composed by Pietro Lichtenthal for Milan, 1818.[8]

But the most congenial setting for Robert's public afterlife was always the historic-heroic stage. We might envisage this stage as having a fixed backdrop, a view of Elizabethan London seen from across the Thames, and side-flats showing the Palace of Westminster on the left and the Tower on the right. From the one to the other there marches the rich Earl and brilliant war hero, reputed lover of a Queen, steadfast across the centuries in heroic character and deportment. His gallant customs never change, and his picturesque costume changes only in so far as he loses, at some moment in the drama, his sword. And then, of course, his head.

The Greeks created tragedy, according to some, in an attempt at reenacting and rationalizing, even explaining away, the disasters which had reportedly happened among their forefathers. Classicist and Romantic dramatists search for motivations, too: they always ask *why* something has happened, why a tragic outcome was inevitable, even logical, in addition to being perhaps 'historically true'. The Essex disaster of 1601 raised the question: what was it that drove this favourite of a powerful Queen to his death? He was suspected of treason, insisted on his innocence and refused to beg for pardon: that was the 'historical' ground for his downfall. But

4. First acted at the Theatre Royal, Drury Lane, in 1681. See John Banks, *The Unhappy Favourite*, ed. with an introduction by Thomas M. H. Blair (New York: Columbia University Press, 1939), pp. 34–49.

5. Printed in Pierre Corneille, *Œuvres complètes suivies des œuvres choisies de Thomas Corneille* (Paris: Firmin-Didot, 1880), pp. 1717–43. On the work, see also chapters 6 and 7 above.

6. For these, and the German versions, see Walter Baerwolff, *Der Graf von Essex im deutschen Drama* (Tübingen, 1919).

7. Vittorio Viviani, *Storia del Teatro Napoletano* (Naples: Guida, 1969), p. 190.

8. For eighteenth-century titles, see Claudio Sartori, *I libretti italiani a stampa dalle origini al 1800*, 6 vols (Cuneo: Bertola and Locatelli, 1993); for the nineteenth century, see Franz Stieger, *Opernlexikon*, Teil I: Titelkatalog (Tutzing: Schneider, 1975). Towards the end of the eighteenth century, the *sujet* partly overlaps with the broad romantic tradition of literature on Elizabeth I and her court. Examples of this are the libretto by C. Federici and Giovanni Schmidt, *Elisabetta d'Inghilterra* (music by Stefano Pavesi, Turin, 1809, and by Gioacchino Rossini, Naples, 1815), derived from Sophia Lee's novel *The Recess*, 1783–5, and of course Walter Scott's *Kenilworth*, 1821, with its operatic derivatives written for Donizetti and Auber. Unrelated in subject matter is Edward Bulwer Lytton, *Devereux: A Tale*, 3 vols (London, 1829), which poses as the autobiography of Morton D., a later member of the clan.

the poets' answers vary: political gain, revenge, greed, *raison d'état*, honour, glory, pride, love, jealousy, terrible accidents and simply *fate* – any combination of them may conspire against Devereux in the history of the plot. The search for motivations also involves his companions on stage. Whether or not they are shown to contrive or permit his death, they, too, are continuously asked 'Why?' Salvadore Cammarano is obsessed by this question ('onde?' in his poetic language). For example, in his first scene, the ladies of the court beseech Sara to reveal the secret of her tears:

> *Dame.*
> Onde la tua mestizia?
> *Sara.*
> Mestizia in me?
> *Dame.*
> Non hai
> Bagnato il sen di lagrime?
> (*Ladies.* What is the reason for your sadness? *S.* Sadness in me? *L.* Are you not drenched in tears?)

The flow of Donizetti's music is interrupted for the first time when a dominant ninth chord dies away on Sara's unaccompanied words of denial 'Mestizia in me?' She does not admit to her sadness – her secret is guarded. It remains guarded until the tremendous *scena ultima*, when Sara – too late – presents Devereux's ring which would have guaranteed his pardon, and Elizabeth is shattered by the almost simultaneous revelations that Sara was her rival, that Devereux is dead and that his best friend Nottingham, Sara's husband, has delayed the presentation of the ring and thus prevented the royal pardon, to avenge his honour:

> *Elis.*
> Questa gemma d'onde avesti?
> Quali smanie! Qual pallore!
> Oh, sospetto . . . e che, potesti
> Forse . . . Ah! parla . . .
> *Sara.*
> Il mio terrore . . .
> Tutto dice . . . Io son . . .
> *Elis.*
> Finisci . . .
> *Sara.*
> Tua rivale, me punisci . . .
> . . .
> *Elis. (a Sara)*
> Tu perversa, tu soltanto
> Lo spingesti nell'avello!
> Onde mai tardar cotanto

THE EARL OF ESSEX

A recarmi quest'anello?
Nott.
Io, regina, la rattenni.
Fui trafitto nell'onor.
Sangue volli, e sangue ottenni.
Elis.
Alma rea! spietato cor!

(*Elis.* Where did you obtain this jewel? What desperation! What paleness! Oh, suspicion . . . and were you capable, perhaps . . . so, speak! *Sara.* My horror says all . . . I am . . . *Elis.* Go on . . . *Sara.* Your rival, punish me! . . . *Elis.* You perverted woman, you alone pushed him in the abyss! Why on earth did you wait so long to bring me this ring? *Nott.* I, my Queen, have held her back; I had been offended in my honour. Blood I wanted, and blood I got. *Elis.* Criminal soul! Pitiless heart!)

We have anticipated most of the story. Here now follows a discussion of the most important French and Italian dramatizations, all of which endeavour to motivate this mysterious and dramatic political event:

1. Gautier de Costes, seigneur de La Calprenède. *Le Comte d'Essex, tragédie,* Paris, 1639 (first acted 1632);
2. Thomas Corneille, *Le Comte d'Essex, tragédie,* Paris, 1678;[9]
3. Antonio Salvi, *Amore e maestà,*[10] *tragedia per musica,* Florence, 1715, and thirty other libretto editions until 1768, mostly under the title *Arsace;*[11]
4. Jacques-Arsène-François-Polycarpe Ancelot, *Élisabeth d'Angleterre, tragédie en 5 actes,* Paris, 1829;
5. Felice Romani, *Il Conte di Essex, melodramma,* Milan, La Scala, 1833 (music by Saverio Mercadante);
6. Salvadore Cammarano, *Roberto Devereux, tragedia lirica,* Naples, S. Carlo, 28 October 1837 (music by Gaetano Donizetti).

Throughout this two-century career on the public stage, Robert Devereux serves two mistresses, French tragedy and Italian opera. Similarly, in each reenactment of his story he tries to balance his dependence on two very different ladies, one of whom is a queen. Is his longevity as a tragic character a cruel punishment which he receives for failing to please both of his mistresses? What seems to determine his career is, in any case, the dilemma not only of his relationships but also of theirs.

The Seigneur de La Calprenède wrote under political circumstances which might have tempted anyone to paint the Tudors as godless tyrants; this time saw the

---

9. I have not been able to see the Essex tragedy by Abbé Claude Boyer, 1672.
10. See also chapters 8 and 9 in this volume.
11. Unrelated are: *Arsace, dramma per musica* by Giovanni de Gamerra, Padua, 1775 and later; *Arsaces,* a tragedy by William Hodson, 1775.

first wave of Mary Stuart tragedies in Catholic countries, and the Earl of Essex could have been presented as yet another victim of Elizabeth Tudor's wrath. To some extent this is what La Calprenède did. But the characterization which he gave to his figures rises far above political propaganda. He liked plots taken from British history: in 1638 he published a *tragédie* on Lady Jane Grey, *Ieanne reyne d'Angleterre*, in 1640 a *tragicomédie*, *Edouard*. His knowledge of English and probably Spanish dramatic literature might have helped him to avoid a partisan position.

La Calprenède's Elizabeth is a proud, resourceful woman, but obsessed by secret passions and fears which only her chambermaid anxiously observes.[12] She never publicly admits what 'secret histories' and gossip in France might then have taken for granted: that she is in love with Devereux. It adds to her stature that her motive for confirming Devereux's sentence is not jealousy but profound disappointment over his apparently disloyal politics, even if the tone of her monologues is often melodramatic (II, 2: 'Tu mourras, tu mourras, monstre d'ingratitude!'). The author, in his dedication of the play to the Princesse de Guimené, stresses the Queen's reputed greatness, and her partial resemblance to the dedicatee, a daring rhetorical gambit from which he extracts himself by claiming that Essex would not have become ungrateful to her, the Princesse.[13] In the preface he asserts that he has not invented anything but that his sources are the older 'Historiens Anglois', on the one hand, and oral history, on the other ('de bonnes memoires que j'en avois receuës de personnes de condition, et qui ont peut estre part à l'Histoire'). He accepts the historical ambiguity of Elizabeth's reputation, almost as if he were saying about her what Schiller says about his Wallenstein, another controversial figure from that period:

Von der Parteien Gunst und Haß verwirrt,
Schwankt sein Charakterbild in der Geschichte . . .
(Confused by partisan favour and hatred, the image of his character oscillates in history).

The consequence of this ambiguity for La Calprenède's Devereux is that he must be guilty of at least something, since his Queen is not downright selfish or cruel. His own political actions are presented as possibly faultless, although it matters little since the Queen is inclined to pardon him anyway. His valiant friend, the Earl of

12.   Act I, scene 3: '*Alix*. Iuste Ciel! quel changement estrange, Que la Reyne est troublée! O Dieu, le teint luy change! Et l'on recognoist bien à voir ses actions, Que son coeur est pressé d'estranges passions. . . .' And several similar scenes thereafter.
13.   'Madame, i'offre une excellente Reyne à une excellente Princesse, et quoy que sa memoire soit en quelque horreur parmy nous, elle est en telle veneration parmy beaucoup d'autres, qu'elle passe dans leur esprit pour la plus grande Princesse qui fut iamais.' Later, he mentions the 'raison d'état' as her only excuse but finishes with the words 'si le Ciel eust adiousté à ses bonnes qualitez une partie des vostres il en eut fait son chef-d'oeuvre, et que s'il eut pourveuë des beautez de l'ame et du corps que vous possedés avec tant d'avantage; Nostre Comte n'eut pas été ingrat aux preuves qu'il avoit receuës de son amitié . . .'.

Southampton, is prepared to die for him. But there is *another woman*: an intrigue, of the dramatist's invention, which was to become a vital ingredient of subsequent versions. Historians had hinted that Devereux fell victim to a court intrigue created by Lord Cecil, Sir Walter Raleigh and others. La Calprenède makes Cecil's wife – Cherchez la femme! – an ex-mistress of Devereux; she, now repudiated and jealous of the Queen, wants to take revenge. To give this Eboli figure the necessary means to bring about the Earl's death, the author introduces a stage-prop, the later famous *ring* which the Queen had given to her favourite as a warrant of her pardon *in extremis*. The Earl, generous and lighthearted, gives it to Madame Cecile to convince her of his true and lasting affections. She does not believe him, but at first resolves to let him live. Later, in accord with her husband, she withholds the ring from the Queen when its significance has become known to her. Jealousy on the part of Lord Cecil does not seem to play a role. Throughout several scenes with Devereux and with Elizabeth, Madame Cecile (who has no name of her own) dissimulates her motives. Thus, Elizabeth has no reason for jealousy. At the end of Act Four, Madame Cecile leaves the stage with her husband, announcing that she has something of great importance to show him. Even the audience are not informed of the fatal intrigue of the two until the last scenes when suddenly Elizabeth is called to hear, in a back room of the palace, the confessions of Madame Cecile, now dying from remorse over her misdeed. This dark and sudden revelation, coming from an underestimated and neglected woman, has probably greater effect on stage than even the preceding scenes, in which the anxiety for the Earl's fate had come to an end with a messenger's explicit account of his beheading. The Queen is left to accuse herself for not having prevented it all. But she had no chance.

It seems worth remembering La Calprenède when assessing later dramatic versions; somehow the tradition could never rid itself entirely of his motives and motivations.

Thomas Corneille applauds himself in his preface for having thrown out the ring, a detail not supported by any historian.[14] Instead, he tries to motivate his tragic catastrophe from a conflict of characters and passions alone. The rival courtiers are again the instigators of Devereux's death, and one of them delays the ultimate request for pardon. But the true motivation of the tragic ending is the character conflict between Essex and Elizabeth: he excessively proud and inflexible, she torn between honour, glory, *raison d'état*, and her terrible jealousy which in the end leads to the catastrophe. The special humiliation reserved for her is that she not only suffers the loss of her friend but does so for the wrong reason – jealousy rather than honour or *raison d'état*. In order to motivate her jealousy, Corneille presents Devereux's relationship with the *other woman* as a reciprocated and lasting one, which is revealed to Elizabeth, on top of all her other troubles, in the middle of the play (Act III, scene 4). The Queen first rages, then forgives, and so forth. The *other woman* now has a name (Henriette, Duchesse d'Irton); she has sacrificed herself for

14. '. . . je suis persuadé que cette bague est de l'invention de monsieur de la Calprenède, du moins je n'en ai rien lû dans aucun historien.'

Devereux's safety by marrying another man – not Lord Cecil – to divert the Queen's attention, a motive which influenced much of the later tradition. With Henriette, this pure, loving soul, a wave of *attendrissement* swamps the stage. The dialogues between the lovers are supposed to leave us in tears, not least when we hear that it is precisely Henriette's love which confirms the Earl's decision not to betray her and rather face death than obtain the Queen's pardon. (A tragic conflict better known from Jean Racine's *Bajazet*.) Henriette has in common with Madame Cecile that she is herself a lady-in-waiting of the Queen, but since she is honest, she suffers correspondingly more from her concealment (just like Racine's Atalide). Only the Earl has not noticeably changed, except that we might take his attachment to Henriette a little more seriously than that to Madame Cecile. Henriette's husband does not appear at all.

When Antonio Salvi exploited Corneille's version for his tragic opera libretto, he probably knew La Calprenède's version too. An idea which he found in the older dramatist is the scene of the trial ('le Comte devant ses juges', Act III), omitted by Corneille. On the other hand, he portrayed the Queen (Statira), the Earl (Arsace) and Henriette (Rosmiri) almost exactly as Corneille had done, ably translating the tragic conflict of ethos and pathos within the Queen herself as one between *amore* and *maestà*. But he must have felt that the omission of Henriette's husband was a loss. Thus he reinstated the Earl's enemy, Lord Cecil, as Rosmiri's husband Mitrane, and in contrast to La Calprenède presented him as explicitly jealous. But since *she* inherits from Corneille's Henriette the ethos of the pure lover, *he* must by necessity be a villain. The resulting marital conflict between the two has surprisingly modern, 'psychological' traits, for example when Rosmiri tests her husband's strength by threatening suicide if he persists in destroying Arsace. In fact, the catastrophe is compounded by her suicide. Unlike Madame Cecile, however, Rosmiri dies accusing the Queen of injustice and tyranny: the tables are turned.[15]

The *nœud* or dramatic nub of La Calprenède's drama is the figure of Madame Cecile: the evil corner of the triangle, whose power is concentrated in a tiny object, the ring. There is a feeling that Elizabeth and Devereux could have been reconciled, not least through the heroic friendship of a Pylades (Southampton). What pushes Devereux over the edge is one of his past *amours* – more an accident than a sin – and the revenge of an offended woman who, however, is ultimately punished. The straightforward morality and atavistic symbolism of this drama are rejected by Corneille, who in good Cartesian manner seeks the fatal conflict within each human soul itself. There is no villain among the principal triangle; they are all enemies of themselves. As a result, action is suspended, accidents are reduced, but also the goal-directedness of the drama is greatly diminished. It somehow ends when enough tears are shed.

15.   This strikingly rebellious motive was facilitated by the transfer of the play's setting from recent European to ancient Persian history. See also chapter 9 in this volume.

Salvi's adaptation is ingenious and convincing; compared with his French predecessors, he represents a shift in taste and morality without being dramatically
weakened by the need to cater for a musical setting. He adds an actual prison scene
for Essex, and elaborates the trial scene. He resuscitates the principle of terror while
not neglecting compassion; love, honour and glory are presented on a high plane.
But there is a certain loss of balance between the characters, at least in comparison
with Thomas Corneille, and the dramatic expedient that drives the tragedy forward
is slightly pleonastic: a *jealous villain*. Moreover, this force operates outside of, and
in addition to, the principal triangle, so that the primary conflict between the Queen
and her ungrateful servant becomes dangerously irrelevant for the outcome. The
other main conflict which Corneille had developed, *l'amore impossibile* between the
Earl and Henriette, seems overshadowed by the plight of the deceived husband.
Both these tendencies were to be increased a century later.

When turning to the nineteenth-century career of Robert Devereux, we
must start with question marks. How could such a subject survive into the
Romantic era? Would it not at least have had to be transformed and remotivated
beyond recognition?

Jacques-Arsène-François-Polycarpe Ancelot (1794–1854) was the husband of a
famous writer and lady of society (Marguerite-Louise-Virginie Ancelot, 1792–
1875), and a prolific dramatist himself who also specialized in the musical theatre.
Nevertheless, his spoken tragedies are described as following classicist models,
which may explain how he became interested in the subject of the Earl of Essex.[16]
It can be shown that his *Élisabeth d'Angleterre* is the model for Romani's and
Cammarano's libretti,[17] and that it is based on all three of the tragedies discussed
so far. While Ancelot's reception of La Calprenède and Thomas Corneille does
not surprise us, his awareness of Salvi, hitherto unrecognized, may suggest how
some of the links between French tragedy and Italian opera survived Metastasian
normalization.

A genealogy or even 'filiation' of all the Essex dramas through history seems
possible with the help of 'connecting variants', of the kind the textual critic uses
when constructing a stemma. For example, connecting variants between Salvi and

---

16. Luciano Salce says of him in the *Enciclopedia dello Spettacolo*: 'Onesto raciniano in ritardo, Ancelot
    fu tradito dalla fecondità e dalla pedissequa imitazione dei modi classici' ('An honest if belated
    Racinian, Ancelot was let down by his productivity and by his slavish imitation of the classical
    modes').
17. In the following discussion, the far-reaching identities of plot between Ancelot's *Élisabeth
    d'Angleterre* and the two Italian libretti are not always specifically mentioned. The connection has
    been overlooked in F. Cella, *Indagini* (n. 2 above), where there is only a generic reference to
    Romani's libretto as the supposed model for Cammarano's. In 1841 Gaetano Rossi based the
    libretto for Donizetti's *Maria Padilla* on an Ancelot tragedy of the same title; see F. Cella, *Indagini*,
    pp. 549–57. John Black, *The Italian Romantic Libretto: A Study of Salvadore Cammarano* (Edin-
    burgh University Press, 1984), pp. 40–3, maintains that the two libretti could well have been
    independent derivations from Ancelot; he quotes the contemporary Neapolitan magazine
    L'omnibus as saying that Cammarano had used an old play by 'Tomasso Corneille', Ancelot and
    Romani as his sources.

La Calprenède – motives not present in Corneille – would be the trial scene, the death of the *other woman*, and the identity of Devereux's enemy with her husband.[18] Those between La Calprenède and Ancelot – motives present neither in Salvi nor Corneille – are the ring and everything that happens with it, plus probably the character of Elizabeth's chambermaid Anna (Alix). The connecting variants between Corneille and Ancelot are numerous, and they often extend to the verbal structures themselves. Ancelot and Salvi are connected by four elements not present in the rest of the tradition: 1. the jealousy of the husband as the principal catalyst; 2. a long scene where the Queen hesitates to sign the death sentence; 3. an actual prison scene for Essex; and 4. two haunting solo scenes for the Queen in the last Act. In the first of these, before the *dénouement* (V, 1), the Queen anxiously awaits in her apartment the return of the negotiators to bring Devereux's request for pardon. This is the more remarkable as Ancelot's Élisabeth had not explicitly invited such a request, whereas in Corneille and Salvi she had done it repeatedly. The other scene is her final monologue, interrupted only briefly by Anna and Lord Cecil, in which she blames Sara (the new name for the *other woman*) and her husband (Nottingham) for Devereux's death: 'Dieu peut pardonner! . . . Mais moi, jamais, jamais!' and then falls into violent self-accusations.

> *Él.*
> Essex me demandait la vie!
> Du fond de sa prison implorant mon sécours,
> Je le vois! . . . Il attend que je sauve ses jours!
> Il songe à ma promesse, et mon nom le console!
> J'ai chargé le bourreau d'acquitter ma parole.
> Sans doute en m'accusant le malheureux est mort! *etc.*

Compare Salvi's concluding *ombra* scene:

> *Statira.*
> Furie, che m'agitate
> Rapitemi all'orrenda
> Faccia del mio delitto . . .
> Ahimè, che in ogni oggetto
> Veggio il teschio d'Arsace, e di Rosmiri
> L'ombra errante, e funesta,
> E in quella parte, e in questa
> Sento per mia cagion pianti, e sospiri. *etc.*
> (Furies, who agitate me, take me away from the horrible face of my crime! Ah, in every object I see the skull of Arsace, and the erring shadow of the dead Rosmiri; wherever I turn, I hear the weeping and sighing I have caused.)

---

18.   This admittedly on condition that they do not also occur in Boyer's version, as yet unknown to me. Obviously, stemmata of dramatic plots are rarely safe since variants are often polygenetic, i.e. identical dramatic ideas often originate independently of each other.

Here, as in the prison scene, we would like to conclude that the model of opera has benefited spoken drama, although it must be kept in mind that no law forbade conventional spoken tragedy to have prison or *ombra* scenes.

The ring and the death warrant, however, are motives leading into the heart of the matter. These are physical objects which carry a great deal of responsibility for people's destinies, almost like fetishes. The ring travels, in Ancelot's tragedy, along the same paths as in La Calprenède. Sara, however, who is now passionate and pure like Henriette, wants to use it to save the Earl's life. She had at first not realized its power, because her generous lover did not tell her about it. She then receives a *letter* from him out of prison telling her to use the ring to obtain the Queen's pardon. Surprised by the Queen herself, she has no time to read the letter and hides it, and when she does read it later it is too late because her husband, alerted to her supposed infidelity, has returned and arrests her in the house. It is amazing what can happen with letters in tragedy: exactly the same as in comedy. The means by which Nottingham has learned of his wife's liaison – a *blue scarf* – might pass as Ancelot's invention: but the object and its travels through several hands are nothing but a variant of Othello's handkerchief.

Salvi's elaborate scene (II, 10) about the Queen's signature on the *death warrant* – she hesitates to sign it and is interrupted several times – is another cliché of historic-heroic drama and was often used in opera librettos.[19] Ancelot shows Elizabeth's resolve at least at the end of the scene, when she signs and also forbids Nottingham to question the Earl one last time outside prison. Nevertheless, she then submits her own judgment to the uncertainty whether or not the *ring* will arrive.

Poor Ancelot! He has to fill his plot with fetishes – letter, ring, death warrant, blue scarf – to bring about the catastrophe, because his characters, overburdened with their histories, are too weak to do it themselves. So many unfortunate accidents are needed here that a coroner, summoned to the bloody scaffold, would almost have to return a verdict of 'accidental death'.

I believe that the two operas based on Ancelot make clearer, in a way, what Devereux's service to Romantic tragedy was. The development of his story over two centuries allowed history to pale into *fate*.

This can be concluded from the evidence of the librettos in various ways. Least significant are the general plotlines. In both adaptations they are more or less the same as in Ancelot; it is certain that Cammarano used the French drama in addition to Romani's libretto, and there are also 'connecting variants' suggesting his independent use of Salvi's *Arsace*.[20] A small but characteristic motive, in turn, seems to connect Romani directly with Salvi.[21] In comparison with the earlier

19. In this particular story, it curiously conflicts with the evidence of the real object. The actual, historical death warrant for the Earl of Essex, which is on permanent display in the British Museum, shows a bold signature 'Elizabeth' proudly written in black ink across the top of the parchment sheet, suggesting anything but hesitation.
20. In Romani's III, 3–5, Essex is shown in prison as in Ancelot, whereas in Cammarano's corresponding scenes II, 4–5, he appears before Elizabeth herself, just as in Salvi's II, 12 but not in Ancelot.
21. The secondary villain, Walter Raleigh, expresses in III, 3 his hope to marry the Queen when Essex is out of the way – apparently an echo of Salvi's Artabano.

dramatizations, the nineteenth-century texts further develop ostensible motivation, and perhaps realistic effect, on the level of detail. As has been observed, this plot relies much on the time element, since the Earl's execution is supposedly the unfortunate result of a fatal delay. Ancelot drives this to an extreme by overemphasizing the delay-motive: Sara is actually locked into her house by her husband. The much cruder timing of the libretto versions only accentuates this use of time for dramaturgical expediency. Character and personal interest, on the other hand, are of little relevance.

What matters more is scenic accentuation. As in many operatic adaptations of spoken dramas, there is the usual shift of emphasis away from verbal reasoning and dialogue to straightforward expression of feelings in arias and choruses. Less of the verbal matter is now used to motivate feelings, more to enhance emotions that are taken for granted. Much of the dialogue is passed from the main characters to ensemble and chorus. The ladies-in-waiting of the Queen, already used by Ancelot, form excited and exciting musical backgrounds; concerted ensembles and scenic verse (open forms in lyrical metres) generally surround the dialogue with a vibrating atmosphere which seems to conjure up the very essence of drama. As regards the soloists, Elizabeth is presented in Ancelot as being jealous already in Act I; but this becomes almost a *colpo di scena* in Donizetti's opera when she, instead of conducting a long interrogation to confirm her suspicions, simply explodes in a love/jealousy aria ('L'amor suo mi fe' beata'). It makes no difference that the person interrogated is Sara, and not the Earl as in Ancelot and Romani. In all three Romantic dramatizations, the question of Elizabeth's or Devereux's moral stature is played down. He is presumed guilty, so the plot can get under way. It matters more to the spectator whether the Queen will find out about him and Sara. (This is, of course, also a strongly *bourgeois* motive.) The operas create an atmosphere so fatalistic that nobody indeed bothers any more about Elizabeth's or Devereux's *Charakterbild in der Geschichte*. Among the questions which these operas return to history, unanswered, is why everything had to happen at all. Ring, letter and blue scarf do not motivate the tragic events, they merely describe the mechanics of inevitability. They do not explain the whole great mystery of tyranny, love and death as the seventeenth-century writers had endeavoured to do.

In these versions there is one case of a changed motivation of character. Cammarano brilliantly solves the problem, tolerated by both Ancelot and Romani, that a *jealous villain* makes the outcome too predictable. Reviving La Calprenède's Pylades-figure, he makes Nottingham a true friend of Devereux, who only out of jealousy becomes his mortal enemy. The hero's destiny turns as Nottingham's motivation turns; neither of them has wanted or indeed deserved it. This striking motive, superbly carried out in Donizetti's setting, makes the figure of Nottingham even more important, not as a character but as an agent of destiny. The Earl of Essex and his motivations are taken even more for granted.

In these operas the hero must die because the history books have decreed it. Love and jealousy must be part of his story because they are part of every opera. The individual, Robert Devereux, is annihilated. It is clear that Romantic opera and drama had to look for a fresh character.

But until that happened, the Earl of Essex had done great service to both his mistresses. To both spoken and musical tragedy, he had presented a dark, unanswered question, a disaster that had happened in the documented past and yet was unexplained. A moralistic or politically tendentious answer having been rejected already by the pioneer dramatist, classicist tragedy endeavoured to motivate Devereux's fate within the categories of character, interest, pathos and ethos. Romantic tragedy perfected the mechanics of plot motivation, but behind this smoke-screen the blind, unanswerable verdict of history reappeared. This was, in a sense, a return to the Greek origins of tragedy: to the fatalistic answer. When Robert Devereux learned from Donizetti that he had to die because he *did* die, he retired from the stage.[22]

22. Devereux's resurrection in William Plomer's and Benjamin Britten's opera *Gloriana* (1953), based on Lytton Strachey's novel *Elizabeth and Essex*, might be considered as part of a different story altogether. It is the story of twentieth-century *Literaturoper*, and thus of modern musical historicism: a cultural attitude which no longer relies on drama to deal with events or texts of the past, but which enjoys its own scientific awareness of history and literature also in the secondary, derationalized form of opera.

Bibliography

Main series

Abert, Anna Amalie, 'Opera in Italy and the Holy Roman Empire (chapters a–e)', in *The Age of Enlightenment 1745–1790*, ed. by Egon Wellesz and Fred W. Sternfeld (London: Oxford University Press, 1973) (*The New Oxford History of Music*, vol. 7), pp. 1–172

Abert, Anna Amalie, 'Mozarts italianità in *Idomeneo* und *Titus*', in *Colloquium 'Mozart und Italien'*, ed. by F. Lippmann, 1978, pp. 205–16

Accademia Nazionale dei Lincei (ed.), *Metastasio (Convegno indetto in occasione del II centenario della morte)* (Rome: Accademia Nazionale dei Lincei, 1985) (Atti dei Convegni Lincei, 65)

Algarotti, Francesco, '*Saggio sopra l'opera in musica*', 2nd edn (1763), in F. Algarotti, *Scritti*, ed. by Giovanni Da Pozzo (Bari: Laterza, 1963)

Antolini, Bianca Maria, 'L'Opera italiana in Francia: intorno all'"Essay sur l'union de la poésie et de la musique" di François-Jean de Chastellux (1765)', in *Napoli e il teatro musicale*, ed. by B. M. Antolini and W. Witzenmann, 1993, pp. 69–96

Antolini, Bianca Maria, and Witzenmann, Wolfgang (eds), *Napoli e il teatro musicale in Europa tra Sette e Ottocento: Studi in onore di Friedrich Lippmann* (Florence: Olschki, 1993)

Arteaga, Stefano, *Le rivoluzioni del teatro musicale italiano*, 3 vols (Bologna, 1783–1788, R Bologna: Forni, n.d.)

Barcham, William L., 'Costume in the Frescoes of Tiepolo and Eighteenth-Century Italian Opera', in *Opera and Vivaldi*, ed. by M. Collins and E. K. Kirk, 1984, pp. 149–69

Barnett, Dene, *The Art of Gesture: The Practices and Principles of Eighteenth-century Acting* (Heidelberg: Winter, 1987)

Baselt, Bernd, 'Thematisch-systematisches Verzeichnis: Bühnenwerke', in *Händel-Handbuch*, 4 vols, ed. by Kuratorium der Georg-Friedrich-Händel-Stiftung, vol. 1 (Leipzig: VEB Deutscher Verlag für Musik, 1978)

Baur-Heinhold, Margarethe, *Baroque Theatre* (London: Thames & Hudson, 1968)

Bédarida, Henri, 'L'opéra italien jugé par un amateur français en 1756', in *Mélanges de musicologie offerts à M. Lionel de la Laurencie* (Paris: Droz, 1933), pp. 185–200

Bellina, Anna Laura, 'Dal mito della corte al nodo dello stato: il "topos" del tiranno', in *Antonio Vivaldi*, ed. by L. Bianconi and G. Morelli, 1982, vol. 2, pp. 297–313

Bellina, Anna Laura, 'Metastasio a Venezia: appunti per una recensione', *Italianistica* 13 (1984), pp. 145–73

Bellina, Anna Laura, Brizi, Bruno, and Pensa, Maria Grazia, *I libretti Vivaldiani: Recensione e collazione dei testimoni a stampa* (Florence: Olschki, 1982)

Bianconi, Lorenzo, 'Die pastorale Szene in Metastasios *Olimpiade*', in *Kongreßbericht Gesellschaft für Musikforschung Bonn 1970* (Kassel, etc.: Bärenreiter, 1971), pp. 185–91

Bianconi, Lorenzo, 'Funktionen des Operntheaters in Neapel bis 1700 und die Rolle Alessandro Scarlattis', in *Colloquium Alessandro Scarlatti Würzburg 1975*, ed. by

W. Osthoff and J. Ruile-Dronke (Tutzing: Schneider, 1979), pp. 91–116

Bianconi, Lorenzo, and Morelli, G. (eds), *Antonio Vivaldi: Teatro musicale, cultura e società*, 2 vols (Florence: Olschki, 1982)

Bianconi, Lorenzo, and Pestelli, G. (eds), *Storia dell'opera italiana*, vols 2, 4–6 (Turin: EdT, 1987–8)

Bianconi, Lorenzo, and Walker, Thomas, 'Production, consumption and political function of seventeenth-century Italian opera', *Early Music History* 4 (Cambridge, 1984), pp. 209–96

Binni, Walter, *L'Arcadia e il Metastasio* (Florence, 1963)

Boyd, Malcolm, *Domenico Scarlatti – Master of Music* (London: Weidenfeld, 1986)

Brockpähler, Renate, *Handbuch zur Geschichte der Barockoper in Deutschland* (Emsdetten, 1964)

Brosses, Charles de, *Lettres familières sur l'Italie (1739–40)*, ed. by Yvonne Bézard, 2 vols (Paris, 1931)

Brown, Howard M., and Weimer, Eric (eds), *Italian Opera 1640–1770*, facs. edn, 60 vols (New York: Garland, Inc., 1977ff.)

Buelow, George J., 'Rhetoric and Music', in *The New Grove Dictionary of Music and Musicians*, ed. by S. Sadie (London: Macmillan, 1980), vol. 15, pp. 793–803

Buelow, George J., 'Mattheson's Concept of "Moduli" as a Clue to Handel's Compositional Process', *Göttinger Händel-Beiträge* 3 (1987), pp. 272–8

Burney, Charles, *Memoirs of the Life and Writings of the Abate Metastasio* (London, 1796)

Cagli, Bruno (ed.), *Le Muse galanti: La musica a Roma nel Settecento* (Rome: Istituto della Enciclopedia Italiana, 1985)

Cagli, Bruno, 'Produzione musicale e governo pontificio', in *Le Muse galanti*, ed. by B. Cagli, 1985, pp. 11–21

Carli Ballola, Giovanni, 'Mozart e l'opera seria di Jommelli, de Majo e Traetta', in *Colloquium 'Mozart und Italien'*, ed. by F. Lippmann, 1978, pp. 138–47

Caruso, Carlo, 'Italian Opera Libretti 1679–1721: Universality and Flexibility of a Literary Genre', in *Alessandro Scarlatti und seine Zeit*, ed. by M. Lütolf, 1995, pp. 21–37

Celletti, Rodolfo, *Storia del Belcanto* (Fiesole: Discanto, 1983)

Celletti, Rodolfo, 'I cantanti a Roma nel XVIII secolo', in *Le muse galanti*, ed. by B. Cagli, pp. 101–7

Clausen, Hans Dieter, 'Der Einfluß der Komponisten auf die Librettowahl der Royal Academy of Music (1720–1729)', in *Zur Dramaturgie der Barockoper: Bericht über die Symposien 1992 und 1993*, ed. by Hans Joachim Marx (Laaber, 1994) (Veröffentlichungen der Internationalen Händel-Akademie, vol. 5), pp. 55–72

Collins, Michael, and Kirk, Elise K. (eds), *Opera and Vivaldi* (Austin: University of Texas Press, 1984)

Colzani, Alberto, Dubowy, Norbert, et al. (eds), *Il melodramma italiano in Italia e in Germania nell'età barocca / Die italienische Barockoper, ihre Verbreitung in Italien und Deutschland (Atti del convegno, Loveno di Menaggio, 1993)* (Como: A.M.I.S., 1995)

Corneille, Pierre, 'Trois discours sur le poème dramatique (1660)', in P. Corneille, *Œuvres complètes*, vol. iii, ed. by Georges Couton (Paris: Gallimard, 1987), pp. 117–90

Cross, Eric, *The Late Operas of Antonio Vivaldi 1727–1738*, 2 vols (Ann Arbor: UMI research press, 1981)

Cross, Eric, 'Text and Music in Vivaldi's Operas', in *Opera and Vivaldi*, ed. by M. Collins and E. Kirk, 1984, pp. 279–307

Dahlhaus, Carl, 'Zum Affektbegriff der frühdeutschen Oper', in *Die frühdeutsche Oper*, ed. by C. Floros et al., 1981, pp. 107–111

Dahlhaus, Carl, 'Drammaturgia dell'opera italiana', in *Storia dell'opera italiana*, ed. by L. Bianconi and G. Pestelli, vol. 6, 1988, pp. 79–162

Dahlhaus, Carl, 'What is a Musical Drama?', *Cambridge Opera Journal* 1 (1989), pp. 95–111

Dahlhaus, Carl, et al. (eds), *Pipers Enzyklopädie des Musiktheaters*, vol. 2 (München-Zürich: Piper, 1987)

Davoli, Susi (ed.), *Civiltà teatrale e settecento emiliano* (Bologna: Mulino, 1986)

Dean, Winton, *Handel and the Opera Seria* (Berkeley and Los Angeles: University of California Press, 1969)

Dean, Winton, and Knapp, J. Merrill, *Handel's Operas 1704–1726* (Oxford: Clarendon Press, 1987)

De Angelis, Marcello, *La felicità in Etruria: Melodramma, impresari, musica, virtuosi: lo spettacolo nella Firenze dei Lorena* (Florence: Ponte alle Grazie, 1990)

Degrada, Francesco, 'Giuseppe Riva e il suo *Avviso ai compositori ed ai cantanti*', *Studien zur italienisch-deutschen Musikgeschichte* 4 (1967) (Analecta musicologica, vol. 4), pp. 112–32

Degrada, Francesco, 'L'opera napoletana fra Seicento e Settecento', in *Storia dell'Opera*, ed. by Guglielmo Barblan and Alberto Basso (Turin: UTET, 1977), vol. i/1 (*L'Opera in Italia*), pp. 237–332

Degrada, Francesco, *Il palazzo incantato: Studi sulla tradizione del melodramma dal Barocco al Romanticismo* I (Fiesole: Discanto, 1979)

Degrada, Francesco, 'Una sconosciuta esperienza teatrale di Domenico Scarlatti: *La Dirindina*', in F. Degrada, *Il palazzo incantato*, 1979, pp. 67–97

Degrada, Francesco, 'Aspetti gluckiani nell'ultimo Hasse', in F. Degrada, *Il palazzo incantato*, 1979, pp. 133–53

Degrada, Francesco, and Muraro, M. T. (eds), *Antonio Vivaldi da Venezia all'Europa* (Milan: Electa, 1978)

Della Seta, Fabrizio, 'Il librettista', in *Storia dell'opera italiana*, ed. by L. Bianconi and G. Pestelli, vol. 4, 1987, pp. 231–91

Della Seta, Fabrizio, and Piperno, Franco (eds), *Francesco Gasparini (1661–1727): Atti del Primo Convegno Internazionale 1978* (Florence: Olschki, 1981)

Delogu, Maria, 'La clemenza di Tito tra Metastasio e Mozart', in *Metastasio e il melodramma*, ed. by E. Sala Di Felice and L. Sannia Nowé, 1985, pp. 131–60

Dent, Edward J., *Alessandro Scarlatti: His Life and Works* (London, 1905), rev. edn by Frank Walker (London, 1960)

Döhring, Sieghart, 'Das Hasse-Bild Rudolf Gerbers: Zur Geschichte der deutschen Seria-Rezeption', in *Colloquium 'Johann Adolf Hasse'*, ed. by F. Lippmann, 1987, pp. 67–77

Durante, Sergio, 'Il cantante', in *Storia dell'opera italiana*, ed. by L. Bianconi and G. Pestelli, vol. 4, 1987, pp. 349–415

Durante, Sergio, 'Alcune considerazioni sui cantanti di teatro del primo settecento e la loro formazione', in *Antonio Vivaldi*, ed. by L. Bianconi and G. Morelli, 1982, vol. 2, pp. 427–81

Durante, Sergio, 'Strutture mentali e vocabolario di un cantore antico/moderno', in *Alessandro Scarlatti und seine Zeit*, ed. by M. Lütolf, 1995, pp. 38–54

Eisenschmidt, Joachim, *Die szenische Darstellung der Opern Händels auf der Londoner Bühne seiner Zeit*, 2 vols (Wolfenbüttel and Berlin, 1940)

Fabbri, Paolo, 'Istituti metrici e formali', in *Storia dell'opera italiana*, ed. by L. Bianconi and G. Pestelli, vol. 6, 1988, pp. 165–233

Fanna, Antonio, and Morelli, Giovanni (eds), *Nuovi studi vivaldiani: Edizione e cronologia critica delle opere*, 2 vols (Florence: Olschki, 1988)

Faustini-Fasini, Eugenio, 'Gli astri maggiori del "bel canto" Napoletano', *Note d'Archivio* 12 (1935), pp. 297–316

Fenlon, Iain, and Carter, Tim (eds), *Con che soavità: Studies in Italian Opera, Song, and Dance, 1580–1740* (Essays Dedicated to Nigel Fortune) (Oxford: Clarendon Press, 1995)

Ferrari, G., et al., 'L'organizzazione teatrale parmense all'epoca del Du Tillot: i rapporti fra la corte e gli impresari', in *Civiltà teatrale*, ed. by S. Davoli, 1986, pp. 357–80

Ferrari, Luigi, *Le traduzioni italiane del teatro tragico francese nei secoli XVII–XVIII* (Paris, 1925)

Fischer, Erik, *Zur Problematik der Opernstruktur: Das künstlerische System und seine Krisis im 20. Jahrhundert* (Wiesbaden: Steiner, 1982) (Beihefte zum Archiv für Musikwissenschaft, vol. 20)

Flaherty, Gloria, *Opera in the Development of German Critical Thought* (Princeton: Princeton University Press, 1978)

Florimo, Francesco, *La scuola musicale di Napoli e i suoi conservatorii*, 4 vols (Naples, 1880–3; R Bologna: Forni, 1969)

Floros, Constantin, et al. (eds), *Die frühdeutsche Oper und ihre Beziehungen zu Italien, England und Frankreich; Mozart und die Oper seiner Zeit* (Laaber, 1981) (Hamburger Jahrbuch für Musikwissenschaft, vol. 5)

Fortune, Nigel (ed.), *Music and Theatre: Studies in Honour of Winton Dean for his 70th Birthday* (Cambridge: Cambridge University Press, 1987)

Freeman, Daniel E., *The Opera Theater of Franz Anton von Sporck in Prague* (New York: Pendragon Press, 1992) (Studies in Czech Music, 2)

Freeman, Robert S., *Opera without Drama: Currents of Change in Italian Opera 1675–1725* (Ann Arbor: UMI Research Press, 1981) (Studies in Musicology, vol. 35)

Freeman, Robert S., 'The travels of Partenope', in *Studies in Music History: Essays for Oliver Strunk*, ed. by Harry S. Powers (Princeton: Princeton University Press, 1968), pp. 356–85

Freeman, Robert S., 'Farinello and His Repertory', in *Studies in Renaissance and Baroque Music in Honor of Arthur Mendel*, ed. by Robert Marshall (Kassel, etc.: Bärenreiter, 1974), pp. 301–30

Fubini, Enrico, *Music and Culture in Eighteenth-Century Europe: A Source Book*, trans. by W. Freis, L. Gasbarrone and M. L. Leone; trans. ed. by Bonnie J. Blackburn (Chicago-London: University of Chicago Press, 1994)

Fubini, Enrico, 'Razionalità e irrazionalità in Metastasio', in *Metastasio e il melodramma*, ed. by E. Sala di Felice and L. Sannia Nowé, pp. 39–53

Gallarati, Paolo, 'Zeno e Metastasio tra melodramma e tragedia', in *Metastasio e il melodramma*, ed. by E. Sala di Felice and L. Sannia Nowé, 1985, pp. 89–104

Gallarati, Paolo, *Musica e maschera: Il libretto italiano del settecento* (Turin: EdT, 1984)

Gerber, Rudolf, *Der Operntypus Johann Adolf Hasses und seine textlichen Grundlagen* (Leipzig, 1925)

Giarrizzo, Giuseppe, 'L'ideologia di Metastasio tra cartesianismo e illuminismo', in *Metastasio*, ed. by Accademia Nazionale dei Lincei, 1985, pp. 43–77

Giazotto, Remo, *Poesia melodrammatica e pensiero critico nel settecento* (Milan: Bocca, 1952)

Gibson, Elizabeth, *The Royal Academy of Music 1719–1728: The Institution and its Directors* (New York & London: Garland, Inc., 1989)

Giuntini, Francesco, *I drammi per musica di Antonio Salvi: Aspetti della 'riforma' del libretto nel primo Settecento* (Bologna: Il Mulino, 1994)

Gronda, Giovanna, 'Metastasiana', *RIdM* 19 (1984), pp. 314–32

Gronda, Giovanna, 'Per una ricognizione dei libretti di Pietro Pariati', in *Civiltà teatrale*, ed. by S. Davoli, 1986, pp. 115–36

Gronda, Giovanna, 'Varianti di un mito classico nella librettistica settecentesca', in *I vicini di Mozart*, ed. by M. T. Muraro and D. Bryant (Florence: Olschki, 1989), pp. 3–18

Gronda, Giovanna, 'Le peripezie di un libretto', in *La carriera di un librettista*, ed. by G. Gronda, 1990, pp. 289–737 [*sic*]

Gronda, Giovanna (ed.), *La carriera di un librettista: Pietro Pariati da Reggio di Lombardia* (Bologna: Il Mulino, 1990)

Gronda, Giovanna, 'Das Arianna-Libretto und seine Vorlagen', in *Gattungskonventionen der Händel-Oper*, ed. by H. J. Marx, 1992, pp. 139–57

Grout, Donald J., *A Short History of Opera* (New York-London, 1947), 2nd, rev. edn, 2 vols (New York, 1965)

Guccini, G., 'Direzione scenica e regía', in *Storia dell'opera italiana*, ed. by L. Bianconi and G. Pestelli, vol. 5, 1988, pp. 123–73

Harris, Ellen T., *Handel and the Pastoral Tradition* (London: Oxford University Press, 1980)

Harris, Ellen T., *The Librettos of Handel's Operas*, facsimile edn with introductions, 13 vols (New York: Garland , Inc., 1989)

Heartz, Daniel, 'Approaching a History of 18th-Century Music', *Current Musicology* 9 (1969), pp. 92–5

Heartz, Daniel, 'Opera and the Periodization of Eighteenth-Century Music', in *IMS 10th*

Congress Report Ljubljana 1967 (Kassel, etc.: Bärenreiter, 1970), pp. 160–8

Heartz, Daniel, 'Mozart's Overture to *Titus* as Dramatic Argument', *MQ* 64 (1978), pp. 29–49

Heartz, Daniel, 'Hasse, Galuppi, and Metastasio', in *Venezia e il melodramma del Settecento* [I], ed. by M. T. Muraro (Florence: Olschki, 1978), pp. 309–39

Heartz, Daniel, 'From Garrick to Gluck: The Reform of Theatre and Opera in the Mid-eighteenth Century', *Proceedings of the Royal Musical Association* 94 (1967–8), pp. 111–27

Heinichen, Johann David, *Der Generalbaß in der Komposition* (Dresden, 1728)

Henze, Sabine, 'Opera seria am kurpfälzischen Hofe: Traettas *Sofonisba*, de Majos *Ifigenia in Tauride*, Bachs *Temistocle*', in *Mannheim und Italien*, ed. by R. Würtz, 1984, pp. 78–96

Henze-Döhring, Sabine, 'Die *Attilio Regolo* – Vertonungen Hasses und Jommellis – ein Vergleich', in F. Lippmann (Hrsg.), *Colloquium 'Johann Adolf Hasse'*, 1987, pp. 131–58

Henze-Döhring, Sabine, 'Zur Gattungstradition von Händels *Ariodante*', in *Gattungs-konventionen*, ed. by H. J. Marx, 1992, pp. 39–62

Hill, John Walter, 'Vivaldi's *Ottone in Villa*', in (Domenico Lalli-) Antonio Vivaldi, *Ottone in villa*, facs. edn, pp. vii–xxxvii

Hortschansky, Klaus, *Parodie und Entlehnung im Schaffen Chr. Willibald Glucks* (Köln: Volk, 1973)

Hortschansky, Klaus, 'Die Rezeption der Wiener Dramen Metastasios in Italien', in *Venezia e il melodramma del Settecento* [I], ed. by M. T. Muraro, 1978, pp. 407–24

Hortschansky, Klaus (ed.), *Christoph Willibald Gluck und die Opernreform* (Darmstadt: Wissenschaftliche Buchgesellschaft, 1989) (Wege der Forschung, vol. 613)

Hucke, Helmut, 'L'*Achille in Sciro* di Domenico Sarri e l'inaugurazione del Teatro di San Carlo', in *Il teatro di San Carlo 1737–1987: L'opera, il ballo*, ed. by B. Cagli and A. Ziino (Naples: Electa, 1987), pp. 21–32

Hucke, Helmut, and Downes, Edward O. D., 'Die neapolitanische Tradition in der Oper / The Neapolitan Tradition in Opera', in *IMS 8th Congress Report New York 1961*, 2 vols (Kassel, etc.: Bärenreiter, 1961), vol. 1, pp. 253–84, and vol. 2, pp. 132–4

Joly, Jacques, *Les fêtes théâtrales de Métastase à la cour de Vienne (1731–67)* (Clermont Ferrand: Presses de l'Université II, 1978)

Joly, Jacques, 'Metastasio e le sintesi della contraddizione', in J. Joly, *Dagli Elisi all'Inferno*, pp. 11–83

Joly, Jacques, 'Le didascalie per la recitazione nei drammi del Metastasio', in *Metastasio*, ed. by Accademia Nazionale dei Lincei, pp. 277–91, also in: J. Joly, *Dagli Elisi all'Inferno*, pp. 95–111

Joly, Jacques, 'Un'ideologia del sovrano virtuoso', in J. Joly, *Dagli Elisi all'Inferno*, pp. 84–94

Joly, Jacques, *Dagli Elisi all'Inferno: Il melodramma tra Italia e Francia dal 1730 al 1850* (Florence: La Nuova Italia, 1990)

Junker, Hermann, 'Zwei Griselda-Opern', in *Festschrift Adolf Sandberger* (Munich , 1918), pp. 51–64

Kanduth, Erika, 'Silvio Stampiglia, poeta Cesareo', in *L'Opera italiana a Vienna*, ed. by M. T. Muraro, pp. 43–63

Krause, Christian Gottfried, *Von der musikalischen Poesie* (Berlin, 1752)

Kropfinger, Klaus, 'Vivaldi as Self-Borrower', in *Opera and Vivaldi*, ed. by M. Collins and E. Kirk, 1984, pp. 308–26

Kubik, Reinhold, *Händels Rinaldo: Geschichte, Werk, Wirkung* (Neuhausen-Stuttgart: Hänssler, 1982)

Kunze, Stefan, 'Die Vertonungen der Arie "Non sò donde viene" von J. Chr. Bach und W. A. Mozart', in *Studien zur italienisch-deutschen Musikgeschichte II*, ed. by Helmut Hucke (Cologne-Graz: Böhlau, 1965) (Analecta Musicologica, vol. 2), pp. 85–111

Kunze, Stefan, 'Die Opera seria und ihr Zeitalter', in *Colloquium 'Johann Adolf Hasse'*, ed. by F. Lippmann, 1987, pp. 1–15

Kunze, Stefan, 'Szenische Aspekte in Händels Opernmusik', in *Händel auf dem Theater: Bericht über die Symposien der Internationalen Händel-Akademie Karlsruhe 1986 und 1987*, ed. by H. J. Marx (Laaber, 1988), pp. 181–92

Kuzmick Hansell, Kathleen, 'Il ballo teatrale e l'opera italiana', in *Storia dell'opera italiana*, ed. by L. Bianconi and G. Pestelli, vol. 5, 1988, pp. 175–306

Landmann, Ortrun, 'Italienische Opernpraxis in Dresden', in *Il melodramma italiano*, ed. by A. Colzani, N. Dubowy et al., pp. 23–30

Leich, Karl, *Girolamo Frigimelica Robertis Libretti: Ein Beitrag insbesondere zur Geschichte des Opernlibrettos in Venedig* (Munich: Katzbichler, 1972) (Schriften zur Musik, 26)

Lenneberg, Hans H., 'Johann Mattheson on Affekt and Rhetoric in Music', *Journal of Music Theory* 2 (1958), pp. 47–84, 193–236

Leopold, Silke, 'Feinds und Keisers *Masagniello furioso*: Eine politische Oper?', in *Die frühdeutsche Oper*, ed. by C. Floros et al., 1981, pp. 55–68

Lindgren, Lowell, *A Bibliographic Scrutiny of Dramatic Works Set by Giovanni and His Brother Antonio Maria Bononcini*, Ph. D. Harvard University, 1972 (Ann Arbor: UMI, 74–25, 641)

Lindgren, Lowell, 'La carriera di Gaetano Berenstadt, contralto evirato (ca. 1690–1735)', in *Rivista Italiana di Musicologia* 19 (1984), pp. 36–112

Lindgren, Lowell, 'Il dramma musicale a Roma durante la carriera di Alessandro Scarlatti (1660–1725)', in *Le Muse galanti*, ed. by B. Cagli, pp. 35–57

Lindgren, Lowell, 'The Staging of Handel's Operas in London', in *Handel. Tercentenary Collection*, ed. by A. Hicks and S. Sadie (London: Macmillan, 1987), pp. 93–119

Lindgren, Lowell, 'Critiques of Opera in London, 1705–1719', in *Il melodramma italiano*, ed. by A. Colzani, N. Dubowy et al., 1995, pp. 145–65

Lippmann, Friedrich (ed.), *Colloquium 'Mozart und Italien' (Rom 1974)* (Cologne: Volk, 1978) (Analecta Musicologica, vol. 18)

Lippmann, Friedrich (ed.), *Colloquium 'Johann Adolf Hasse und die Musik seiner Zeit' (Siena 1983)* (Laaber, 1987) (Analecta Musicologica, vol. 25)

Lippmann, Friedrich, 'Hasses Arienstil und seine Interpretation durch Rudolf Gerber', in *Colloquium 'Johann Adolf Hasse'*, ed. by F. Lippmann, 1987, pp. 17–65

Lühning, Helga, '*Titus'-Vertonungen im 18. Jahrhundert: Untersuchungen zur Tradition der Opera seria von Hasse bis Mozart* (Laaber: Arno Volk – Laaber Verlag, 1983) (Analecta Musicologica, 20)

Lühning, Helga, 'Cosroes Verzweiflung. Regel und Erfindung in Hasses Seria-Arien', in *Colloquium 'Johann Adolf Hasse'*, ed. by F. Lippmann, 1987, pp. 79–130

Lütolf, Max (ed.), *Alessandro Scarlatti und seine Zeit* (Berne: Haupt, 1995)

Maffei, Scipione, *De' teatri antichi e moderni e altri scritti teatrali*, ed. by Laura Sannia Nowé (Modena: Mucchi, 1988)

Mamy, Sylvie, 'La diaspora dei cantanti veneziani nella prima metà del Settecento', in *Nuovi studi vivaldiani*, ed. by A. Fanna and G. Morelli, vol. 2, pp. 591–631

Mangini, Nicola, *I teatri di Venezia* (Milan, 1974)

Mangini, Nicola, 'I teatri Veneziani al tempo della collaborazione di Galuppi con Goldoni', in *Galuppiana 1985*, ed. by M. T. Muraro and F. Rossi, pp. 133–42 (Florence, 1986).

Marcello, Benedetto, *Il teatro alla moda* (Venice: Pinelli, 1720), ed. by Andrea d'Angeli (Milan, 1927)

Marcialis, Maria Teresa, 'Il melodramma o le trasgressioni della tragedia', in *Metastasio e il melodramma*, ed. by E. Sala di Felice and L. Sannia Nowé, 1985, pp. 225–46

Markstrom, Kurt Sven, 'The Operas of Leonardo Vinci, Napoletano', PhD diss. (Graduate Department of Music, University of Toronto, 1993)

Martello, Pier Jacopo, *Della tragedia antica e moderna* (Rome, 1715), in P. J. Martello, *Scritti critici e satirici*, ed. by Hannibal S. Noce (Bari: Laterza, 1963)

Marx, Hans Joachim, 'Geschichte der Hamburger Barockoper: Ein Forschungsbericht', *Hamburger Jahrbuch für Musikwissenschaft* 3 (1978), pp. 7–34

Marx, Hans Joachim, 'Politische und wirtschaftliche Voraussetzungen der Hamburger Barockoper', in *Die frühdeutsche Oper*, ed. by C. Floros et al., 1981, pp. 81–8

Marx, Hans Joachim (ed.), *Gattungskonventionen der Händel-Oper: Bericht über die Symposien 1990 und 1991* (Laaber, 1992) (Veröffentlichungen der Internationalen Händel-Akademie, vol. 4)

Marx, Hans Joachim (ed.), *Zur Dramaturgie der Barockoper: Bericht über die Symposien 1992 und 1993* (Laaber, 1994) (Veröffentlichungen der Internationalen Händel-Akademie, vol. 5)

Mattheson, Johann, *Die neueste Untersuchung der Singspiele* (Hamburg, 1744)

McCleave, Sarah Y., 'Dance in Handel's Italian Operas: The Collaboration with Marie Sallé', unpubl. PhD Diss. (King's College, University of London, 1993)

McClymonds, Marita P., 'Mattia Verazi and the Opera at Mannheim, Stuttgart, and Ludwigsburg', in *Crosscurrents and the Mainstream in Italian Serious Opera, 1730–1790*, ed. by Don J. Neville, 2 vols (London, Ontario: Faculty of Music, 1982) (= *Studies in Music from the Unversity of Western Ontario*, 7/1–2), pp. 99–136

McClymonds, Marita P., 'Haydn and the Opera Seria Tradition: *Armida*', in *Napoli e il teatro musicale*, ed. by B. M. Antolini and W. Witzenmann, 1993, pp. 191–206

McClymonds, Marita P., and Heartz, D, 'Opera seria', in *The New Grove Dictionary of Opera*, ed. by S. Sadie (London: Macmillan, 1992), vol. 3, pp. 698–707

Messina, Costantino, et al., *Sogni e favole io fingo: Teatro pubblico e melodramma a Roma all'epoca di Metastasio* (Exhibition Catalogue, Rome, Palazzo Venezia, 1983–4) (Rome: Ministero per i beni culturali e ambientali, 1983)

Metastasio, Pietro, 'Estratto dell'arte poetica d'Aristotile e considerazioni su la medesima' (1773), in P. Metastasio, *Tutte le opere*, vol . 2 (Milan, 1965), pp. 957–1117

Metastasio, Pietro, *Tutte le opere*, ed. by Bruno Brunelli, 5 vols, 2nd edn (Milan: Mondadori, 1953–65)

Millner, Frederick L., *The Operas of Johann Adolf Hasse* (Ann Arbor: UMI research press, 1979)

Mioli, Piero, ' "Non più reggina, ma pastorella": Sulla drammaturgia vocale medio e tardo-barocca nella *Griselda*, da Scarlatti a Vivaldi', in *Nuovi studi vivaldiani*, ed. by A. Fanna and G. Morelli, vol. 1, pp. 83–116

Monelle, Raymond, 'Gluck and the Festa Teatrale', *Music & Letters* 54 (1973), pp. 308–25

Monelle, Raymond, 'The Rehabilitation of Metastasio', *Music & Letters* 57 (1976), pp. 268–91

Monelle, Raymond, 'Recitative and Dramaturgy in the Dramma per Musica', *Music & Letters* 59 (1978), pp. 245–67

Müller von Asow, Erich H., *Die Mingottischen Opernunternehmungen 1732 bis 1756* (Dresden: Hille, 1915); 2nd edn as *Angelo und Pietro Mingotti: Ein Beitrag zur Geschichte der Oper im XVIII. Jahrhundert* (Dresden: Bertling, 1917)

Muraro, Maria Teresa (ed.), *Venezia e il melodramma del Settecento* [I] (Florence: Olschki, 1978)

Muraro, Maria Teresa (ed.), *Venezia e il melodramma del Settecento* [II] (Florence: Olschki, 1981)

Muraro, Maria Teresa (ed.), *L'Opera italiana a Vienna prima del Metastasio* (Florence: Olschki, 1990)

Muresu, Gabriele, 'Metastasio e la tradizione poetica italiana', in *Metastasio*, ed. by Accademia Nazionale dei Lincei, pp. 111–46

Neville, Don J. (ed.), *Crosscurrents and the Mainstream of Italian Serious Opera, 1730–1790*, 2 vols (London (Ontario): Department of Music History, 1982) (Studies in Music, 7, vols 1/2, 1982)

Neville, Don J., 'Moral Philosophy in the Metastasian Dramas', in *Crosscurrents and the Mainstream*, ed. by D. J. Neville, 1982, pp. 28–46

Osthoff, Wolfgang, 'Zur musikalischen Tradition der tragischen Gattung im italienischen Theater (16.–18. Jahrhundert)', in *Studien zur Tradition in der Musik. Festschrift Kurt von Fischer zum 60. Geburtstag*, ed. by Hans Heinrich Eggebrecht and Max Lütolf (Munich: Katzbichler, 1973) pp. 121–43

Osthoff, Wolfgang, '*Attilio Regolo*: Metastasios musikdramatische Konzeptionen und Hasses Ausführung', in *Dresdener Operntraditionen* (Dresden, 1986), pp. 147–73

Pagano, Roberto, *Scarlatti Alessandro e Domenico: due vite in una* (Milano: Mondadori, 1985)

Pagano, Roberto, Bianchi, Lino, and Rostirolla, Giancarlo, *Alessandro Scarlatti* (Turin: ERI, 1972)

Paratore, Ettore, 'L'*Andromaque* del Racine e la *Didone abbandonata* del Metastasio', in *Scritti in onore di Luigi Ronga* (Milan: Ricciardi, 1973), pp. 515–47

Petrocchi, Giorgio (ed.), *Orfeo in Arcadia: Studi sul Teatro a Roma nel Settecento* (Rome: Istituto della Enciclopedia Italiana, 1984)

Petrocchi, Giorgio, 'Un melodramma romano del Metastasio' [i.e. *Catone in Utica*], in *Orfeo in Arcadia: Studi sul Teatro a Roma nel Settecento*, ed. by G. Petrocchi, 1984, pp. 39–46

Piperno, Franco, 'Buffe e buffi (Considerazioni sulla professionalità degli interpreti di scene buffe ed intermezzi)', *RIdM* 18 (1982), pp. 240–84

Piperno, Franco,'Impresariato collettivo e strategie teatrali: Sul sistema produttivo dello spettacolo operistico settecentesco', in *Civiltà teatrale*, ed. by S. Davoli, 1986, pp. 345–65

Piperno, Franco, 'Il sistema produttivo, fino al 1780', in *Storia dell'opera italiana*, ed. by L. Bianconi and G. Pestelli, vol. 4, 1987, pp. 1–75

Piperno, Franco, 'Venezia e Vienna: Produzione e circolazione dello spettacolo operistico', in *L'Opera italiana a Vienna*, ed. by M. T. Muraro, 1990, pp. 115–25

Pirrotta, Nino, and Ziino, Agostino (eds), *Händel e gli Scarlatti a Roma: Atti del convegno internazionale di studi, Roma 1985* (Florence: Olschki, 1987)

Planelli, Antonio, *Dell'opera in musica* (Naples, 1772, R Fiesole: Discanto, 1981)

Prota-Giurleo, Ulisse, 'Leonardo Vinci', *Il Convegno musicale* 2 (1965), pp. 3–11

Quadrio, Francesco Saverio, *Della storia e della ragione d'ogni poesia*, 5 vols (Bologna and Milan, 1741–52)

Questa, Cesare, *Semiramide redenta* (Urbino: Quattro Venti, 1989)

Raguenet, François, *Parallèle des Italiens et des François en ce qui regarde la musique et les opéra* (Paris: Moreau, 1702)

Reimer, Erich, *Die Hofmusik in Deutschland, 1500–1800* (Wilhelmshaven: Noetzel, 1991)

Roberts, John H., 'Handel's and Jennens's Italian opera manuscripts', in *Music and Theatre*, ed. by N. Fortune, 1987, pp. 159–202

Robinson, Michael, *Naples and Neapolitan Opera* (Oxford: Clarendon Press, 1972)

Rolandi, Ulderico, *Il libretto per musica attraverso i tempi* (Rome, 1951)

Rosselli, John, *The Opera Industry in Italy from Cimarosa to Verdi* (Cambridge: Cambridge University Press, 1984)

Rosselli, John, 'The Castrati as a Professional Group and a Social Phenomenon, 1550–1850', *Acta Musicologica* 60 (1988), pp. 143–79

Rosselli, John, *Singers of Italian Opera: The History of a Profession* (Cambridge: Cambridge University Press, 1992)

Ruhnke, Martin, 'Zum Rezitativ der Opera seria vor Hasse', in *Colloquium 'Johann Adolf Hasse'*, ed. by F. Lippmann, 1987, pp. 159–86

Sala Di Felice, Elena, 'L'arbitro dei destini: Ideologia e drammaturgia in Metastasio', in E. Sala Di Felice, *Metastasio*, pp. 149–68

Sala Di Felice, Elena, *Metastasio: Ideologia, drammaturgia, spettacolo* (Milan: Franco Angeli, 1983)

Sala Di Felice, Elena, 'L'*Ezio* di Metastasio', in *Orfeo in Arcadia*, ed. by G. Petrocchi, 1984, pp. 47–62

Sala Di Felice, Elena, 'Virtù e felicità alla corte di Vienna', in *Metastasio e il melodramma*, ed. by E. Sala Di Felice and L. Sannia Nowé, 1985, pp. 55–87

Sala Di Felice, Elena, 'Alla vigilia del Metastasio: Zeno', in *Metastasio*, ed. by Accademia Nazionale dei Lincei, pp. 79–109

Sala Di Felice, Elena, 'Zeno da Venezia a Vienna: Dal teatro impresariale al teatro di corte', in *L'Opera italiana a Vienna*, ed. by M. T. Muraro, pp. 65–114

Sala Di Felice, Elena, and Sannia Nowé Laura (eds), *Metastasio e il melodramma* (Padua: Liviana Editrice, 1985)

Sannia Nowé, Laura, 'Una voce sul melodramma nelle discussioni del primo settecento (S. Maffei)', in *Metastasio e il melodramma*, ed. by E. Sala Di Felice and L. Sannia Nowé,

1985, pp. 247–70

Sartori, Claudio, *I libretti italiani a stampa dalle origini al 1800*, 6 vols (Cuneo: Bertola & Locatelli, 1993)

Scheibe, Johann Adolph, *Critischer Musicus* (Leipzig, 1745)

Scherer, Jacques, *La dramaturgie classique en France* (Paris: Nizet, 1950)

Selfridge-Field, Eleanor, 'Marcello, Sant'Angelo and *Il Teatro alla Moda*', in *Antonio Vivaldi*, ed. by L. Bianconi and G. Morelli, 1982, vol. 2, pp. 533–46

Selfridge-Field, Eleanor, 'Opera Criticism and the Venetian Press', in *Opera and Vivaldi*, ed. by M. Collins and E. Kirk, 1984, pp. 179–90

Selfridge-Field, Eleanor, *Pallade Veneta: Writings on Music in Venetian Society 1650–1750* (Venice: Fondazione Levi, 1985)

Smith, Patrick J., *The Tenth Muse: A Historical Study of the Opera Libretto* (London, 1971)

Sonneck, Oscar G. T., 'Die drei Fassungen des Hasseschen *Artaserse*', *Sammelbände der Internationalen Musikgesellschaft* 14 (1912–13), 226–42

Strohm, Reinhard, 'Hasse, Scarlatti, Rolli', *Studien zur italienisch-deutschen Musikgeschichte* 10 (Cologne, 1975) (Analecta Musicologica, 15), pp. 220–57

Strohm, Reinhard, *Italienische Opernarien des frühen Settecento (1720–1730)*, 2 vols (Cologne: Volk, 1976) (Analecta Musicologica, 16)

Strohm, Reinhard, *Die italienische Oper im 18. Jahrhundert* (Wilhelmshaven: Heinrichshofen, 1979)

Strohm, Reinhard, 'Die *tragedia per musica* als Repertoirestück: Zwei Hamburger Opern von G. M. Orlandini', in *Die frühdeutsche Oper*, ed. by C. Floros et al., pp. 37–54

Strohm, Reinhard, 'Aspetti sociali dell'opera italiana del primo Settecento', *Musica/Realtà* 2 (1981), pp. 117–41

Strohm, Reinhard, 'Vivaldi's Career as an Opera Producer', in *Antonio Vivaldi*, ed. by L. Bianconi and G. Morelli, 1982, vol. 1, pp. 11–63 (also in R. Strohm, *Essays*, pp. 122–63)

Strohm, Reinhard, *Essays on Handel and Italian Opera* (Cambridge: Cambridge University Press, 1985)

Strohm, Reinhard, 'Handel's pasticci', in R. Strohm, *Essays on Handel*, 1985, pp. 164–211

Strohm, Reinhard, 'Leonardo Vinci's *Didone abbandonata* (Rome 1726)', in R. Strohm, *Essays on Handel*, 1985, pp. 213–24

Strohm, Reinhard, 'Metastasio's *Alessandro nell'Indie* and its earliest settings', in R. Strohm, *Essays on Handel*, 1985, pp. 232–48

Strohm, Reinhard, 'Vivaldi's and Handel's settings of *Giustino*', in *Music and Theatre*, ed. by N. Fortune, 1987, pp. 131–58

Strohm, Reinhard, 'Johann Adolf Hasses Oper *Cleofide* und ihre Vorgeschichte', in *Johann Sebastian Bachs Spätwerk und dessen Umfeld*, ed. by C. Wolff, 1988, pp. 170–6

Strohm, Reinhard, 'Tradition und Fortschritt in der Opera seria', in *Christoph Willibald Gluck und die Opernreform*, ed. by K. Hortschansky, 1989, pp. 325–52

Strohm, Reinhard, 'Scarlattiana at Yale', in *Händel e gli Scarlatti a Roma*, ed. by N. Pirrotta and A. Ziino, 1987, pp. 113–52

Strohm, Reinhard, 'The Critical Edition of Vivaldi's *Giustino* (1724)', in *Nuovi studi vivaldiani*, ed. by A. Fanna and G. Morelli, 1988, vol. 1, pp. 399–415

Strohm, Reinhard, 'Auf der Suche nach dem Drama im "Dramma per musica": die Bedeutung der französischen Tragödie', in *De Musica et Cantu: Studien zur Geschichte der Kirchenmusik und Oper Helmut Hucke zum 60. Geburtstag*, ed. by Peter Cahn and Ann-Katrin Heimer (Hildesheim: Olms, 1993), pp. 481–93

Strohm, Reinhard, 'Händel und Italien – ein intellektuelles Abenteuer', *Göttinger Händel-Beiträge* 5 (1993), pp. 5–43

Strohm, Reinhard, 'Wien und die mitteleuropäische Opernpflege der Aufklärungszeit', in *Europa im Zeitalter Mozarts*, ed. by Moritz Csáky and Walter Pass (Vienna, etc.: Böhlau, 1995), pp. 391–6

Surian, Elvidio, 'Metastasio, i nuovi cantanti, il nuovo stile: verso il classicismo', in *Venezia e il melodramma del Settecento* [I], ed. by M. T. Muraro, 1978, pp. 341–62

Surian, Elvidio, 'L'operista', in *Storia dell'opera italiana*, ed. by L. Bianconi and G. Pestelli, vol. 4, 1987, pp. 293–345

Talbot, Michael, *Vivaldi*, 2nd edn (London: Dent, 1993)

Talbot, Michael, 'Vivaldi and the Empire', *Informazioni e Studi Vivaldiani* 8 (1987), pp. 31–50

Talbot, Michael, *Tomaso Albinoni: The Venetian Composer and His World* (Oxford: Clarendon Press, 1990)

Termini, Olga, 'From *Ariodante* to *Ariodante*', in Carlo Francesco Pollarolo, *Ariodante*, introduction, pp. ix–lxxiv

Termini, Olga, 'The Role of Diction and Gesture in Italian Baroque Opera', *Performance Practice Review* 6 (1993), pp. 146–57

Timms, Colin, 'George I's Venetian palace and theatre boxes in the 1720s', in *Music and Theatre*, ed. by N. Fortune, pp. 95–130

Viale Ferrero, Mercedes, *Filippo Juvarra scenografo e architetto teatrale* (Turin: Pozzo, 1970)

Viale Ferrero, Mercedes, 'Antonio e Pietro Ottoboni e alcuni melodrammi da loro ideati o promossi a Roma', in *Venezia e il melodramma nel Settecento* [I], ed. by M. T. Muraro, 1978, pp. 271–94

Viale Ferrero, Mercedes, 'Scene di Filippo Juvarra per il *Lucio Papirio* di Francesco Gasparini (Roma, Teatro Capranica, 1713–1714)', in *Francesco Gasparini*, ed. by F. Della Seta and F. Piperno, 1981, pp. 245–57

Viale Ferrero, Mercedes, 'Luogo teatrale e spazio scenico', in *Storia dell'opera italiana*, ed. by L. Bianconi and G. Pestelli, vol. 5, 1988, pp. 1–122

Viale Ferrero, Mercedes, 'Le didascalie sceniche nei drammi per musica di Zeno', in *L'Opera italiana a Vienna*, ed. by M. T. Muraro, 1990, pp. 271–85

Viale Ferrero, Mercedes, 'Scenotecnica e macchine al tempo di Alessandro Scarlatti', in *Alessandro Scarlatti und seine Zeit* , ed. by M. Lütolf, 1993, pp. 55–77

Villatico, Dino, 'In margine al *Demetrio* di Metastasio: fonti francesi del melodramma metastasiano', in *Nuovi studi vivaldiani*, ed. by A. Fanna and G. Morelli, 1988, vol. 1, pp. 273–84

Weimer, Eric, *Opera seria and the Evolution of Classical Style 1755–1772* (Ann Arbor: UMI Research Press, 1984) (Studies in Musicology, vol. 78)

Weiss, Piero, 'Pier Jacopo Martello on Opera (1715): An Annotated Translation', *Musical Quarterly* 66 (1980), pp. 378–403

Weiss, Piero, 'Teorie drammatiche e "infranciosamento": motivi della "riforma" melodrammatica nel primo Settecento', in *Antonio Vivaldi*, ed. by L. Bianconi and G. Morelli, vol. 1, 1982, pp. 273–96

Weiss, Piero, 'Metastasio, Aristotle, and the Opera seria', *Journal of Musicology* 1 (1982), pp. 385–94; Italian version in *Metastasio e il mondo musicale*, ed. by M. T. Muraro (Florence: Olschki, 1986), pp. 1–12

Weiss, Piero, 'Neoclassical Criticism and Opera', in *Studies in the History of Music II* (New York: Broude Bros., 1984), pp. 1–30

Weiss, Piero, 'Baroque Opera and the Two Verisimilitudes', in *Music and Civilization: Essays in Honor of Paul Henry Lang* (New York, 1984), pp. 117–26

Weiss, Piero, 'La diffusione del repertorio operistico nell'Italia del settecento: il caso dell'opera buffa', in *Civiltà teatrale e settecento emiliano*, ed. by S. Davoli, 1986, pp. 241–56

Wiel, Taddeo, *I teatri musicali veneziani del settecento* (Venice, 1897), ed. by R. Strohm (Leipzig: Peters Reprints, 1979)

Wiesend, Reinhard, 'Metastasios Revisionen eigener Dramen und die Situation der Opernmusik in den 1750er Jahren', *Archiv für Musikwissenschaft* 40 (1983), pp. 255–75

Wiesend, Reinhard, *Studien zur opera seria von Baldassare Galuppi: Werksituation und Überlieferung – Form und Satztechnik – Inhaltsdarstellung*, 2 vols (Tutzing: Schneider, 1984)

Wiesend, Reinhard, 'Baldassare Galuppi fra opera seria e opera buffa', in *Galuppiana*, ed. by M. T. Muraro and F. Rossi, 1986, pp. 153–64

Wiesend, Reinhard, 'Zum Ensemble in der Opera seria', in *Colloquium 'Johann Adolf Hasse'*, ed. by F. Lippmann, 1987, pp. 187–222

Wiesend, Reinhard, 'Tonartendisposition und Rollenhierarchie in Hasses Opern', in *Colloquium 'Johann Adolf Hasse'*, ed. by F. Lippmann, 1987, pp. 223–31

Wolff, Christoph (ed.), *Johann Sebastian Bachs Spätwerk und dessen Umfeld: Bericht über das wissenschaftliche Symposion (61. Bachfest, Duisburg, 1986)* (Kassel, etc.: Bärenreiter, 1988)

Wolff, Hellmuth Christian, *Die Barockoper in Hamburg (1678–1738)*, 2 vols (Wolfenbüttel: Möseler, 1957)

Wolff, Hellmuth Christian, *Oper: Szene und Darstellung von 1600 bis 1900* (Leipzig, 1968)

Wolff, Hellmuth Christian, 'Johann Adolf Hasse und Venedig', in *Venezia e il melodramma nel Settecento* [I], ed. by M. T. Muraro, 1978, pp. 295–308

Wolff, Hellmuth Christian, 'Vivaldi und der Stil der italienischen Oper', *Acta musicologica* 40 (1968), pp. 179–86

Würtz Roland (ed.), *Mannheim und Italien – zur Vorgeschichte der Mannheimer: Bericht über das Mannheimer Kolloquium im März 1982* (Mainz: Schott, 1984)

Wynne, Shirley, 'Baroque Manners and Passions in Performance', in *Opera and Vivaldi*, ed. by M. Collins and E. Kirk, pp. 170–7

Yorke-Long, Alan, *Music at Court: Four Eighteenth-Century Studies* (London, 1954)

Zaslaw, Neal, 'When is an Orchestra not an Orchestra?', *Early Music* 16 (1988), pp. 483–90

Zechmeister, Gustav, *Die Wiener Theater nächst der Burg und nächst dem Kärntnertor von 1747 bis 1776* (Wien-Graz: Böhlau 1971) (Theatergesch. Österreichs, Bd III/2)

Zelm, Klaus, 'Die Sänger der Hamburger Gänsemarkt-Oper', *Hamburger Jahrbuch für Musikwissenschaft* 3 (1978), pp. 35–73

Zeno, Apostolo, *Lettere di Apostolo Zeno Cittadino Veneziano*, 6 vols, 2nd edn (Venice: Sansoni, 1786)

Zeno, Apostolo, *Poesie drammatiche*, 10 vols (Venice: Pasquali, 1744)

Scores

Hasse, Johann Adolf, *Siroe re di Persia*, facs. edn, in *Italian Opera, 1640–1770*, ed. by H. M. Brown and E. Weimer, vol. 33

Pergolesi, Giovanni Battista, *Adriano in Siria*, ed. by Dale Monson (New York and Milan: Pendragon Press, 1986) (Pergolesi, *Complete Works*, ed. by B. S. Brook, F. Degrada and H. Hucke, vol. 3)

Pollarolo, Carlo Francesco, *Ariodante* (Venice, 1718), facs. edn, ed. by O. Termini (Milan: Ricordi, 1986) (Drammaturgia Musicale Veneta, vol. 13)

Sarri, Domenico, *Arsace*, facs. edn, in *Italian Opera, 1640–1770*, ed. by H. M. Brown and E. Weimer, vol. 22

Scarlatti, Alessandro, *Griselda*, ed. by Donald J. Grout, in *The Operas of Alessandro Scarlatti*, vol. 3 (Cambridge/Mass.: Harvard University Press, 1975) (Harvard Publications in Music, 8)

Scarlatti, Alessandro, *La Caduta de' Decemviri*, ed. by Hermine W. Williams, in *The Operas of Alessandro Scarlatti*, ed. by D. J. Grout, vol. 6 (Cambridge/Mass.: Harvard University Press, 1980) (Harvard Publications in Music, 11)

Vinci, Leonardo, *Didone abbandonata*, facs. edn, in *Italian Opera, 1640–1770*, ed. by H. M. Brown and E. Weimer, vol. 29

Vivaldi, Antonio, *Giustino*, ed. by Reinhard Strohm, 2 vols (Milan: Ricordi, 1991) (Istituto Italiano Antonio Vivaldi)

Vivaldi, Antonio, *La Griselda*, facs. edn, in *Italian Opera, 1640–1770*, ed. by H. M. Brown and E. Weimer, vol. 35

Vivaldi, (Domenico Lalli-)Antonio, *Ottone in villa*, facs. edn (Milan: Ricordi, 1983) (Drammaturgia Musicale Veneta, vol. 12)

Index

Titles

Abdolomino 48, 273n
Achille in Sciro 41, 97, 101, 109, 110n, 108–17, 284
Acis and Galatea 256
Adelaide 102
Admeto 212
Adriano in Siria 21, 240–3 (pl. 11), 279, 284, 295
Alceste 27, 237
Alcina 256, 258, 260
Aldiso 75, 76n
Alessandro nell'Indie 18, 21, 74, 99–102, 284;
    (Corselli) 98–9; (Hasse) 79, 99–100, 278, 286;
    (Schiassi) 100; (Vinci) 99, 112
Alessandro Severo 50
Almira 263
Alonso e Cora 29
Amadigi 206
Gli amanti generosi 65
Ama più chi men si crede 2
Amare per regnare 72
Ambleto (Zeno) 35, 47–8
Amleto (Foppa) 29
Amor d'un ombra e gelosia d'un aura (Narciso) 43, 46
Amore e maestà 21, 45, 72–4, 128n, 165–91, 197 (pl.
    9), 297, 300–4
L'amor eroico tra pastori 124, 268n
L'amor tirannico 35, 42, 46, 102
Amor vince l'odio, overo Timocrate 66–7, 167
L'amor volubile e tiranno (Dorisbe) 35, 39
Anagilda 40
Andromaque (Racine) 167, 287
Angelica 72
Angelica ed Orlando 3
L'anima del filosofo (Orfeo ed Euridice) 28
Annibale 74, 79, 98
Antigona 20, 68, 167–9, 171
Antigono tutore di Filippo 169
Antiochus (T. Corneille) 167
Argeno 75–6
Argippo 49
Arianna e Teseo 73, 76, 205, 228–30
Arianna in Creta 76, 220–36, 256, 261, 266
Arianna in Nasso 76
Ariodante 167, 255–69, 264–5 (pl. 12)
Armida 28
Armide (Quinault) 175n
Arminio 20, 36, 57–9 (pl. 2a–b), 102, 167, 276n
Arminius (Campistron) 57, 167
Arsace 72–3, 168–72, 197 (pl. 9), 297
Arsilda regina di Ponto 139

Artaserse 22–3, 96, 277, 284; (Hasse) (1730) 22,
    73–4, 78–9, 98, 112, 114, 276–8, (1740) 278;
    (Vinci) 74, 78, 96, 101–2, 276–7
Ascanio in Alba (Parini) 28
Astarto 35, 47–8
Astianatte 20, 50, 167
Astinome 35, 51–2
L'Astrobolo 40
Atalanta 81, 265
Ataulfo 35, 41–2
Atenaide (Metastasio) 4
L'Atenaide (Zeno) 163n
Attalo 274
Attilio Regolo (Gigli) 40
Attilio Regolo (Metastasio) 21, 170, 274, 284–5

Bajazet (Racine) 125–33, 140–55, 162–3, 207, 300
Barilotto e Slapina 65
Berenice (Pasqualigo) 69–70
Bérénice (Racine) 18, 46
Berenice regina d'Egitto (Salvi) 35, 50–1, 167, 265
Britannicus (Racine) 276

Cajo Fabricio 280–1
Calliroë 28
Candace 100
Il carceriere di se stesso 167
Catone in Utica 10n, 15–16, 73–4, 77–8, 168–9
Le Cid (P. Corneille) 68, 131
Cimene 68
Cinna (P. Corneille) 287
Cirene 70n
Il Ciro (Ottoboni) 41
Il Ciro (Noris) 35, 49
Ciro riconosciuto 3, 284
La clemenza d'Augusto 287
La clemenza di Tito 21, 29, 60, 95, 100, 113, 170, 238,
    284–93, 289 (pl. 14)
Cleofida (Handel, *Poro*) 91
Cleofide (Hasse) 278
Le Comte d'Essex (T. Corneille) 125–33, 144, 147,
    156–60, 167, 173, 177–97, 180 (pl. 8), 295, 297–305
Le Comte d'Essex (La Calprenède) 126, 294, 297–303
El Conde de Sex (Coello) 294
Il Conte di Essex (Romani) 297, 301–4
La costanza in amor vince l'inganno 41
La costanza trionfante degli amori, e degli odii 139, 153
Crispo 35, 54–5
La critica teatrale (L'opera seria) 75

Il Dafni   3
Dalisa   79
Damiro e Pitia   75
Demetrio   18–19, 22–3, 79, 98, 101, 114, 278–80
Demofoonte   21, 100, 283–4
Didone abbandonata   21, 63, 71–4, 77, 100–1, 168–71, 173–5, 244–7
La Dirindina   25, 47–8, 174n
Don Chisciotte in Sierra Morena   3
Don Giovanni   95
Don Sanche d'Aragon (P. Corneille)   168
Dorilla in Tempe   3, 261
Dorisbe   35, 38–9, 40–1

Elfrida   27
Elisa   66
Élisabeth d'Angleterre (Ancelot)   297, 301–5
Elpidia   70, 71n
Elpina e Silvano   47
Endimione   72
Enea in Caonia   289
Engelberta   35, 39–40
Eraclea   79
Eraclio   41, 43
Ercole sul Termodonte   36
Erminia   52
Ernelinda   41n
L'Eroe Cinese   21
Etearco   52
Euristeo   79, 289
Evergete   76n
Ezio   21, 23, 73–4, 77, 79n, 275–8, 282–3, 287–90

Faramondo   19
Farnace re di Ponto   97, 100–8
La fede ne' tradimenti   19–20
La fede riconosciuta   41
La fede tradita e vendicata   20, 35, 41n, 42
Le festin de pierre (T. Corneille)   125, 131
Flavio Anicio Olibrio   75
La Frascatana   63

La Galatea   72–3
Le geôlier de soi-mesme (T. Corneille)   167
Gerone tiranno di Siracusa   274
Giulio Cesare in Egitto (Bussani)   46n
Giulio Cesare nell' Egitto (Ottoboni)   42, 46n
Giulio Flavio Crispo   68, 169
Giustino (Beregan-Pariati)   36, 57, 139n, 247–51, 266, 276n
Il Gran Tamerlano (Salvi)   35, 167
Griselda (Rolli)   54–6
Griselda (Zeno)   33, 35, 37–8, 53–6, 66, 102, 139, 156n, 268

Héraclius (P. Corneille)   41, 67

Idaspe   78
Idomeneo re di Creta   28–9
Ifigenia in Aulide (Capeci)   42
Ifigenia in Aulide (Verazi)   26
Ifigenia in Tauri (Capeci)   42
Ifigenia in Tauride (Pasqualigo)   20, 68–9, 71, 169
Imeneo (in Atene)   4, 69n, 75
L'impresario delle isole Canarie   25, 48, 174
L'incoronazione di Dario   139
Gl' inganni felici   124, 178n
L'innocenza giustificata   26
Ipermestra   22
Ippolito ed Aricia   26
Issipile   91

Leucippe e Teonoe   169
La libertà nociva   2
Lotario   167
Lucio Papirio   35, 43–5
Lucio Silla   28
Lucio Vero   19

Madama Dulcinea e il cuoco   42
Marco Attilio Regolo   35, 51–2, 170n
Maximien (T. Corneille)   277
Medonte re d'Epiro   4, 29
Meride e Selinunte   75, 76n
La Merope   23, 156, 202
Mithridate (Racine)   68, 74
Mitridate (Vanstryp)   74
Mitridate (Zeno)   74, 78
Mitridate Eupatore   170n, 174
Mitridate re di Ponto (Q. Gasparini)   28
Mitridate re di Ponto vincitor di se stesso (Pasqualigo)   68
Montezuma   6, 26

Narciso   46
Nerina   100
Nerone   3, 169
Nerone fatto Cesare   139, 157
Nino   36, 57, 97–8, 100

L'Olimpiade   1, 28, 74, 101, 178n, 261, 274, 283–4, 288–9
Onorio   78
L'Orazio   25
Oreste   36, 57, 256
Orfeo ed Euridice (Badini)   28
Orfeo ed Euridice (Calzabigi)   4, 27, 240n
Orlando   206, 211–12, 219, 255, 258–63, 255–6, 269
Orlando finto pazzo   139, 157, 163n
Orlando furioso   93, 157, 163n
L'Orlando, ovvero la gelosa pazzia   40–1, 46, 211
Orlando Paladino   3
Gli orti esperidi   72, 75
Ottone in villa   139n

Paride ed Elena   27
Partenope   69–71
Il pastor d'Anfriso   169
Il pastor fido   41, 68, 256, 265, 268
Le pazzie d'Orlando   3
Pertharite (P. Corneille)   167
Phèdre (Racine)   55, 68, 125
Pimpinone   39n
Piramo e Tisbe   28
Il Pirro   35, 50
Pisistrato   67
Il pomo d'oro   91
Poro   258n
La pravità castigata   95
Prima la musica e poi le parole   25
Proserpina rapita   42
Publio Cornelio Scipione   35, 42, 171

Radamisto   102, 257
Il re pastore   3, 21, 28, 48, 273, 284, 288, 292
Regulus (Pradon)   40, 52, 170n
Rinaldo   65
I rivali generosi (Elpidia)   70n
Roberto Devereux   294, 296–7, 301–4
Rodelinda   167, 264
Rosimonda   169
(La) Rosmira fedele   69–70
Ruggiero   28

Scanderbeg 139
Scipione 167
Semiramide 26
Semiramide riconosciuta 21, 23, 73–4, 77, 98, 261
La serva padrona 84, 96
Sesostrate 273
Sesostri re d'Egitto 50, 169
Siface 21, 72–3, 75
Silla dittatore 72
Siroe re di Persia 15, 21, 72–4, 100, 163, 211–12, 243–7, 281–2
Sofonisba 3, 26
Il sogno di Scipione 4
Sosarme 167
Stratonica 167

Talestri, regina delle Amazzoni 85
Tamerlan (Pradon) 50, 167
Tamerlano 169
Telemaco 21, 35, 51
Télémaque (Campra) 51
Temistocle 284
Teodorico 49
Teodosio il giovane 40
Terpsicore 256, 258
Teseo 208n
Tetide in Sciro 41, 110
Teuzzone 6, 121–33, 134–64, 135 (pl. 7), 165
Thesée 208n
Tieteberga 139
Il Tigrane (Lalli) 49

Tigrane (Silvani) 274–6, 281
Timocrate (T. Corneille) 167
Timocrate (Salvi-Lalli) 66–7
I Tindaridi 26
Tite et Bérénice (P. Corneille) 46
Tito e Berenice 35, 43–6 (pl. 1a–b), 69
Tito Manlio 65
Tito Sempronio Gracco 35, 53
Titus l'Empereur 46
Tolomeo et Alessandro, overo la corona disprezzata 40, 46
Tolomeo re d'Egitto 207, 211–19, 269
Il Trace in catena 35, 49–50
Il trionfo della fedeltà 85
Il trionfo della libertà 3, 169
Il trionfo di Camilla, regina de' Volsci 48, 70n
Il trionfo di Clelia 285
Il trionfo di Flavio Olibrio 75
Turno Aricino 35, 53

The Unhappy Favourite (Banks) 176n, 294–5

Venere placata 98, 100
I veri amici 67, 76n
Il Vincislao 35, 49
La virtù negli amori 57
La virtù nel cimento 139
La virtù trionfante dell'amore e dell'odio 36

Zenobia 284

Names and subjects

Abert, Hermann 67
absolutism 272–3
Accademia dell'Arcadia 19–20, 24, 34, 44–5, 51, 53, 55, 69, 85, 122–4, 173, 293n, 263–4, 268
Accademia de'Quirini 44–5, 51, 55, 166, 173
acting and gesture 96, 191–2, 224–6 (pl. 10)
Addison, Joseph 24, 202–3
Adimari, Lodovico 167n, 168
affections in music 18–19, 123, 138, 221, 277, 290–2
Alari, Paola 40
Albani family 51–3
Albinoni, Tommaso 20, 39n, 63, 67, 71–2, 78, 169–71
Aldobrandini, Pompeo 42–3
Algarotti, Francesco 14n, 25–7, 63, 205n, 237–9, 272
Alibert, Conte Antonio d' 173
allegory 158, 221–3, 260, 266–7, 281–2, 292
Amadei, Filippo 40, 171
Ambreville, Anna 156
Ancelot, Jacques A. F. P. 184, 297, 301–5
Ancelot, Marguerite L. V. 301
Andreozzi, Gaetano 29
Anfossi, Pasquale 28
Angiolini, Gasparo 11
Ansbach 87
Araya, Francesco 65, 77
Archi, Giovanni Antonio 42–3
architects, *see* scenography
Arena, Giuseppe 109n
argomento 237–51
aria 12–14, 18–19, 27–9, 72, 112–17, 123, 134, 150–62, 226–30, 243, 274–7, 282–3; (borrowed a.) 139, 155–7, 162, 257, 287–92; (dance a.) 228–36, 242–3, 248–50, 261, 280; (dialogue a.) 204, 215–18; (entrance a.) 160, 213–15, 217, 265; (exit a.) 187–90, 192, 213; (a. keys and modes) 227–9, 238, 243; (monologue a.) 150–62; (*ombra* a.) 14, 126,

216, 243, 281; (parody and transfer) 136, 244, 251, 287–92; (pastoral a.) 273–4, 277; (a. and recitative) 202–5; (sentence a.) 204, 216, 277; (a. and sinfonia) 243–50; (a. tables) 105–7, 137–9, 213–15; (text setting) 23; (a. theory) 202–5; (a. types) 215–17
Ariosto, Lodovico 255–8, 263–9
Ariosti, Attilio 86
Aristotle 2, 17–18, 126–7, 131, 165–7, 201–10, 239, 267
Armellini, Mario 69n
Arteaga, Stefano 25
Augsburg 94–5
Auletta, Pietro 25, 63, 74
azione teatrale per musica 3, 262

Bach, Johann Christian 7, 10, 15–16, 28
Bach, Johann Sebastian 87
Badia, Carlo Agostino 51
Badini, Carlo Francesco 3, 22
ballet 11, 27, 42, 49, 53, 55, 86, 91, 255–6, 258–63, 269
Bambini, Eustachio 7, 64, 94–5
Banks, John 176n, 294–5
Barlocci, Giangualberto 2, 57
Bartoli, Bartolomeo 55
Baselt, Bernd 257
Basso, Andrea 67
Bayreuth 84, 87, 89
Beard, John 257n
Belisani troupe 67
Benti-Bulgarelli, Marianna 21, 69n, 72–4, 171–2, 174
Beregan, Niccolò 247
Berenstadt, Gaetano 9n
Berlin 7, 22, 26, 63, 84, 87, 89, 93
Bernacchi, Antonio 42, 55, 172

Bernardoni, Pietro Antonio 41, 43
Berscelli, Matteo 46, 49, 171
Bianconi, Lorenzo 98n
bienséances see decorum, morality
Bioni, Antonio 93
La Birba 42
Birke, Joachim 85
Boccaccio, Giovanni 55
Bohemia 7, 93–5
Boileau-Despréaux, Nicolas 202
Boldini, Giovanni 78, 277
Bologna 8, 20, 22, 64, 67
Bonlini, Carlo 66
Bonn 94–5
Bononcini, Antonio Maria 47, 67n
Bononcini, Giovanni 7, 19, 86; *Abdolomino* 48;
   Astarto 35, 47–8; *Crispo* 35, 54–5; *Erminia* 52;
   Etearco 52; *Griselda* 54–5; *Il trionfo di
   Camilla* 48, 70n
Bordoni, Faustina 7, 22, 76, 79, 106, 171, 264 (pl. 12),
   285
Borghese family 43, 47–9
Borghi, Gaetano 42
borrowing *see* arias, borrowed
Bourbon, House of 7, 38–9, 98–100, 108–10
Boyer, Claude 297n
Braccioli, Grazio 20, 93
Breitkopf, Gottlob Immanuel 85
Britain 7–8, 28, 77
Brooke, Henry 295
Broschi detto Farinelli, Carlo 7, 10n, 22, 76–8, 98,
   100, 110
Broschi, Riccardo 65, 77–8
Brunswick 8, 82–3, 88–90
Brusa, Giovanni Francesco 69n, 73
Brussels 94–5
Buckworth, John 77
Buini, Giuseppe Maria 20, 67
Burlington, Earl of 48
Burney, Charles 8, 63, 70n, 74n
Busenello, Giovanni Francesco 175
Bussani, Girolamo 36

Caffarelli *see* Majorano
Caldara, Antonio 7, 21–2, 35, 40–1, 43–8, 88, 108,
   242n
Calliroë 28
Calzabigi, Ranieri de' 3, 7, 11, 25, 27, 205n;
   Alceste 27, 237; *La critica teatrale (L'opera
   seria)* 25; *Elfrida* 27; *Paride ed Elena* 27
Cammarano, Salvatore 184, 294n, 296–7, 301–5
Campistron, Jean-Gualbert de 57, 167
Campra, André 51, 91
Canal family 11, 53
Capeci, Carlo Sigismondo 19, 21, 34, 46, 52; *Amor
   d'un'ombra e gelosia d'un' aura* 43, 46; *La clemenza
   d'Augusto* 287; *Ifigenia in Aulide* 42; *Ifigenia in
   Tauri* 42; *Marco Attilio Regolo* 170n; *L'Orlando,
   ovvero la gelosa pazzia* 40–1, 46, 211;
   Telemaco 21, 35, 51; *Tetide in Sciro* 41, 110; *Tito e
   Berenice* 35, 43–6, 69; *Tolomeo ed Alessandro, overo
   la corona disprezzata* 40, 46, 211–19
Capelli, Giovanni Maria 68, 169
Capranica family 33–8, 42, 49, 51, 60
Carestini, Giovanni 75, 78
Carlo Borbone, King of Naples 98–9, 101n
Carl Philipp, Count Palatinate 87
Carreras, Juan-José 98n
Cassani, Vincenzo 72
Casti, Giovanni Battista 25
castratos 8–9, 24, 37, 72–4, 46, 76–8, 113

Cato Uticensis 68
Cavalli, Francesco 121
Cavana, Giambattista 60
Cavana, Giovanni Battista 40, 43
cavat(in)a 161, 163
Cecil, Lord 297
Cesti, Antonio 91
Charles VI (III) of Habsburg 39, 42, 88
Chastellux, François-Jean de 14, 25
Chelleri, Fortunato 67
Chiarini, Pietro 109n
chorus 71, 110–11, 123, 163, 191, 205, 241, 250,
   255–6, 259, 262–2, 269
Christina, Queen of Sweden 175
Ciampi, Francesco 78
Cicognini, Giacinto Andrea 168
Cigna-Santi, Vittorio Amedeo 28
Cimarosa, Domenico 28
classicism 27, 101, 110–12, 295
Coburg 87
Coello, Antonio 294
Coke, Edward 79
Colloredo-Wallsee, Johann Baptist 67n
Coltellini, Marco 27–8
comédie héroïque 3n, 168
comedy, spoken 2, 46, 168, 208–9
comic opera 4, 90, 208
Comito, Giuseppe 72
commedia dell'arte 4, 24, 201, 295
commedia per musica 1, 21, 64, 66, 168, 262
componimento drammatico per musica 3–4
Constantinople 247
Conti, Antonio 76n
Conti, Francesco Bartolomeo 3, 21, 88, 91
Copenhagen 7
Cordans, Bartolomeo 78
Corneille, Pierre 12, 17, 19, 67, 74n, 124, 128 (pl. 5),
   131–2, 173, 295; (parties intégrantes) 127, 221, 239;
   Le Cid 68, 131; *Cinna* 287; *Don Sanche
   d'Aragon* 168; *Héraclius* 41, 67; *Pertharite* 167;
   Tite et Bérénice 46; *Trois discours sur le poème
   dramatique* 239
Corneille, Thomas 19, 66, 163, 165; *Antiochus* 167;
   Le Comte d'Essex 125–33, 144, 147, 156–60, 167,
   173, 177–97, 180 (pl. 8), 295, 297–305; *Le festin de
   pierre* 125, 131; *Le geôlier de soi-mesme* 167;
   Maximien 277; *Timocrate* 167
Corradini, Francesco 113n
Corselli, Francesco 7, 23, 78, 97–117; *Achille in
   Sciro* 108–17; *Farnace* 100–8; *Nino* 97–8, 100;
   Venere placata 98, 100
Cortona, Antonio 101n
Costa, Rosa 95
Costanzi, Giovanni Francesco 49
Crescimbeni, Giovanni Maria 24, 122–3, 203n, 209
Croce, Benedetto 62
Cuvilliés, François 88
Cuzzoni, Francesca 106
Cyprus 212

Dahlhaus, Carl 18
Da Ponte, Lorenzo 17n
Darmstadt 87
D'Astorga, Emanuele 66
Daun, Wirich 172
D'Averara, Pietro 69
David, Domenico 19, 35, 41–2, 122, 124, 173
Dean, Winton 257–8, 265
De Brosses, Charles 8, 63
De Carli, A. 125
decorum 12, 20, 24, 211–19, 160, 268

Degrada, Francesco 47n, 62
Della Seta, Fabrizio 44
della Stella, Giovanna 95
Denmark 7
Dent, Edward J. 61
Denzio, Antonio 7, 93–5
De Sanctis, Francesco 209n
Descartes, René 15, 18
deus ex machina 205–6
Devereux, Robert *see* Essex
dialogue 194–5, *see also* aria (dialogue), recitative
Diderot, Denis 63
Di Majo, Francesco 10, 28
Döbricht, Daniel 89
Donizetti, Gaetano 184, 294, 296–7
Downes, Edward O. D. 61
drama, French spoken 19, 24, 85, 165–8, *see also*
  tragédie
drama, Greek *see* tragedy, Greek
drama, Italian spoken 4, 40, 202, 272
drama, theory of 17–18, 24, 122, 126–8, 131, 134–6,
  165–8, 201–10, 218, 221, 239, 271
dramaturgy 220–36, 244–5, 267, *see also* drama,
  theory of
dramma per musica (genre definition) 1–3, 121–5,
  270–1; (spoken performances) 136
Dresden 7, 22–3, 94–5, 83, 88–9, 278
Durante, Francesco 63n
Durastanti, Margherita 170–1
Durazzo, Giacomo 7, 26–7
Durlach-Karlsruhe 87
Düsseldorf 7, 87
Du Tillot, Guillaume-Léon 7, 26

Edesimo, Evandro 25
Einstein, Alfred 237
Elizabeth I 126, 173–5, 294–5, 298, 303
ensembles, operatic 14, 53, 58–9 (pl. 2a–b), 103–4,
  107–8, 150, 217, 231, 277
Essex, Earl of 126, 294–305
Eximeno, Antonio 25
exotic subjects 6, 27, 76, 125, 129, 175–6, 243, 262

Fab(b)ri, Annibale Pio 40, 52, 99, 100–3, 108
Fabri, Antonio Pio 282n
Facchinelli, Lucia 73
Fago, Nicola 65, 67
Farinelli *see* Broschi, Carlo
Febi armonici troupe 64
Feo, Francesco 72–3, 197 (pl. 9)
Ferdinand VI of Spain 117
festa teatrale per musica 3–4, 21n
finance and economy 5, 8, 34, 86–90, 92–3, 256
Fiorillo, Ignazio 65, 77
Florence 49–50, 99, 166–8, 170–1
Florimo, Francesco 61
Fontana, Giacinto 42, 47, 49, 53, 55, 78–9
Foppa, Giuseppe 29
Forcellini, Giacinta 99
France 3, 6, 8, 24, 27, 39–40, 122, 100, 108–9, 257
Franchi, Carlo 168
Frankfurt 94–5
Frederick II, King of Prussia 26
French drama, tragedy *see* drama, *tragédie*
French opera *see tragédie lyrique*
Frigimelica-Roberti, Girolamo 3, 20, 122, 124, 169–
  70, 174
Frugoni, Innocenzo 7, 22, 26
Fubini, Enrico 271
funesto fine 165–76, 180, *see also tragedia per musica*
Fux, Johann Joseph 7, 21

Gallas, Count Wenzel 47–9, 51
Galliari brothers 11
Galli Bibiena family 11, 49, 55, 242 (pl. 11), 289 (pl.
  14)
Galuppi, Baldassarre 7, 22–3, 26–7, 48, 78, 98,
  117
Gamerra, Giovanni de 4, 28–9
Garrick, David 295
Gasparini, Francesco 19, 35, 43, 47–51, 57, 167;
  Amore e maestà 172; *Il Ciro* 35, 49; *Lucio
  Papirio* 35, 43–5; *Il Pirro* 35, 50; *Sesostri* 169;
  Tamerlano 169; *Il Trace in catena* 35, 49–50; *Il
  Vincislao* 35, 49
Gasparini, Michelangelo 72, 170–1, 202
Gassmann, Florian Leopold 25
Gdansk 81
Genevesi, Domenico 48–9
Genoa 65
Gerber, Rudolf 61
Germany 81–96
Ghezzi, Pier Leone 11
Giacomelli, Geminiano 22, 74, 78, 97–9
Giay, Giovanni Antonio 74, 78, 171
Gigli, Girolamo 168; *Anagilda (La fede
  ne'tradimenti)* 19–20, 40; *La Dirindina* 25, 47–8,
  174n
Giordano, Carmine 65
Giovannini, Francesco 109, 113
Girò, Anna 105
Giusti, Anna Maria 40
Giusti, Girolamo 6
Gizzi, Domenico 21, 51, 73, 77
Gluck, Christoph Willibald 7, 23, 26–7, 89, 95, 121,
  205n, 237; *Alceste* 27, 237–8; *Orfeo ed Euridice* 4,
  27, 240n
Goldoni, Carlo 25, 66–7, 201–2
Gotha 87
Gottsched, Johann Christoph 24, 81–6, 201–3
Graun, Karl Heinrich 7, 22, 26, 283
Gravina, Gian Vincenzo 24, 45, 166, 170
Graz 94, 100
Grétry, André E. M. 26, 63
Grimaldi, Nicolò 21, 65, 67n, 72–4, 76–77, 171–2
Grimani family 66, 68–9, 79
Grimani, Vincenzo 39, 40n, 124
Gronda, Giovanna 62n, 228n
Gualandi Campioli, Margherita 163
Guarini, Giambattista 256, 265, 268
Guglielmi, Pietro 3

Habsburg, House of 7, 20, 38, 42, 48, 51, 57, 87–8,
  108–9
Halle 82–3
Hamburg 7, 9, 22, 82–4, 89–92, 169, 171
Handel, George Frideric 7, 21, 46, 48, 52n, 62, 77,
  90–1, 106, 170–1; (finales) 205; (pasticcio operas)
  70n, 77, 98, 256, 261; (and Salvi) 167, 264–5; (and
  singers) 113, 256; (style) 283; *Acis and
  Galatea* 256; *Admeto* 212; *Alcina* 256, 258, 260;
  Almira 263; *Amadigi* 206; *Arianna in Creta* 76,
  220–36, 256, 261, 266; *Ariodante* 167, 255–69;
  Arminio 167; *Atalanta* 265; *Berenice regina
  d'Egitto* 167, 265; *Catone* 77; *Cleofida (Poro)* 91;
  Giulio Cesare in Egitto 46n; *Lotario* 167;
  Oreste 256; *Orlando* 206, 211–12, 219, 258n, 261,
  263–6, 269; *Il pastor fido* 41, 256; *Poro* 258n;
  Radamisto 102, 257; *Rinaldo* 65; *Rodelinda* 167,
  264; *Scipione* 167; *Semiramide riconosciuta* 77, 98,
  261; *Sosarme* 167; *Terpsicore* 256, 258;
  Teseo 208n; *Titus l'Empereur* 46; *Tolomeo re
  d'Egitto* 207, 211–19, 269

Hanover 7, 86–7
Hans Wurst 201
Harris, Ellen T. 212, 256–8, 263, 265
Hasse, Johann Adolf 7, 10, 15, 17n, 22, 26–7, 62–5, 71, 84, 89, 113, 270–93; (and the dramma per musica) 270–93; (and Faustina Bordoni) 79; (and Venice) 71, 78–9, 98–9, 286; *Alessandro nell'Indie* 79, 98–100, 278, 286; *Artaserse* (1730) 22, 74, 78–9, 98, 112, 114, 276–7, 278n, (1740) 278; *Attalo* 274; *Attilio Regolo* 285; *Cajo Fabricio* 280–1; *La clemenza di Tito* 286–93; *Cleofide* 278; *Dalisa* 79; *Demetrio* 79, 98–9, 101, 114, 278–80; *Enea in Caonia* 289; *Euristeo* 79, 289; *Ezio* (1730) 275–7, (1755) 282–3, 288–90; *Gerone tiranno di Siracusa* 274; *Ipermestra* 22; *L'Olimpiade* 288–9; *Piramo e Tisbe* 28; *Il re pastore* 288, 292; *Ruggiero* 28; *Sesostrate* 273; *Siroe re di Persia* (1733) 100, 243–7, 281–2, (1763) 281–2; 'Solitario bosco ombroso' 56; *Tigrane* 274–6, 281; *Il trionfo di Clelia* 285
Haym, Nicola 202, 211–19
Heartz, Daniel 61–2, 238
Heidegger, John James 170–1
Heidelberg 87
Heinichen, Johann David 89, 221–2
Heinse, Wilhelm 26
Henze-Döhring, Sabine 258, 261
Heras, Maria 109, 113
Herb(er)stein, Barbara 172
Hill, Aaron 24
Hill, John 139
Hiller, Johann Adam 26
Hollywood 29
Homer 110
Horatius Cocles 6
Hucke, Helmut 61, 109n
humanism 3

impresario 9–10, 51, 60, 64, 80, 90, 92–6, 125, 174
Innocent XII, Pope 33
Innocent XIII, Pope 57
Innsbruck 87
intermedi, mythological 172, 174
intermedi pastorali 47
intermezzi comici per musica 2, 20, 25, 40, 42, 49, 52, 65, 84–5, 89, 91–2, 95, 167–8, 172, 174, 208

Joly, Jacques 270n
Jommelli, Niccolò 7, 10, 15, 22–3, 26, 64
Jones, Henry 295
Juvarra, Filippo 11, 34, 40–1, 43–6 (pl. 1a–b)

Kassel 87
Keiser, Reinhard 86, 91, 257n
key structures *see* aria (keys and modes)
Kiesewetter, Raphael Georg 61
Kleinertz, Rainer 97n
Krause, Christian Gottfried 14n, 23n, 25
Kretzschmar, Hermann 61
Kubik, Reinhold 227n
Kunze, Stefan 29, 224
Kusser, Johann Sigismund 86
Kuzmick Hansell, Kathleen 262–3

La Calprenède, Gautier de *Le Comte d'Essex* 126, 294, 297–303
Lalli, Domenico 21, 66–7, 75–79, 101; *L'amor tirannico* 35, 42, 66, 102; *Argeno* 75–6; *Argippo* 49; *Dalisa* 79; *Damiro e Pitia* 75; *Elisa* 66; *Imeneo in Atene* 75; *Onorio* 78; *Pisistrato* 67; *Tigrane* 49; *Timocrate* 66–7; *Il*

trionfo di Flavio Olibrio 75–6; *I veri amici* 67, 76n
Lampugnani, Giovanni Battista 22, 100
Lancret, Nicolas 180 (pl. 8)
Lang, Franciscus 225 (pl. 10)
Lang, Paul Henry 258
Lapis, Santo 94–5
Latilla, Gaetano 3, 22, 63
Leipzig 7, 82–4, 90, 93
Lemer, Gaetano 34, 45, 54–5, 57
Leo, Leonardo 21, 60, 62, 64–7, 72, 75–6, 79; *Achille in Sciro* 109; *Argeno* 76; *Arianna e Teseo* 73, 76, 229; *Catone in Utica* 10n, 77–8; *La clemenza di Tito* 100; *Demetrio* 98n, 101; *Evergete* 76n; *Farnace* 100n; *La Frascatana* 63; *L'Olimpiade* 101; *Pisistrato* 67
Lessing, Gotthold Ephraim 295
liaison des scènes 187, 207–8, 213–6, 218
libretto editions 56, 77–8, 81, 103, 107–10, 135 (pl. 7), 212, 239, 258n
libretto prefaces 168, 172–3, 177–8, 268n
libretto-writing 134–64, 165–6, 177–97
licenza 102, 110, 174, 205
Lichtenthal, Pietro 295
lieto fine 19, 125, 127, 130, 133, 155, 169, 209
Lindgren, Lowell 54, 211n
Lisbon 11, 289 (pl. 14)
Livorno 166
Locatelli, Giovanni Battista 7, 23, 94–5
London (city) 56, 63, 65, 70; 295; (Covent Garden Theatre) 255–8; (Drury Lane Theatre) 295; (Haymarket operas) 7–9, 22–3, 27, 41, 46, 54–5, 98–100, 169–71 255–6, 258; (Opera of the Nobility) 76, 78–9; (Royal Academy of Music) 77, 211
Lotti, Antonio 2, 19, 101, 136
Lucchini, Antonio Maria 3, 20, 101, 247, 261; *Farnace re di Ponto* 97, 100–8
Lübeck 95
Lütolf, Max 33n
Lully, Jean-Baptiste 208n, 260, 263

Madrid 7–8, 23, 97–117, 294
Maffei, Scipione 24, 202
magic, *merveilleux* 24, 51, 205–6
Magni, Paolo 125
Majorano detto Caffarelli, Gaetano 22, 100–1, 103, 106, 108
Mancia, Luigi 86
Mancinelli, Costanza 109, 113
Mancini, Francesco 35, 39, 49–50, 65
Mancini, Rosa 99–100, 103, 108
Mannheim 7, 22, 26, 87, 95
Mantua 135–6
Marcello, Benedetto 10–11, 25, 67, 84
Maria Antonia Walpurgis 85, 89
Maria Casimira of Poland 34, 36, 38, 40–1, 43
Maria Theresa of Austria 88, 108, 273
Marino, Giambattista 164
Markstrom, Kurt 70n, 73n, 74n
Marmontel, Jean François 14n, 26
Martello, Pier Jacopo 13–14, 20, 24–5, 153
Marx, Hans Joachim 85n, 86, 90–1
Mattheson, Johann 14n, 24, 82–3, 90–1, 202; *Arsace* 171; *Critica musica* 69n; *Der musikalische Patriot* 91n; *Die neueste Untersuchung der Singspiele* 25n, 84–5; *Der vollkommene Kapellmeister* 91
Mauro family 11
Mazarin, Cardinal 40
Mazzolà, Catterino 29
Mazzoni, Antonio 289 (pl. 14)

McCleave, Sarah Y.   259–60
McClymonds, Marita P.   29
Medici, House of   51, 166–7
Mele, Giovanni Battista   113n
melodramma   1
Mercadante, Saverio   297
Metastasio, Pietro   3–4, 14, 20–3, 84–5, 121, 127, 301;
(arias)   203–5, 245; (ballet)   261; (on
drama)   204n, 207–8; (dramas performed without
music)   135n; (early works)   6, 21, 72, 101–2; (and
Hamburg)   91; (and Hasse)   79, 270–93;
(pastoral)   261; (poetics)   219, 239; (portrait)   285
(pl. 13); (and Prague)   95; (and singers)   72–4, 78–
9; (on rulers and states)   270–93; (and Salvi)   167;
(serenatas)   72, 75; (and Spain)   99, 109–110; (and
Venice)   71–9; (and Vienna)   88; (on
women)   145; (works)   9, 12, 17n, 21, 25–6, 75,
261n, 285 (pl. 13); (youth)   45, 48, 52n, 166, 172–4;
Achille in Sciro   97, 101, 108–17, 284; *Adriano in
Siria*   21, 240–3, 279; *Alessandro nell'Indie*   18, 21,
74, 79, 98–102, 112, 278, 284, 287; *Artaserse*   22–3,
73–4, 78–9, 96, 101–2, 112, 276–8, 287; *Atenaide*   4;
Attilio Regolo   21, 170, 285; *Catone in Utica*   15, 21,
73–4, 77–8, 168–70; *Ciro riconosciuto*   3, 284; *La
clemenza di Tito*   21, 29, 100, 170, 238, 284–93, 289
(pl. 14); *Demetrio*   18–19, 22–3, 79, 98, 101, 114,
278–80; *Demofoonte*   21, 100, 283–4; *Didone
abbandonata*   21, 63, 71–4, 77, 100–1, 168–71, 173–
5, 244–7; *L'Eroe Cinese*   21; *Ezio*   21, 23, 73–4, 77,
79, 275–8, 282–4, 287–90; *La Galatea*   72–3;
L'impresario delle isole Canarie   25, 48, 174;
Ipermestra   22; *Issipile*   91, 279n; *L'Olimpiade*   21,
101, 178n, 261, 274, 283–4, 288–9; *Il re pastore*   3,
21, 28, 48, 273, 284, 288, 292; *Ruggiero*   28;
Semiramide riconosciuta   21, 73, 77, 261; *Siface*   21,
72–3, 75; *Siroe re di Persia*   15, 21, 72–4, 100, 211–
12, 243–7, 281–2; *Il sogno di Scipione*   4;
Temistocle   284; *Il trionfo di Clelia*   285;
Zenobia   284
Micheli, Benedetto   36, 57
Michetti, Nicola   38, 49
Migliavacca, Giovanni Ambrogio   22
Milan   26–7, 73, 125, 135–6, 295
Millner, Frederick   281
Mingotti, Angelo   7, 23, 64, 94–5
Mingotti, Pietro   7, 23, 64, 84–5, 89, 94–5, 100
Mingotti Valentini, Regina   89
Mizler, Lorenz Friedrich   82
Modena   202
Monari, Clemente   125
Moniglia, GianAndrea   168
monologue   134, 150–62, 184–6, 204, 213–18, 285
Montagnana, Antonio   109, 113
Montesquieu, Charles-Louis de   8
Monteverdi, Claudio   18, 111
Monticelli, Maria Marta   99
morality, ethos   36–7, 90, 110, 130–3, 210–11, 218–19,
266, 268–9, 272–3
Moretti, Ferdinando   29
Morselli, Adriano   124
Moser, Hans Joachim   84, 86
Mucci, Teresa   153
Munich   22, 55n, 67, 75, 88, 94–5, 166
Muratori, Lodovico Antonio   24, 83–5, 122–5, 203,
211, 271
music   110–12
mythology   4, 27, 51, 101, 110, 112, 212

Naples   7, 9, 20–2, 27, 39, 50, 99, 174, 273; (court and
nobility)   98, 101n, 174, 277; (musicians)   61–80,
247; (opera houses)   38–9, 49, 64, 67, 101n, 109,

172; (Real Cappella)   50, 64–6, 72
national themes   85, 202, 284–5
Negri, Maria Rosa   257n
Nicolini, Filippo   7, 88, 94–5
Noris, Matteo   49, 52, 170n
Noverre, Jean-Georges   11

Olivero, Pietro Domenico   197 (pl. 9)
ombra arias *see* aria (*ombra* a.)
opera buffa   1–2, 4–5, 7, 10, 28, 89, 95, 117
opera houses   5, 33–4
opera seasons   9
opera seria   1–3
Opéra-Studio Genève   33
opera, theories of   270–1
oratorio   36
orchestration   28, 51, 110–11, 114–15, 238, 241, 245,
282–3, 292
Orefice, Antonio   35, 39, 65
Orlandini, Giuseppe Maria   3, 20–1, 67, 90, 167;
L'amor tirannico   35; *Antigona*   68–9, 167–9, 171;
Arsace   72–3, 169–71; *Ataulfo*   35, 41–2;
Berenice   69–70; *Farnace*   101n; *La fede tradita e
vendicata*   41n, 42; *Griselda*   139n; (intermezzi per
musica)   167; *Ifigenia in Tauride*   68–9, 169;
Merope   156; *Nerone*   3, 169; *Nino*   36, 57;
Teuzzone   139; *La virtù nel cimento*   139
Orsi, Gian Gioseffo   125, 202
Ossi, Giovanni   49–50
Ottoboni, Antonio   42, 46n
Ottoboni, Pietro   20, 34, 38–41, 43–4, 75, 123–4, 268n
overture   227, 232–4, 237–8, 246

Pacini, Antonio   55
Paganelli, Giuseppe Antonio   101n
Pagano, Roberto   66
Paisiello, Giovanni   27–8
Paita, Giovanni   48–9
Palazzi, Giovanni   20
Palermo   64
Palomba, Antonio   25
Paradisi, Domenico   42
Pariati, Pietro   3, 20, 39n, 47–8, 88, 93, 101, 122, 125;
Arianna e Teseo (Teseo in Creta)   73, 76, 205, 228–
30; *Astarto*   35; *Giustino*   247, 276n; (intermezzi per
musica)   167; *Sesostri re d'Egitto*   50, 169
Parini, Giuseppe   28
Paris   63, 95
Parma   7, 22, 26, 64, 97–100, 166
parody *see* aria (parody and transfer)
Pasqualigo, Benedetto   20, 68–9, 169
Pasquini, Giovan Claudio   22
pasticcio opera   11, 43, 70, 73, 77, 93, 95, 98, 136,
256–7, 261
pastoral themes   2, 4, 6, 41, 48, 55–6, 101, 122–4,
134n, 169, 207–8, 212, 219, 243, 246, 256–62, 265–9,
273–4, 279, 284
patrons   34–5, 38–9, 43, 47, 49–51, 57, 67, 75, 77, 80,
87–90, 93
Pepusch, Johann Christoph   48
Perez, Davide   10, 23
performance   10, 17, 27, 96, 136, 138, 147–50, 191–2,
224–6 (pl. 10)
Pergolesi, Giambattista   22, 26, 62–3, 71, 77, 117;
Adriano in Siria   240–3; *La serva padrona*   84
Perti, Giacomo Antonio   167
Peruzzi, Anna Maria   100–1, 103–9, 113
Peruzzi, Antonio   7, 93–5
Pesaro   286
Pescetti, Giambattista   22, 74, 78
Peter Leopold of Tuscany   5

Petrarch 5
Petrolli, Catterina 40
Petrosellini, Domenico Ottavio 35, 51
Piacenza 97
Piantanida brothers 125, 169
Piazzon, Giovanni 169
Piccinni, Niccolò 7, 28
Piedz, Anna Maria de 40
Pioli, Giovan Domenico 35, 38
Piovene, Agostino 3, 20; 101; *Nerone* 3, 169; *Publio Cornelio Scipione* 35, 42; *Tamerlano* 169
Pisa 99
Pistocchi, Francesco Antonio 86
Planelli, Antonio 14, 25
poetry, operatic 12, 152–5, 158–62
Pola, Fra Camillo 67, 74
Poland 49, 88–9; *see also* Maria Casimira, Sobieski family
Polani, Girolamo 171
political themes 6, 174, 270–93
Pollarolo, Antonio 100, 169
Pollarolo, Carlo Francesco 3, 19, 43; *Ariodante* 264–5 (pl. 12); *Astinome* 35, 51–2; *Eraclio* 43; *Giulio Cesare nell'Egitto* 42; *Il pastor d'Anfriso* 169; *Proserpina rapita* 42; *Publio Cornelio Scipione* 35, 42–3; *Rosimonda* 169; *Tito Manlio* 65
Porpora, Nicola 4, 7, 21–2, 51, 60, 64–6, 72–6, 79, 91, 113; *Angelica* 72, 75; *Annibale* 74, 79, 98; *Arianna e Teseo* 73, 76, 230; *Arianna in Nasso* 76; *Berenice regina d'Egitto* 35, 50–1; *Damiro e Pitia* 75; *Didone abbandonata* 72; *Ezio* 74, 77; *Flavio Anicio Olibrio* 75; *Imeneo (in Atene)* 69n, 75; *Meride e Selinunte* 75, 76n; *Mitridate* 74; *Gli orti esperidi* 72, 75; *Semiramide riconosciuta* 77; *Siface* 72–3, 75
Porsile, Giuseppe 65
Porta, Giovanni 20, 49, 67; *Aldiso* 75; *Amare per regnare* 72; *Antigono tutore di Filippo* 169; *Farnace* 100, 101n; *Siroe re di Persia* 73; *Il trionfo di Flavio Olibrio* 75–6
Porta, Nunziato 28
Portugal 7, 23, 57
Pradon, Jean-Nicholas 19; *Regulus* 40, 52, 170n; *Tamerlan* 50, 167
Prague 8–9, 23, 93–5
Prato 99
Pratolino, Villa di 8, 51, 166–7
Predieri, Luc'Antonio 47, 167
prison scenes 159–62, 301–3
Prota, Ignazio 65
Prota-Giurleo, Ulisse 62
Pulvini Faliconti, Giuseppe 60

Quadrio, Francesco Saverio 25
Quaglio family 11
Quantz, Johann Joachim 73n, 92
Querelle des bouffons 26, 63, 95
Quinault, Philippe 19, 48; *Armide* 175n; *Thesée* 208n

Racine, Jean 12, 19, 124–5, 128, 132 (pl. 6), 163, 165; *Andromaque* 167, 287; *Bajazet* 125–33, 140–55, 162–3, 207, 300; *Bérénice* 18, 46; *Britannicus* 276; *Mithridate* 68, 74; *Phèdre* 55, 68, 125
Raguenet, François 23n, 25, 202, 268
Raleigh, Sir Walter 297
Ralph, James 295
Rameau, Jean-Philippe 26, 85, 258
Rapaccioli, Giovanni 38
recitative (accompanied) 27–8, 63n, 102, 104, 107–8, 163, 206, 259, 274, 278, 285; (simple) 12–13, 17n,

71–2, 123–5, 134–6, 138, 143–50, 203, 285
Reggio Emilia 8, 166
reforms of opera 23–9, 47, 90–1, 122–5, 203–5, 211
Reichardt, Johann Friedrich 26
revisions and versions 56, 108, 136–8, 257, 278, 278n, 280–1, 287
rhetoric 17, 136, 145–8, 159–60, 222–4, 238–9
Ricciardi, Domenico 295
Riccoboni, Luigi 202
Rich, John 255
Rinaldo da Capua 2, 22
Ristori, Giovanni Alberto 93
Riva, Giuseppe 25, 211
Rizzi, Domenico 75
Robatti, Bernardo 51, 53
Robinson, Michael F. 62
Rogatis, Francesco de 29
roles, hierarchy of 9–10, 46, 55–6, 99–101, 106, 113, 178, 185, 218
Rolli, Paolo 34, 45, 47–9, 54–6, 76
Romani, Felice 184, 297, 301, 303–4
romanticism 29, 256–7, 266, 295, 301, 303–5
Rome (ancient) 6, 46, 53, 55, 69, 102, 170, 207, 241, 280, 284; (opera business) 8–9, 21, 33–60, 64–5, 74, 79, 211n; (Teato Alibert o delle Dame) 49–60, 74, 77–8, 101, 172–3; (Teatro Capranica), 33–60, 44–5 (pl. 1a–b), 74n, 166; (Teatro della Pace) 50, 52
Rossini, Gioacchino 295n
Rotrou, Jean 49
Rousseau, Jean-Jacques 6, 63
Rudolstadt 84
Ruspoli, Francesco Maria 34, 38–42, 47–50, 54–6
Ruspoli, Isabella Cesi 50, 54–5, 57
Russia 7, 28, 94–5

Sacchini, Antonio 7, 28
Saint-Évremont, Charles de 83, 85, 202
St Petersburg 7
Sala di Felice, Elena 211, 280
Saletti, Lorenzo 99–100, 103, 108
Salieri, Antonio 7, 25, 28
Salvi, Antonio 19–20, 45, 72, 101, 122, 124 167–9, 203; (and Handel) 167, 264–5; *Adelaide* 102; *Amore e maestà (Arsace)* 21, 45, 72–4, 128n, 165–91, 197 (pl. 9), 297, 300–4; *Amor vince l'odio, overo Timocrate* 66–7, 167; *Ariodante (Ginevra principessa di Scozia)* 255–69; *Arminio* 20, 36, 57–9, 102, 167, 276n; *Astianatte* 20, 50, 167; *Berenice regina d'Egitto* 35, 50–1; *Il carceriere di se stesso* 167; *Il Gran Tamerlano* 35, 167; *Lucio Papirio* 35, 43–6; *Publio Cornelio Scipione* 171; *Rodelinda* 167; *Sosarme (Dionisio re di Portogallo)* 167; *Stratonica* 167
Salzburg 87
Salzdahlum 8
San Giovanni in Persiceto 8
Sarò, Antonio 55
Sarri, Domenico 21, 62, 65, 79; *Achille in Sciro* 101, 109; *Arsace* 72, 172; *Didone abbandonata* 21, 71–74n, 169, 171; *Endimione* 72; *L'impresario delle isole Canarie* 25; *Partenope* 70–1; *Siroe re di Persia* 72
Sarti, Giuseppe 4, 7, 28
Sassani, Matteo 65
satyre 3, 25, 91
Saxony *see* Dresden
Scalzi, Carlo 51, 257n
Scarlatti, Alessandro 3, 14, 19, 33–41, 49–59, 62, 64–5, 78; (and Salvi) 167; *L'amor volubile e tiranno (Dorisbe)* 35, 39; *Arminio* 36, 57–9 (pl. 2a–b); *Il Ciro* 41; *La fede riconosciuta (Dorinda)* 41;

Griselda 33, 35, 37–8, 53–6, 266; *Marco Attilio Regolo* 35, 50–1; *Mitridate Eupatore* 170n, 174; *Telemaco* 21, 35, 51; *Teodosio il giovane* 40n; *Il Tigrane* (Lalli) 49; *Tito Sempronio Gracco* 35, 53; *Il trionfo della libertà* 3, 169; *Turno Aricino* 35, 53; *La virtù negli amori* 57
Scarlatti, Domenico 50, 97; *Ambleto* 35, 47–8; *Amor d'un'ombra e gelosia d'un'aura* 43, 46; *Berenice regina d'Egitto* 35, 50–1; *La Dirindina* 25, 47–8; *Ifigenia in Aulide* 42; *Ifigenia in Tauri* 42; *L'Orlando, overo la gelosa pazzia* 41, 46; *Tetide in Sciro* 41, 110; *Tolomeo et Alessandro* 40, 46
scene buffe 172, 174
scenography 38, 42–6 (pl. 1a–b), 49, 76n, 86, 102–3, 109, 112–13, 134n, 174, 176, 206–7, 221–2, 224, 242 (pl. 11), 285, 289 (pl. 14); *see also* stage-sets
Scheibe, Johann Adolph 82–3, 287
Schering, Arnold 82–5, 91–2, 96
Schiassi, Gaetano Maria 78, 100
Schiedermair, Ludwig 83, 85–6, 90–1
Schiller, Friedrich 297
Schneider, Herbert 269
Schönborn, Johann Philipp Franz 67
Schubart, Christian Friedrich Daniel 26, 63
Scotland 267–8
Scott, Walter 295n
Scotti, Annibale 98
Sellitti, Giuseppe 65, 77
Senesino, Francesco Bernardi detto 76, 79, 170–1
serenata 4, 72, 90
Serino, Nicola 172
Shakespeare, William 29
Silvani, Francesco 2, 20, 35, 41, 67, 101, 274
sinfonia 237–51, 259, 266
singers 9, 40, 42, 46–9, 67, 72–80, 90, 99–101, 106–8, 171–2, 256–7, 278
Singspiel 85, 92
Sobieski family 40n
Sografi, Antonio Simone 29
Soler, Antonio 97
Spain 7, 23, 38, 42, 64, 97–117, 167
speech-act 136, 148, 150, 155, 158, 162
Sporck, Franz Anton von 93
Stampa, Claudio Nicola 75
stage direction 48, 77
stage-sets 179, 186–7, 213–8, 241–3, 259, 265–7
Stampiglia, Luigi Maria 70
Stampiglia, Silvio 4, 19, 65–6, 69–71, 122, 203; *Abdolomino* 48, 273n; *Cirene* 70n; *Eraclea* 70; *Imeneo* 4, 69n, 75; *Partenope (La Rosmira fedele)* 69–71; *Tito Sempronio Gracco* 35, 53; *Il trionfo di Camilla* 48, 70n; *Turno Aricino* 35, 53
Steele, Richard 54–6
Steffani, Agostino 7, 86
Strungk, Nikolaus Adam 89
Stuart, James Francis 173
Stuttgart 7, 22, 26, 84, 87–9, 93
Suarez, Pietro 169
Sweden 7
Swiney, Owen 70, 76

Tagliazucchi, Giovan Pietro 22, 26
Telemann, Georg Philipp 89, 91
Tempesti, Domenico 46
Terradellas, Domenico 23
Tesi, Vittoria 99–101, 103, 106, 108, 109n
Thomas, Johannes 126
Tocco, Leonardo 69n
Tocco, Niccolò del 69–70
Tollini, Domenico 42–3
Torri, Pietro 55n

Tosi, Pier Francesco 25
Traetta, Tommaso 3, 7, 26, 28
tragedia per musica 3, 20, 63, 68–9, 72, 77, 91, 209
tragédie, French 19, 24, 134–5, 138, 143–62, 165–8, 177–97, 207, 239–40, 260, 262, 287, 297–305
tragédie lyrique 7–8, 24, 51, 85, 123, 134, 166, 208, 257, 260–3, 265
tragedy, German 295
tragedy, Greek 204–5, 295, 305
tragedy, spoken 2, 12, 17, 24, 81, 121–97, 207, 239–40, 260, 262
tragicomedy 3
translations 124, 126, 171, 194
Trombetta, Emanuella 109, 113
Trotti, Marchese 42
troupes, travelling 7, 9, 95 (pl. 4)
Tullio, Francesco Antonio 3
Turin 8, 79, 166, 171, 197 (pl. 9)

Uffenbach, Johann Friedrich Armand von 82
Uttini, Elisabetta 99–100, 103, 108–9, 113

Valesio, Francesco 39–40
Vanbrugh, John 48
Vanstryp, Filippo 74, 79
Vellani, Domenico 50n
Venice 4–5, 8–10, 20, 22, 41, 61–80, 97–9, 174, 276; (Ospedale degli Incurabili) 75, 79; (Teato San Benedetto) 5, 168, 295; (Teatro San Cassiano) 5, 136; (Teatro San Giovanni Grisostomo) 5, 68, 171–2 (pl. 3)
Verazi, Mattia 3, 22; *Calliroë* 28; *Ifigenia in Aulide* 26; *Sofonisba* 3, 26
Verdi, Giuseppe 262
verisimilitude 12, 24, 134, 138, 148–50, 160, 174, 201–7, 212–19, 262
Versailles 86
Vicenza 20
Vienna 7–8, 11, 20–3, 26, 51, 64–5, 86–90, 108, 242n, 261, 279, 285
Vignati, Giuseppe 70n, 231
Vignola, Giuseppe 65
Villati, Leopoldo de 22
Villifranchi, Cosimo 166, 168
Vinci, Leonardo 21–2, 26, 60, 62–3, 71–5, 77–9; *Alessandro nell'Indie* 99, 112; *Artaserse* 74, 78, 101, 276–7; *Catone in Utica* 15–16, 169; *Elpidia* 70; *Eraclea* 79; *Farnace* 100–1, 104, 107; *Rosmira fedele* 69–71; *Silla dittatore* 72; *Siroe re di Persia* 72–4, 244–7
Vivaldi, Antonio 3, 20, 22, 62–3, 66, 78–9, 98–9, 101; (concertos) 250n; (and Prague) 93–5; (recitatives) 146–50; (sources) 136n; *Arsilda regina di Ponto* 139; *L'Atenaide* 163n; *La costanza trionfante degli amori, e degli odii* 139, 153–4; *Dorilla in Tempe* 3, 261; *Ercole sul Termodonte* 36; *Farnace* 101, 104–5; *Giustino* 57, 139n, 247–51, 266; *Griselda* 66, 139n, 156n; *L'incoronazione di Dario* 139; *L'inverno* 163; *Nerone fatto Cesare* 139, 157; *L'Olimpiade* 15n; *Orlando finto pazzo* 139, 157, 163n; *Orlando furioso* 93, 157, 163n; *Ottone in villa* 139n; *La primavera* 250; *Scanderbeg* 139; *Siroe* 163; *Teuzzone* 134–64 (pl. 7); *Tieteberga* 139
Vogler, Georg Joseph 63
Voltaire (François-Marie Arouet) 6, 26

Wagner, Richard 238
Walker, Frank 61
Warsaw 278, 281–2
Weaver, John 259–60

wedding scenes   100–2, 108–10, 183, 262
Weiss, Piero   64, 122
Weissenfels   82–3, 87, 89
Wich, Johann von   90
Wilderer, Johann Hugo   86
Wiel, Taddeo   65
Wolff, Hellmuth Christian   85n, 86, 90–1, 260
women and gender   36–7, 110, 112, 145, 181–2, 246,
   299–300
women performers   40, 105, 113
Wroclaw (Breslau)   95

Young, Cecilia   257n

Zanelli, Ippolito   35, 57

Zanetti, Antonio Maria   264 (pl. 12)
Zeno, Apostolo   (dramas in general)   6, 18–20, 48, 66,
   69, 88, 93, 101, 165, 280; (arias and recitatives;
   style)   134–64; (dramaturgy; libretto reform)   121–
   33, 134, 202–3; *Alessandro Severo*   50; *Ambleto*   35,
   47–8; *Astarto*   35, 47–8; *Cajo Fabricio*   280–1;
   Engelberta   35, 39–40; *Euristeo*   79, 289;
   Faramondo   19; *Flavio Anicio Olibrio*   75;
   Griselda   33, 35–8, 53–6, 66, 102, 156n, 268;
   Gl'inganni felici   124, 178n; *Lucio Vero*   19; *Meride
   e Selinunte*   75–6; *La Merope*   156, 202; *Il
   Pirro*   35, 50; *Poesie drammatiche*   136; *I rivali
   generosi (Elpidia)*   70n; *Teuzzone*   121–33, 134–64;
   Vincislao   35, 49
Zeno, Pier Caterino   69